Ao Haru Ride

The scent of air after rain...
In the light around us, I felt your heartbeat.

1

IO SAKISAKA

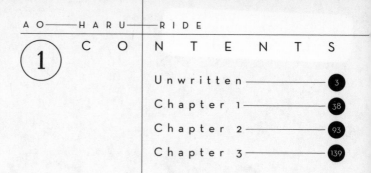

AO——HARU——RIDE

CONTENTS

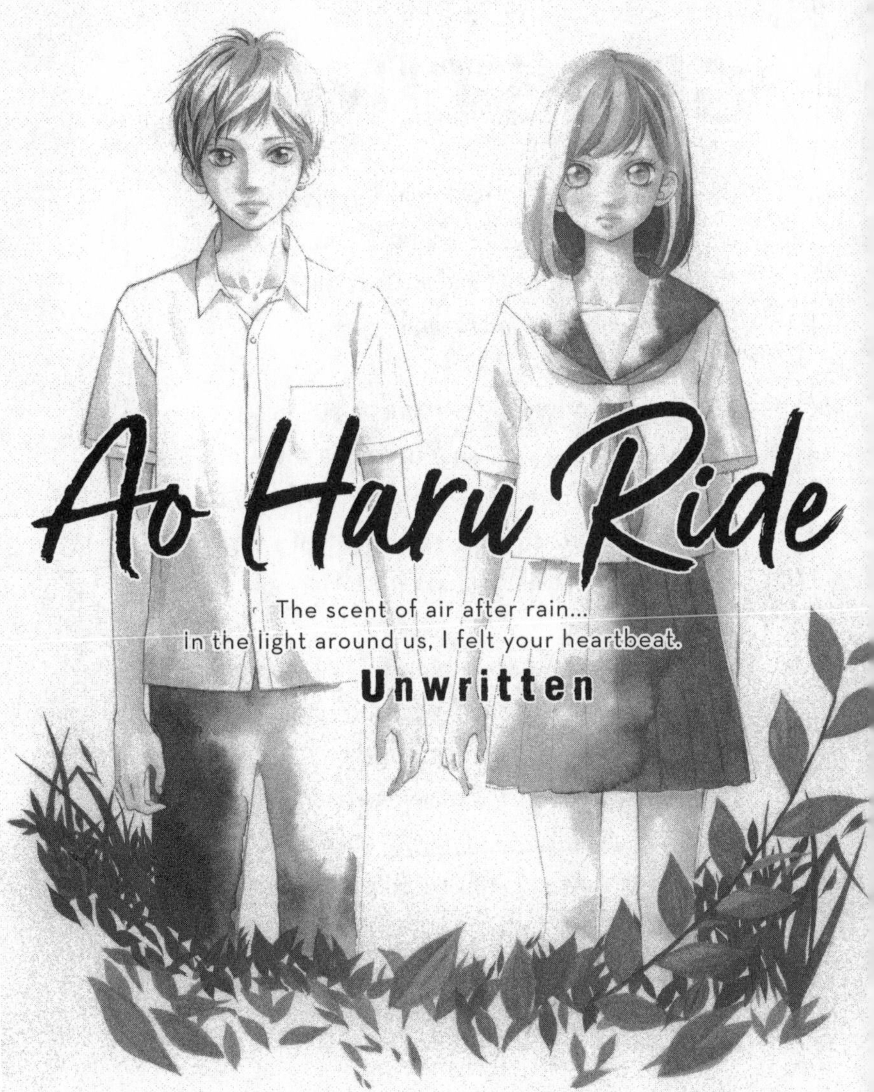

Ao Haru Ride

The scent of air after rain...
In the light around us, I felt your heartbeat.

Unwritten

IO SAKISAKA

GREETINGS

Hi! I'm Io Sakisaka. Thank you for picking up a copy of *Ao Haru Ride* volume 1. I imagine there are many of you who are reading this for the first time—nice to meet you!

I find myself strangely nervous about this new serialization, but it is what it is regardless of how nervous I'm feeling. I'm going to focus on the parts that excite me—at least that's what I've been desperately telling myself.

Even I don't know everything there is to know about the characters yet. What I do know is that I want to see them grow and make choices as they move through the many experiences I draw. I'd like to take the same perspective as a reader would and slowly reveal the characters as I go. I hope you'll come along for the ride!

Enjoy *Ao Haru Ride*, and please read through to the end!

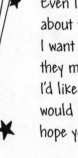

Io Sakisaka

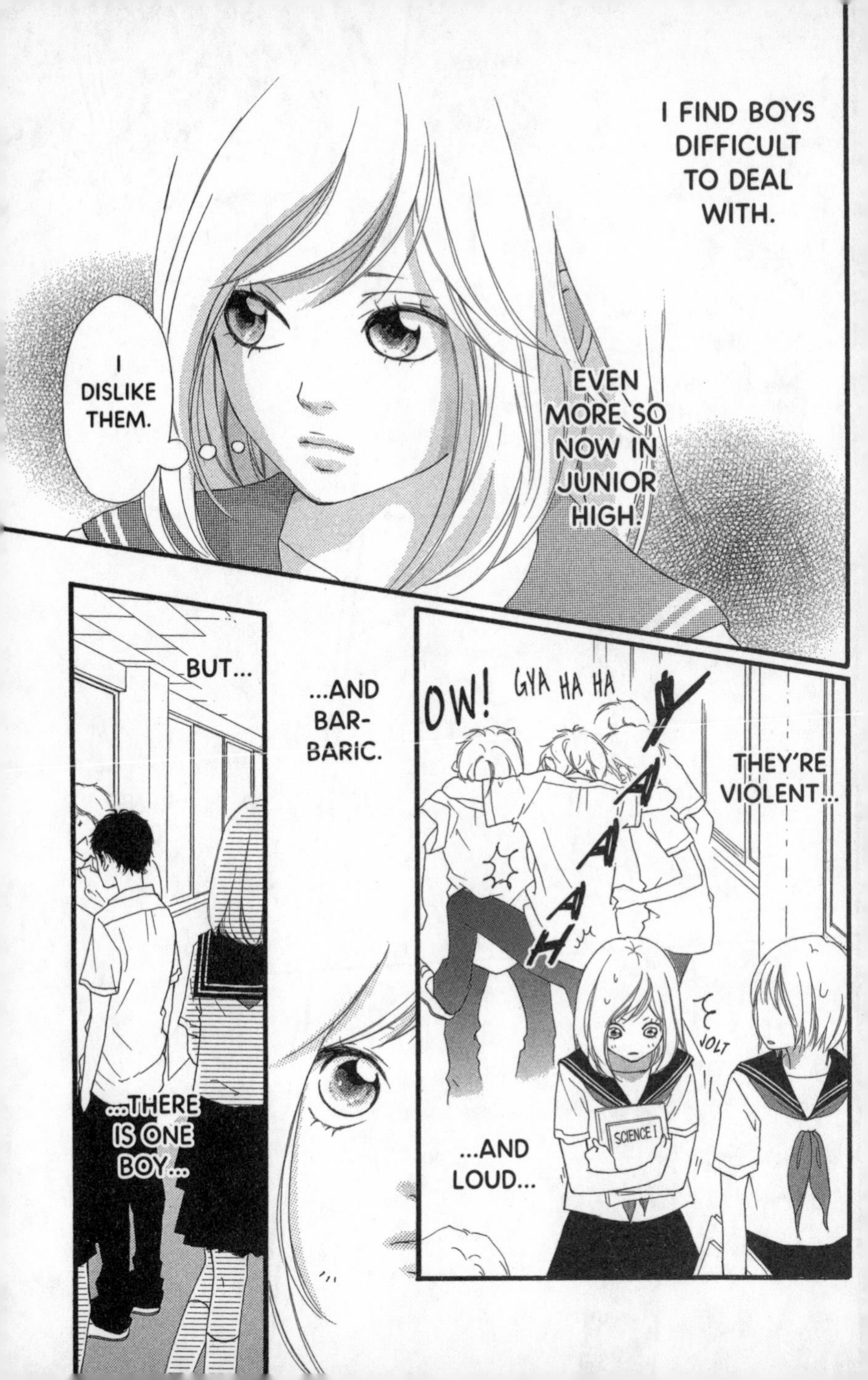
I FIND BOYS DIFFICULT TO DEAL WITH.
EVEN MORE SO NOW IN JUNIOR HIGH.
I DISLIKE THEM.
YAAAAH
THEY'RE VIOLENT...
GYA HA HA
OW!
JOLT
...AND LOUD...
...AND BAR-BARIC.
BUT...
...THERE IS ONE BOY...

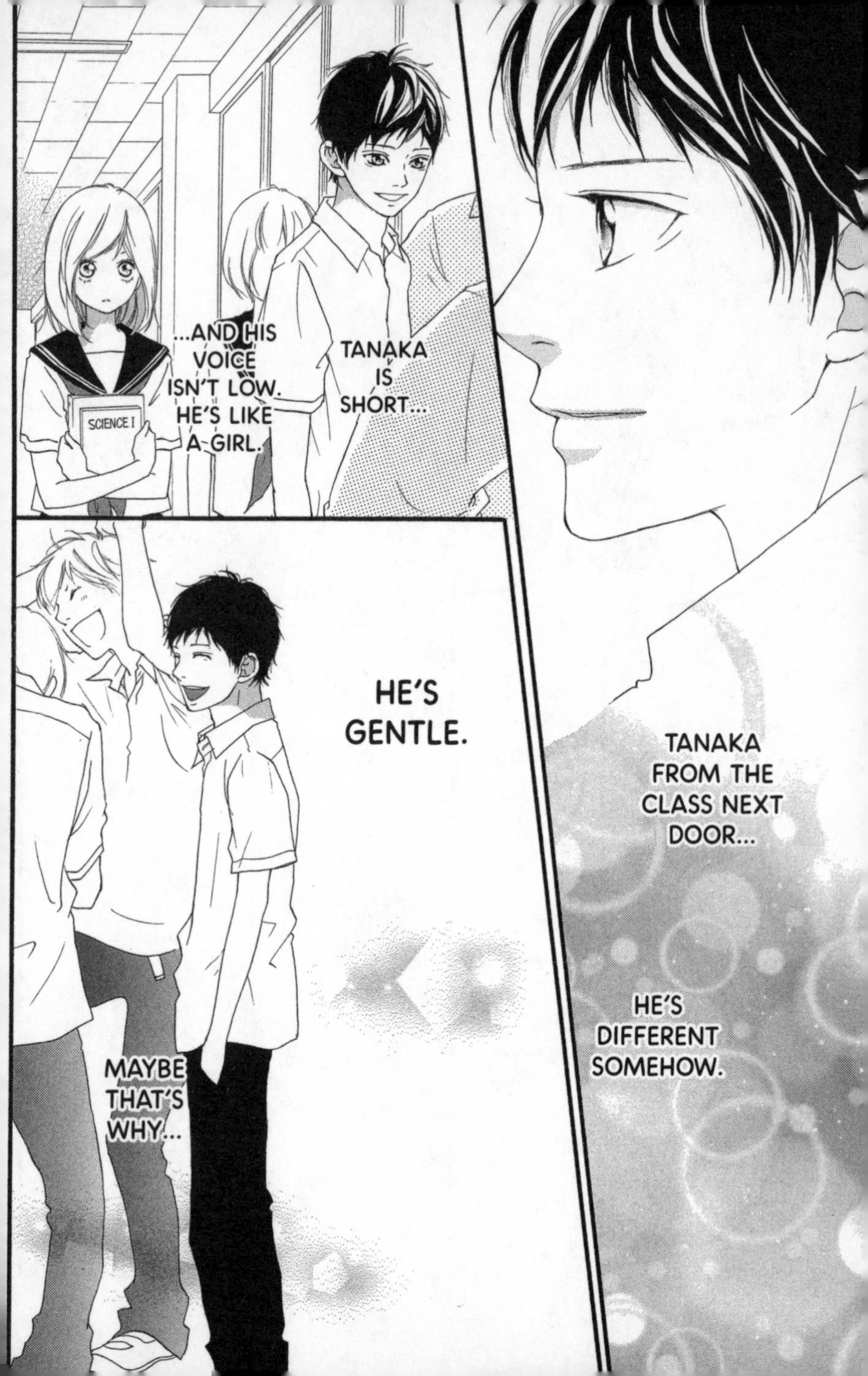
TANAKA FROM THE CLASS NEXT DOOR...
HE'S DIFFERENT SOMEHOW.
TANAKA IS SHORT...
...AND HIS VOICE ISN'T LOW. HE'S LIKE A GIRL.
SCIENCE I
HE'S GENTLE.
MAYBE THAT'S WHY...

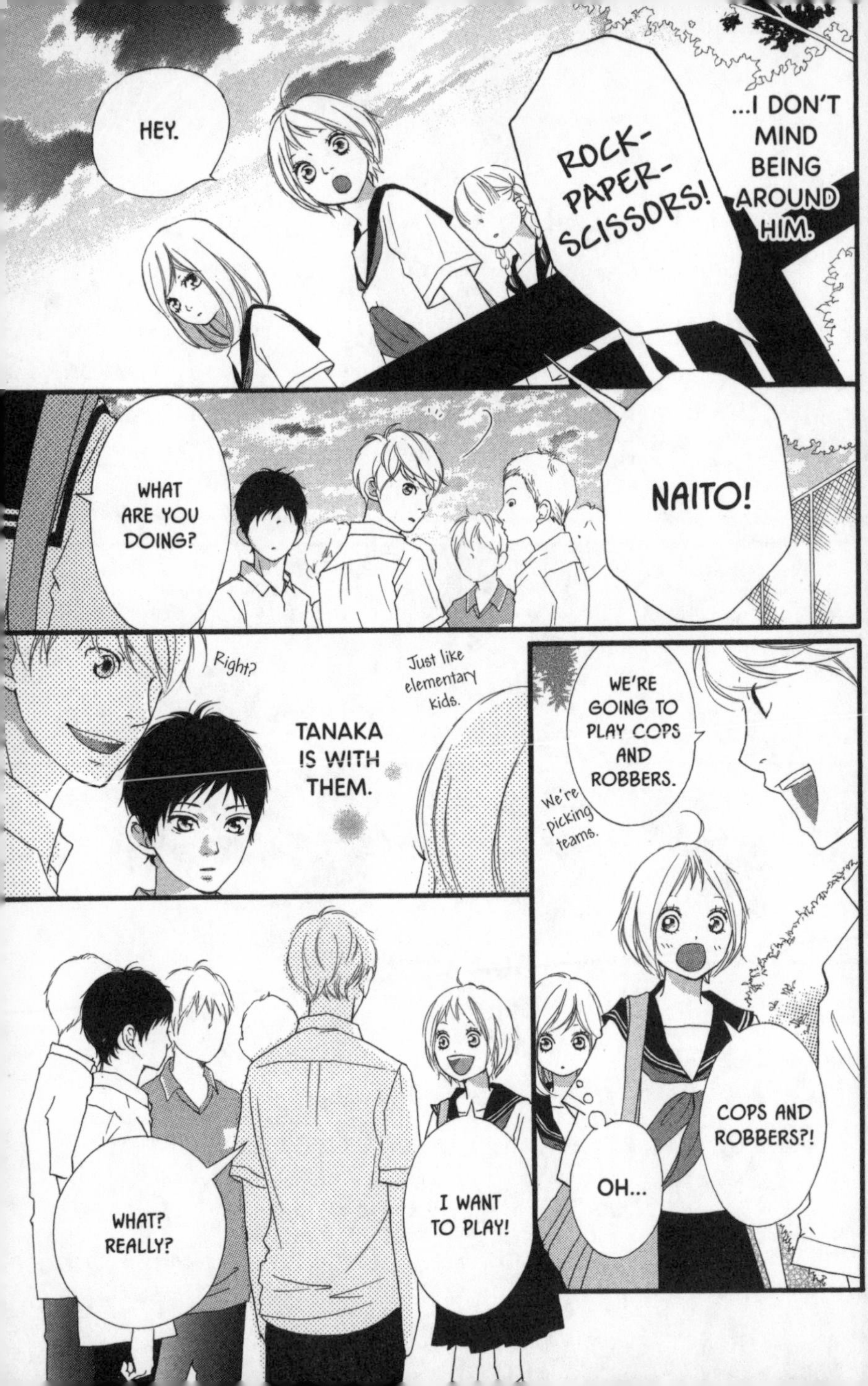
...I DON'T MIND BEING AROUND HIM.
ROCK-PAPER-SCISSORS!
HEY.
NAITO!
WHAT ARE YOU DOING?
WE'RE GOING TO PLAY COPS AND ROBBERS.
We're picking teams.
COPS AND ROBBERS?!
OH...
Just like elementary kids.
TANAKA IS WITH THEM.
Right?
I WANT TO PLAY!
WHAT? REALLY?

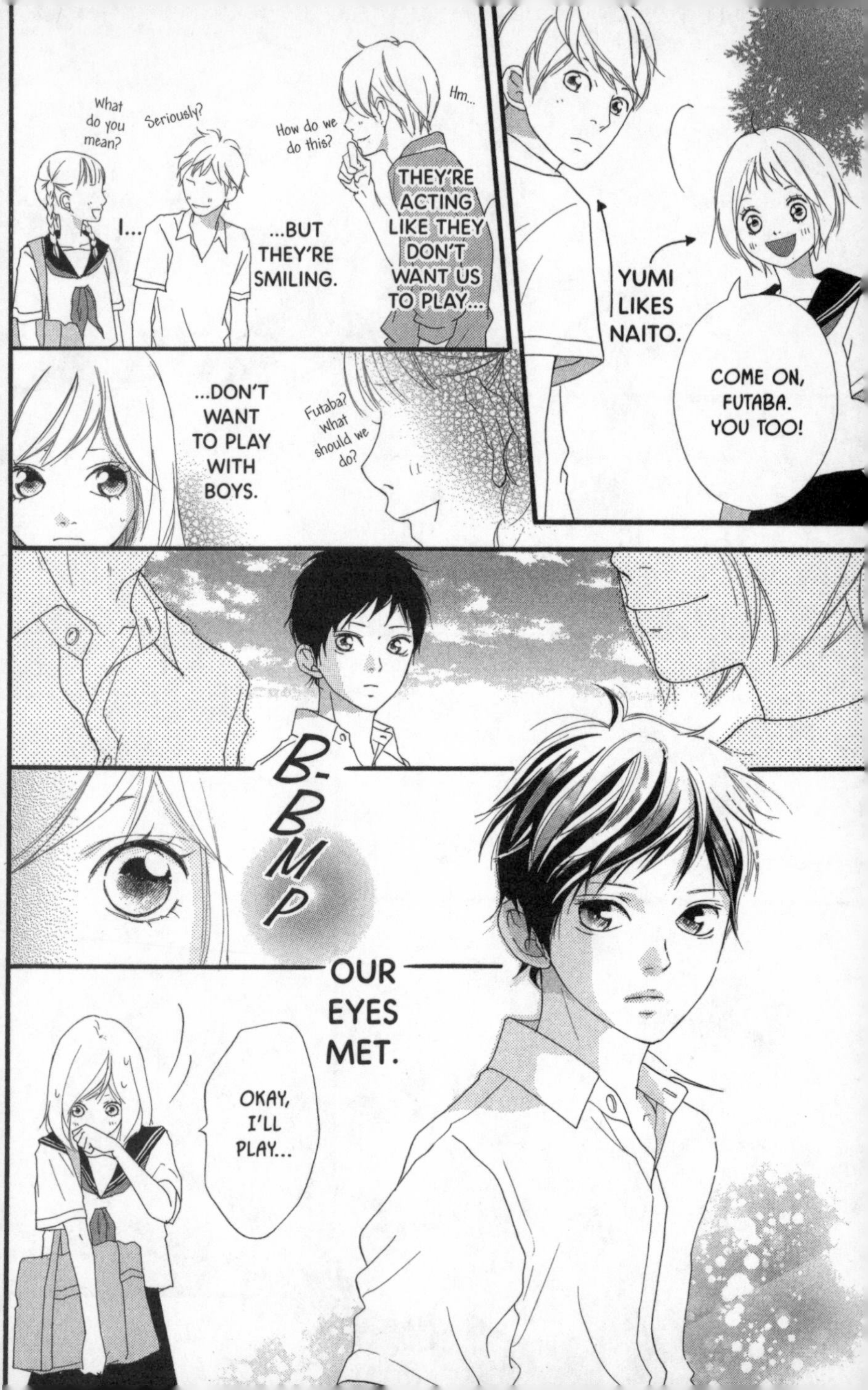

YUMI LIKES NAITO.
COME ON, FUTABA. YOU TOO!
Hm...
How do we do this?
THEY'RE ACTING LIKE THEY DON'T WANT US TO PLAY...
Seriously?
...BUT THEY'RE SMILING.
What do you mean?
I...
Futaba? what should we do?
...DON'T WANT TO PLAY WITH BOYS.
B-BMP
OUR EYES MET.
OKAY, I'LL PLAY...

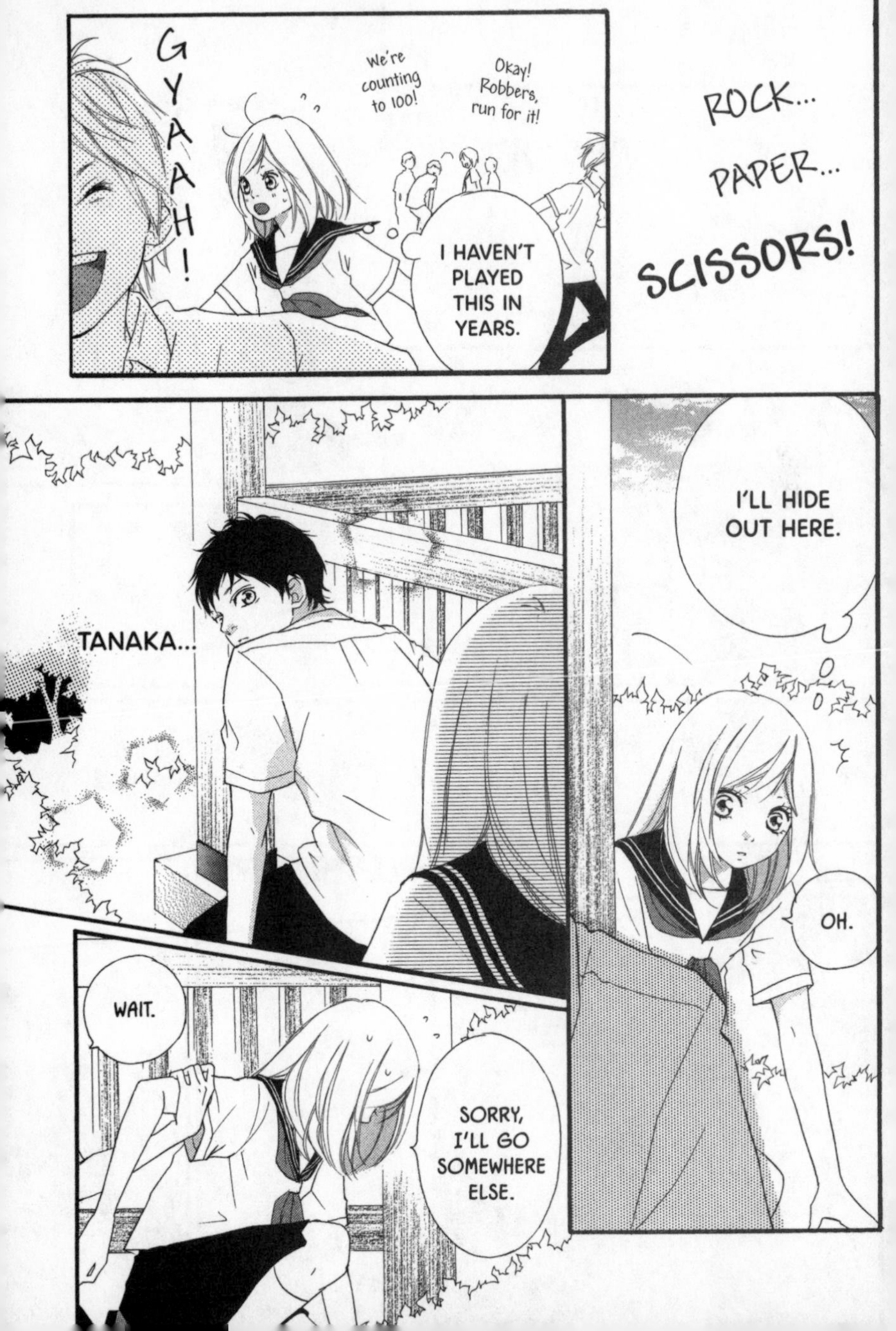
ROCK...
PAPER...
SCISSORS!
Okay! Robbers, run for it!
We're counting to 100!
I HAVEN'T PLAYED THIS IN YEARS.
GYAAH!
I'LL HIDE OUT HERE.
OH.
TANAKA...
SORRY, I'LL GO SOMEWHERE ELSE.
WAIT.

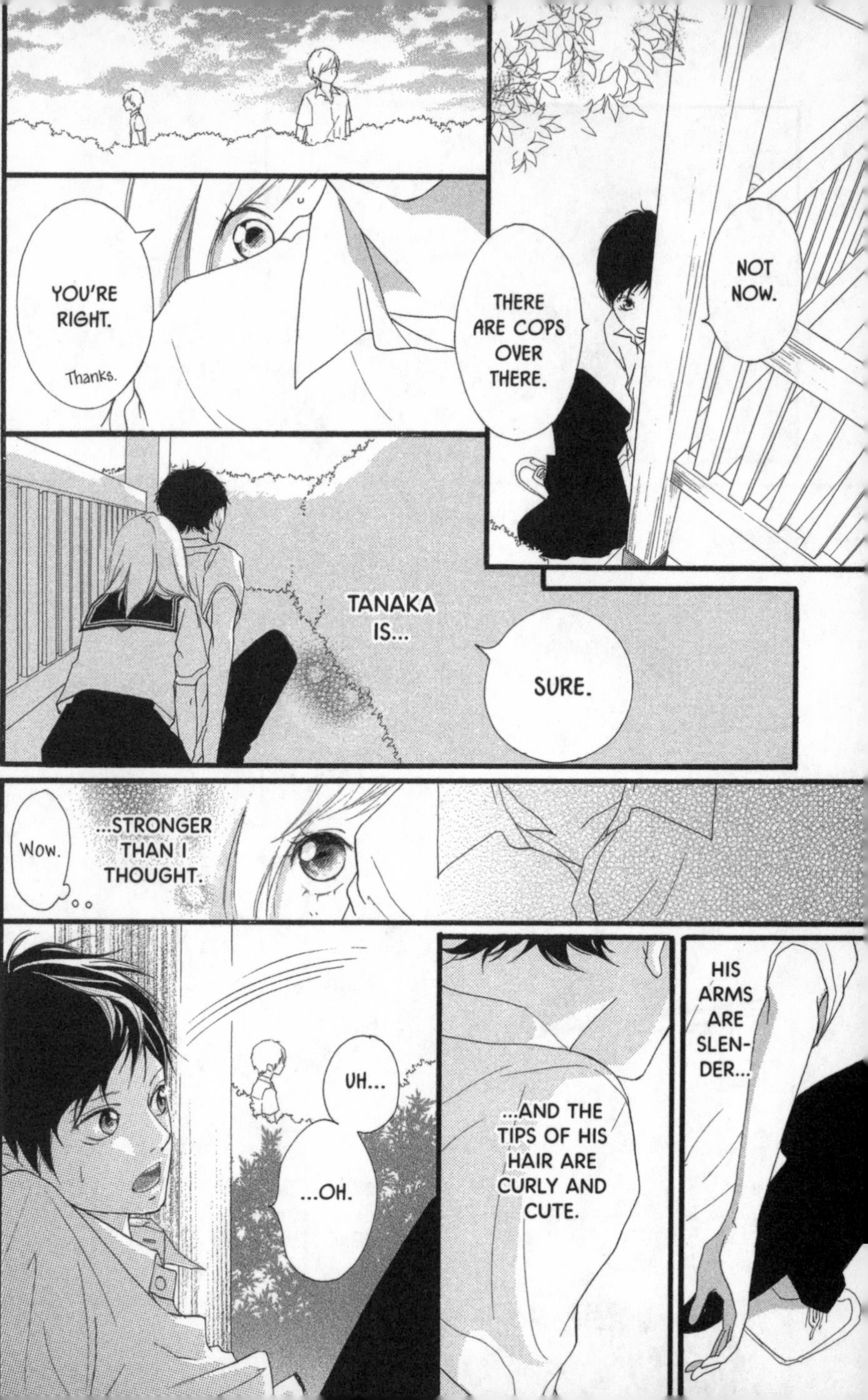
NOT NOW.
THERE ARE COPS OVER THERE.
YOU'RE RIGHT.
Thanks.
TANAKA IS...
SURE.
...STRONGER THAN I THOUGHT.
Wow.
HIS ARMS ARE SLEN-DER...
...AND THE TIPS OF HIS HAIR ARE CURLY AND CUTE.
UH...
...OH.

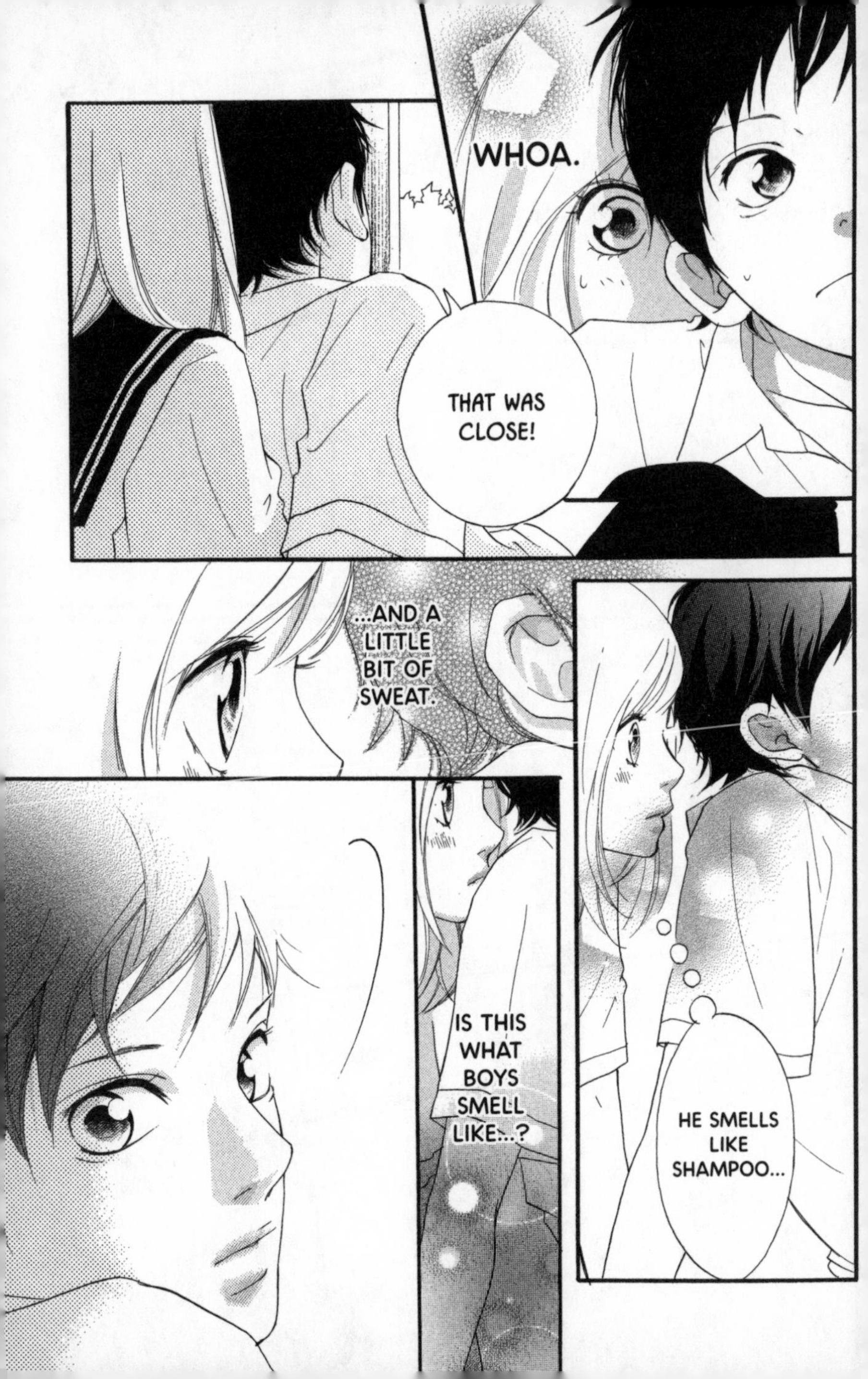
WHOA.
THAT WAS CLOSE!
...AND A LITTLE BIT OF SWEAT.
HE SMELLS LIKE SHAMPOO...
IS THIS WHAT BOYS SMELL LIKE...?

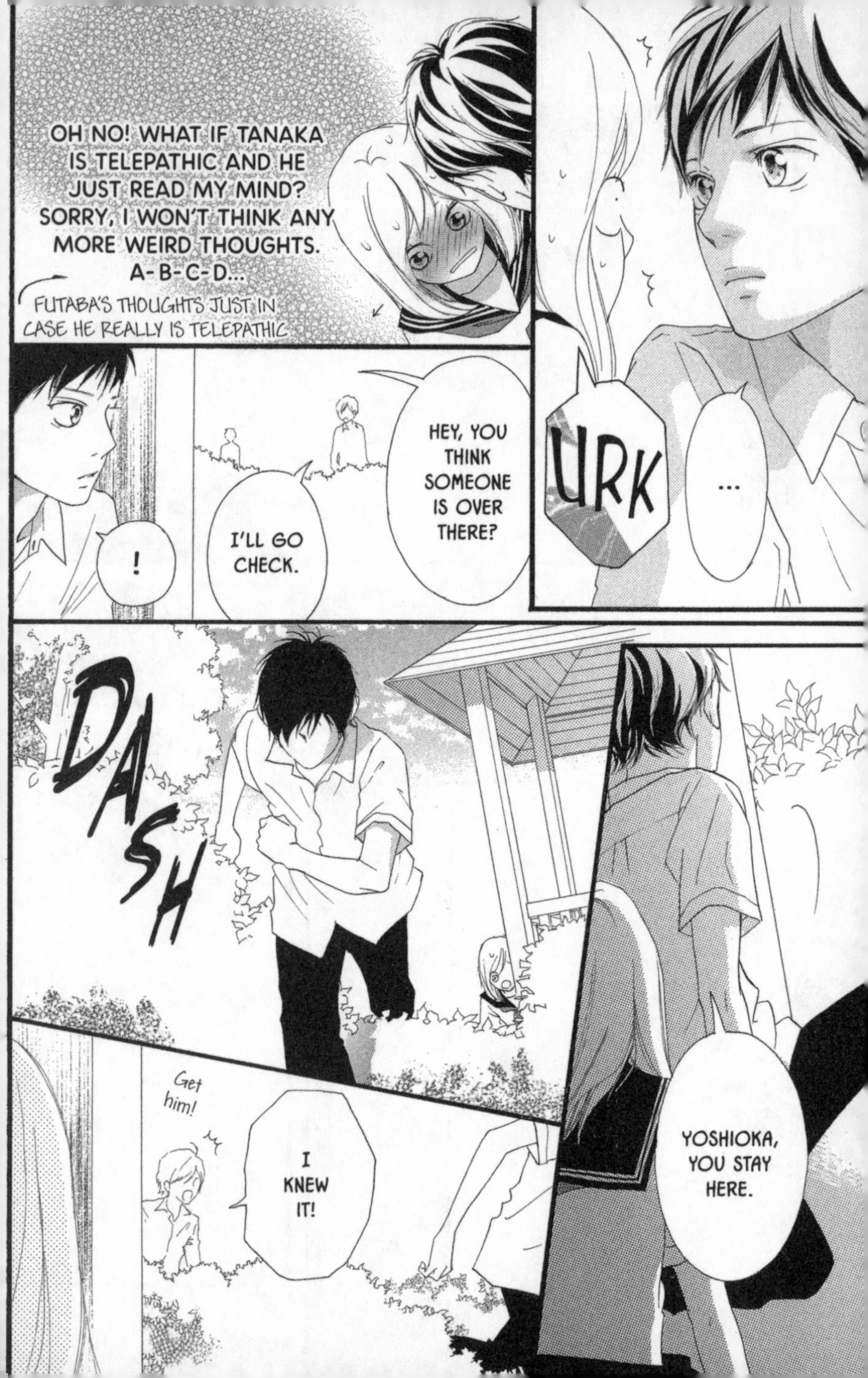
...
URK
OH NO! WHAT IF TANAKA IS TELEPATHIC AND HE JUST READ MY MIND? SORRY, I WON'T THINK ANY MORE WEIRD THOUGHTS. A-B-C-D...
FUTABA'S THOUGHTS JUST IN CASE HE REALLY IS TELEPATHIC
HEY, YOU THINK SOMEONE IS OVER THERE?
I'LL GO CHECK.
!
YOSHIOKA, YOU STAY HERE.
DASH
I KNEW IT!
Get him!

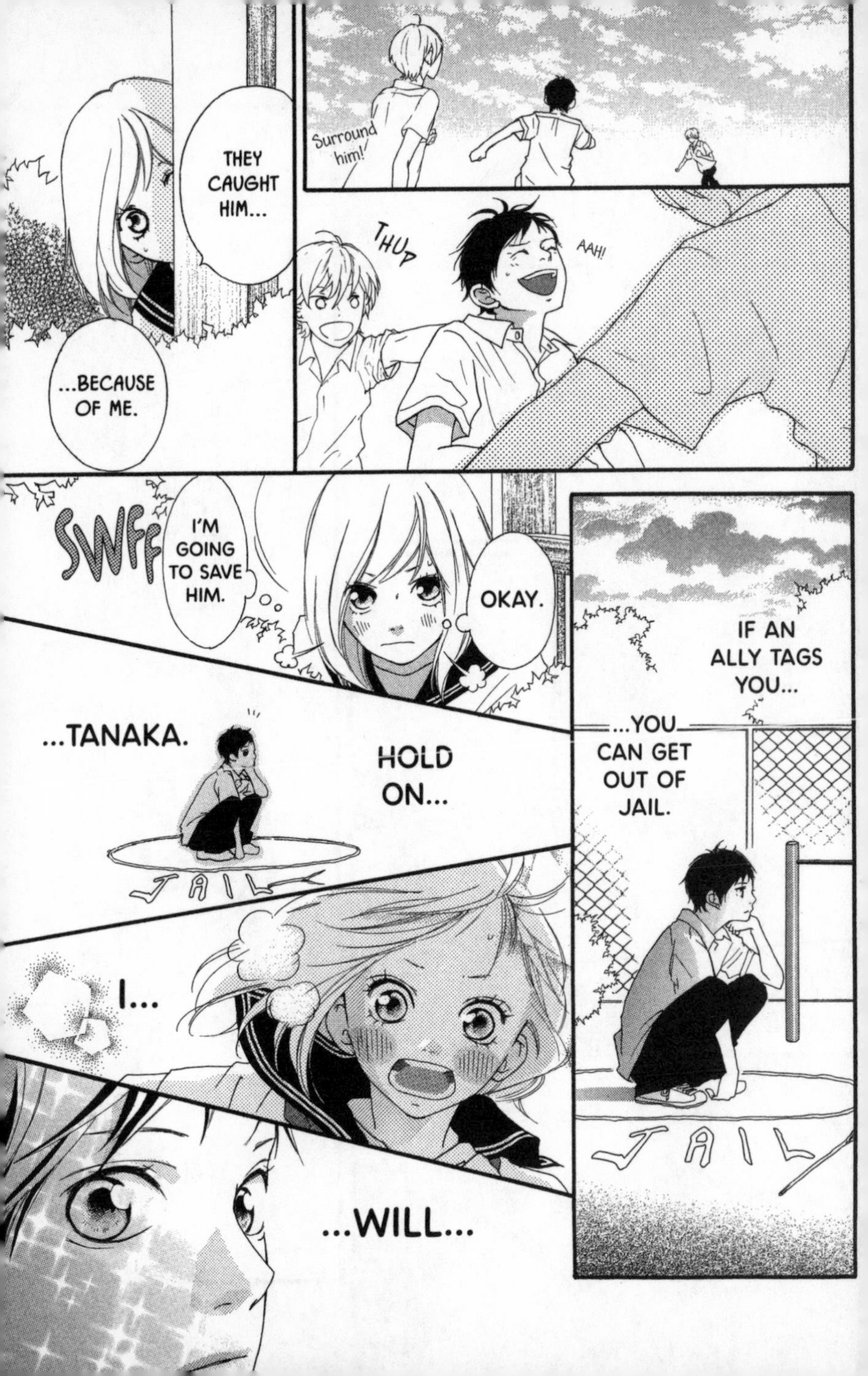
Surround him!
THUD
AAH!
THEY CAUGHT HIM...
...BECAUSE OF ME.
IF AN ALLY TAGS YOU...
...YOU CAN GET OUT OF JAIL.
JAIL
OKAY.
I'M GOING TO SAVE HIM.
SWFF
HOLD ON...
...TANAKA.
JAIL
I...
...WILL...

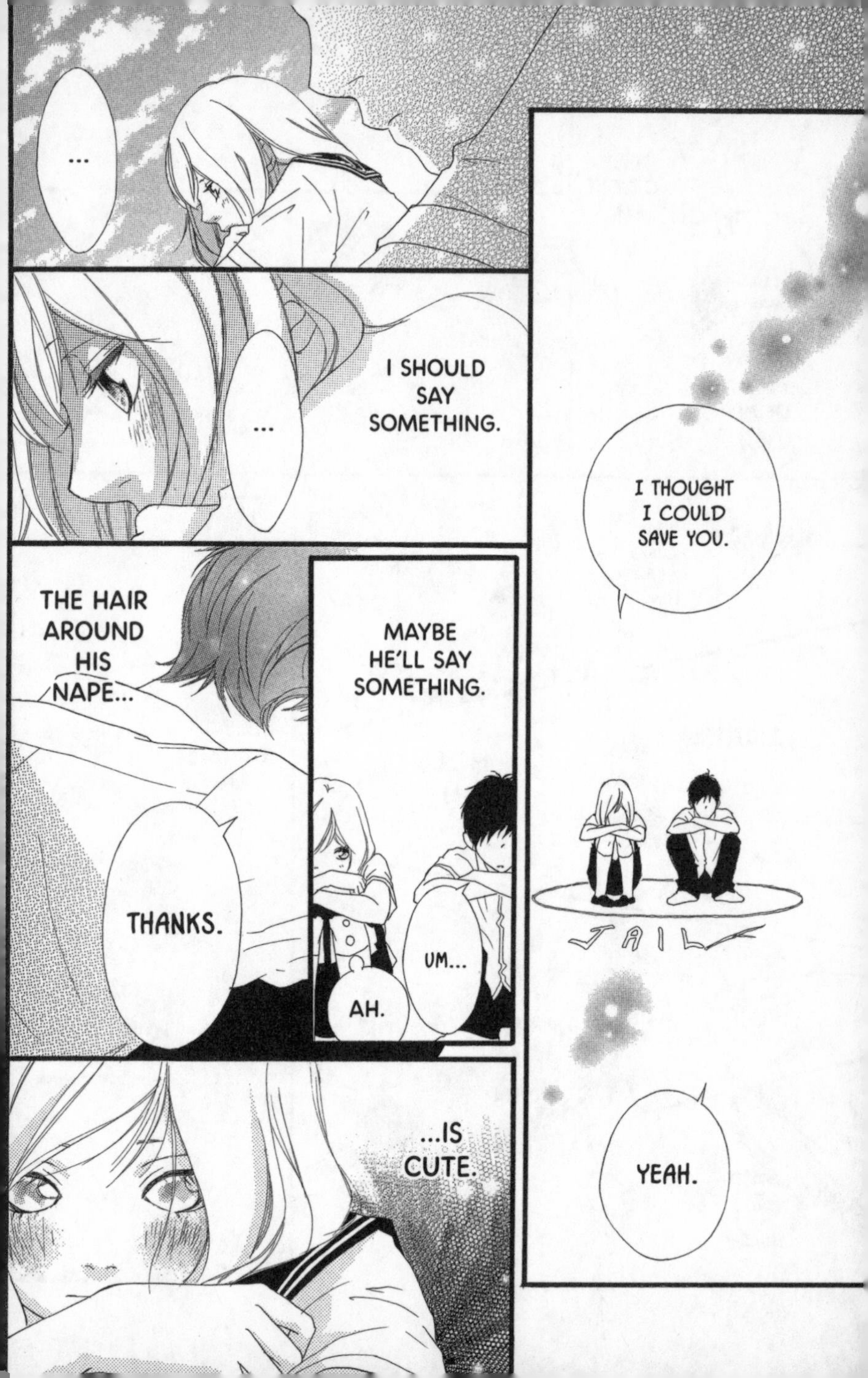
...
I THOUGHT I COULD SAVE YOU.
JAIL
YEAH.
I SHOULD SAY SOMETHING.
...
THE HAIR AROUND HIS NAPE...
MAYBE HE'LL SAY SOMETHING.
UM...
AH.
THANKS.
...IS CUTE.

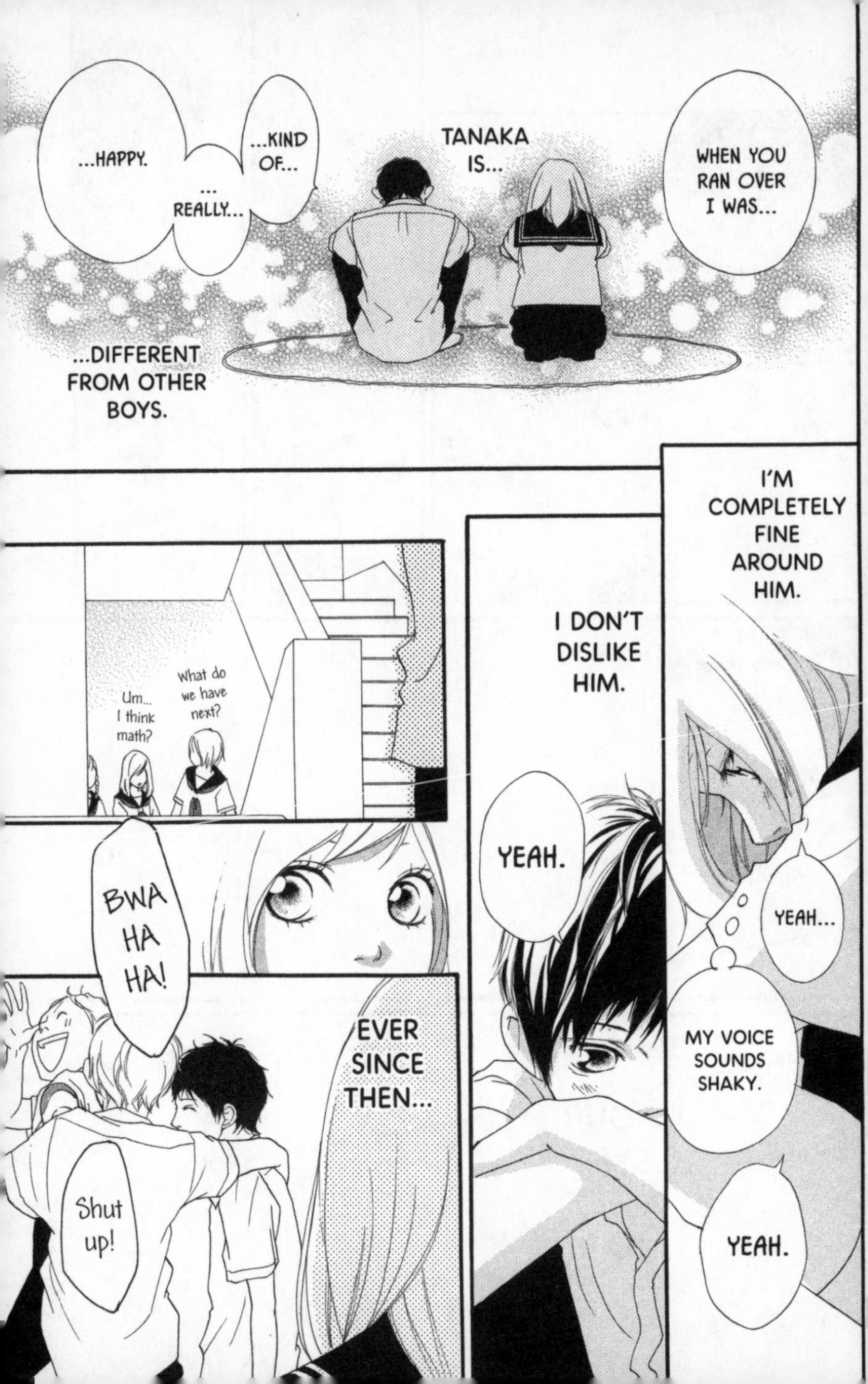
WHEN YOU RAN OVER I WAS...
TANAKA IS...
...KIND OF...
...REALLY...
...HAPPY.
...DIFFERENT FROM OTHER BOYS.
I'M COMPLETELY FINE AROUND HIM.
YEAH...
MY VOICE SOUNDS SHAKY.
YEAH.
I DON'T DISLIKE HIM.
YEAH.
What do we have next?
Um... I think math?
BWA HA HA!
EVER SINCE THEN...
Shut up!

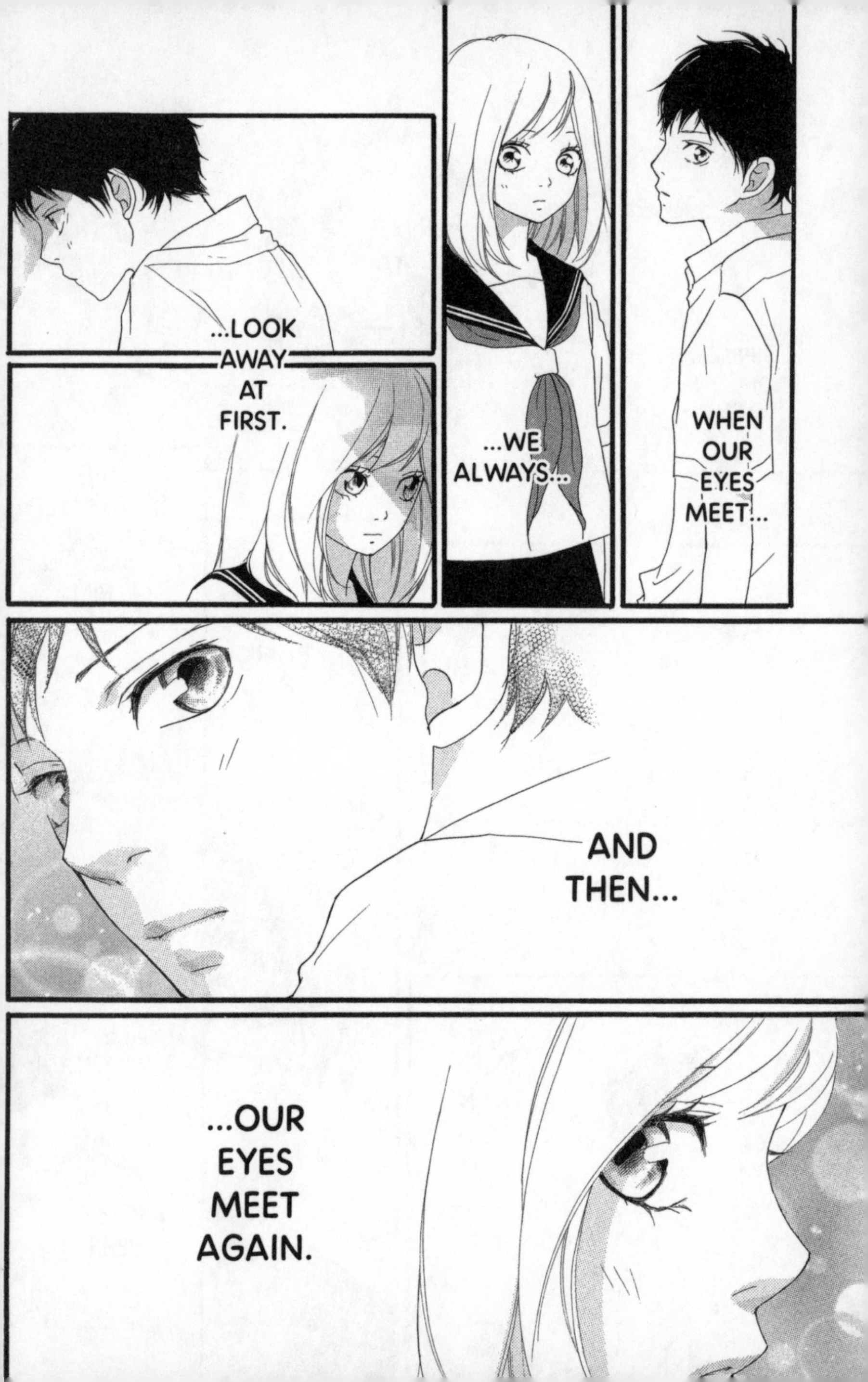
WHEN OUR EYES MEET...
...WE ALWAYS...
...LOOK AWAY AT FIRST.
AND THEN...
...OUR EYES MEET AGAIN.

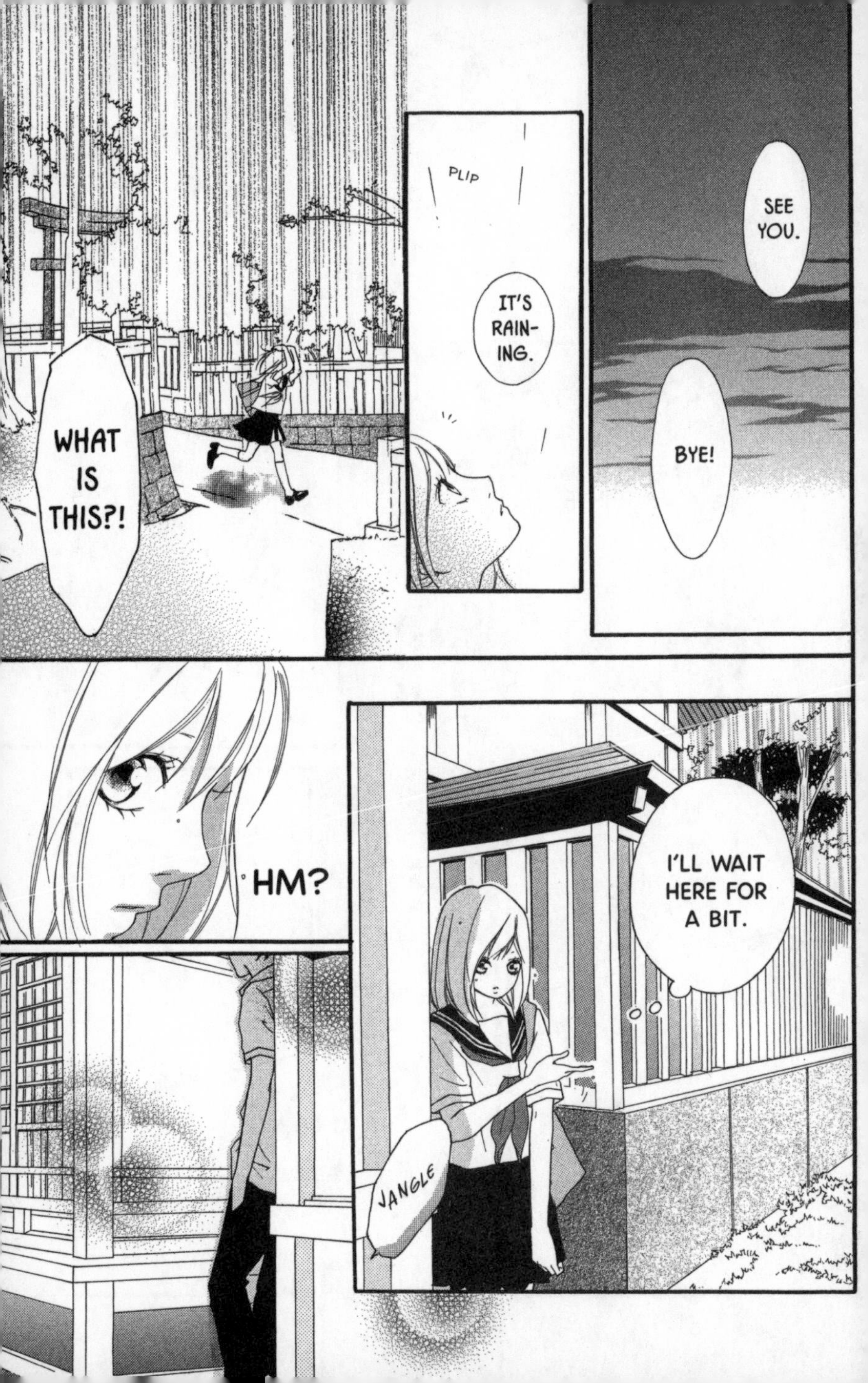
SEE YOU.
BYE!
PLIP
IT'S RAIN-ING.
WHAT IS THIS?!
I'LL WAIT HERE FOR A BIT.
JANGLE
HM?

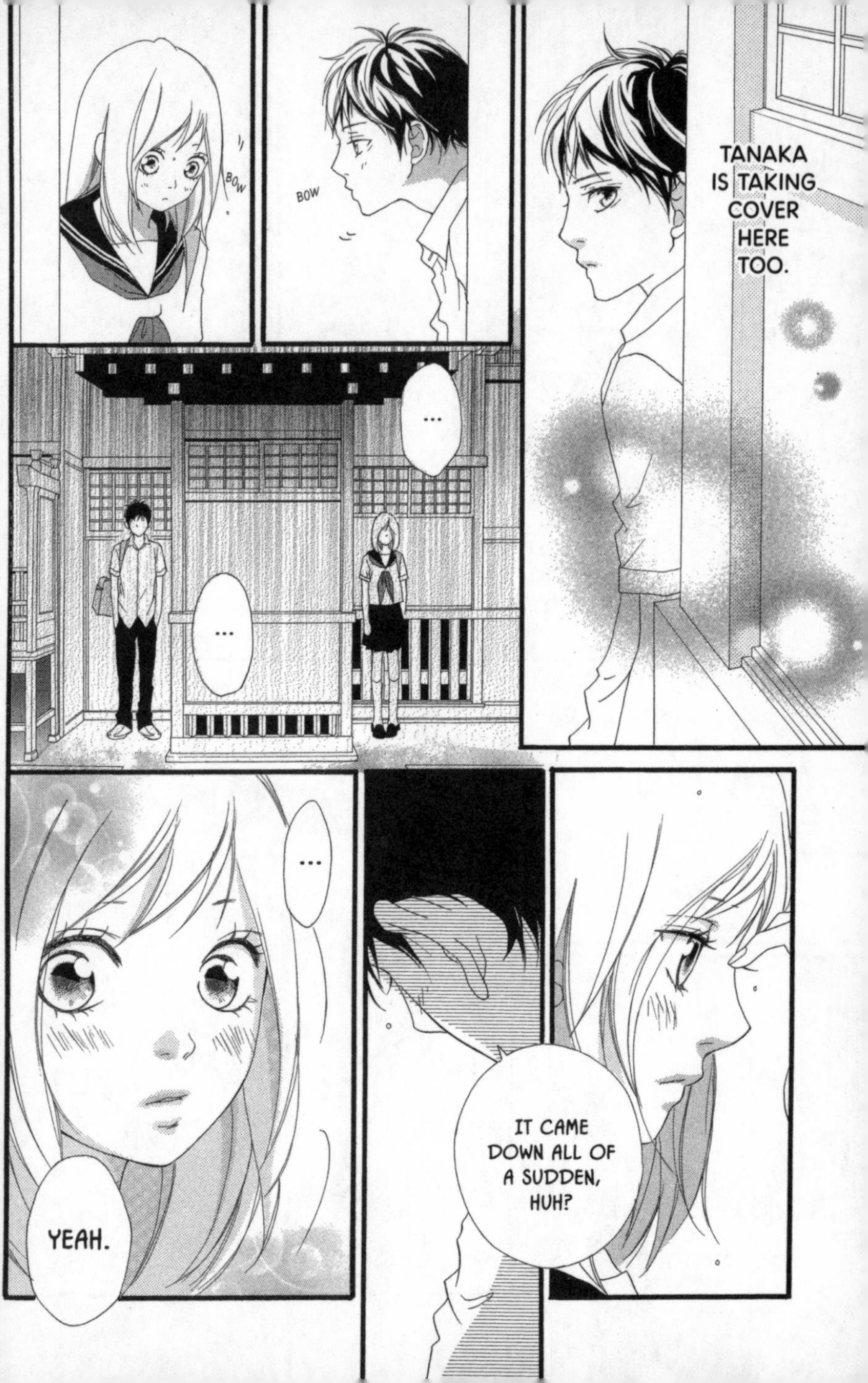
TANAKA IS TAKING COVER HERE TOO.
BOW
BOW
...
...
IT CAME DOWN ALL OF A SUDDEN, HUH?
...
YEAH.

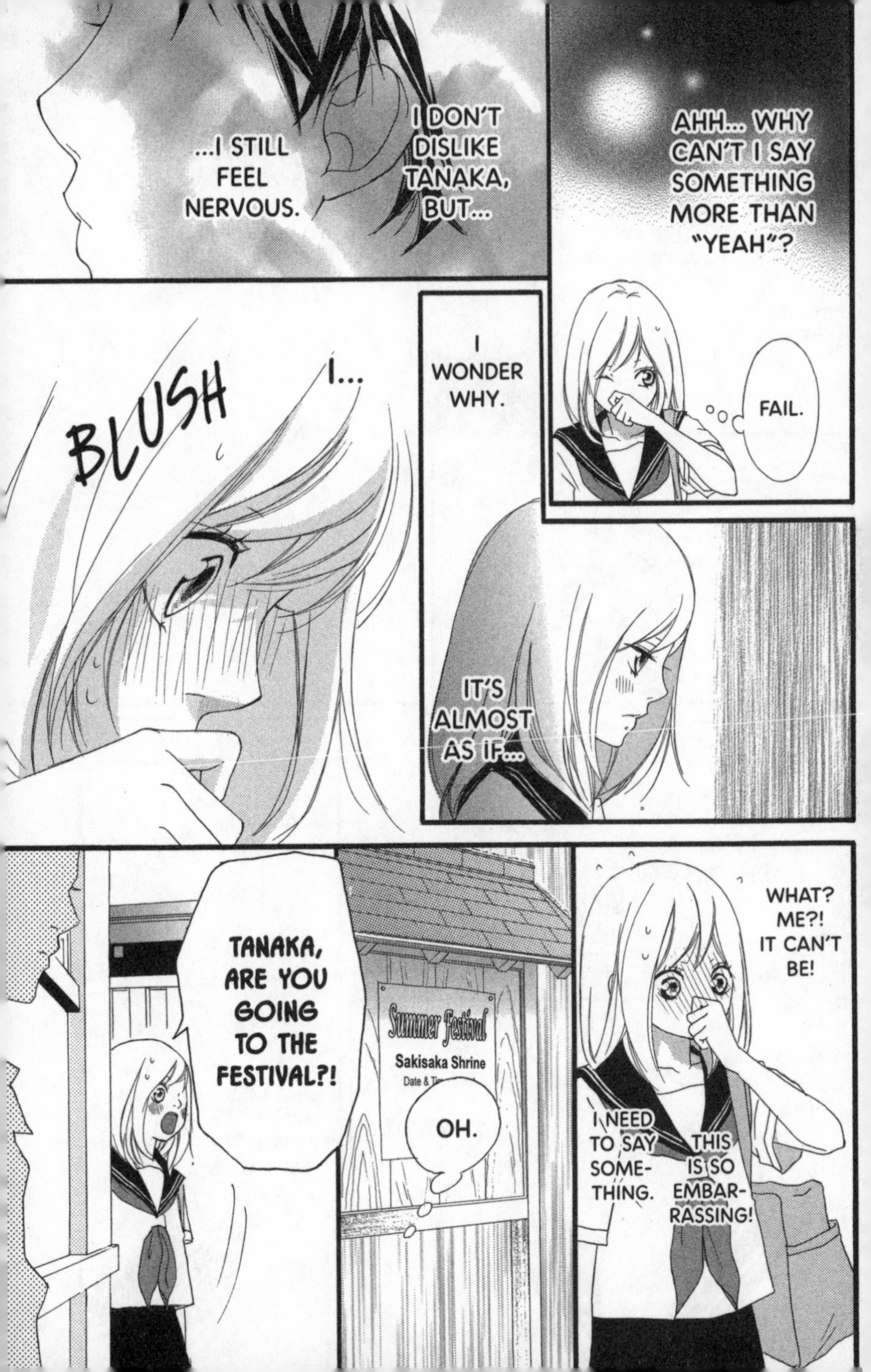
AHH... WHY CAN'T I SAY SOMETHING MORE THAN "YEAH"?
I DON'T DISLIKE TANAKA, BUT...
...I STILL FEEL NERVOUS.
FAIL.
I WONDER WHY.
IT'S ALMOST AS IF...
BLUSH
I...
WHAT? ME?! IT CAN'T BE!
THIS IS SO EMBARRASSING!
I NEED TO SAY SOME-THING.
TANAKA, ARE YOU GOING TO THE FESTIVAL?!
Summer Festival
Sakisaka Shrine
OH.

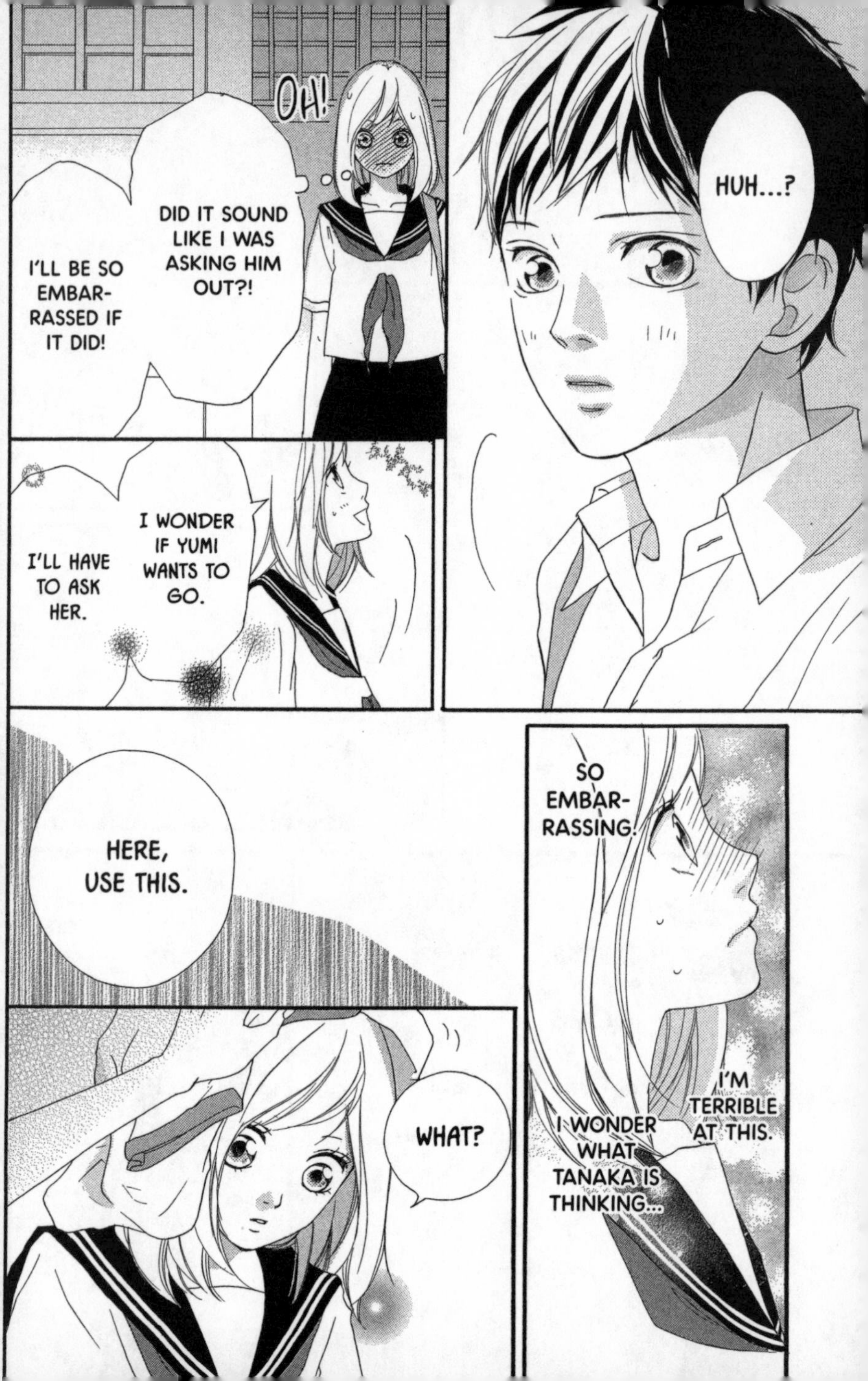
HUH...?
OH!
DID IT SOUND LIKE I WAS ASKING HIM OUT?!
I'LL BE SO EMBARRASSED IF IT DID!
I WONDER IF YUMI WANTS TO GO.
I'LL HAVE TO ASK HER.
SO EMBARRASSING.
I'M TERRIBLE AT THIS.
I WONDER WHAT TANAKA IS THINKING...
HERE, USE THIS.
WHAT?

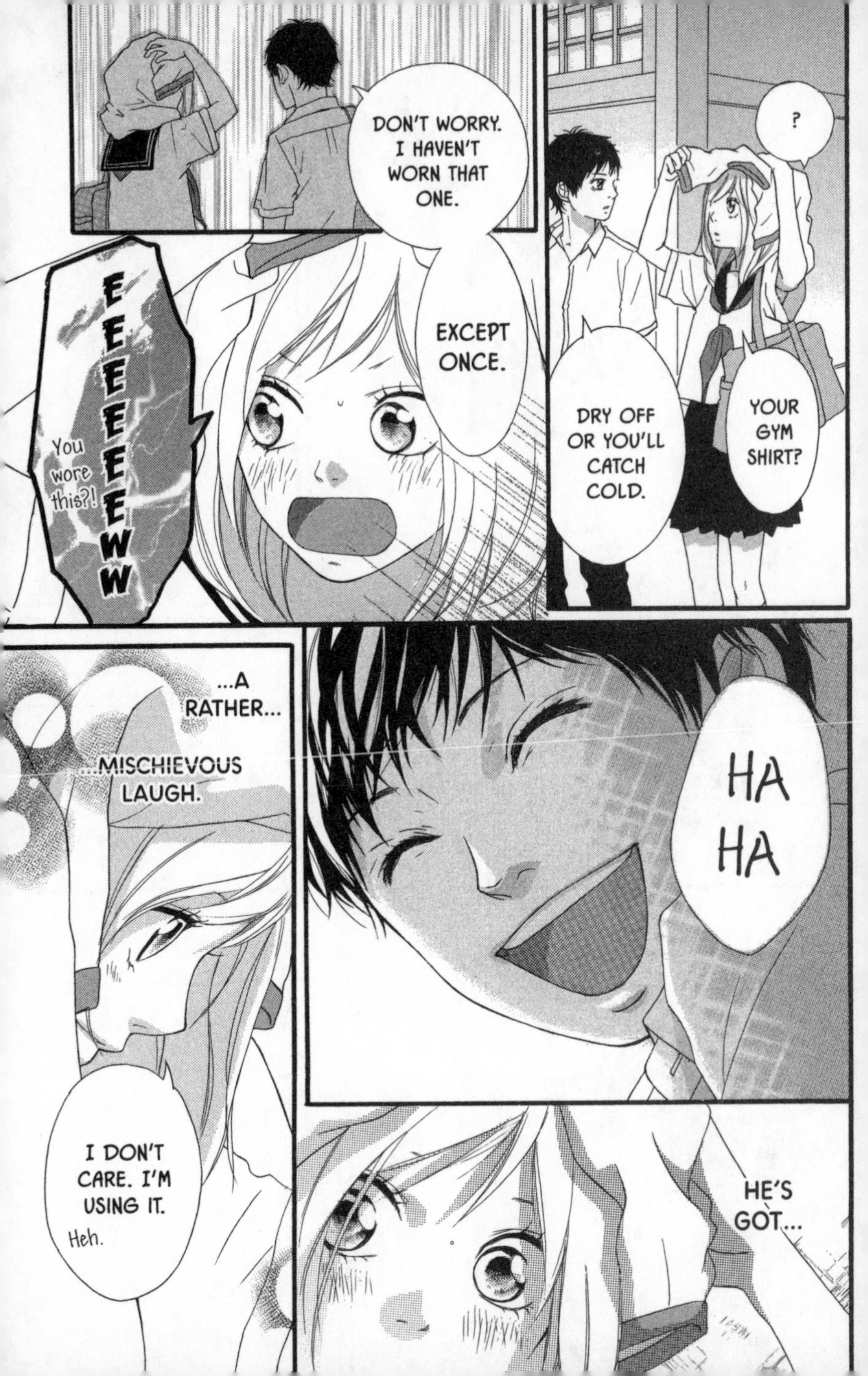
?
YOUR GYM SHIRT?
DRY OFF OR YOU'LL CATCH COLD.
DON'T WORRY. I HAVEN'T WORN THAT ONE.
EXCEPT ONCE.
EEEEEEEEWW
You wore this?!
HA HA
HE'S GOT...
...A RATHER...
...MISCHIEVOUS LAUGH.
I DON'T CARE. I'M USING IT.
Heh.

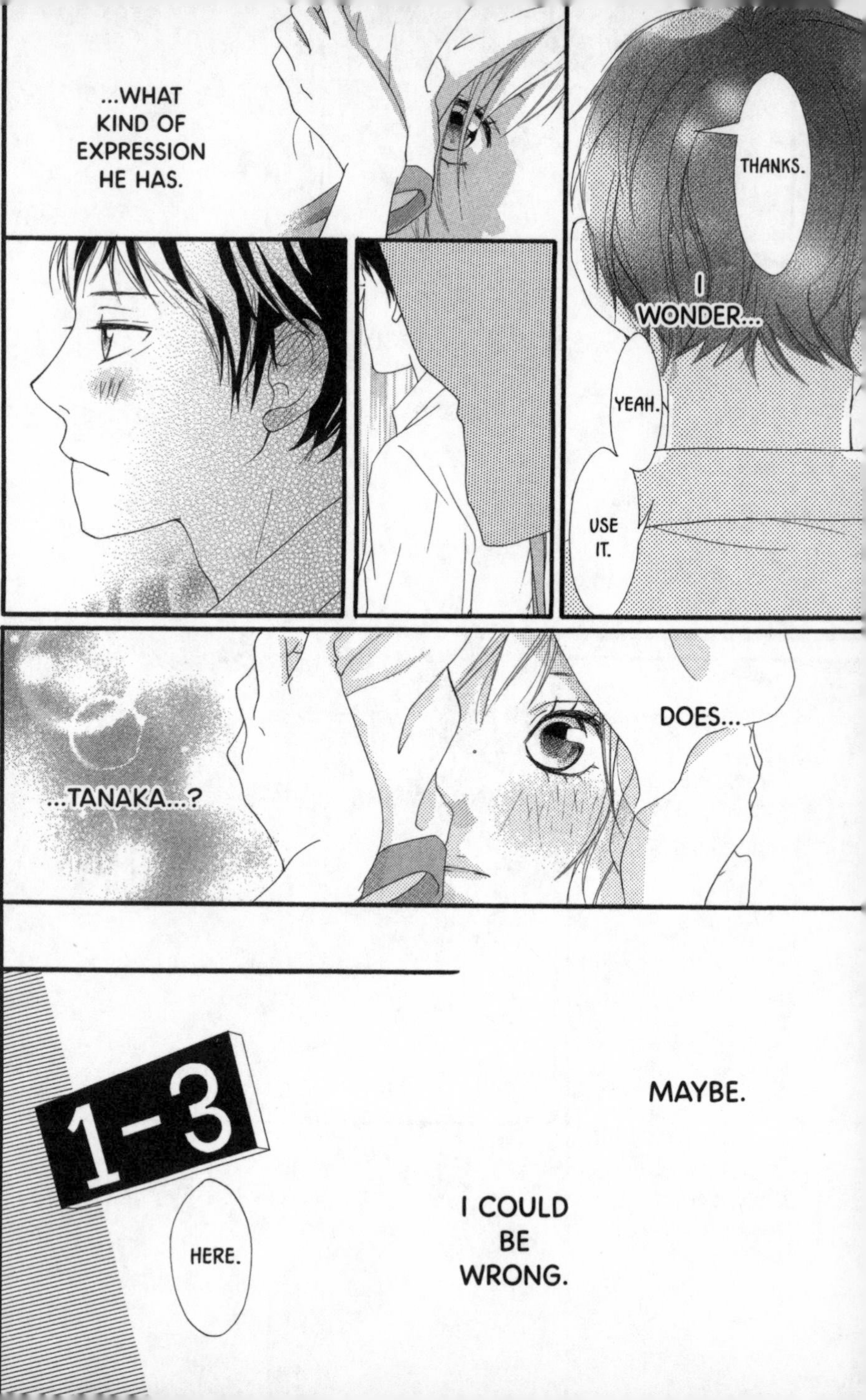
THANKS.
I WONDER...
YEAH.
USE IT.
...WHAT KIND OF EXPRESSION HE HAS.
DOES...
...TANAKA...?
MAYBE.
I COULD BE WRONG.
1-3
HERE.

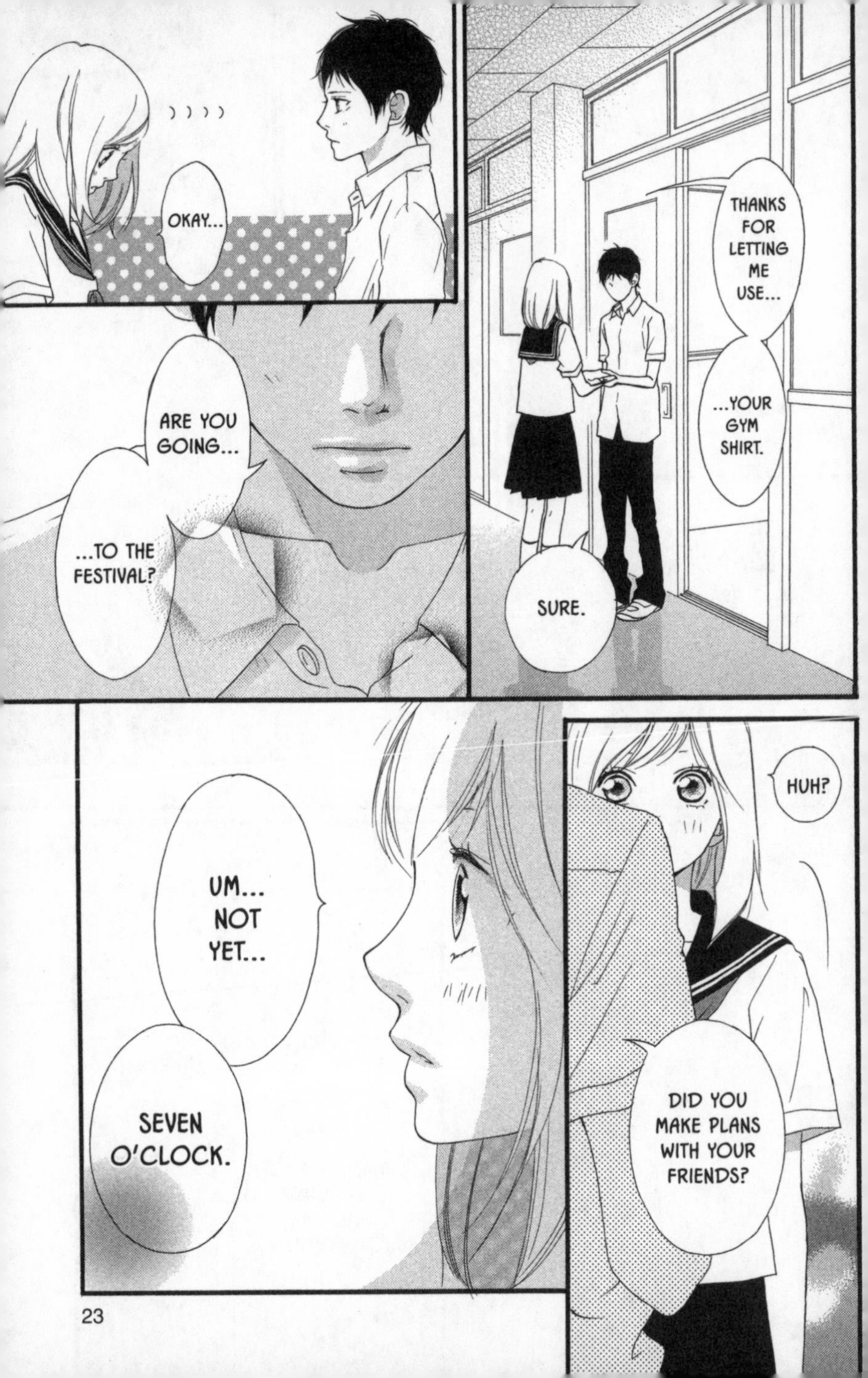
THANKS FOR LETTING ME USE...
...YOUR GYM SHIRT.
SURE.
OKAY...
ARE YOU GOING...
...TO THE FESTIVAL?
HUH?
DID YOU MAKE PLANS WITH YOUR FRIENDS?
UM... NOT YET...
SEVEN O'CLOCK.

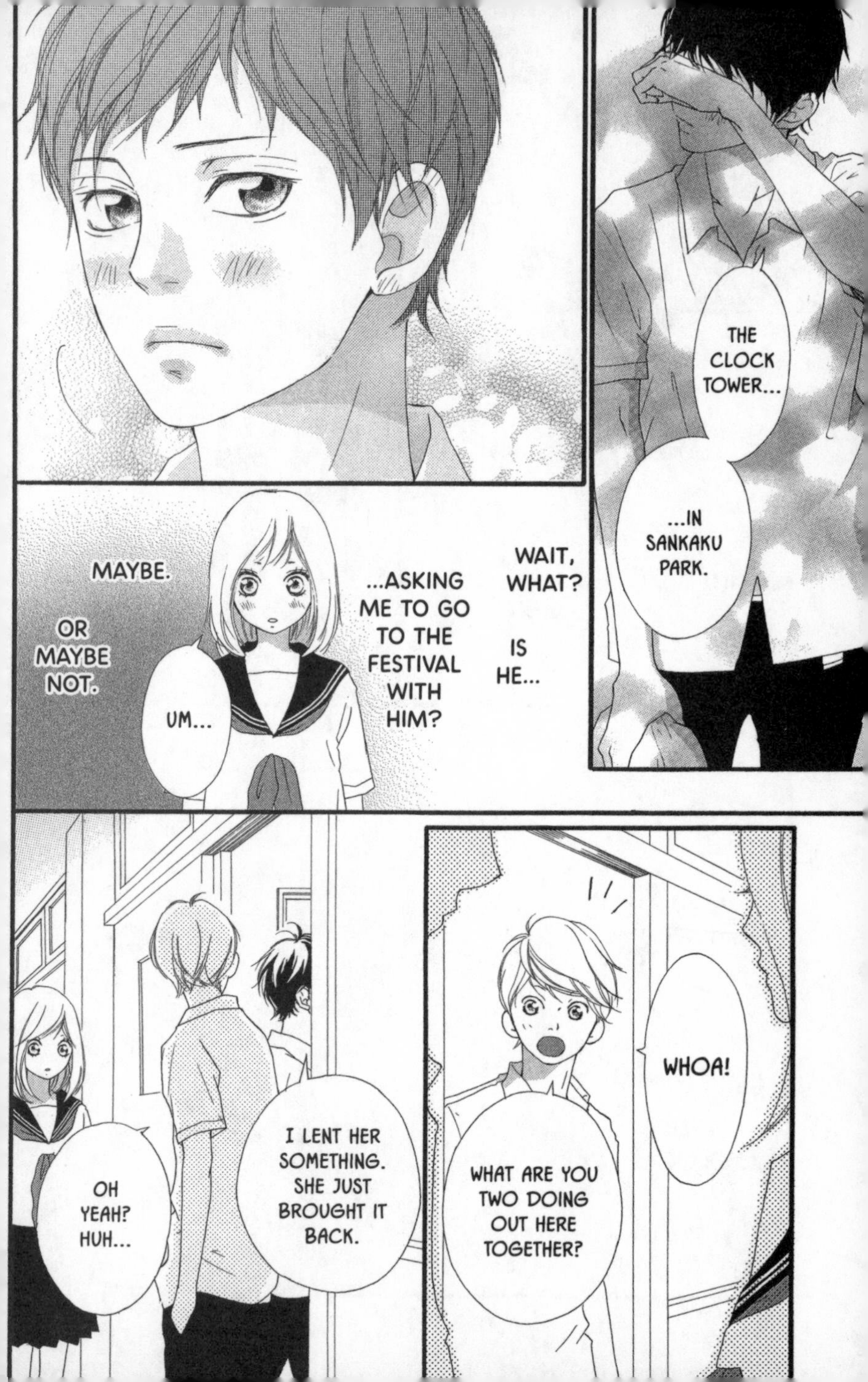
THE CLOCK TOWER...
...IN SANKAKU PARK.
WAIT, WHAT?
IS HE...
...ASKING ME TO GO TO THE FESTIVAL WITH HIM?
UM...
MAYBE.
OR MAYBE NOT.
WHOA!
WHAT ARE YOU TWO DOING OUT HERE TOGETHER?
I LENT HER SOMETHING. SHE JUST BROUGHT IT BACK.
OH YEAH? HUH...

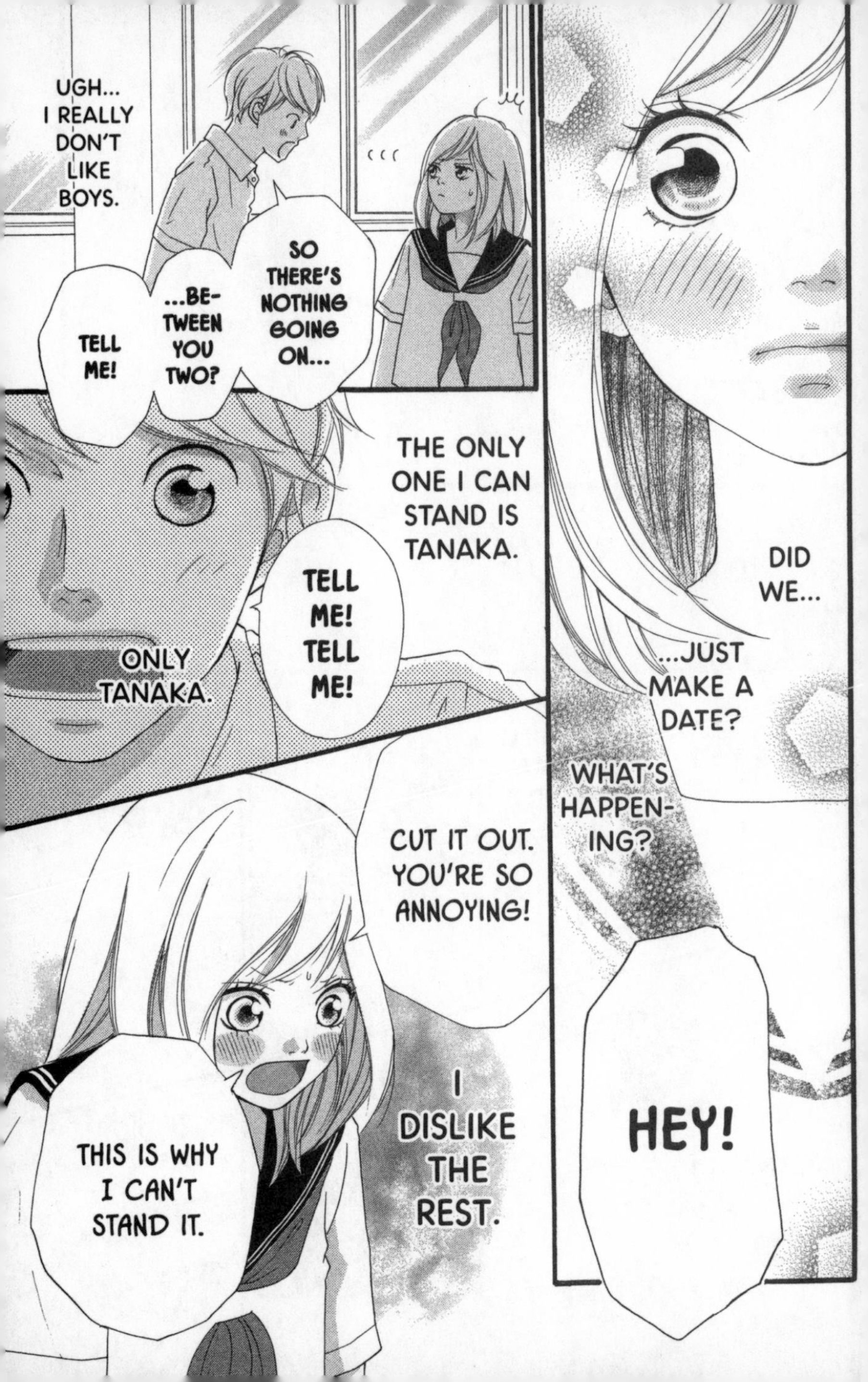
DID WE...
...JUST MAKE A DATE?
WHAT'S HAPPENING?
HEY!
UGH... I REALLY DON'T LIKE BOYS.
SO THERE'S NOTHING GOING ON...
...BE-TWEEN YOU TWO?
TELL ME!
THE ONLY ONE I CAN STAND IS TANAKA.
TELL ME! TELL ME!
ONLY TANAKA.
CUT IT OUT. YOU'RE SO ANNOYING!
I DISLIKE THE REST.
THIS IS WHY I CAN'T STAND IT.

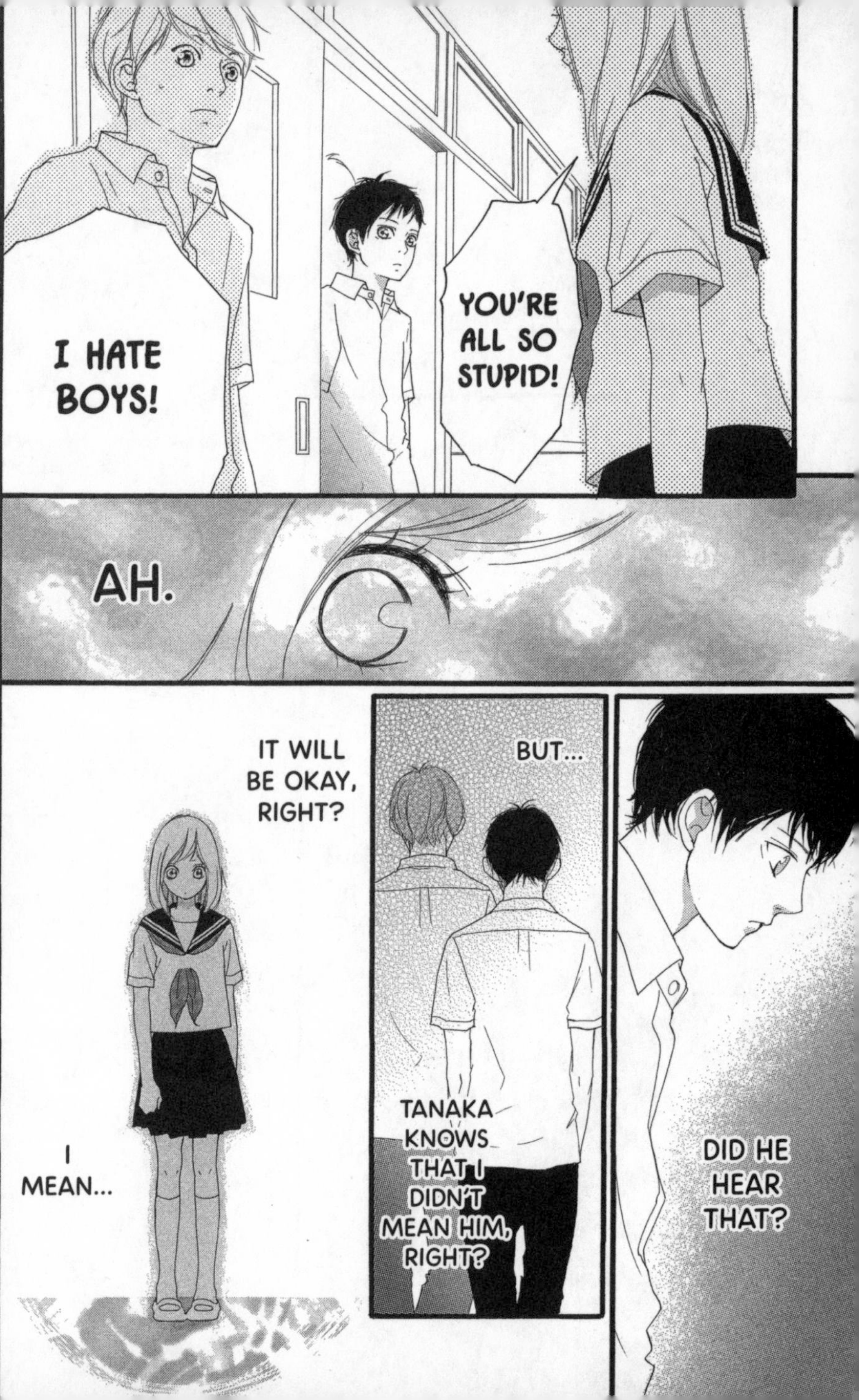
YOU'RE ALL SO STUPID!
I HATE BOYS!
AH.
DID HE HEAR THAT?
BUT...
TANAKA KNOWS THAT I DIDN'T MEAN HIM, RIGHT?
IT WILL BE OKAY, RIGHT?
I MEAN...

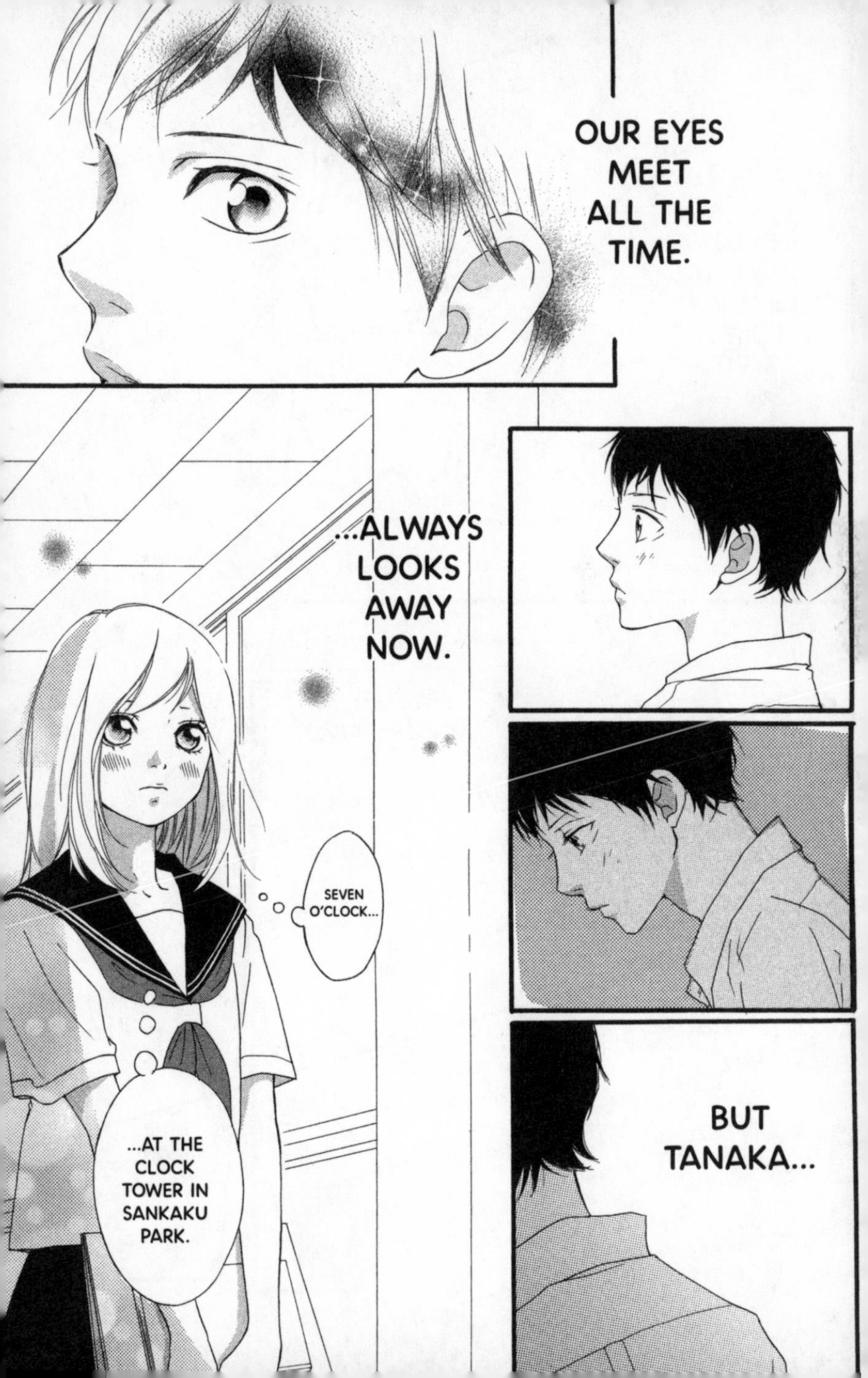
OUR EYES MEET ALL THE TIME.
BUT TANAKA...
...ALWAYS LOOKS AWAY NOW.
SEVEN O'CLOCK...
...AT THE CLOCK TOWER IN SANKAKU PARK.

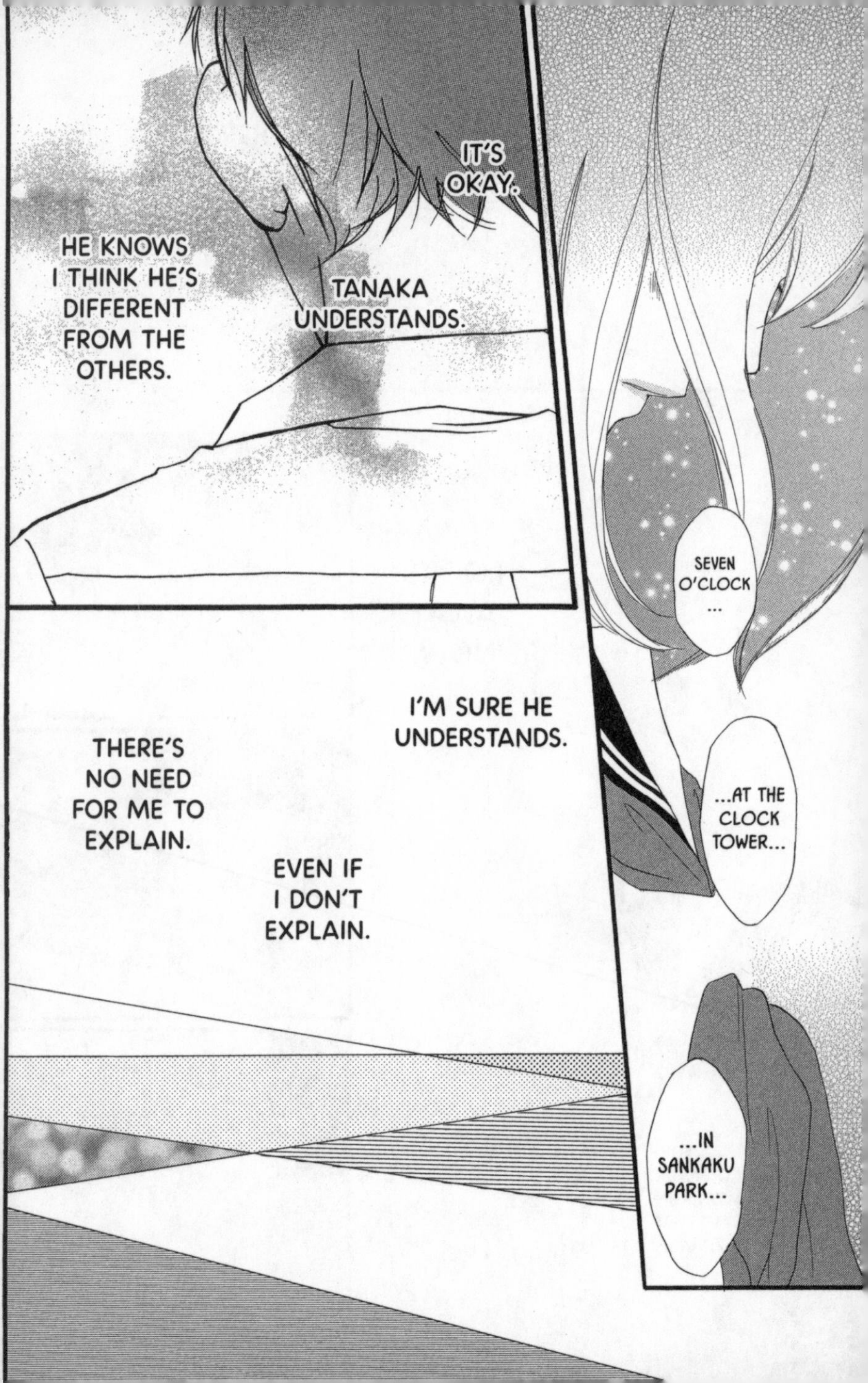
SEVEN O'CLOCK ...
...AT THE CLOCK TOWER...
...IN SANKAKU PARK...
IT'S OKAY.
TANAKA UNDERSTANDS.
HE KNOWS I THINK HE'S DIFFERENT FROM THE OTHERS.
I'M SURE HE UNDERSTANDS.
THERE'S NO NEED FOR ME TO EXPLAIN.
EVEN IF I DON'T EXPLAIN.

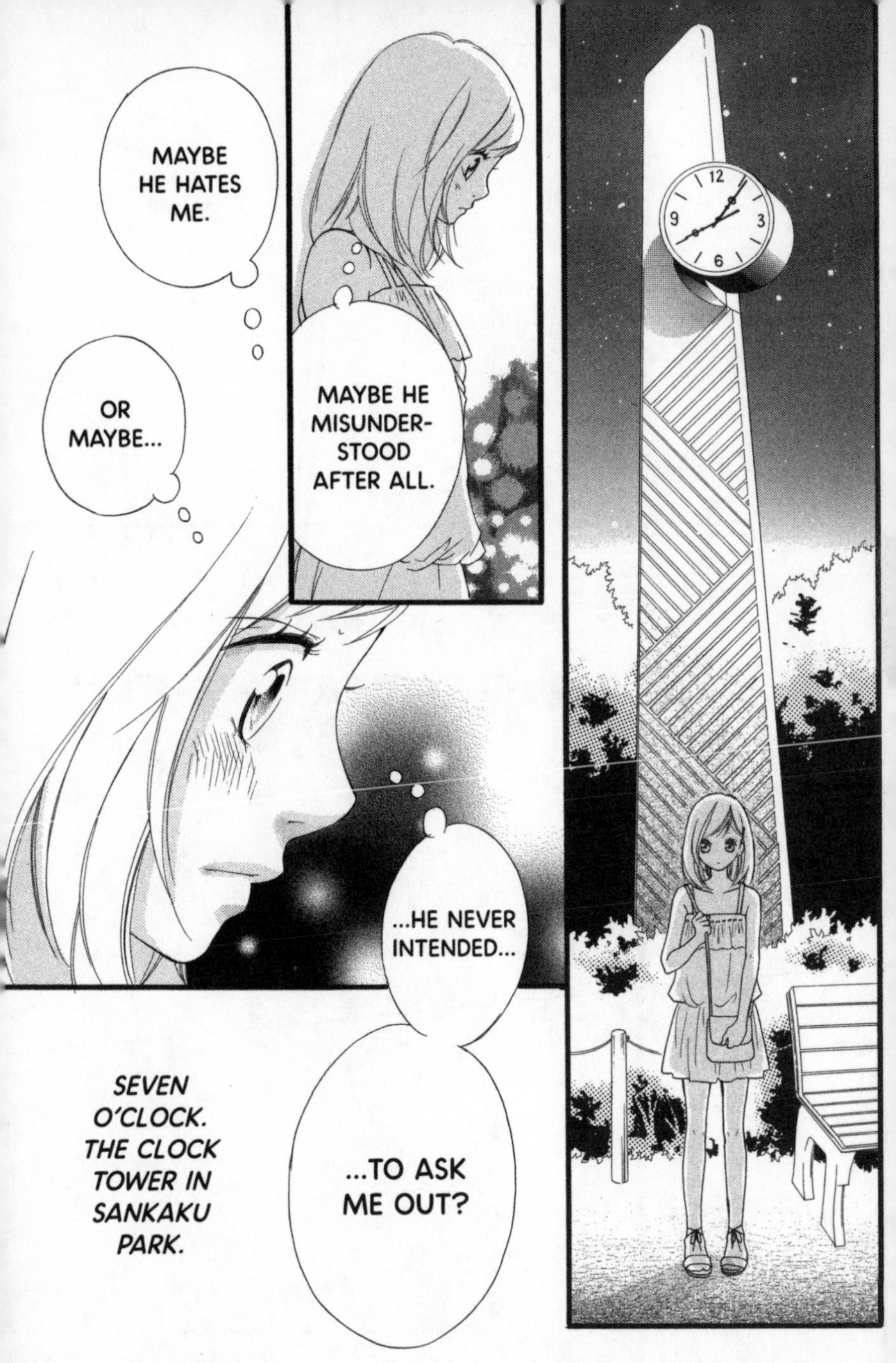
MAYBE HE MISUNDERSTOOD AFTER ALL.
MAYBE HE HATES ME.
OR MAYBE...
...HE NEVER INTENDED...
...TO ASK ME OUT?
SEVEN O'CLOCK. THE CLOCK TOWER IN SANKAKU PARK.

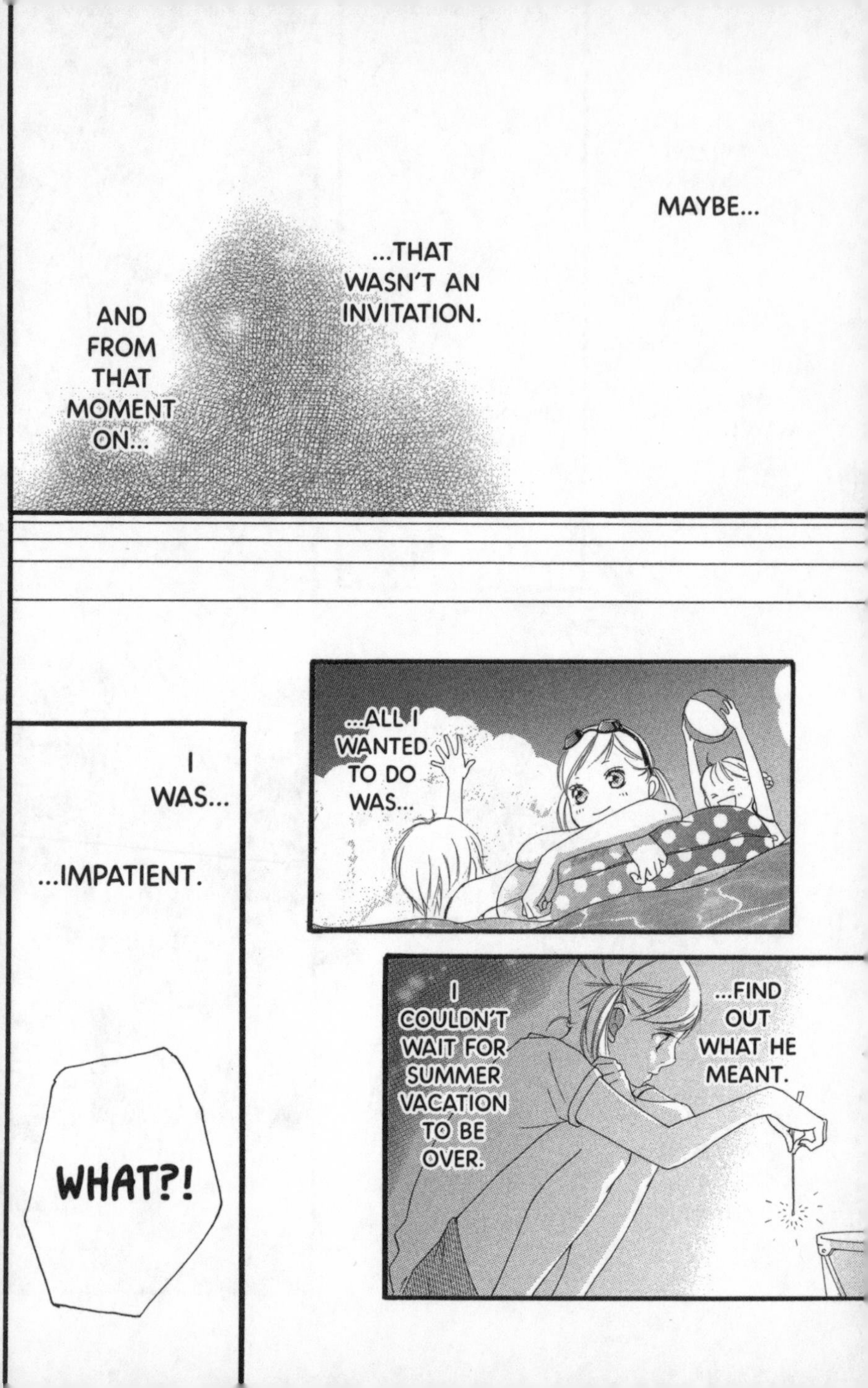
MAYBE...
...THAT WASN'T AN INVITATION.
AND FROM THAT MOMENT ON...
...ALL I WANTED TO DO WAS...
...FIND OUT WHAT HE MEANT.
I COULDN'T WAIT FOR SUMMER VACATION TO BE OVER.
I WAS...
...IMPATIENT.
WHAT?!

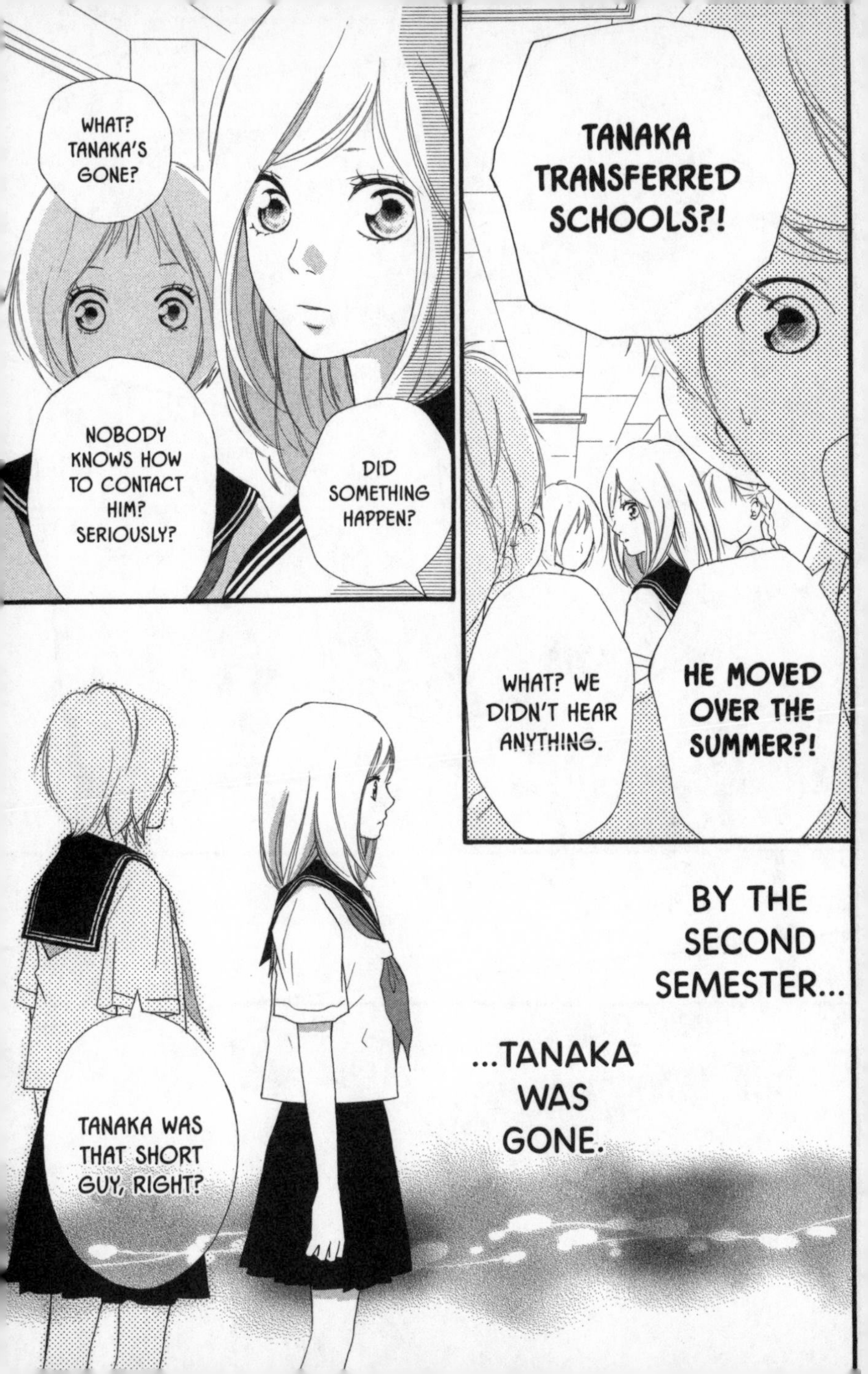
TANAKA TRANSFERRED SCHOOLS?!
HE MOVED OVER THE SUMMER?!
WHAT? WE DIDN'T HEAR ANYTHING.
WHAT? TANAKA'S GONE?
DID SOMETHING HAPPEN?
NOBODY KNOWS HOW TO CONTACT HIM? SERIOUSLY?
BY THE SECOND SEMESTER...
...TANAKA WAS GONE.
TANAKA WAS THAT SHORT GUY, RIGHT?

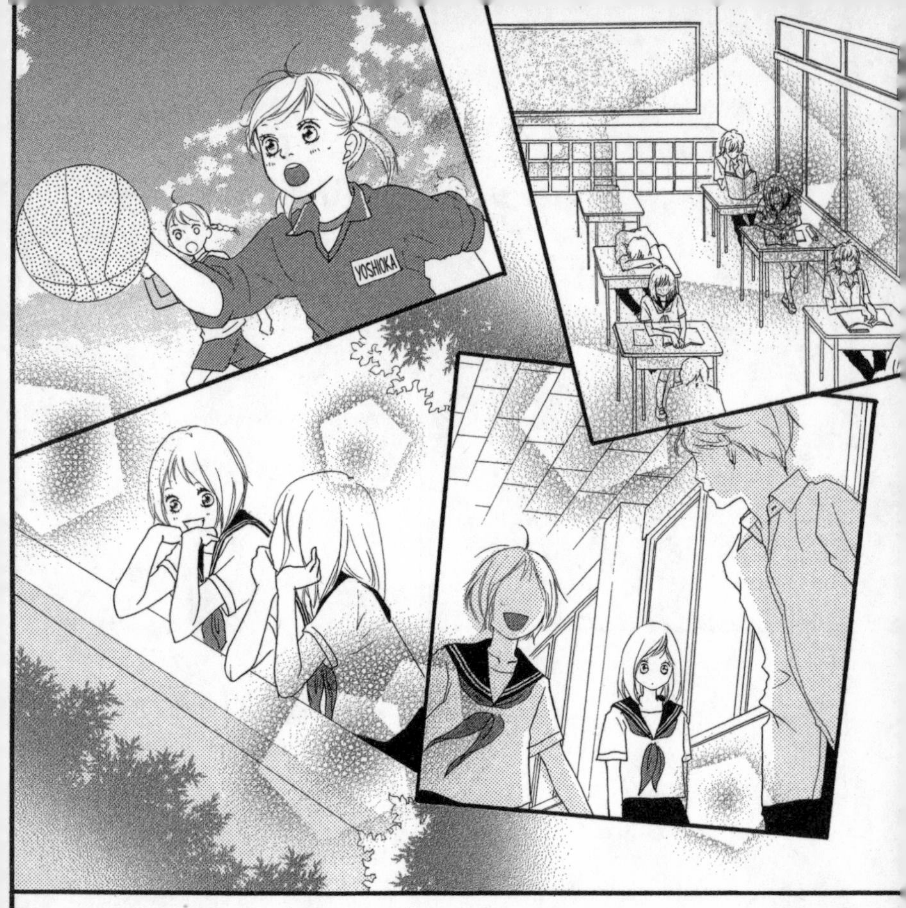
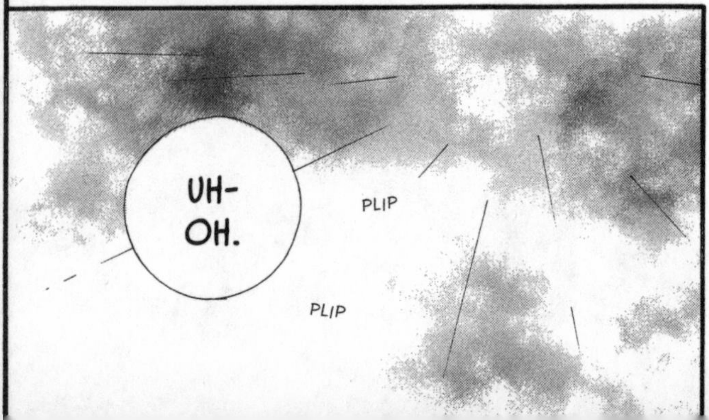
UH-OH.
PLIP
PLIP

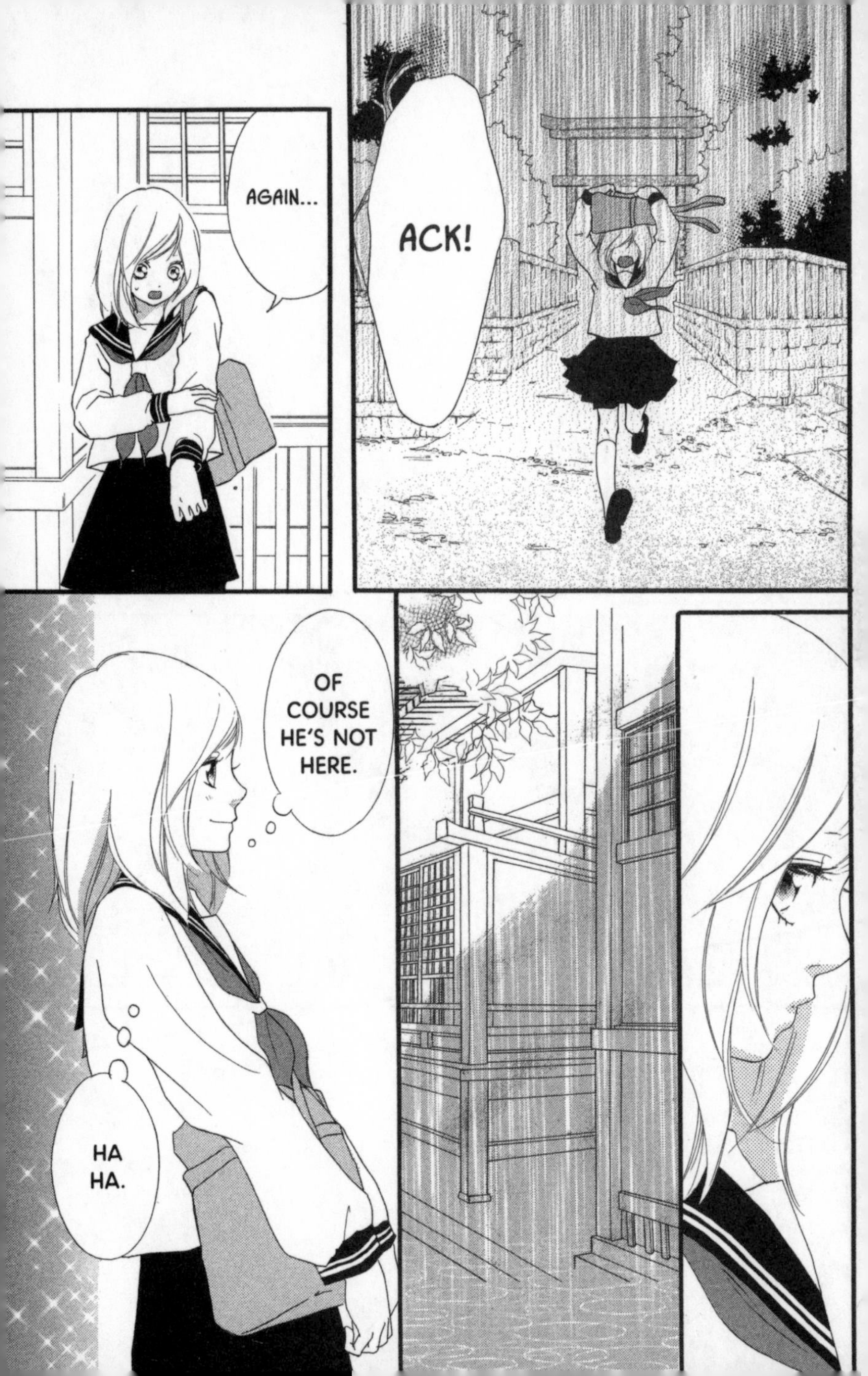
ACK!
AGAIN...
OF COURSE HE'S NOT HERE.
HA HA.

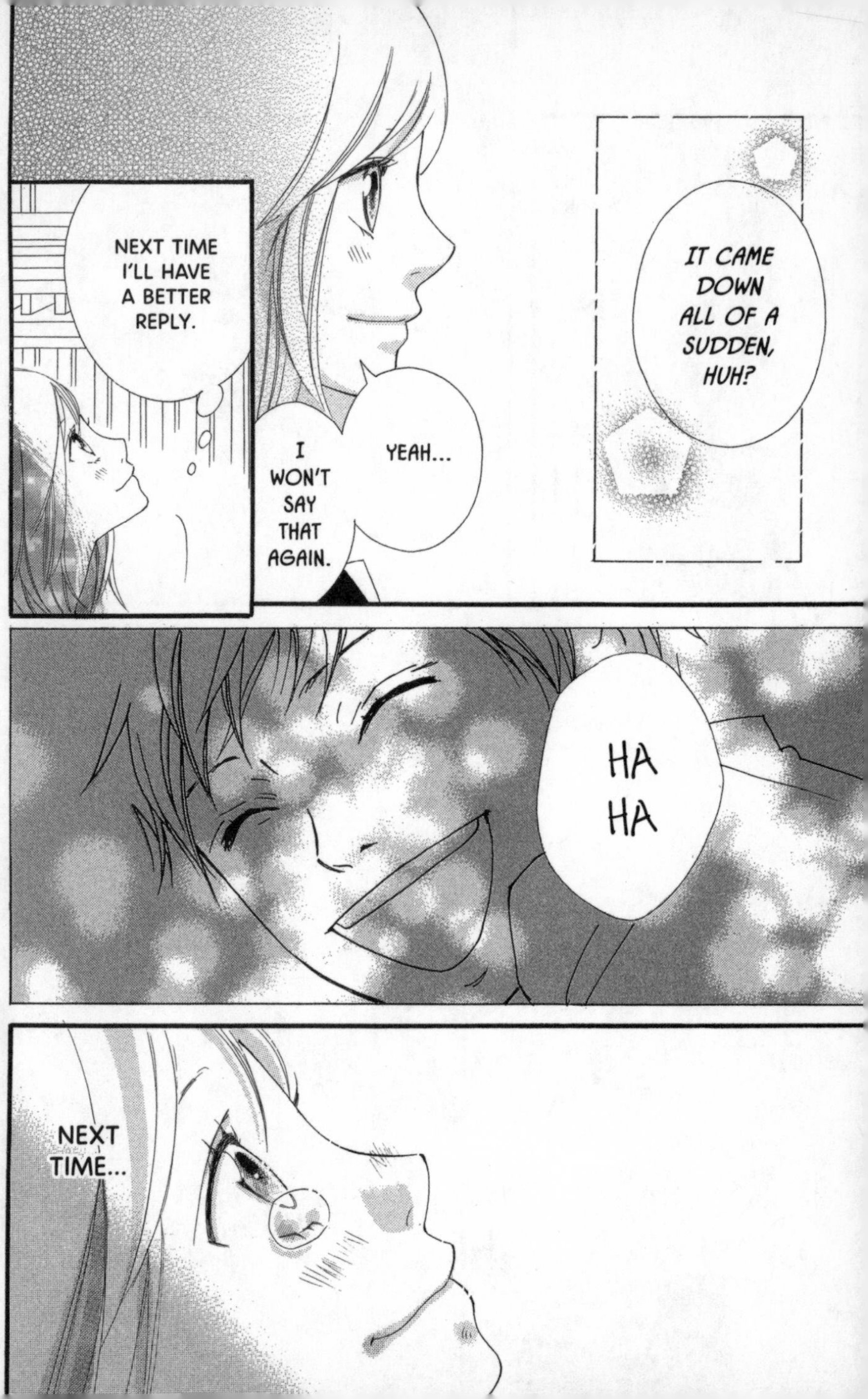
IT CAME DOWN ALL OF A SUDDEN, HUH?
YEAH...
I WON'T SAY THAT AGAIN.
NEXT TIME I'LL HAVE A BETTER REPLY.
HA HA
NEXT TIME...

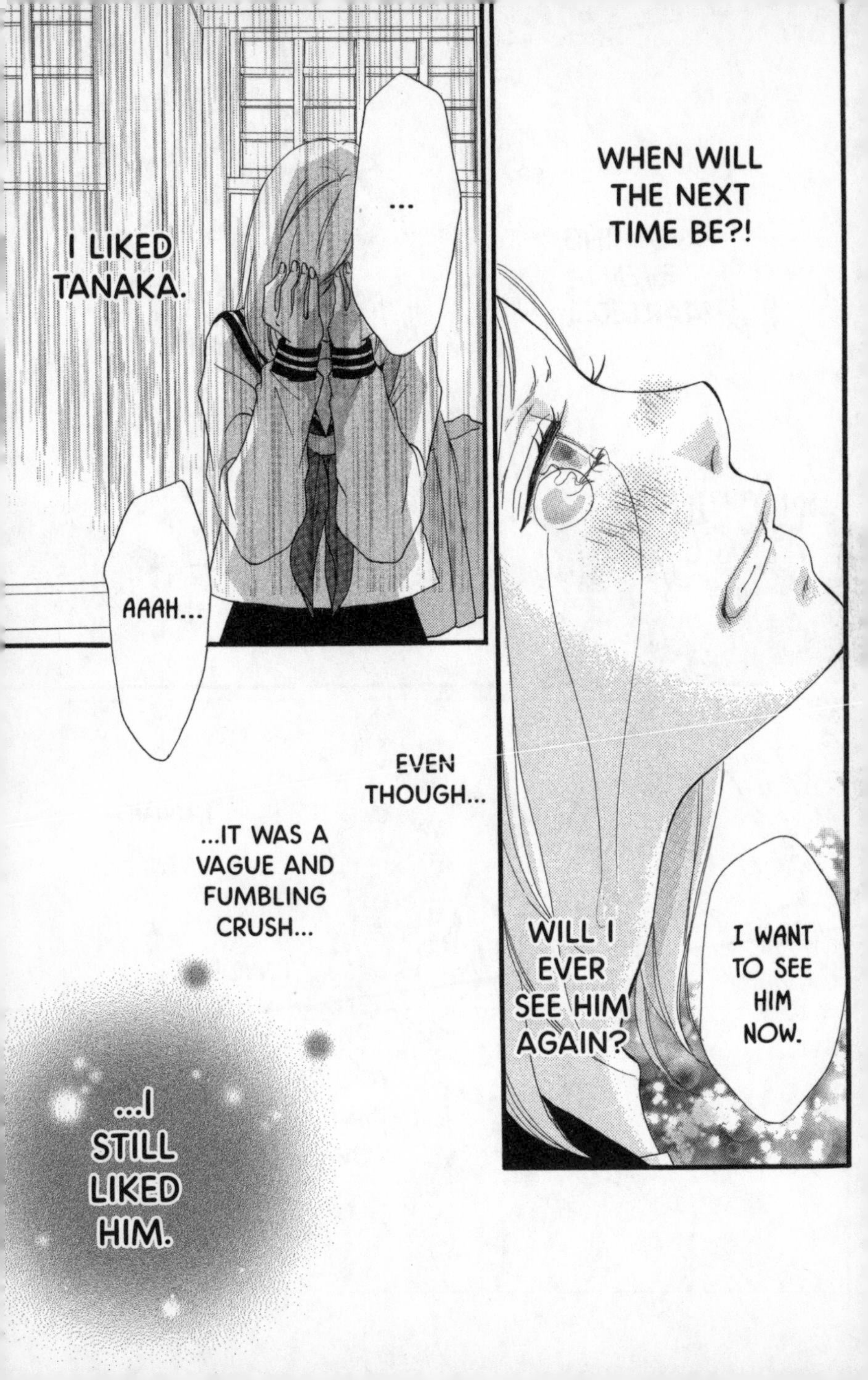
WHEN WILL THE NEXT TIME BE?!
I WANT TO SEE HIM NOW.
WILL I EVER SEE HIM AGAIN?
...
I LIKED TANAKA.
AAAH...
EVEN THOUGH...
...IT WAS A VAGUE AND FUMBLING CRUSH...
...I STILL LIKED HIM.

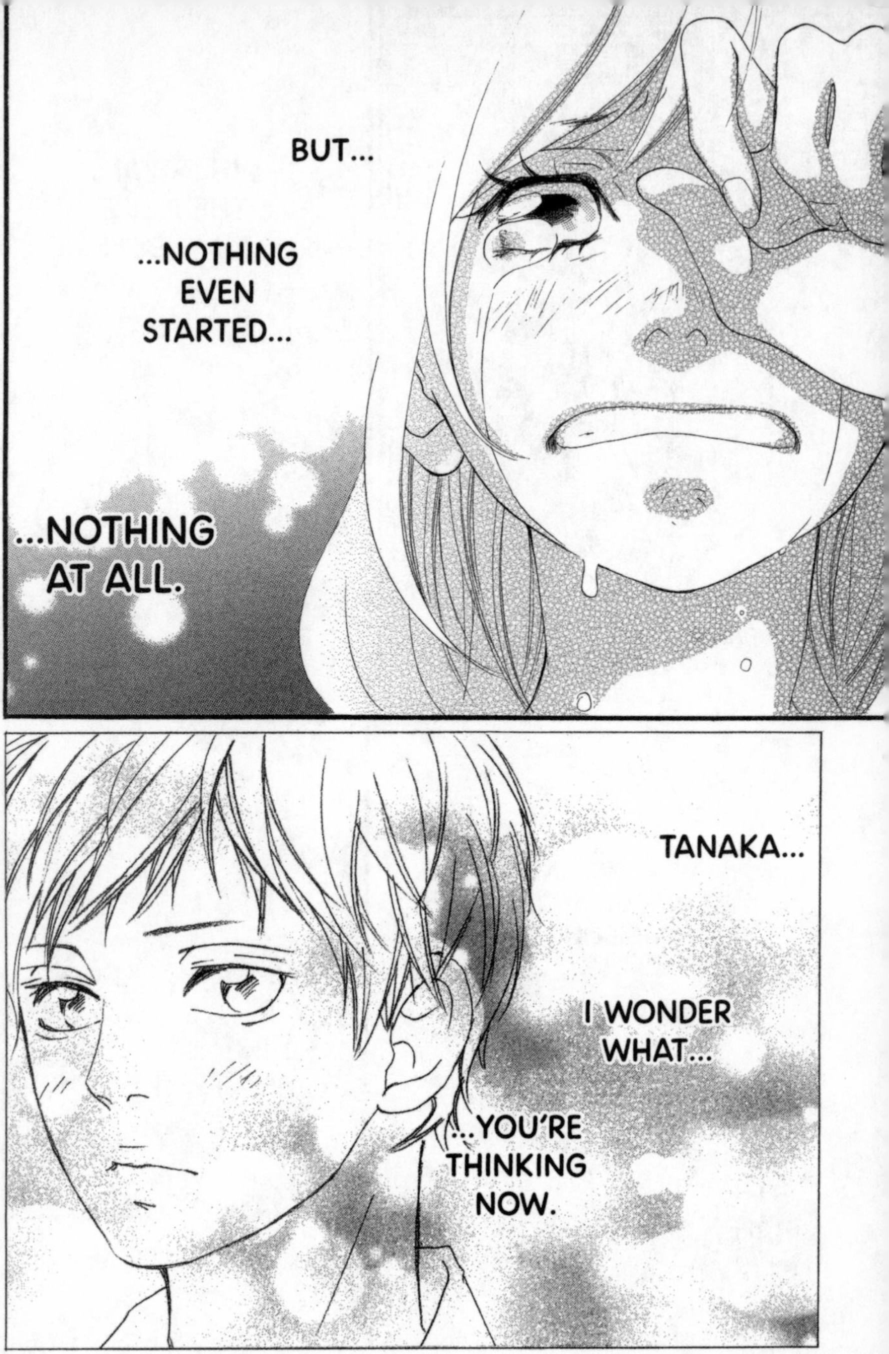
BUT...
...NOTHING EVEN STARTED...
...NOTHING AT ALL.
TANAKA...
I WONDER WHAT...
...YOU'RE THINKING NOW.

Right away people sent letters and tweets, asking about the meaning of the Japanese title *Aoharaido*. So I'd like to take a moment to answer.

Aoharaido = youth + ride

The Japanese kanji for "youth"* can also be read as *aoharu,* and I imagine that the characters are on a ride through their youth, giving it all that they can. Compared to *aoharuraido,* when you say it out loud, *aoharaido* is easier to say and more impactful, so that became the title of the series.

Writing this story reminds me of my own high school days, and while I look back at the many things that I would've liked to have done better, I also remember that I felt overwhelmed at the time, and I was doing the best I could. (Although I still feel overwhelmed.)

Sometimes you're optimistic, sometimes you're pessimistic, and sometimes you just can't see clearly, which is overwhelming in itself. Overwhelmed by both the good and the bad. To me, that's what I picture when I think of youth. What about you?

*The kanji for "youth" is 青春 (seishuun). The *ao haru* reading means "blue spring."

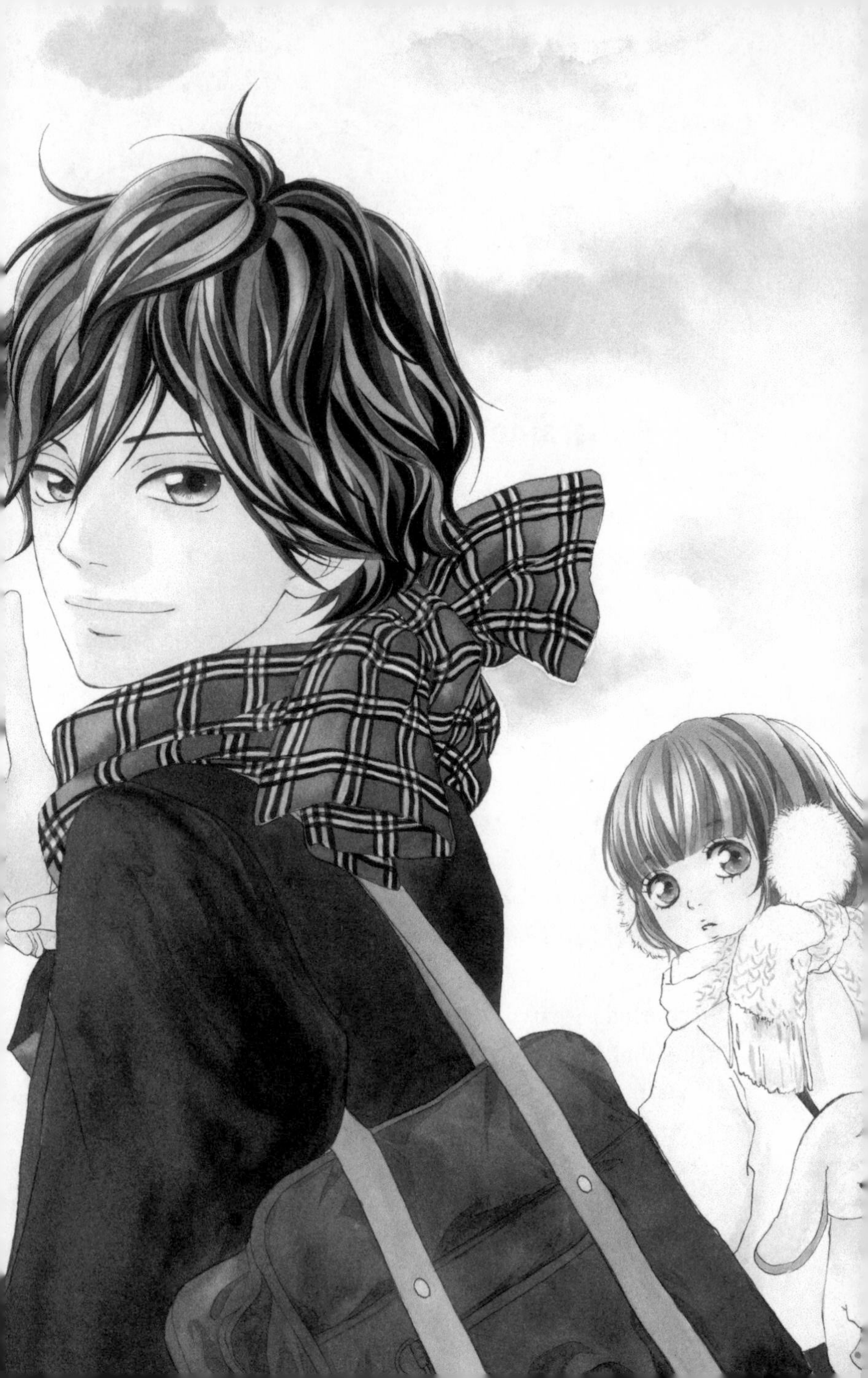

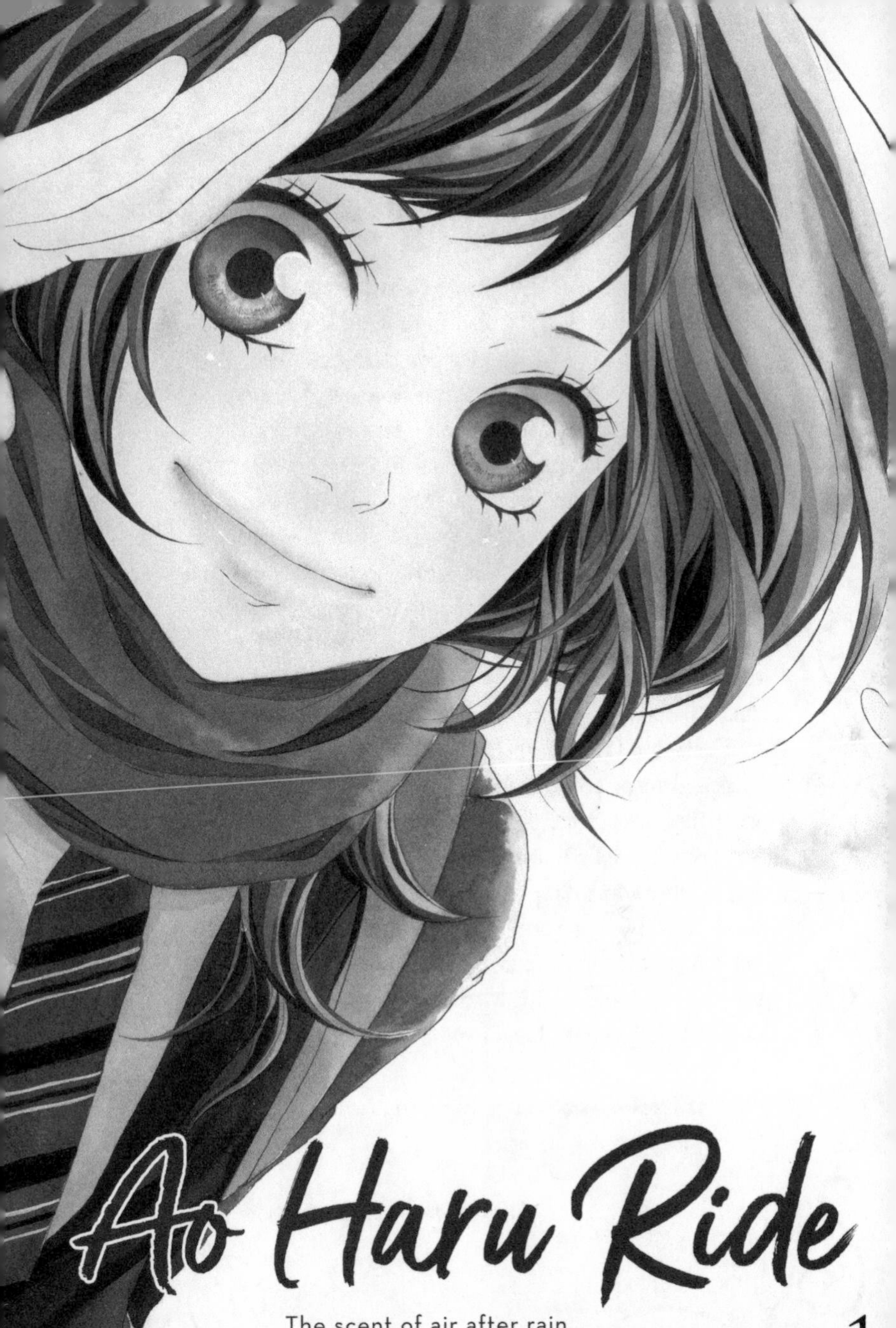
Ao Haru Ride

The scent of air after rain...
In the light around us, I felt your heartbeat.

CHAPTER 1

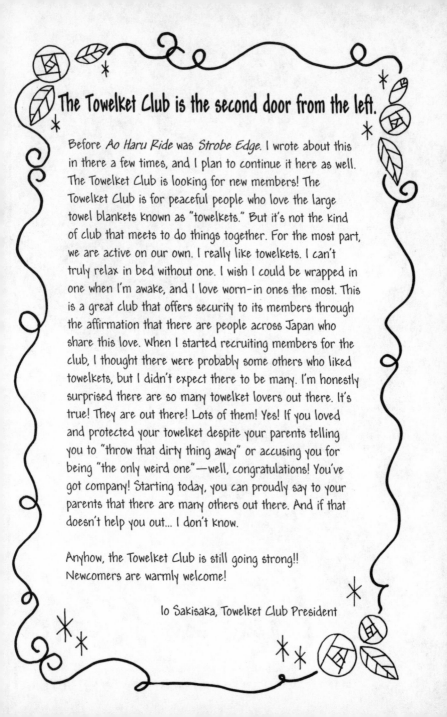

The Towelket Club is the second door from the left.

Before *Ao Haru Ride* was *Strobe Edge*. I wrote about this in there a few times, and I plan to continue it here as well. The Towelket Club is looking for new members! The Towelket Club is for peaceful people who love the large towel blankets known as "towelkets." But it's not the kind of club that meets to do things together. For the most part, we are active on our own. I really like towelkets. I can't truly relax in bed without one. I wish I could be wrapped in one when I'm awake, and I love worn-in ones the most. This is a great club that offers security to its members through the affirmation that there are people across Japan who share this love. When I started recruiting members for the club, I thought there were probably some others who liked towelkets, but I didn't expect there to be many. I'm honestly surprised there are so many towelket lovers out there. It's true! They are out there! Lots of them! Yes! If you loved and protected your towelket despite your parents telling you to "throw that dirty thing away" or accusing you for being "the only weird one"—well, congratulations! You've got company! Starting today, you can proudly say to your parents that there are many others out there. And if that doesn't help you out... I don't know.

Anyhow, the Towelket Club is still going strong!! Newcomers are warmly welcome!

Io Sakisaka, Towelket Club President

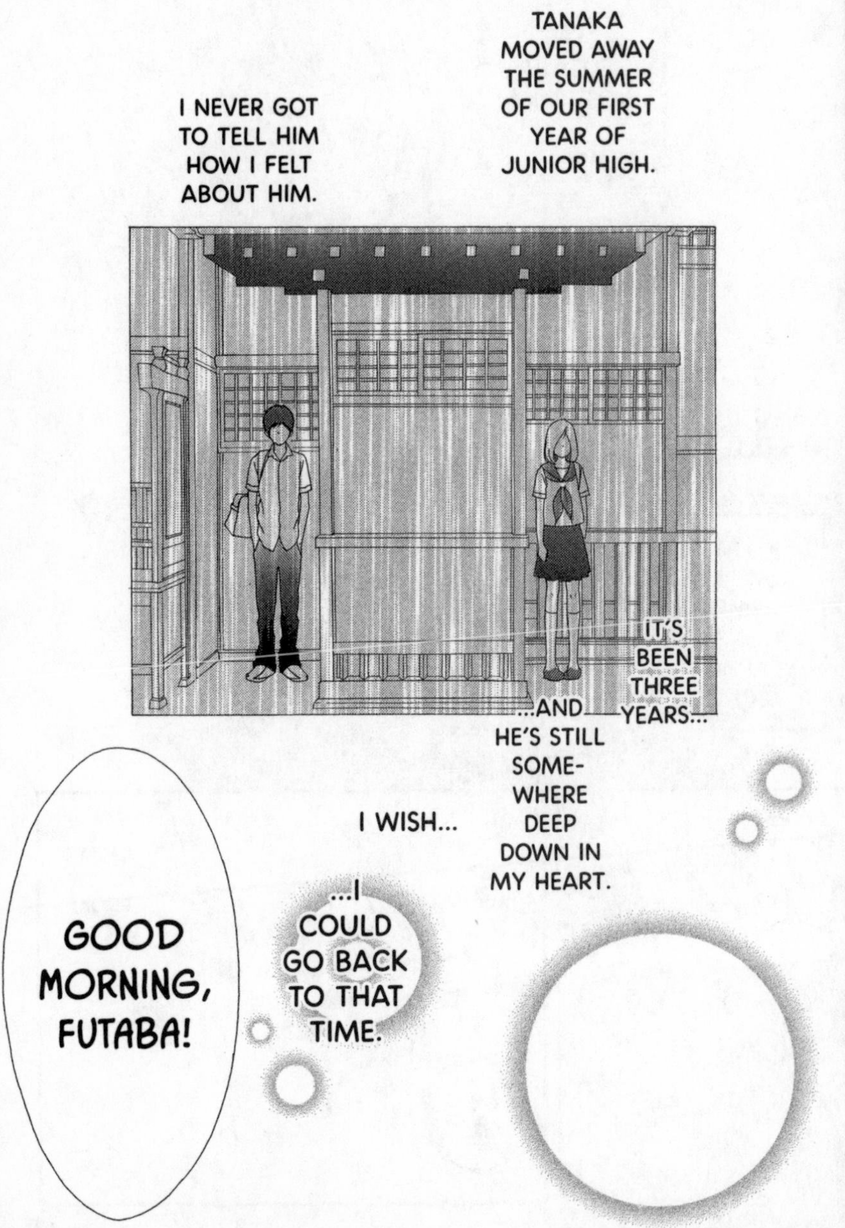
TANAKA MOVED AWAY THE SUMMER OF OUR FIRST YEAR OF JUNIOR HIGH.
I NEVER GOT TO TELL HIM HOW I FELT ABOUT HIM.
IT'S BEEN THREE YEARS...
...AND HE'S STILL SOME-WHERE DEEP DOWN IN MY HEART.
I WISH...
...I COULD GO BACK TO THAT TIME.
GOOD MORNING, FUTABA!

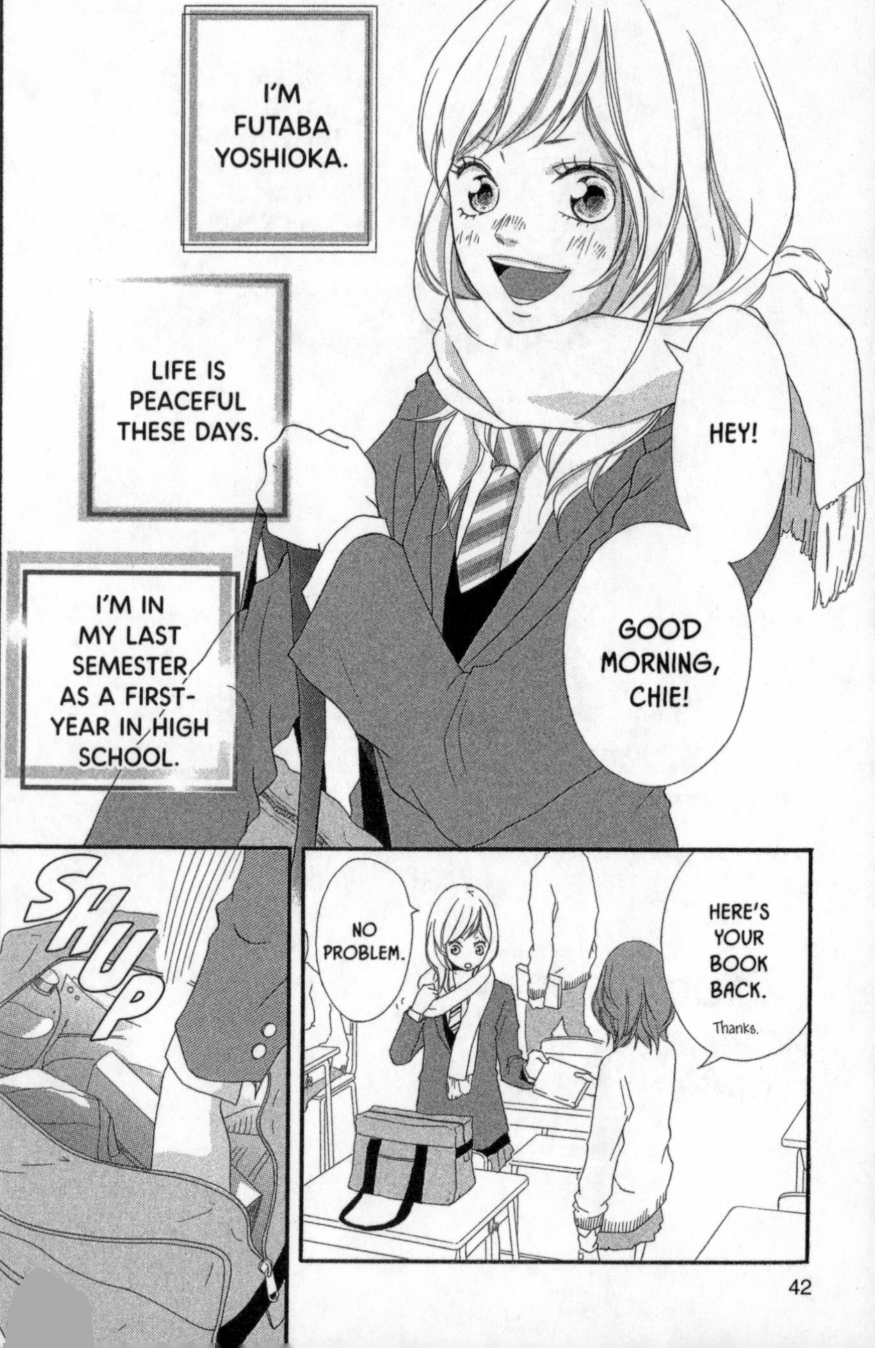
I'M FUTABA YOSHIOKA.
LIFE IS PEACEFUL THESE DAYS.
HEY!
GOOD MORNING, CHIE!
I'M IN MY LAST SEMESTER AS A FIRST-YEAR IN HIGH SCHOOL.
HERE'S YOUR BOOK BACK.
Thanks.
NO PROBLEM.
SHUP

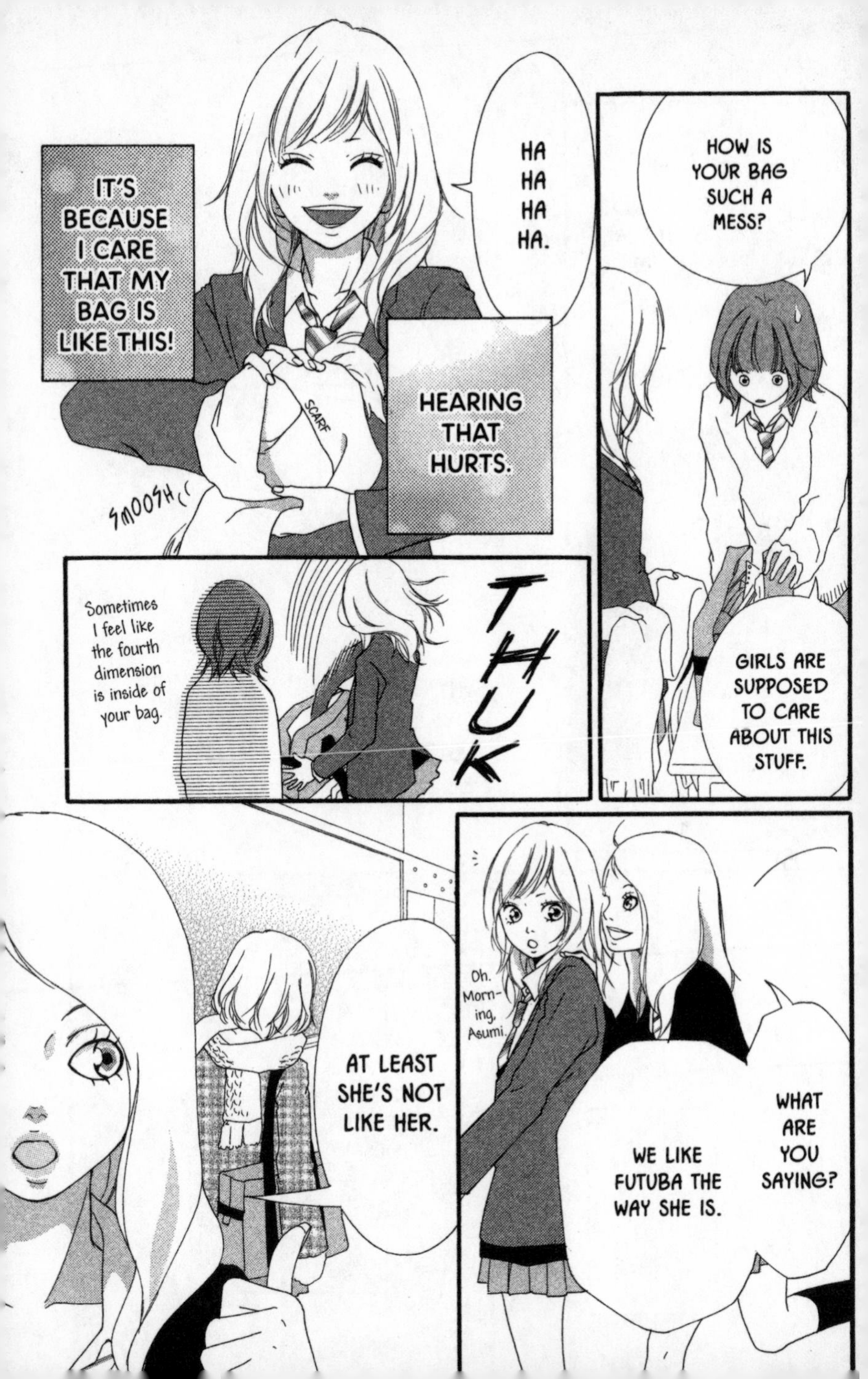
HOW IS YOUR BAG SUCH A MESS?
GIRLS ARE SUPPOSED TO CARE ABOUT THIS STUFF.
HA HA HA HA.
IT'S BECAUSE I CARE THAT MY BAG IS LIKE THIS!
HEARING THAT HURTS.
SCARF
SMOOSH
THUK
Sometimes I feel like the fourth dimension is inside of your bag.
Oh. Morning, Asumi.
WHAT ARE YOU SAYING?
WE LIKE FUTUBA THE WAY SHE IS.
AT LEAST SHE'S NOT LIKE HER.

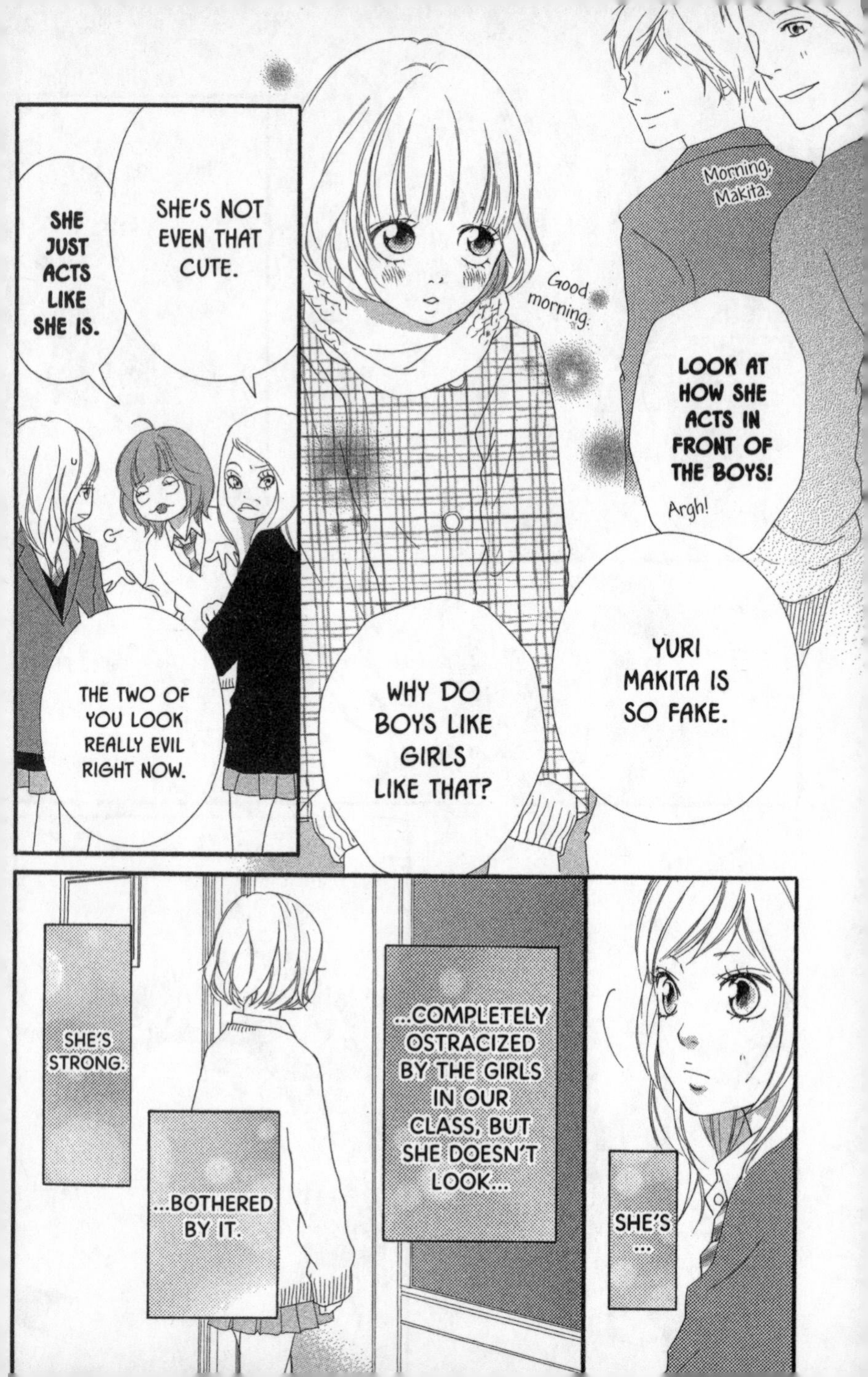
Morning, Makita.
Good morning.
LOOK AT HOW SHE ACTS IN FRONT OF THE BOYS!
Argh!
YURI MAKITA IS SO FAKE.
WHY DO BOYS LIKE GIRLS LIKE THAT?
SHE'S NOT EVEN THAT CUTE.
SHE JUST ACTS LIKE SHE IS.
THE TWO OF YOU LOOK REALLY EVIL RIGHT NOW.
SHE'S ...
...COMPLETELY OSTRACIZED BY THE GIRLS IN OUR CLASS, BUT SHE DOESN'T LOOK...
...BOTHERED BY IT.
SHE'S STRONG.

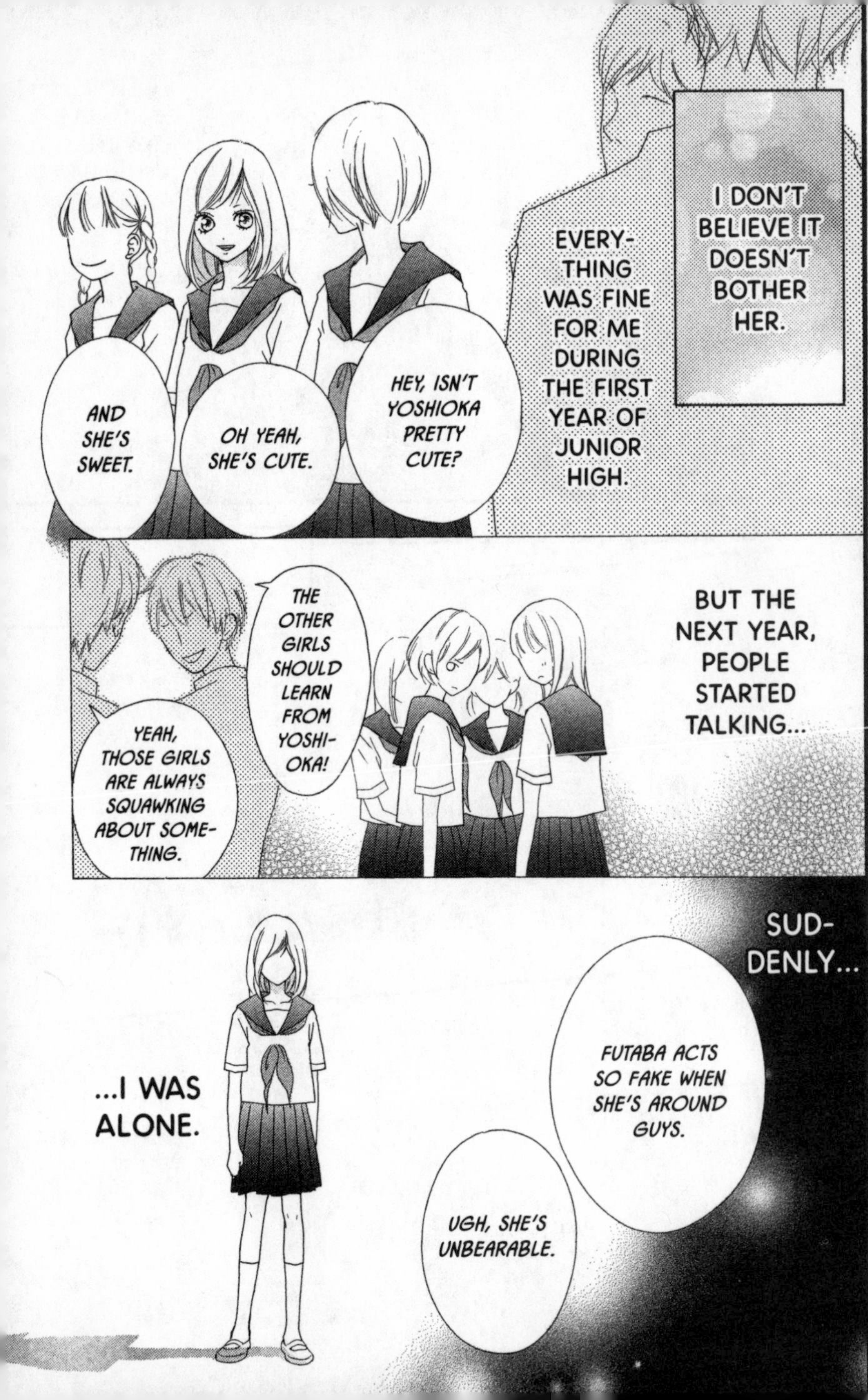
I DON'T BELIEVE IT DOESN'T BOTHER HER.
EVERYTHING WAS FINE FOR ME DURING THE FIRST YEAR OF JUNIOR HIGH.
HEY, ISN'T YOSHIOKA PRETTY CUTE?
OH YEAH, SHE'S CUTE.
AND SHE'S SWEET.
BUT THE NEXT YEAR, PEOPLE STARTED TALKING...
THE OTHER GIRLS SHOULD LEARN FROM YOSHIOKA!
YEAH, THOSE GIRLS ARE ALWAYS SQUAWKING ABOUT SOMETHING.
SUDDENLY...
FUTABA ACTS SO FAKE WHEN SHE'S AROUND GUYS.
UGH, SHE'S UNBEARABLE.
...I WAS ALONE.

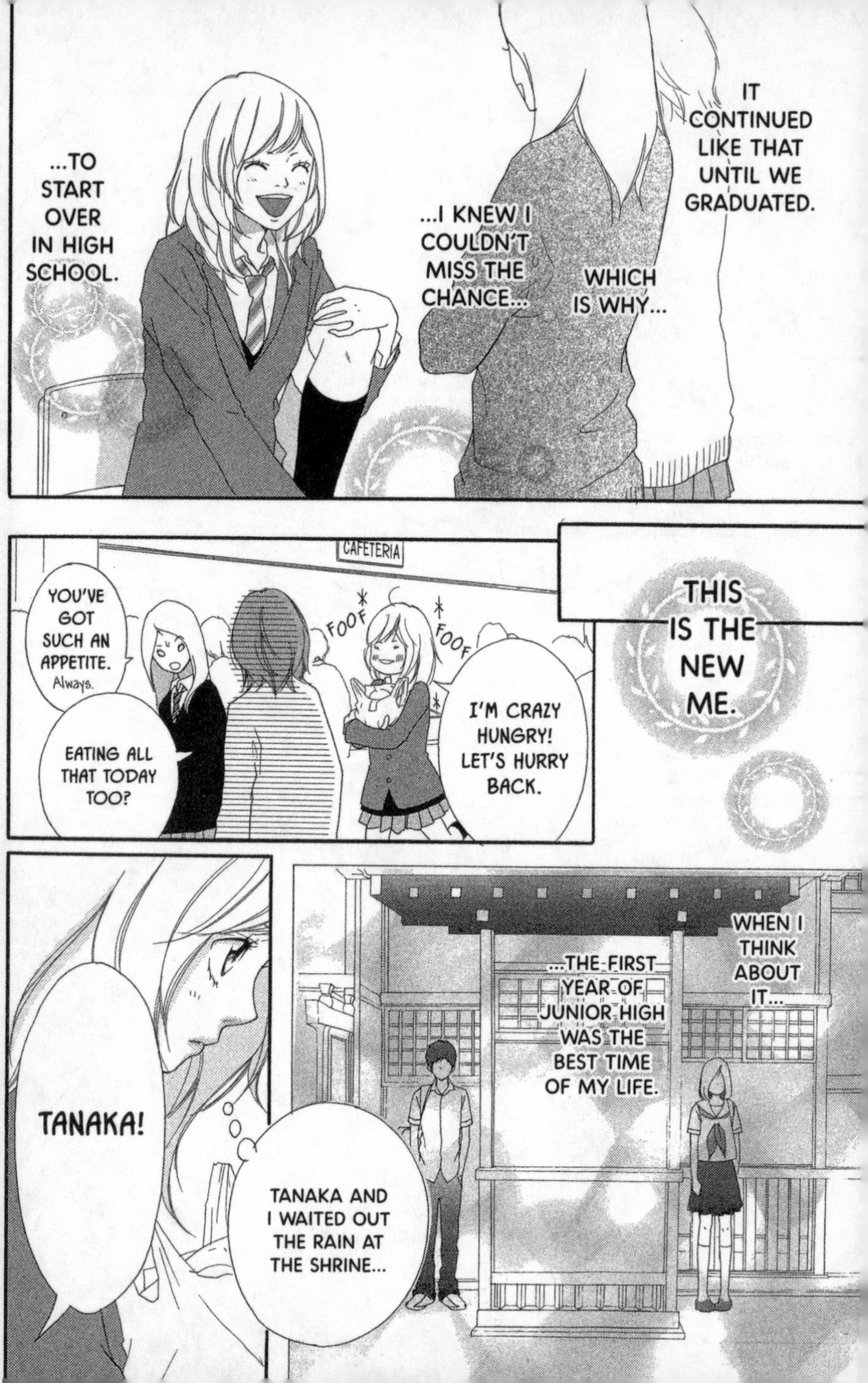
IT CONTINUED LIKE THAT UNTIL WE GRADUATED.
WHICH IS WHY...
...I KNEW I COULDN'T MISS THE CHANCE...
...TO START OVER IN HIGH SCHOOL.
THIS IS THE NEW ME.
CAFETERIA
FOOF
FOOF
I'M CRAZY HUNGRY! LET'S HURRY BACK.
YOU'VE GOT SUCH AN APPETITE.
Always.
EATING ALL THAT TODAY TOO?
WHEN I THINK ABOUT IT...
...THE FIRST YEAR OF JUNIOR HIGH WAS THE BEST TIME OF MY LIFE.
TANAKA AND I WAITED OUT THE RAIN AT THE SHRINE...
TANAKA!

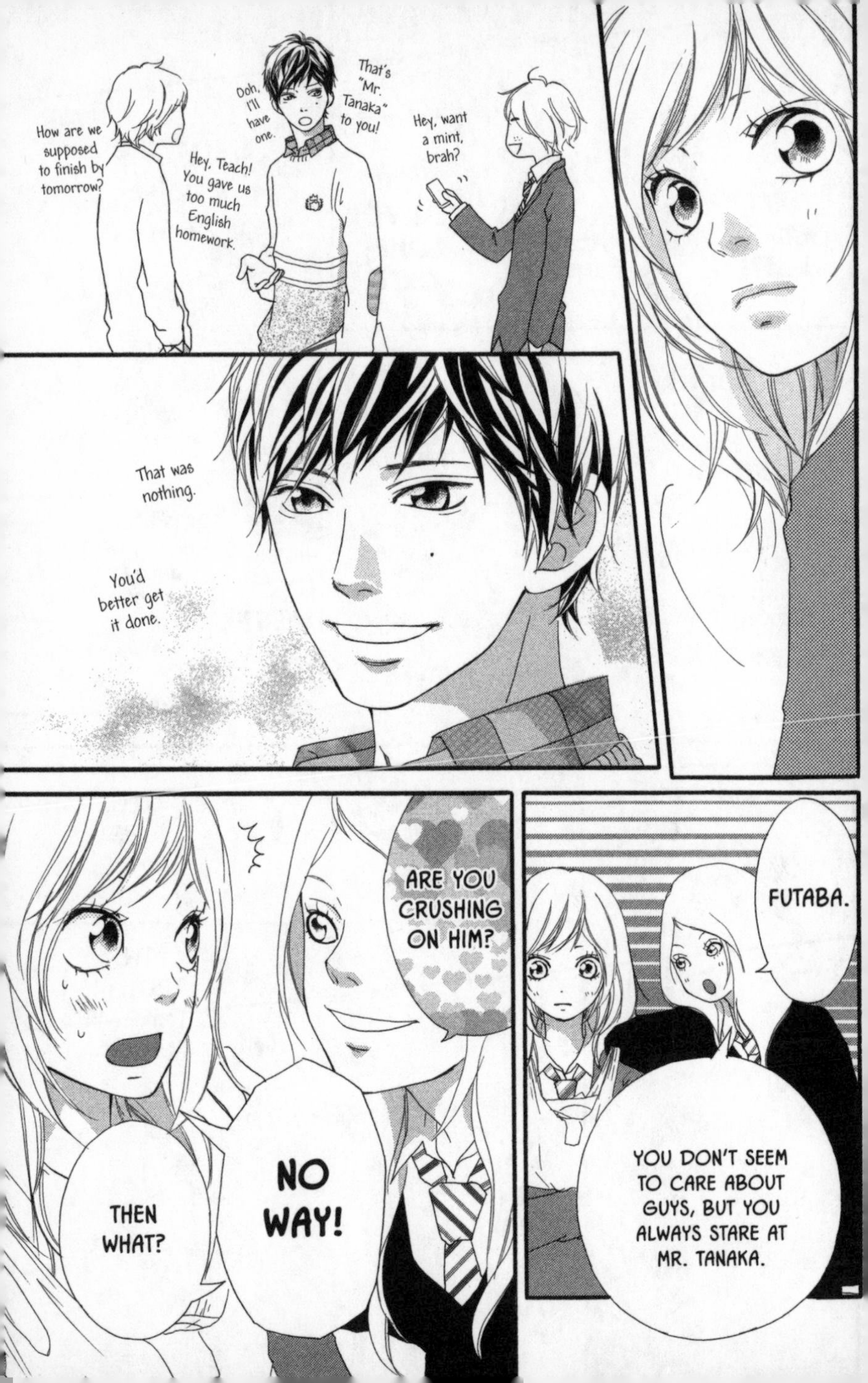
Hey, want a mint, brah?
That's "Mr. Tanaka" to you!
Ooh, I'll have one.
Hey, Teach! You gave us too much English homework.
How are we supposed to finish by tomorrow?
That was nothing.
You'd better get it done.
FUTABA.
YOU DON'T SEEM TO CARE ABOUT GUYS, BUT YOU ALWAYS STARE AT MR. TANAKA.
ARE YOU CRUSHING ON HIM?
NO WAY!
THEN WHAT?

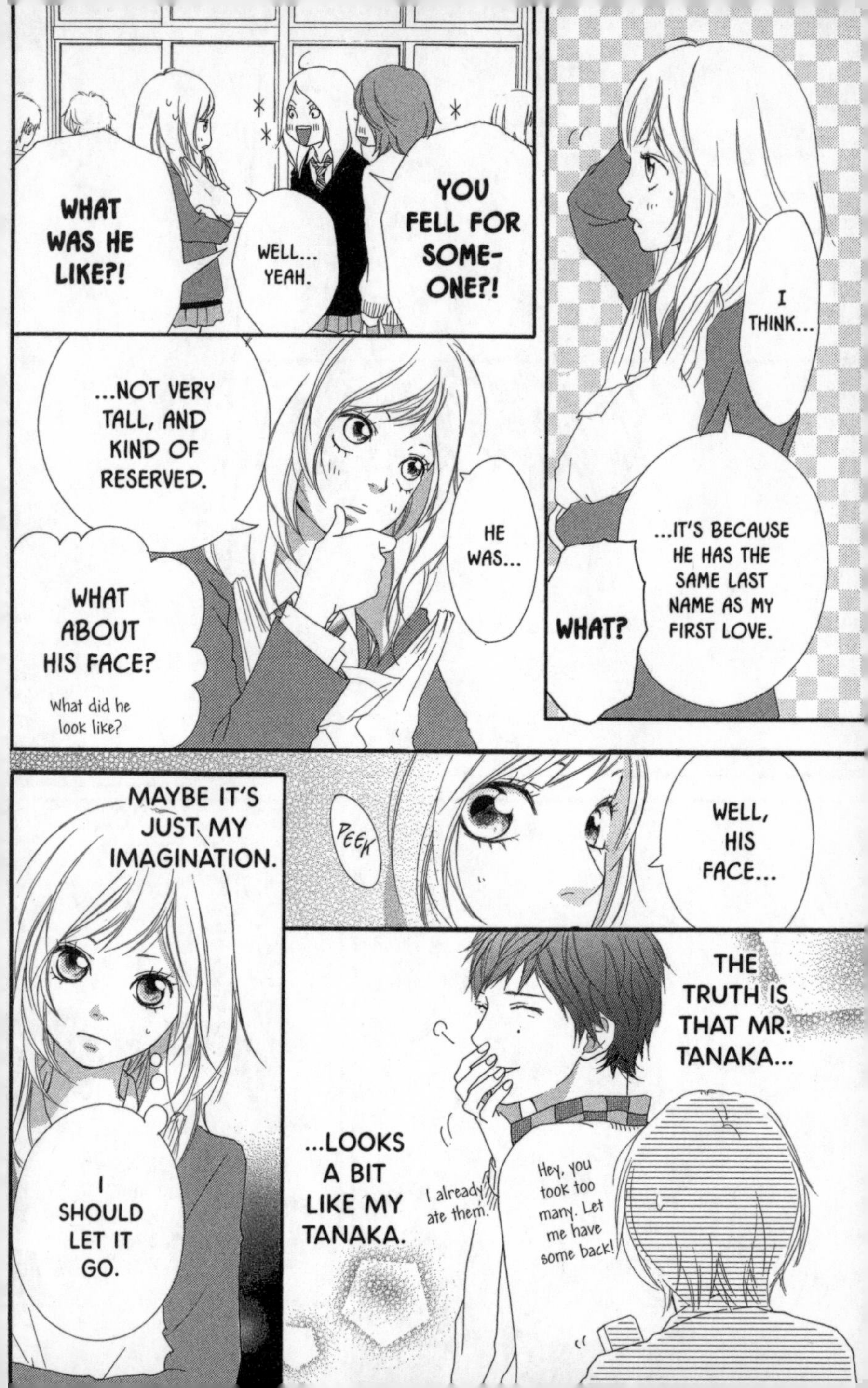
I THINK...
...IT'S BECAUSE HE HAS THE SAME LAST NAME AS MY FIRST LOVE.
WHAT?
YOU FELL FOR SOME-ONE?!
WELL... YEAH.
WHAT WAS HE LIKE?!
HE WAS...
...NOT VERY TALL, AND KIND OF RESERVED.
WHAT ABOUT HIS FACE?
What did he look like?
WELL, HIS FACE...
PEEK
THE TRUTH IS THAT MR. TANAKA...
Hey, you took too many. Let me have some back!
I already ate them.
...LOOKS A BIT LIKE MY TANAKA.
MAYBE IT'S JUST MY IMAGINATION.
I SHOULD LET IT GO.

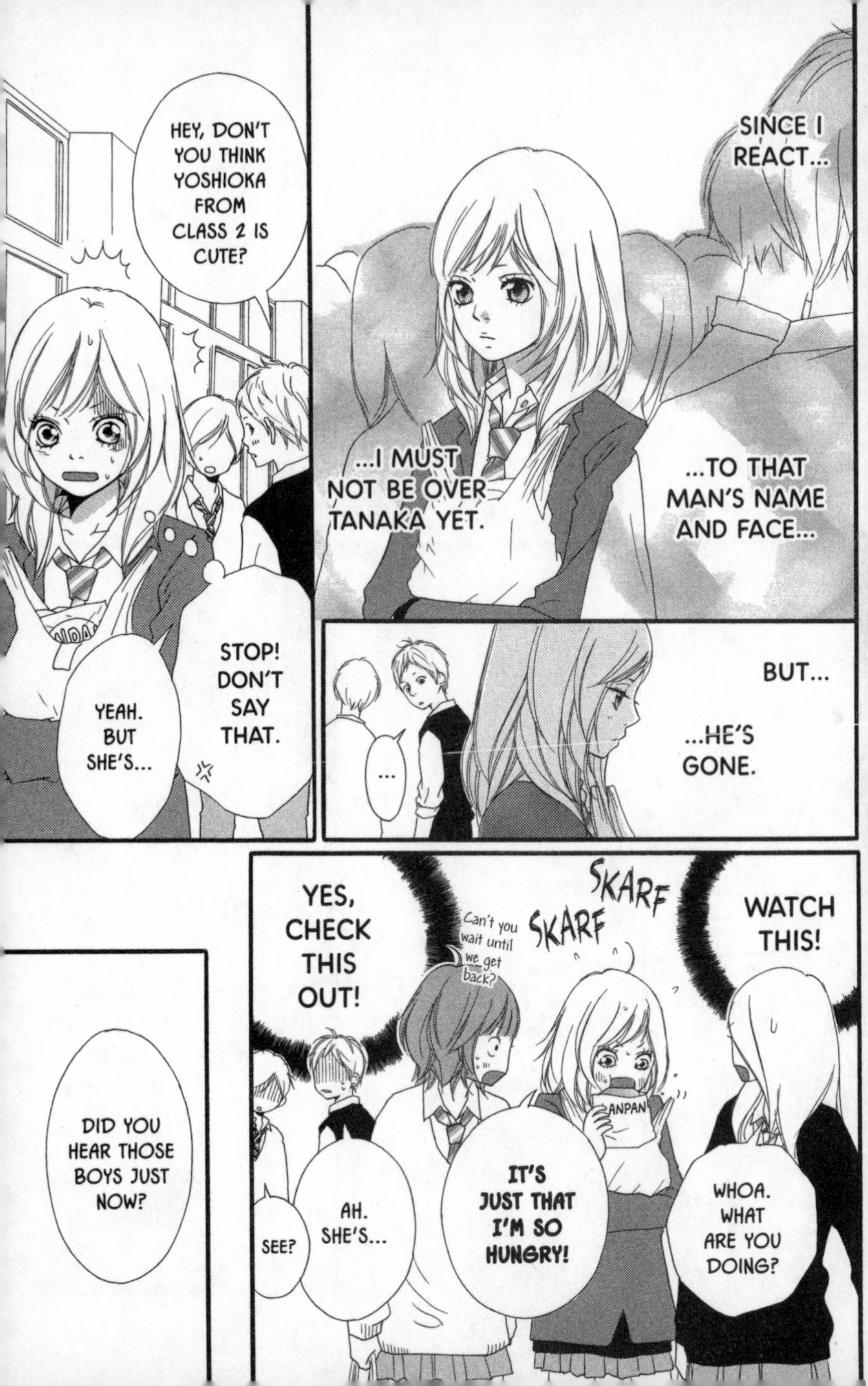
SINCE I REACT...
...TO THAT MAN'S NAME AND FACE...
...I MUST NOT BE OVER TANAKA YET.
BUT...
...HE'S GONE.
...
HEY, DON'T YOU THINK YOSHIOKA FROM CLASS 2 IS CUTE?
STOP! DON'T SAY THAT.
YEAH. BUT SHE'S...
WATCH THIS!
SKARF
SKARF
Can't you wait until we get back?
YES, CHECK THIS OUT!
WHOA. WHAT ARE YOU DOING?
ANPAN
IT'S JUST THAT I'M SO HUNGRY!
AH. SHE'S...
SEE?
DID YOU HEAR THOSE BOYS JUST NOW?

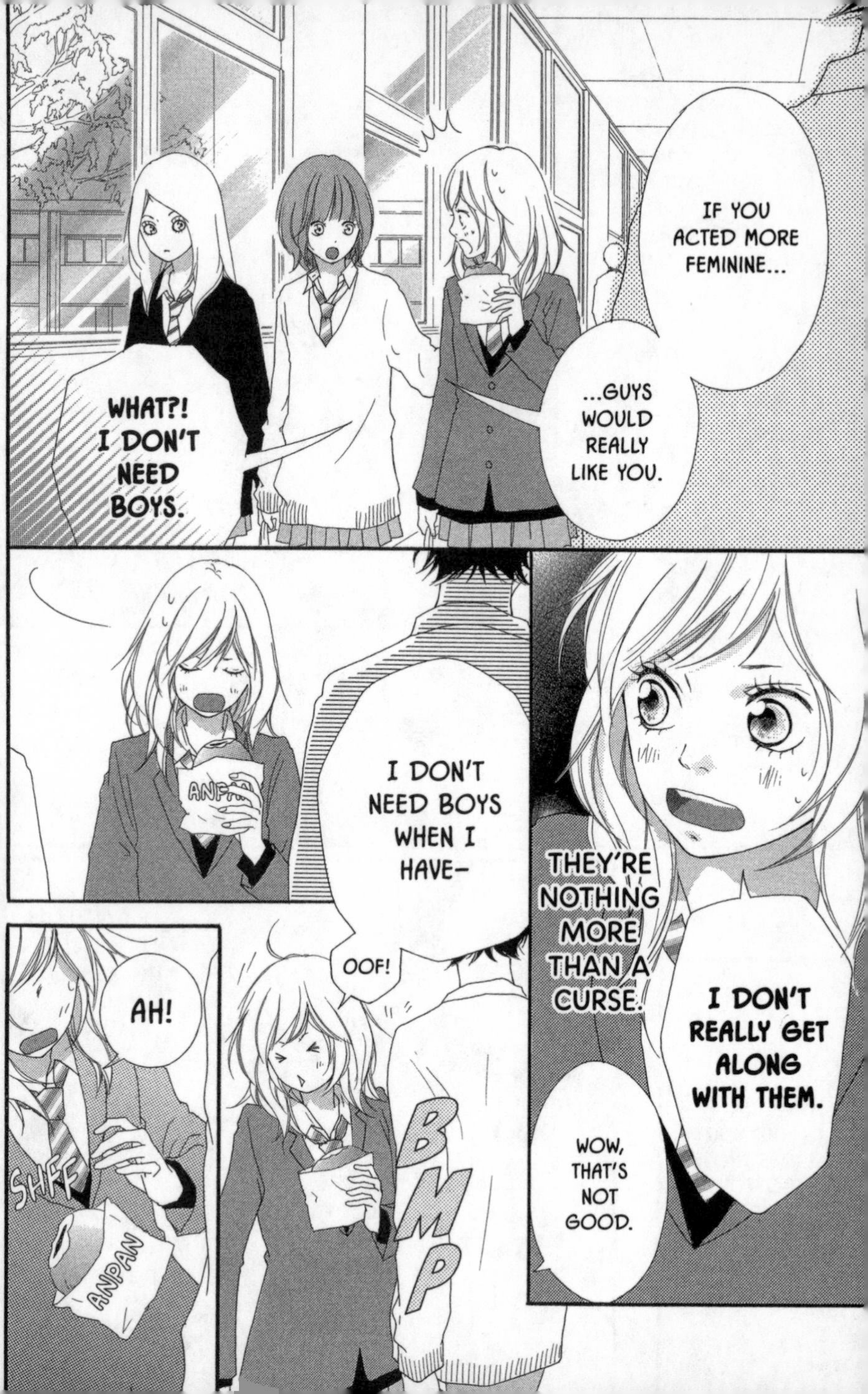
IF YOU ACTED MORE FEMININE...
...GUYS WOULD REALLY LIKE YOU.
WHAT?! I DON'T NEED BOYS.
THEY'RE NOTHING MORE THAN A CURSE.
I DON'T REALLY GET ALONG WITH THEM.
WOW, THAT'S NOT GOOD.
I DON'T NEED BOYS WHEN I HAVE–
BMP
OOF!
AH!
SHFF
ANPAN

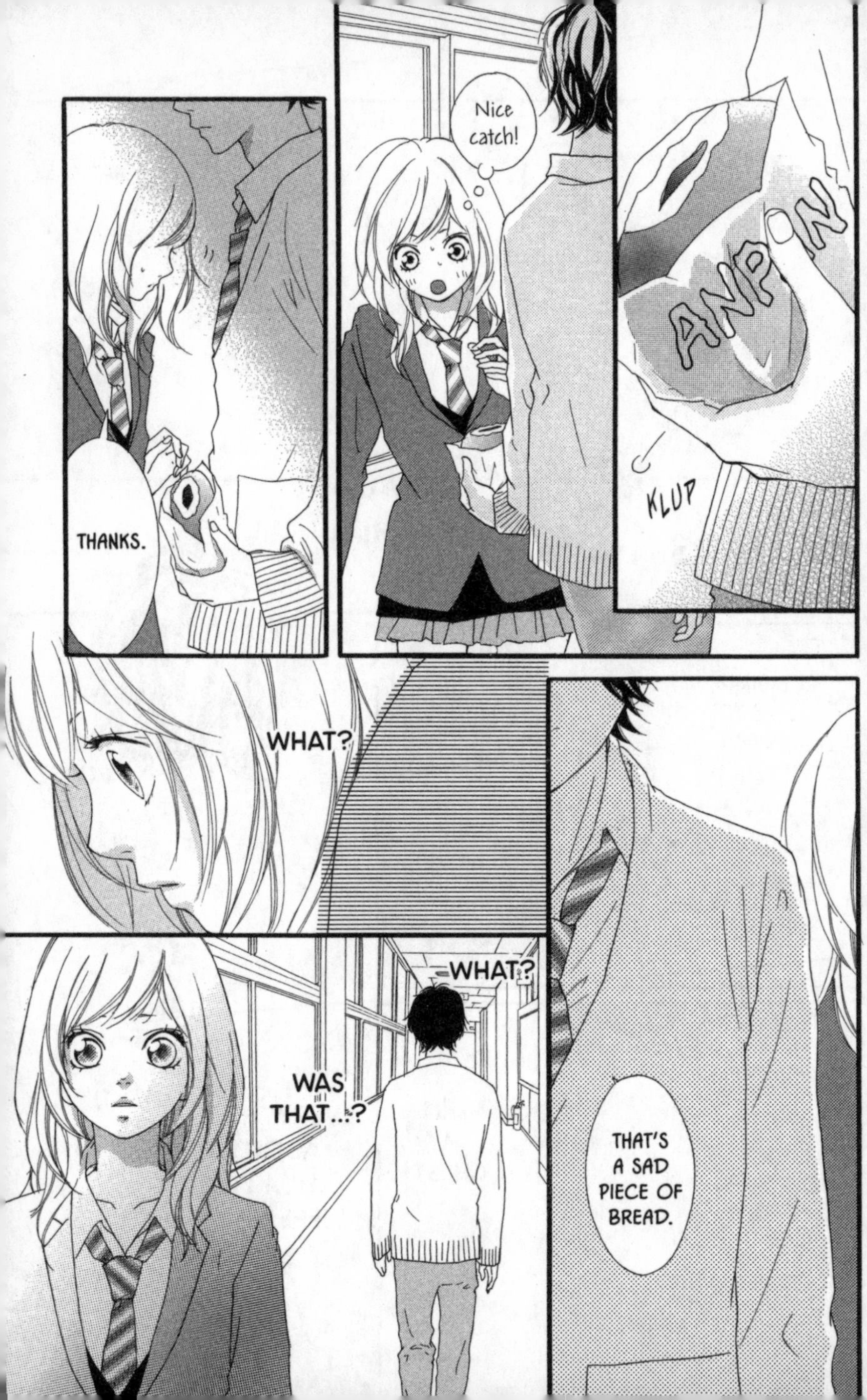
ANPON
KLUP
Nice catch!
THANKS.
THAT'S A SAD PIECE OF BREAD.
WHAT?
WHAT?
WAS THAT...?

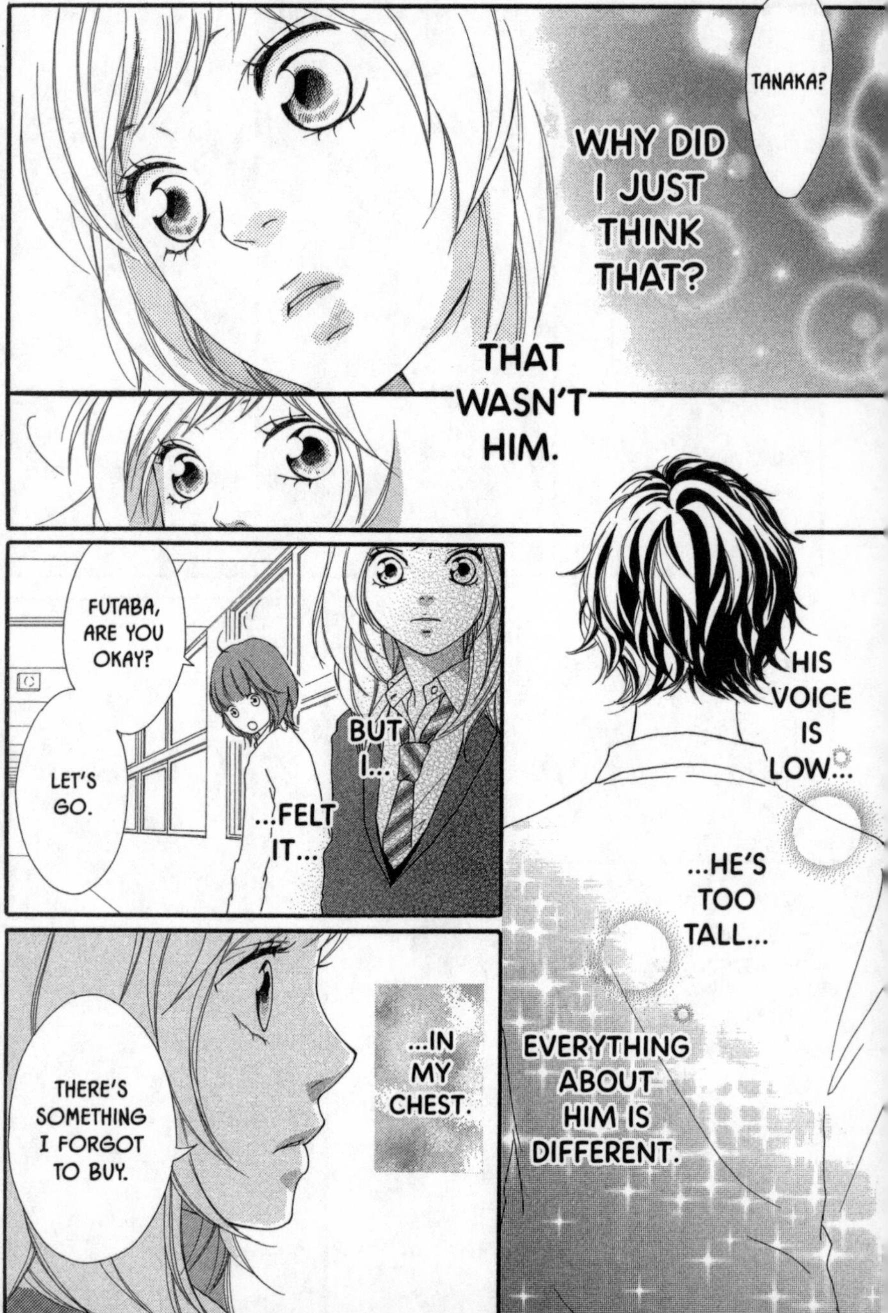
TANAKA?
WHY DID I JUST THINK THAT?
THAT WASN'T HIM.
HIS VOICE IS LOW...
...HE'S TOO TALL...
EVERYTHING ABOUT HIM IS DIFFERENT.
BUT I...
FUTABA, ARE YOU OKAY?
...FELT IT...
LET'S GO.
...IN MY CHEST.
THERE'S SOMETHING I FORGOT TO BUY.

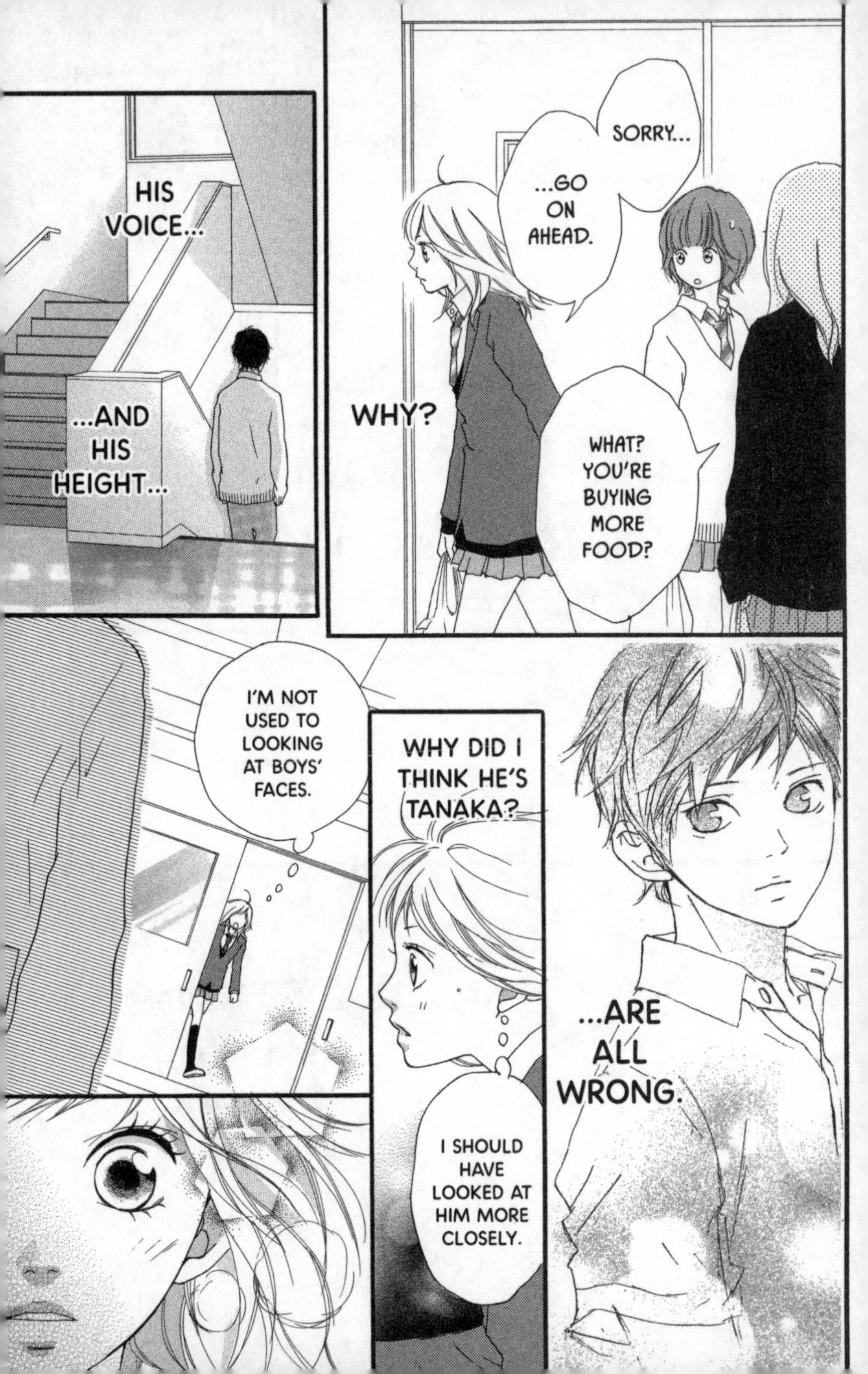
SORRY...
...GO ON AHEAD.
WHAT? YOU'RE BUYING MORE FOOD?
WHY?
HIS VOICE...
...AND HIS HEIGHT...
...ARE ALL WRONG.
WHY DID I THINK HE'S TANAKA?
I SHOULD HAVE LOOKED AT HIM MORE CLOSELY.
I'M NOT USED TO LOOKING AT BOYS' FACES.

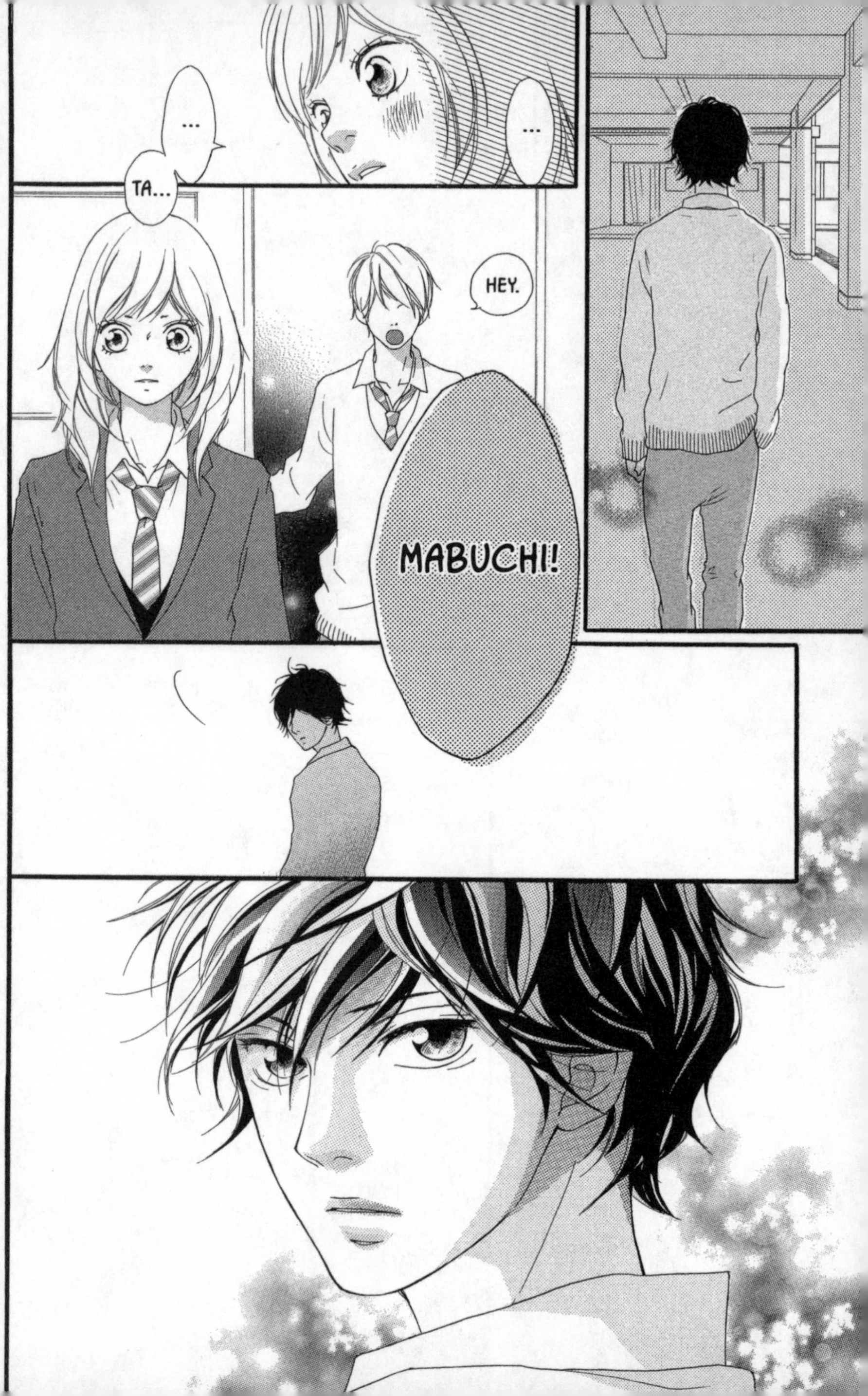
...
...
TA...
HEY.
MABUCHI!

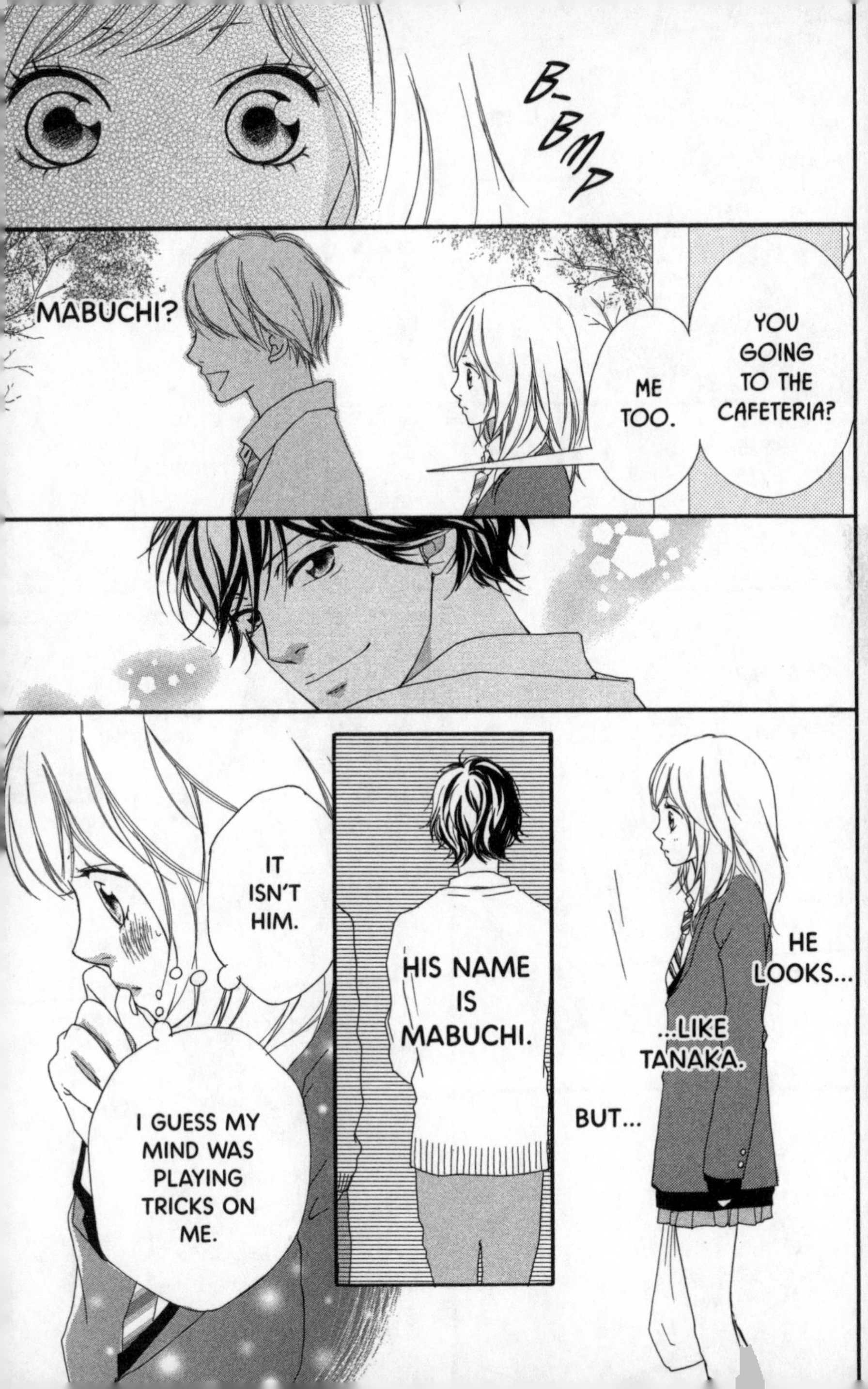
B-BMP
YOU GOING TO THE CAFETERIA?
ME TOO.
MABUCHI?
HE LOOKS...
...LIKE TANAKA.
BUT...
HIS NAME IS MABUCHI.
IT ISN'T HIM.
I GUESS MY MIND WAS PLAYING TRICKS ON ME.

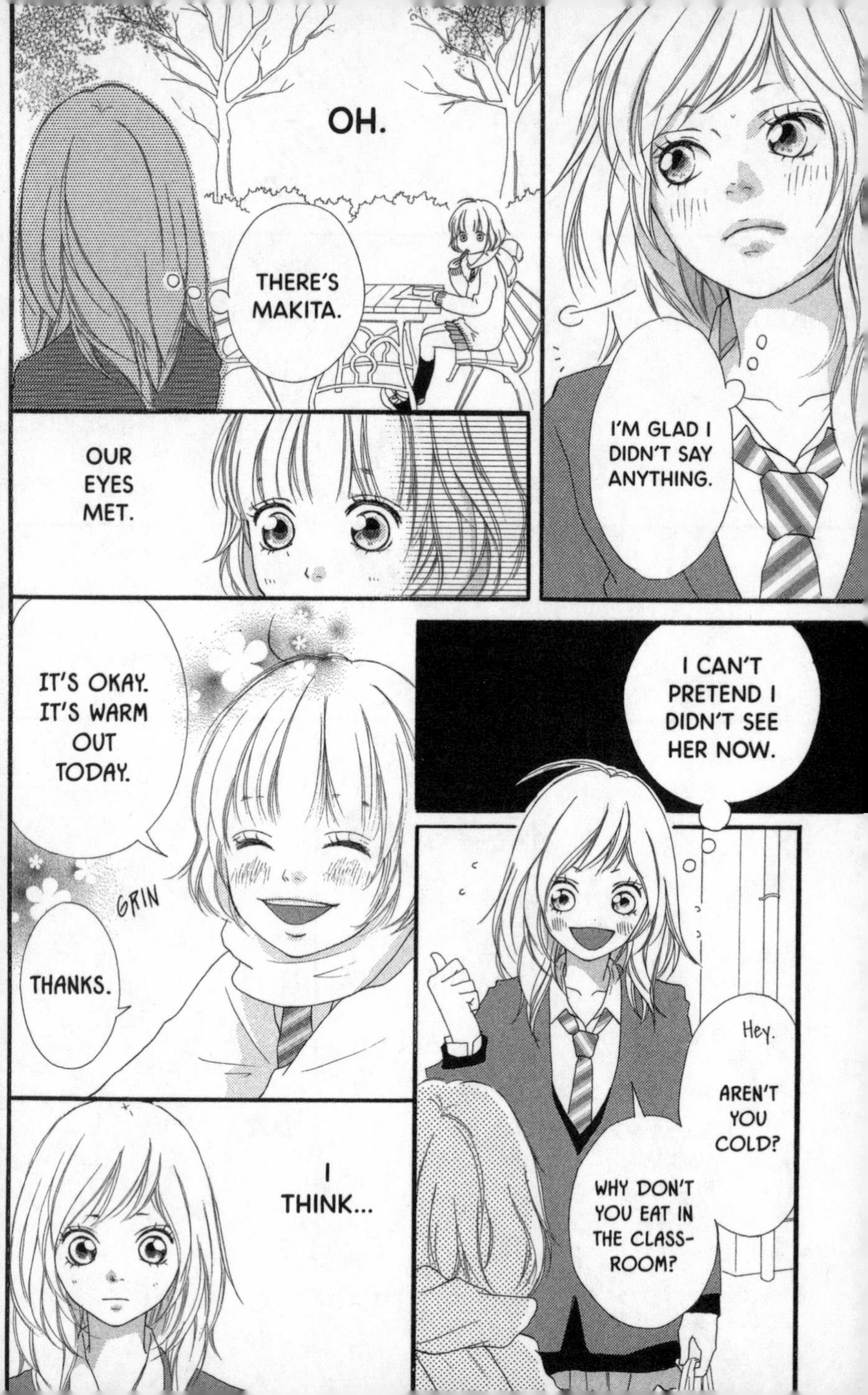
I'M GLAD I DIDN'T SAY ANYTHING.
OH.
THERE'S MAKITA.
OUR EYES MET.
I CAN'T PRETEND I DIDN'T SEE HER NOW.
Hey.
AREN'T YOU COLD?
WHY DON'T YOU EAT IN THE CLASS-ROOM?
IT'S OKAY. IT'S WARM OUT TODAY.
GRIN
THANKS.
I THINK...

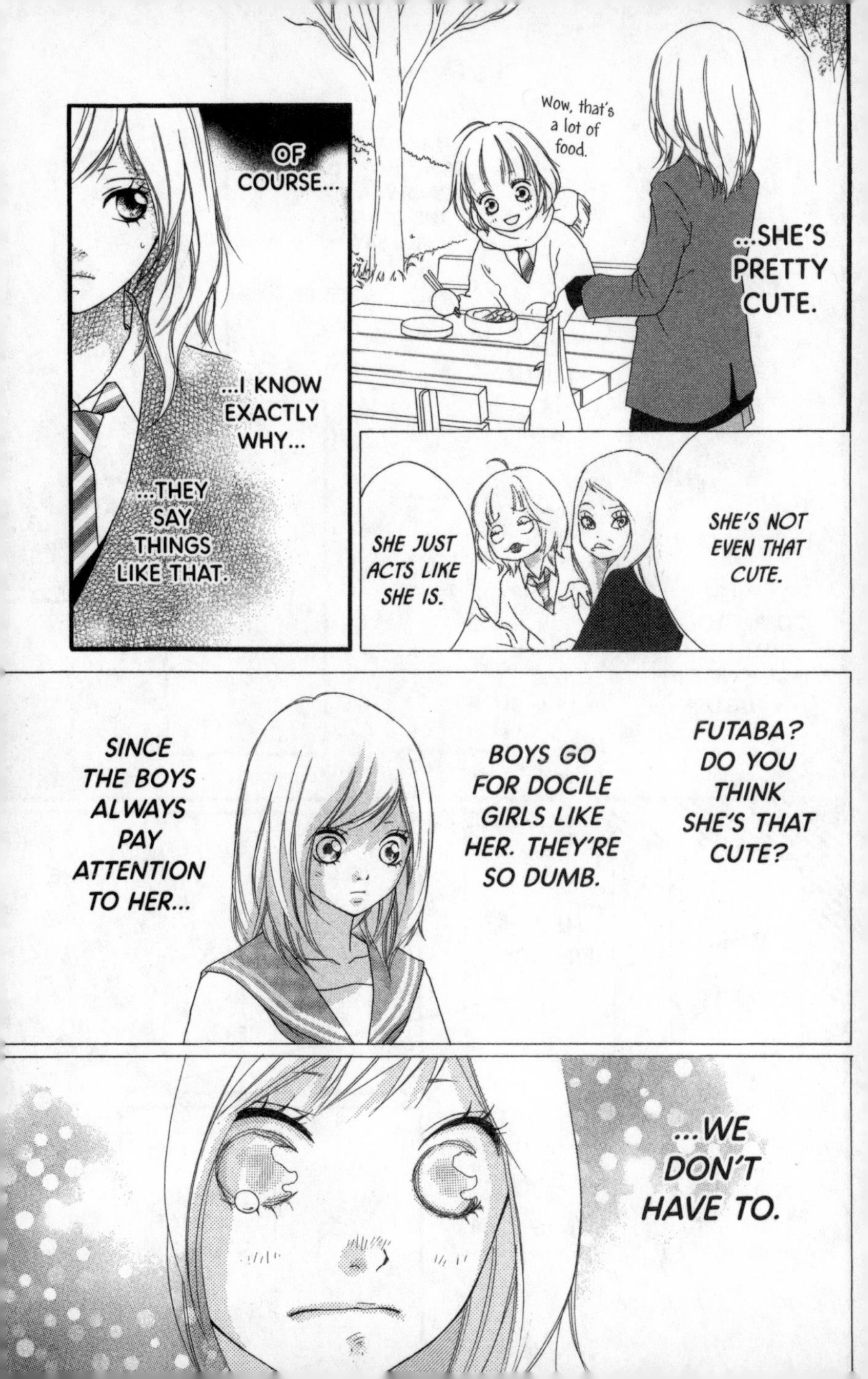
Wow, that's a lot of food.
...SHE'S PRETTY CUTE.
SHE'S NOT EVEN THAT CUTE.
SHE JUST ACTS LIKE SHE IS.
OF COURSE...
...I KNOW EXACTLY WHY...
...THEY SAY THINGS LIKE THAT.
FUTABA? DO YOU THINK SHE'S THAT CUTE?
BOYS GO FOR DOCILE GIRLS LIKE HER. THEY'RE SO DUMB.
SINCE THE BOYS ALWAYS PAY ATTENTION TO HER...
...WE DON'T HAVE TO.

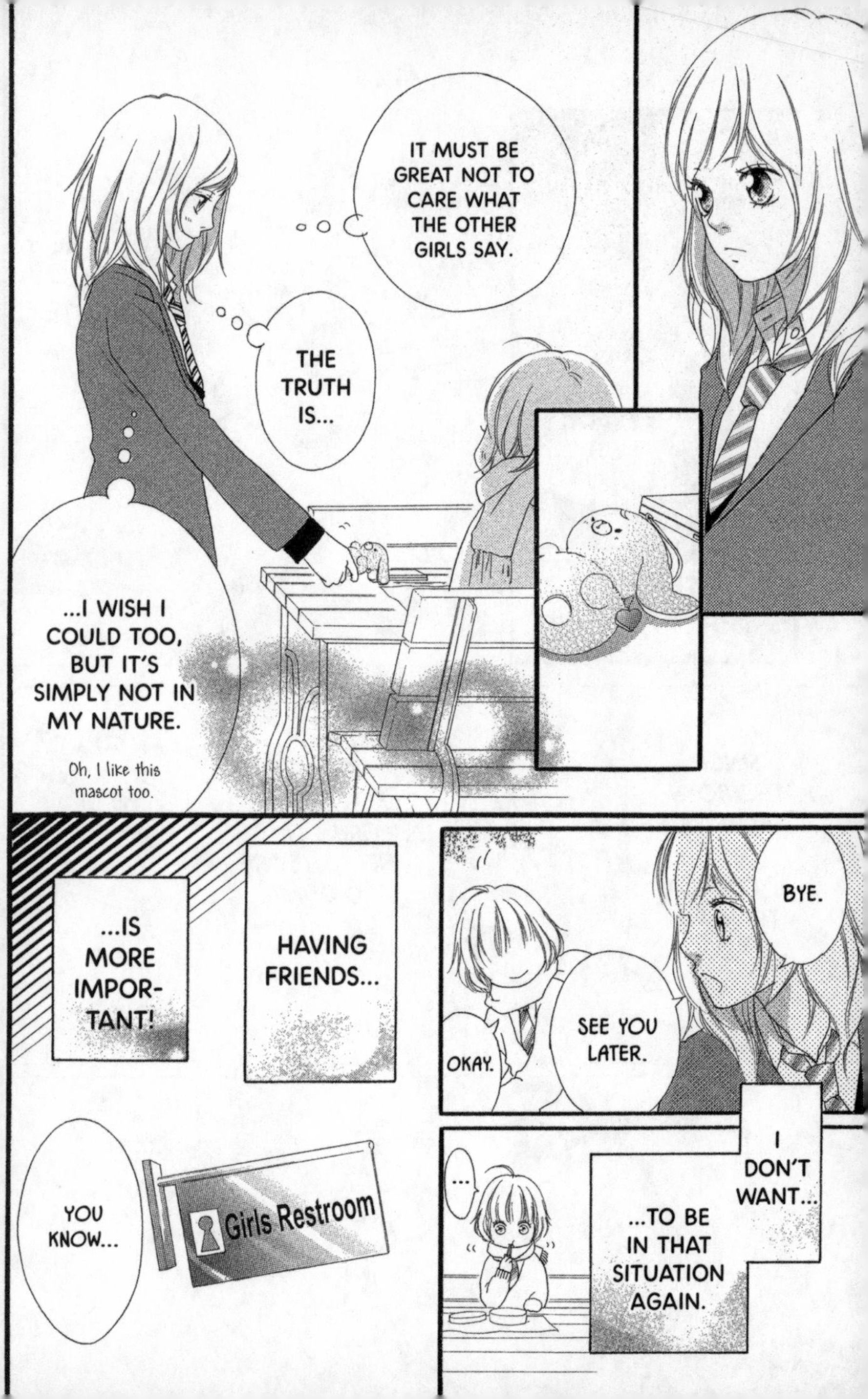
IT MUST BE GREAT NOT TO CARE WHAT THE OTHER GIRLS SAY.
THE TRUTH IS...
...I WISH I COULD TOO, BUT IT'S SIMPLY NOT IN MY NATURE.
Oh, I like this mascot too.
BYE.
SEE YOU LATER.
OKAY.
HAVING FRIENDS...
...IS MORE IMPORTANT!
I DON'T WANT...
...
...TO BE IN THAT SITUATION AGAIN.
Girls Restroom
YOU KNOW...

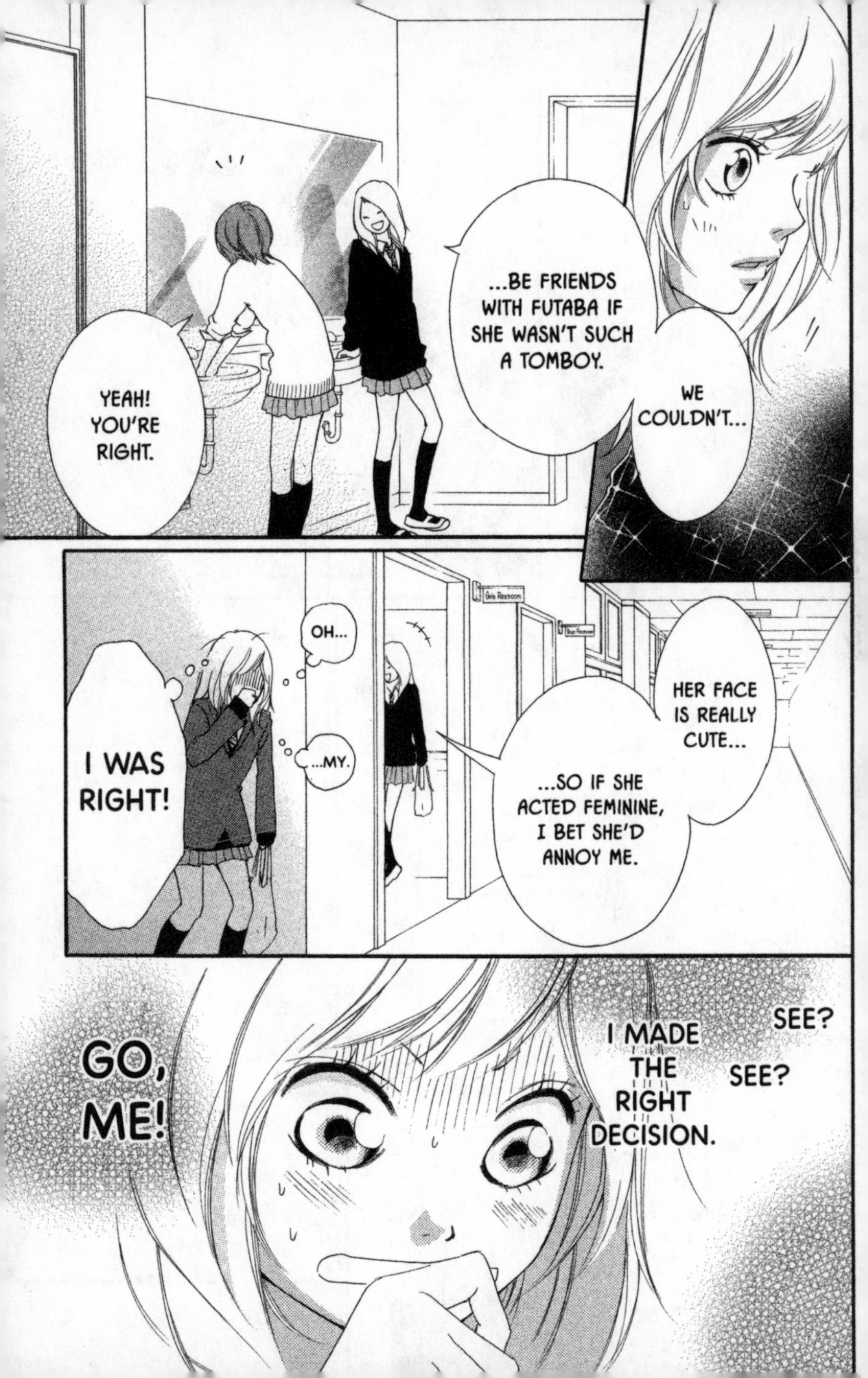
WE COULDN'T...
...BE FRIENDS WITH FUTABA IF SHE WASN'T SUCH A TOMBOY.
YEAH! YOU'RE RIGHT.
HER FACE IS REALLY CUTE...
...SO IF SHE ACTED FEMININE, I BET SHE'D ANNOY ME.
OH...
...MY.
I WAS RIGHT!
SEE?
SEE?
I MADE THE RIGHT DECISION.
GO, ME!

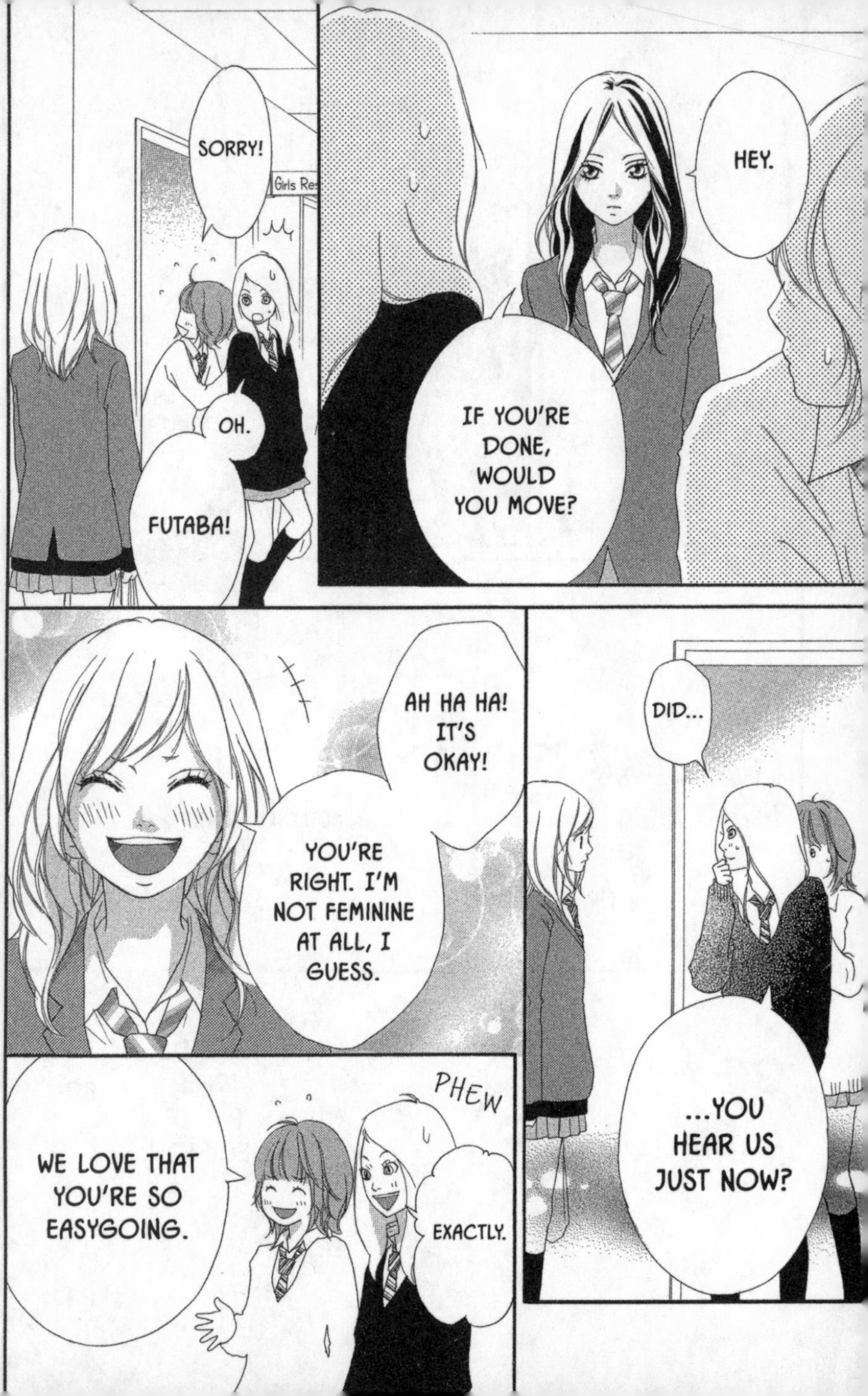
HEY.
IF YOU'RE DONE, WOULD YOU MOVE?
SORRY!
Girls Res
OH.
FUTABA!
DID...
...YOU HEAR US JUST NOW?
AH HA HA! IT'S OKAY!
YOU'RE RIGHT. I'M NOT FEMININE AT ALL, I GUESS.
PHEW
EXACTLY.
WE LOVE THAT YOU'RE SO EASYGOING.

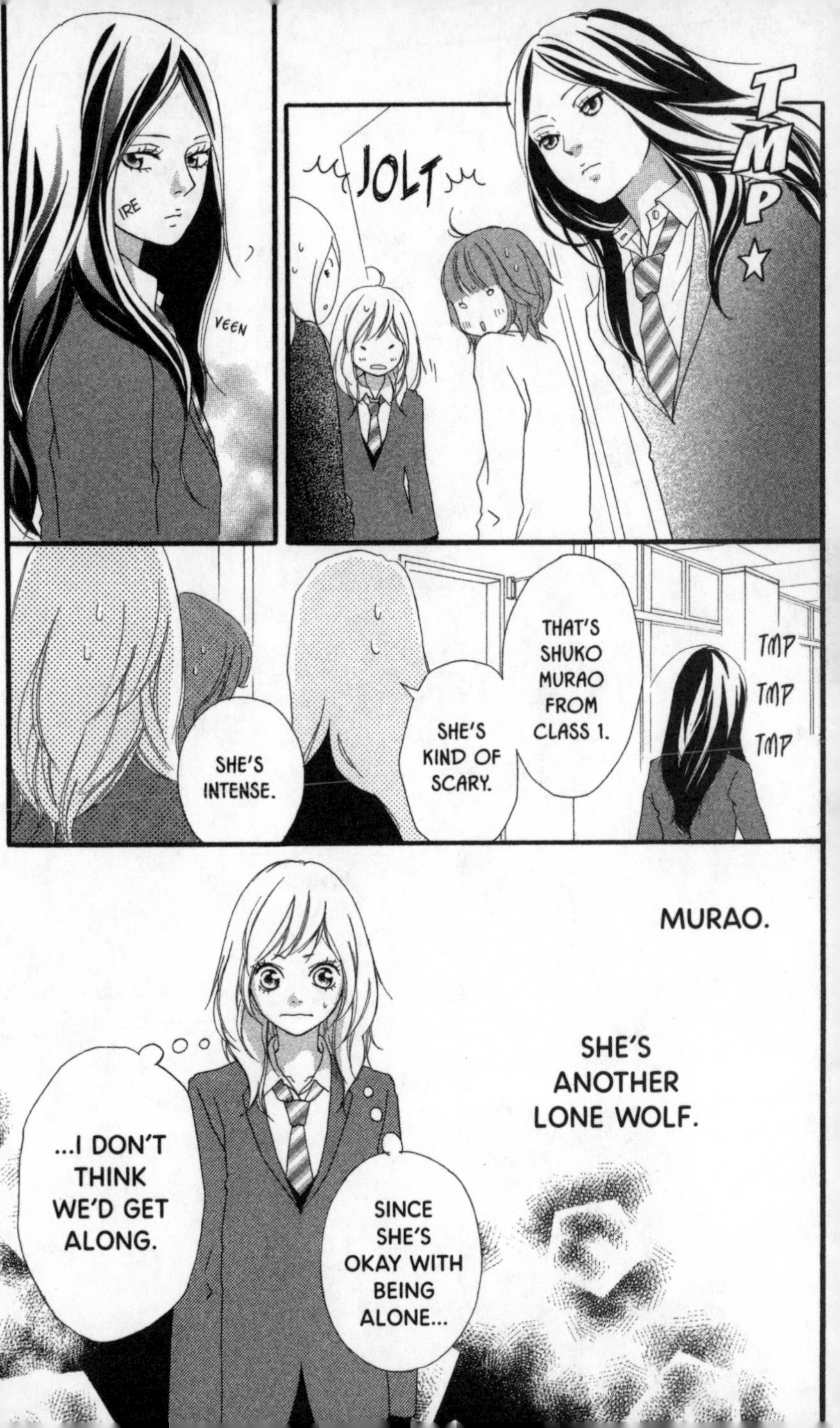
TMP☆
JOLT
IRE
VEEN
TMP TMP TMP
THAT'S SHUKO MURAO FROM CLASS 1.
SHE'S KIND OF SCARY.
SHE'S INTENSE.
MURAO.
SHE'S ANOTHER LONE WOLF.
SINCE SHE'S OKAY WITH BEING ALONE...
...I DON'T THINK WE'D GET ALONG.

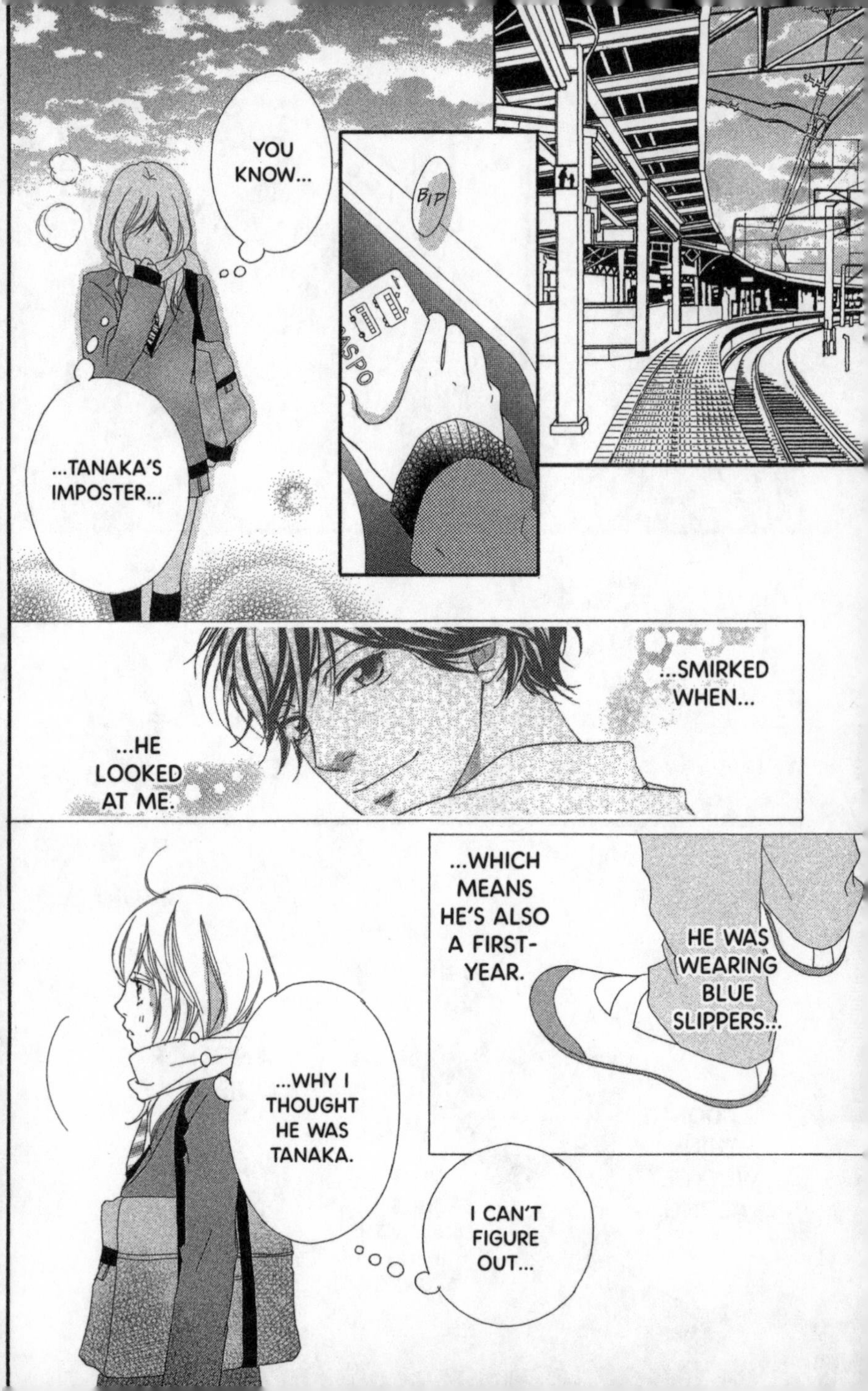
BIP
YOU KNOW...
...TANAKA'S IMPOSTER...
...SMIRKED WHEN...
...HE LOOKED AT ME.
HE WAS WEARING BLUE SLIPPERS...
...WHICH MEANS HE'S ALSO A FIRST-YEAR.
I CAN'T FIGURE OUT...
...WHY I THOUGHT HE WAS TANAKA.

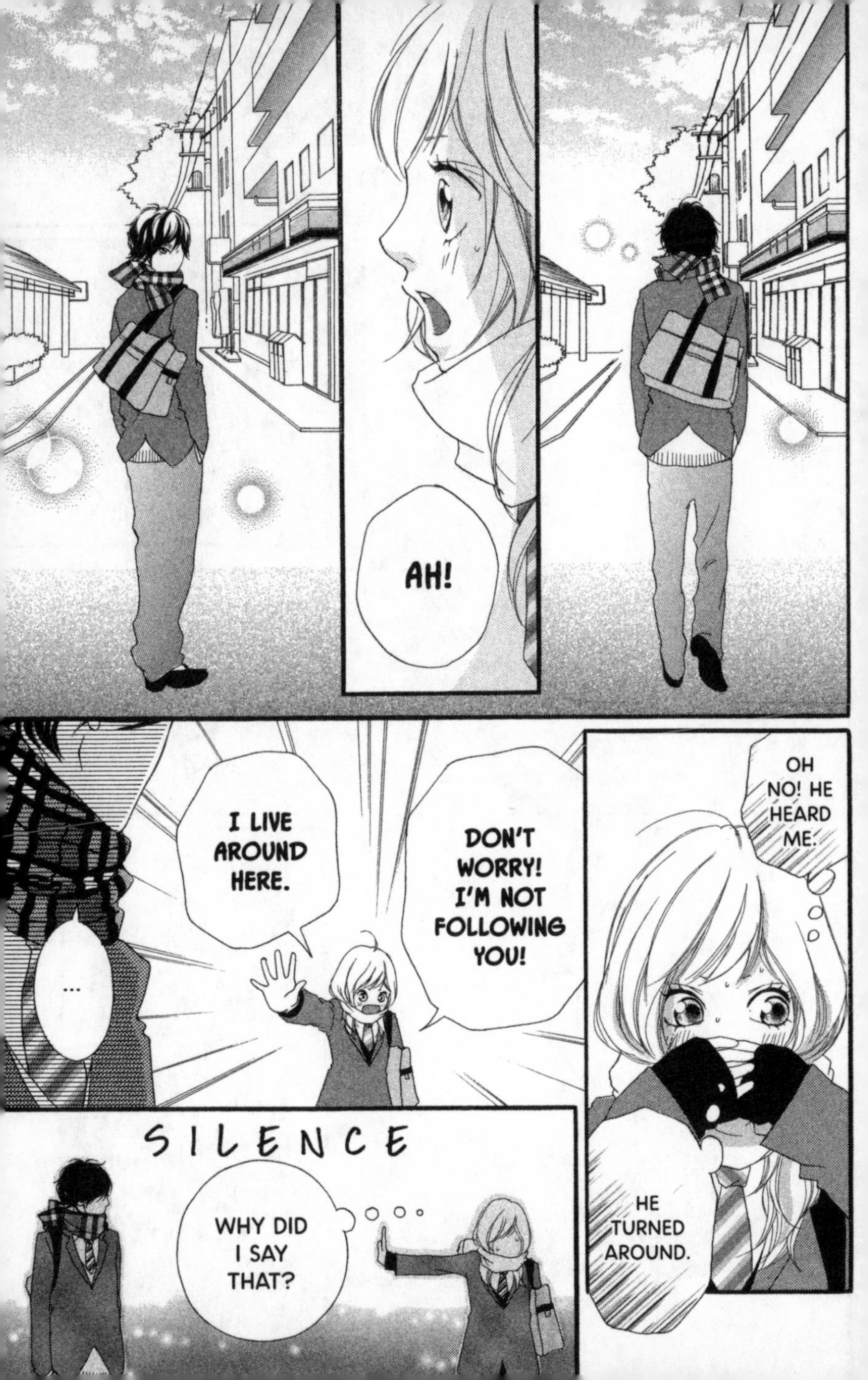
AH!
OH NO! HE HEARD ME.
HE TURNED AROUND.
DON'T WORRY! I'M NOT FOLLOWING YOU!
I LIVE AROUND HERE.
...
SILENCE
WHY DID I SAY THAT?

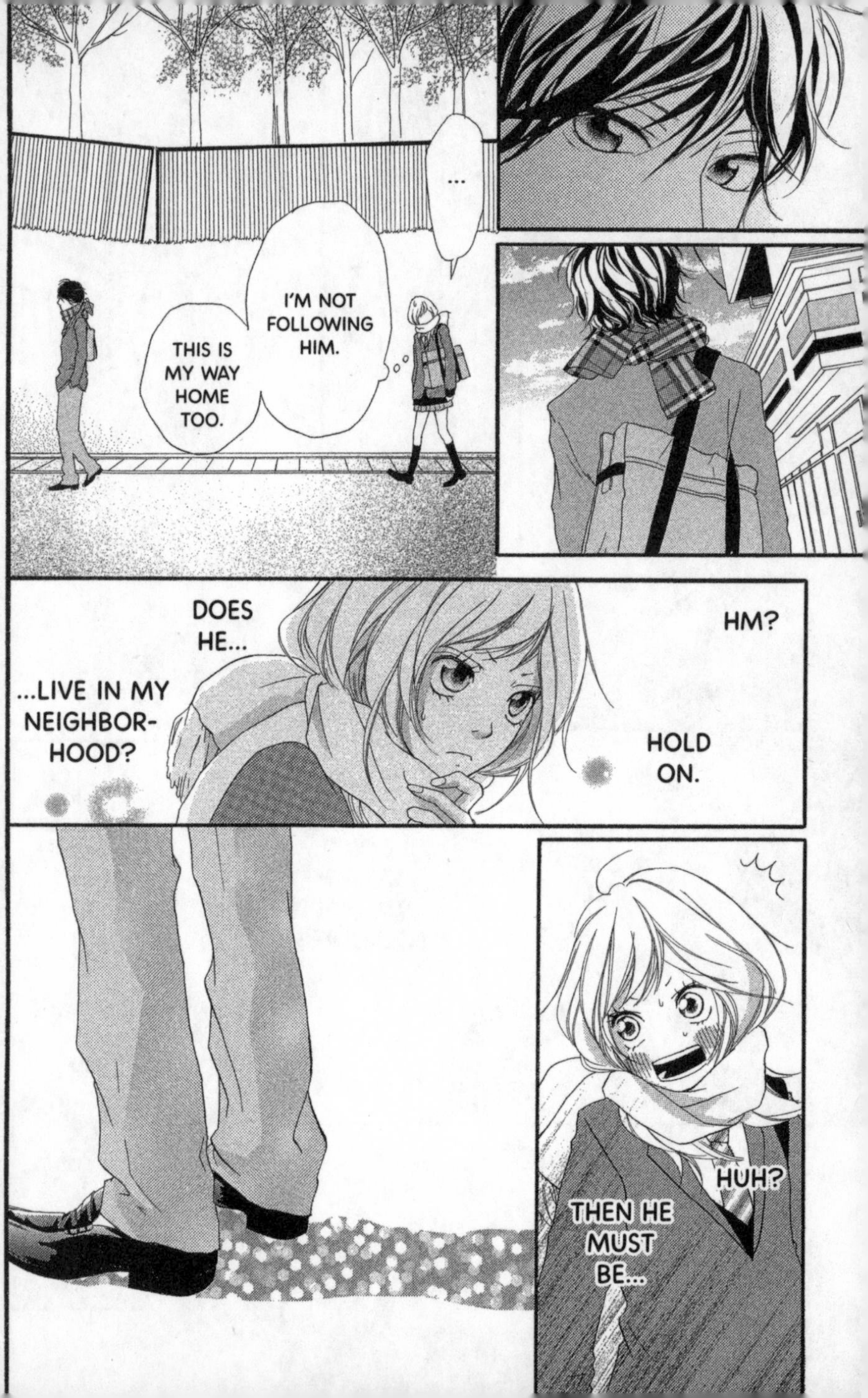
...
I'M NOT FOLLOWING HIM.
THIS IS MY WAY HOME TOO.
HM?
HOLD ON.
DOES HE...
...LIVE IN MY NEIGHBOR-HOOD?
HUH?
THEN HE MUST BE...

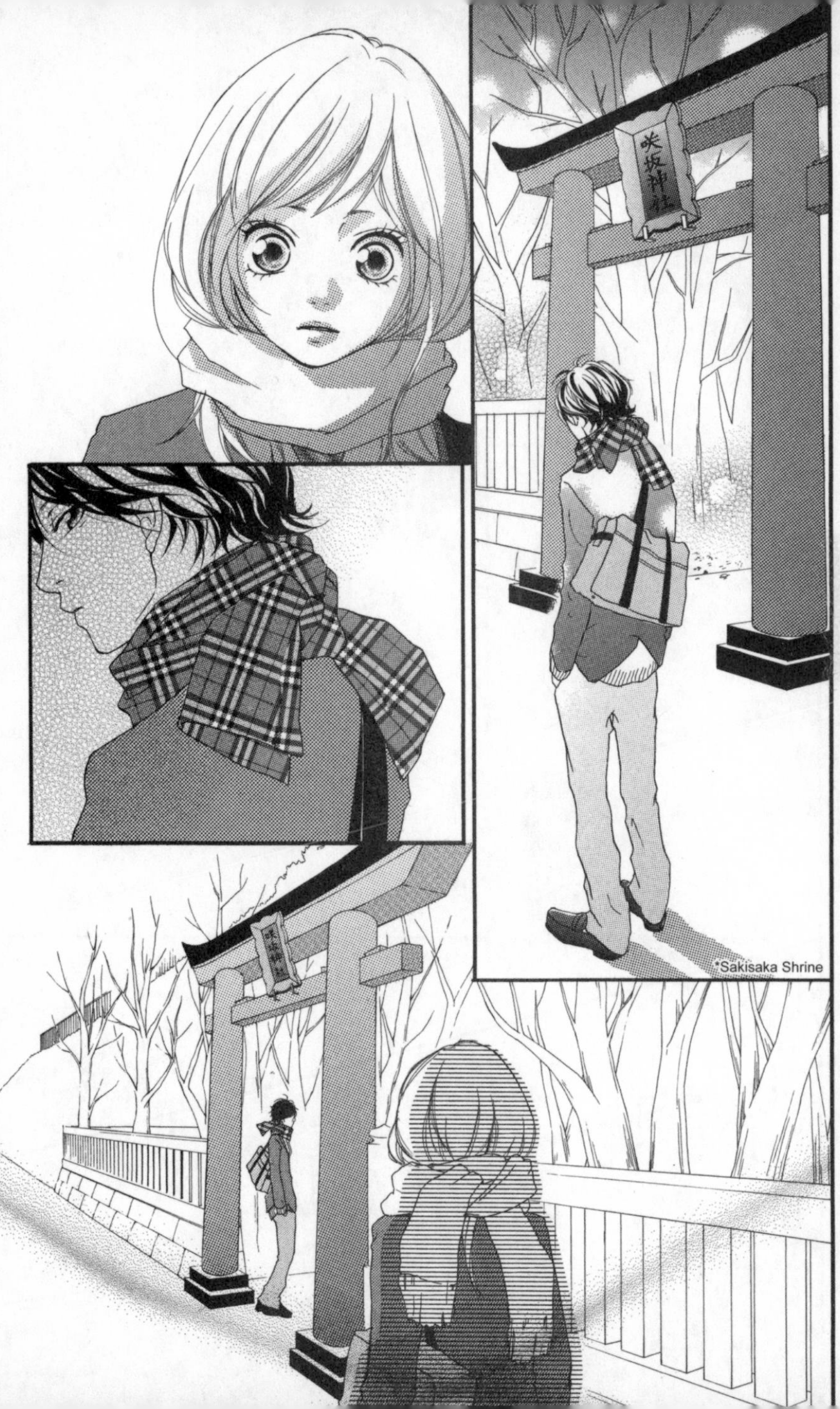
咲坂神社
*Sakisaka Shrine

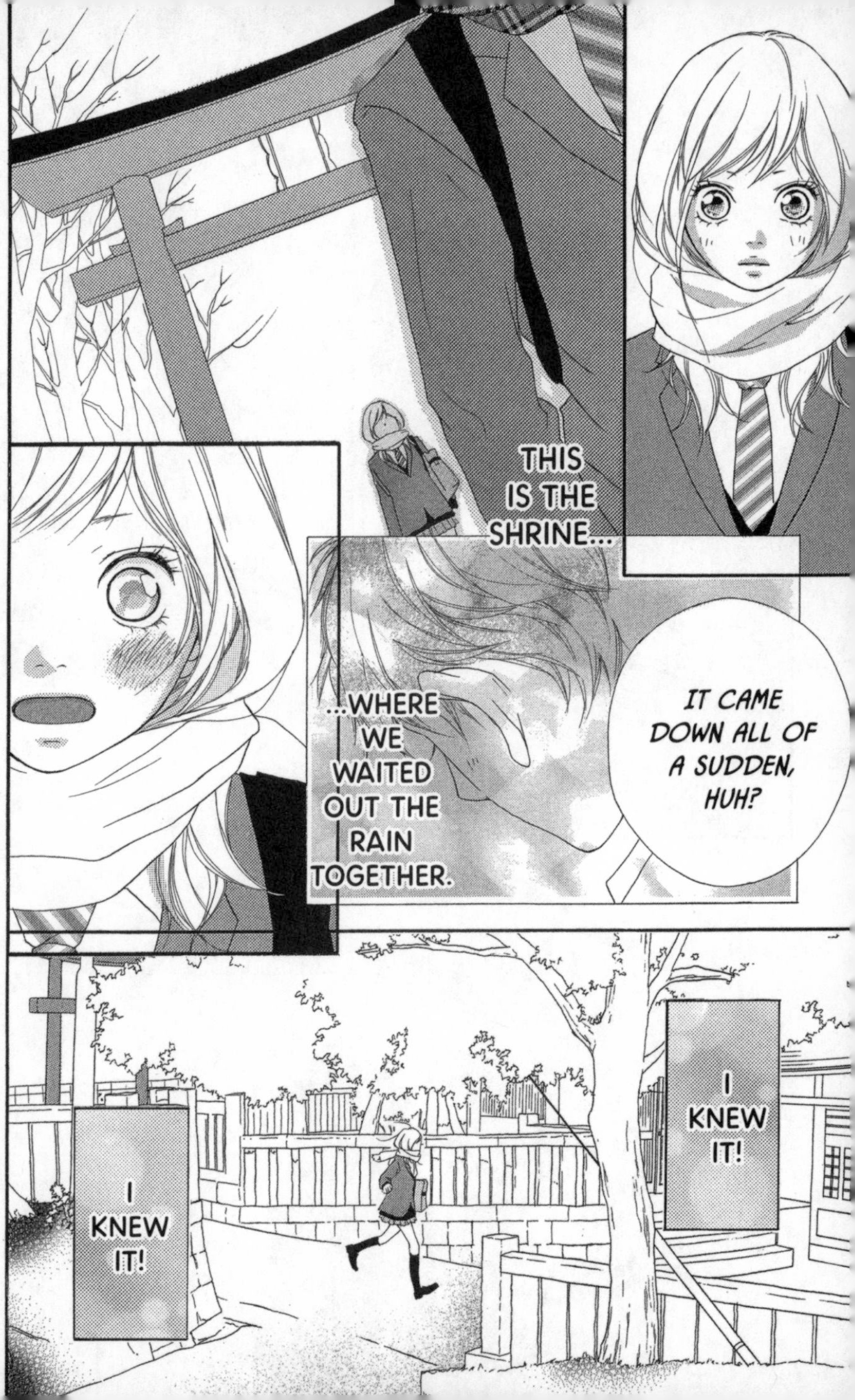
THIS IS THE SHRINE...
IT CAME DOWN ALL OF A SUDDEN, HUH?
...WHERE WE WAITED OUT THE RAIN TOGETHER.
I KNEW IT!
I KNEW IT!

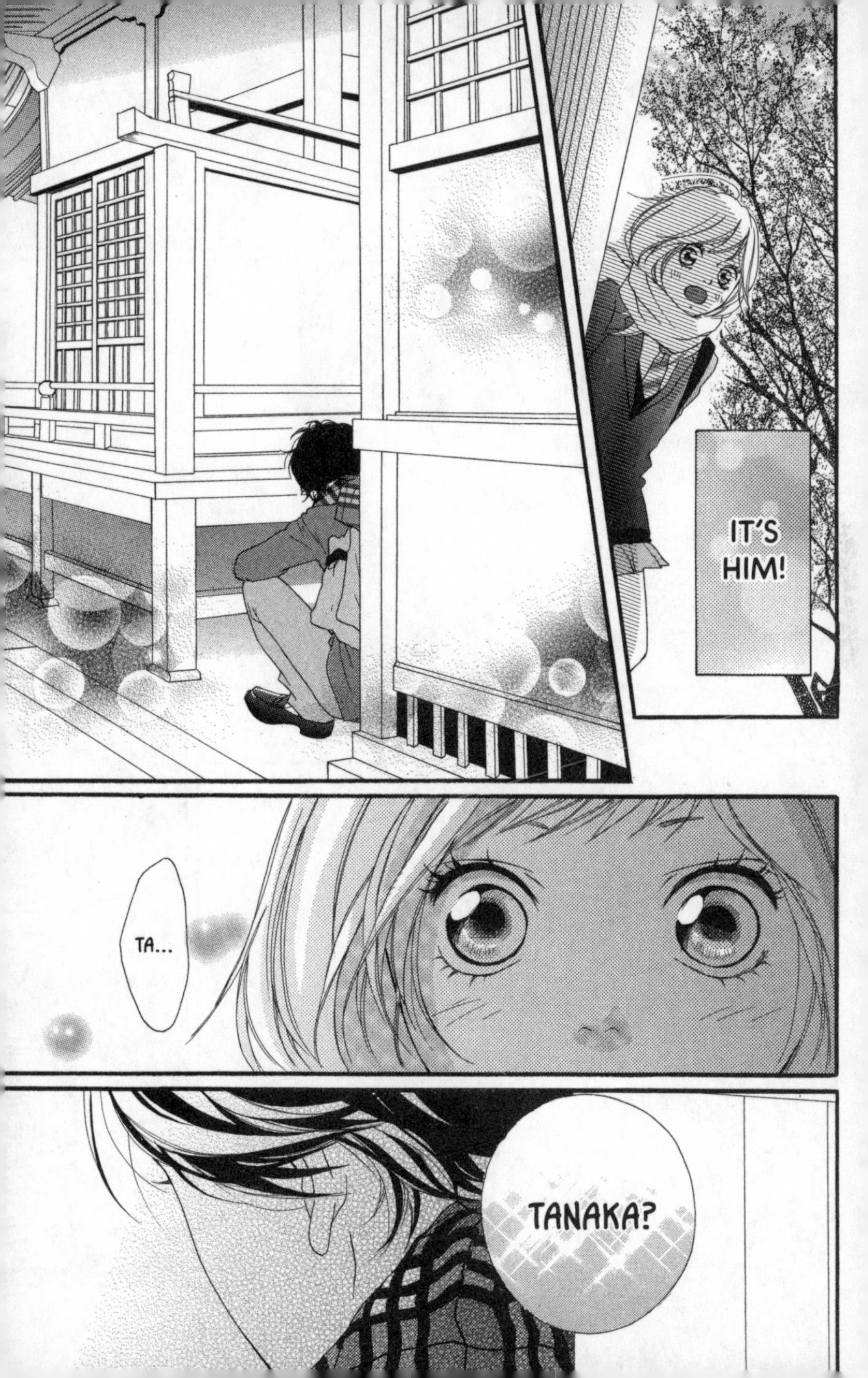
IT'S HIM!
TA...
TANAKA?

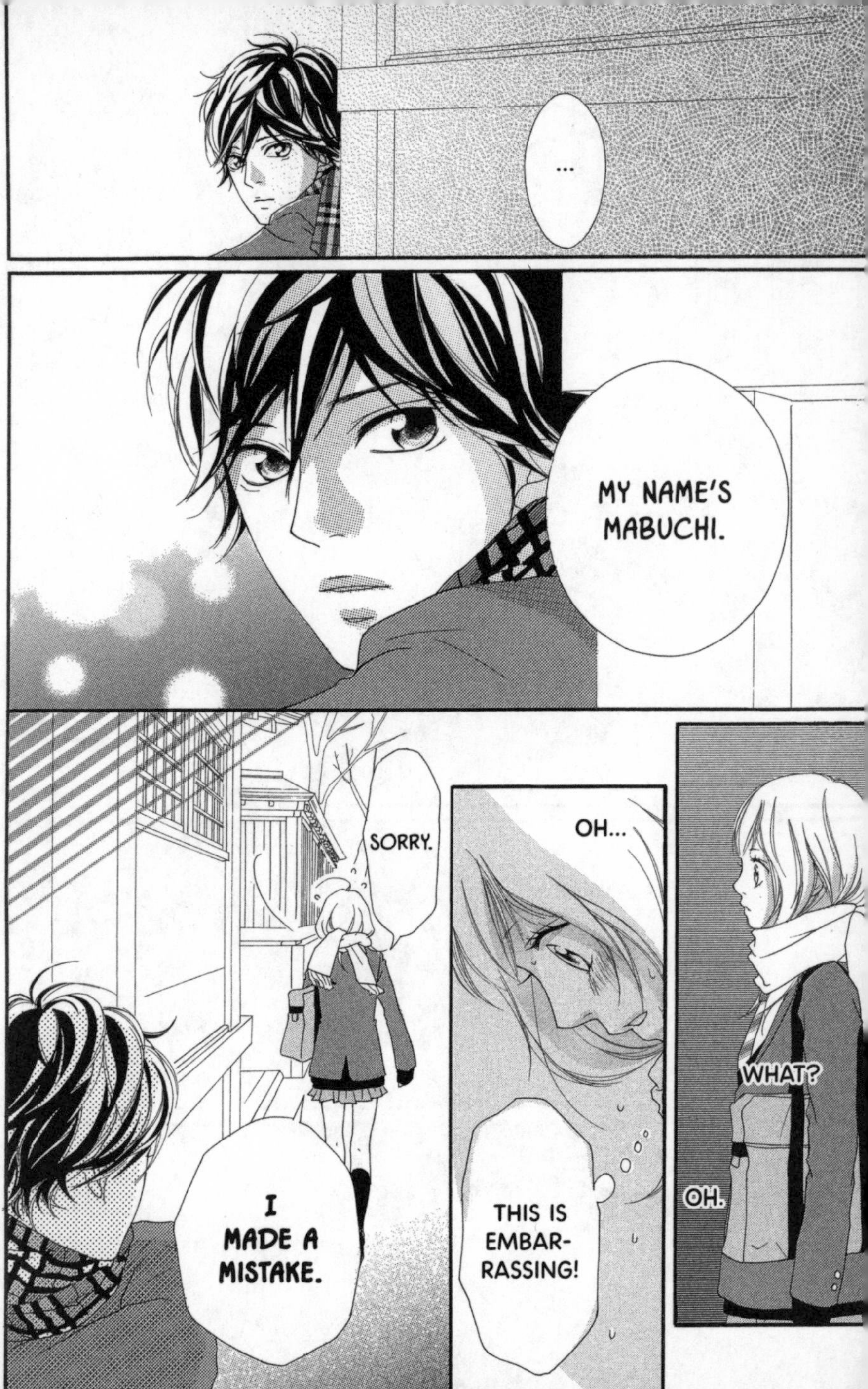
...
MY NAME'S MABUCHI.
WHAT?
OH.
OH...
THIS IS EMBARRASSING!
SORRY.
I MADE A MISTAKE.

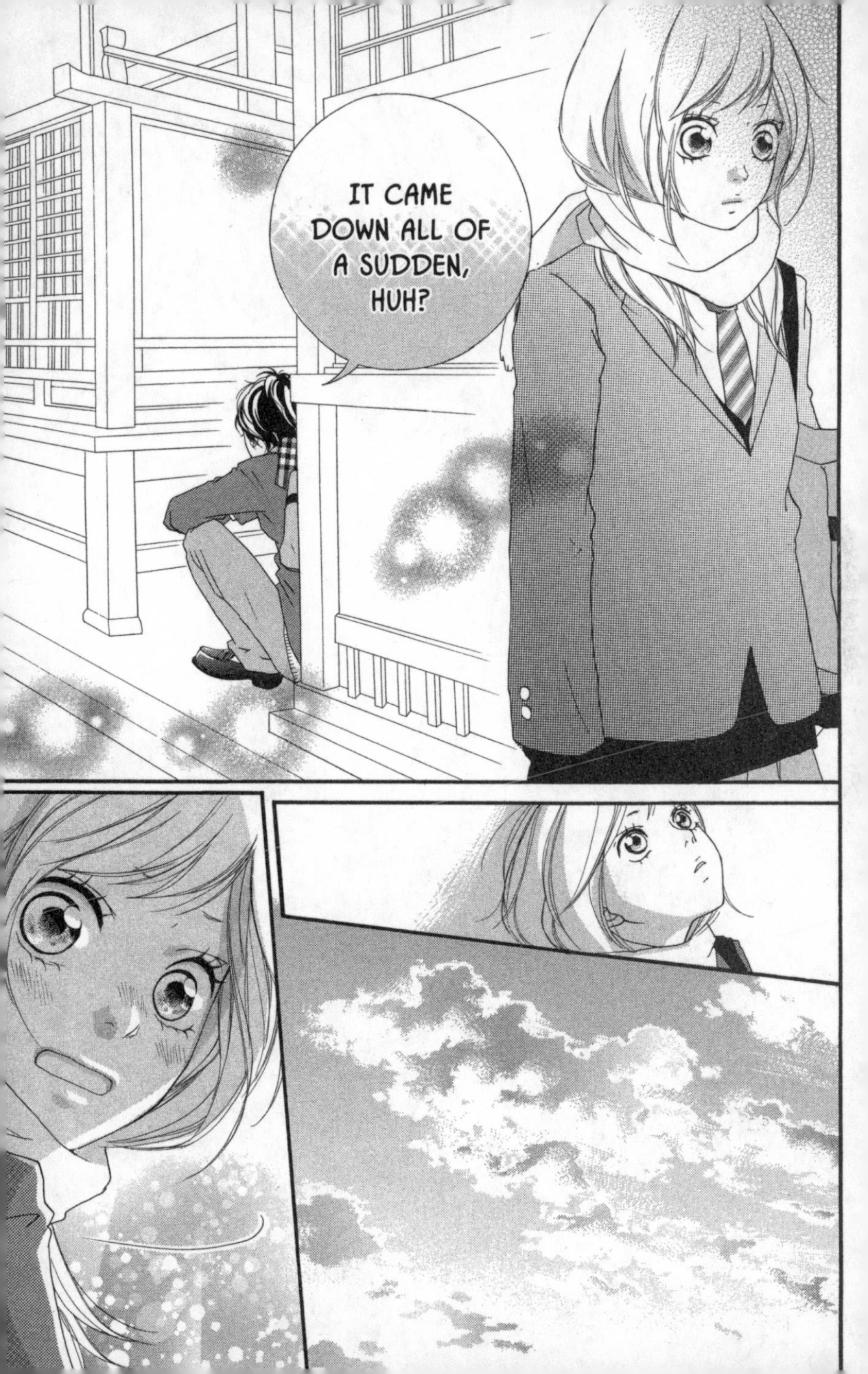
IT CAME DOWN ALL OF A SUDDEN, HUH?

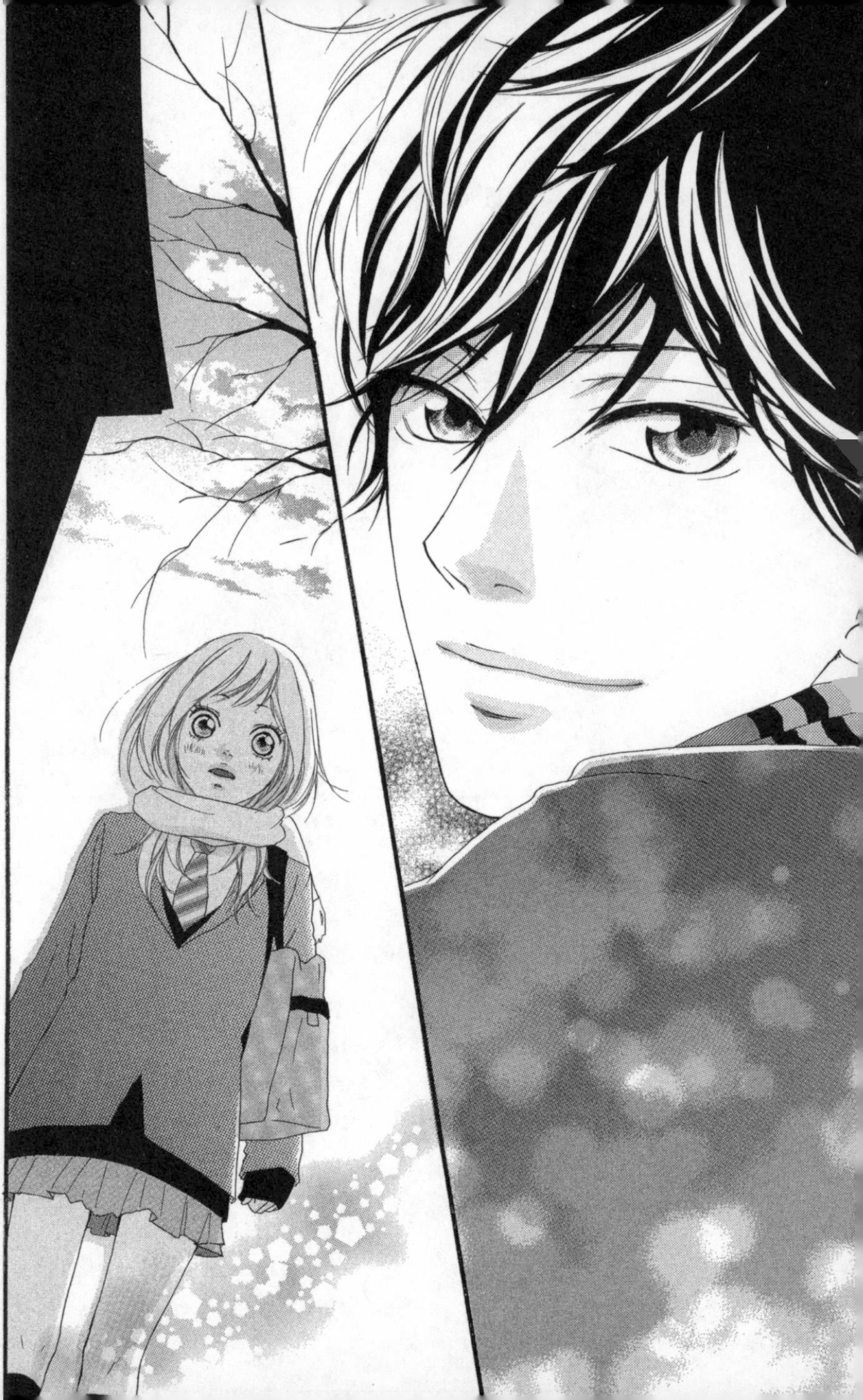

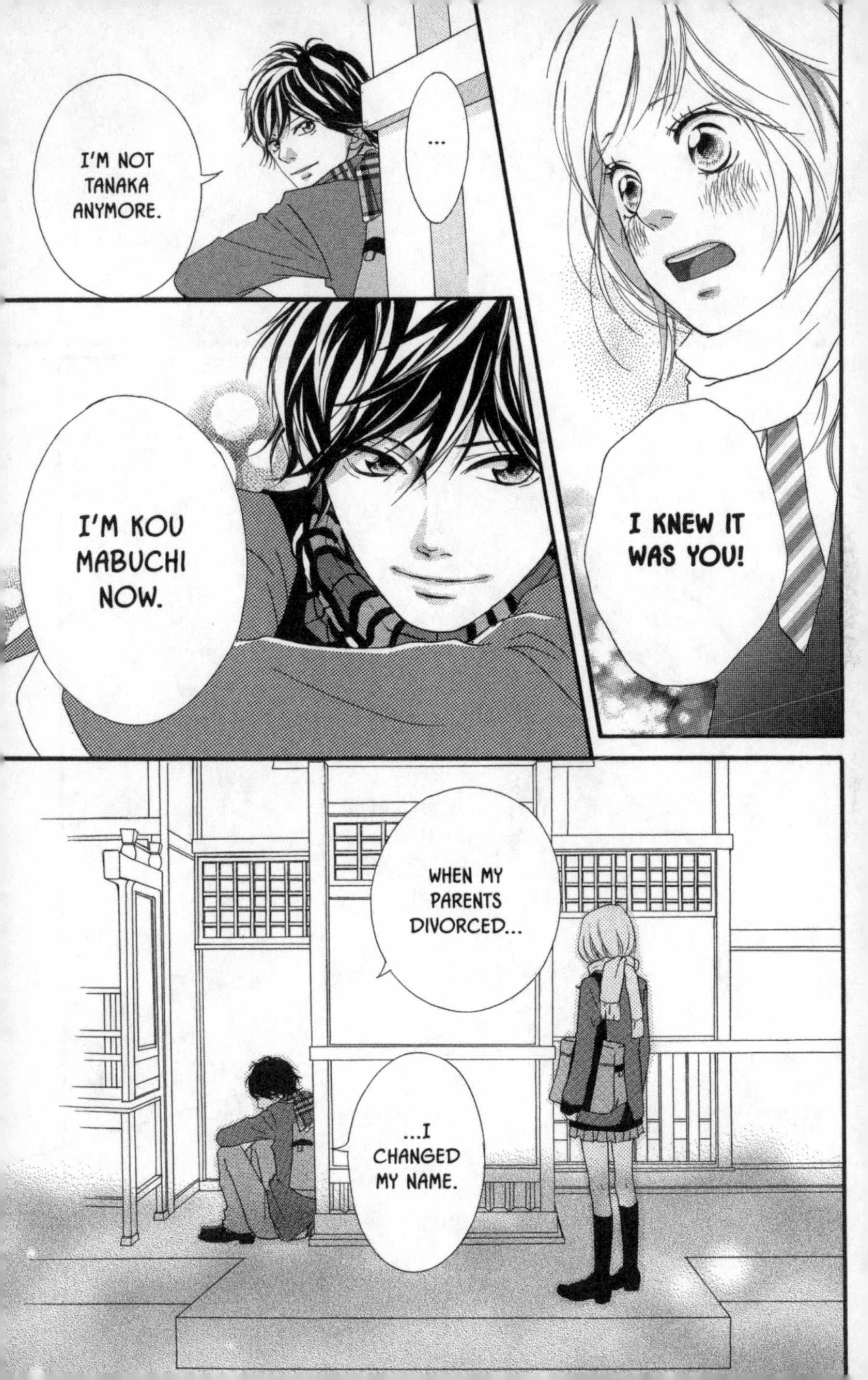
I KNEW IT WAS YOU!
...
I'M NOT TANAKA ANYMORE.
I'M KOU MABUCHI NOW.
WHEN MY PARENTS DIVORCED...
...I CHANGED MY NAME.

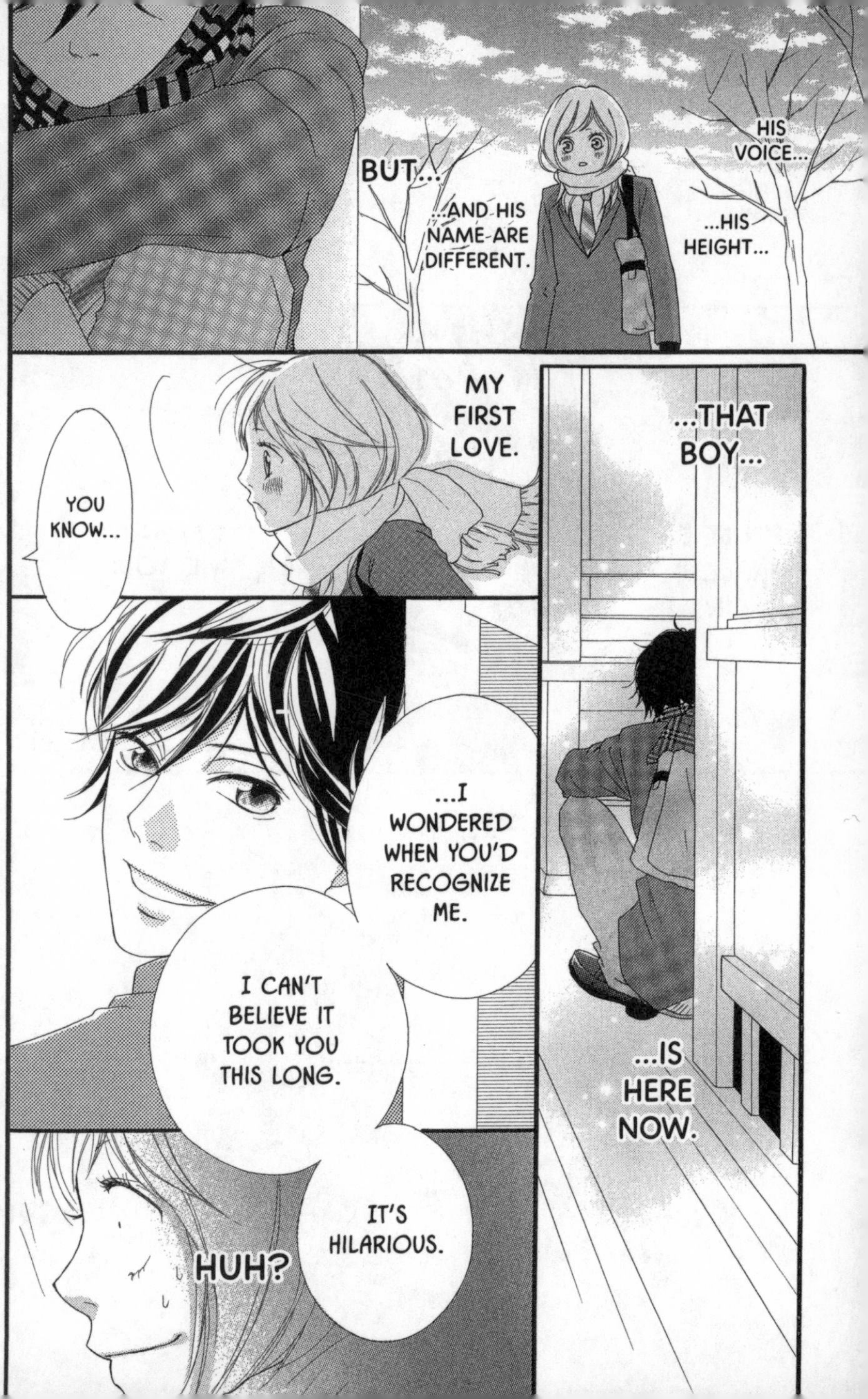
HIS VOICE...
...HIS HEIGHT...
BUT...
...AND HIS NAME ARE DIFFERENT.
...THAT BOY...
...IS HERE NOW.
MY FIRST LOVE.
YOU KNOW...
...I WONDERED WHEN YOU'D RECOGNIZE ME.
I CAN'T BELIEVE IT TOOK YOU THIS LONG.
IT'S HILARIOUS.
HUH?

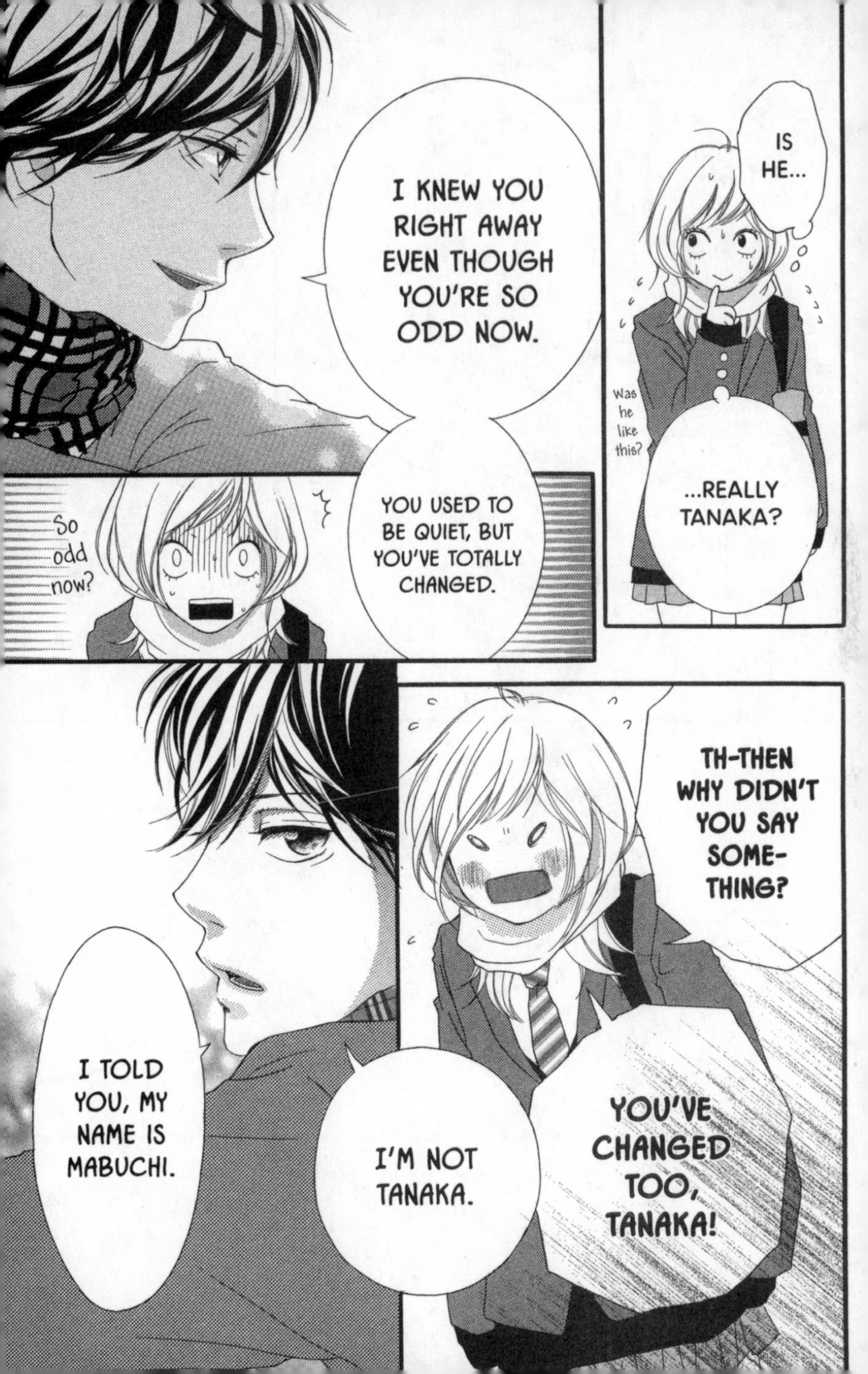
IS HE...
...REALLY TANAKA?
Was he like this?
I KNEW YOU RIGHT AWAY EVEN THOUGH YOU'RE SO ODD NOW.
YOU USED TO BE QUIET, BUT YOU'VE TOTALLY CHANGED.
So odd now?
TH-THEN WHY DIDN'T YOU SAY SOME-THING?
YOU'VE CHANGED TOO, TANAKA!
I'M NOT TANAKA.
I TOLD YOU, MY NAME IS MABUCHI.

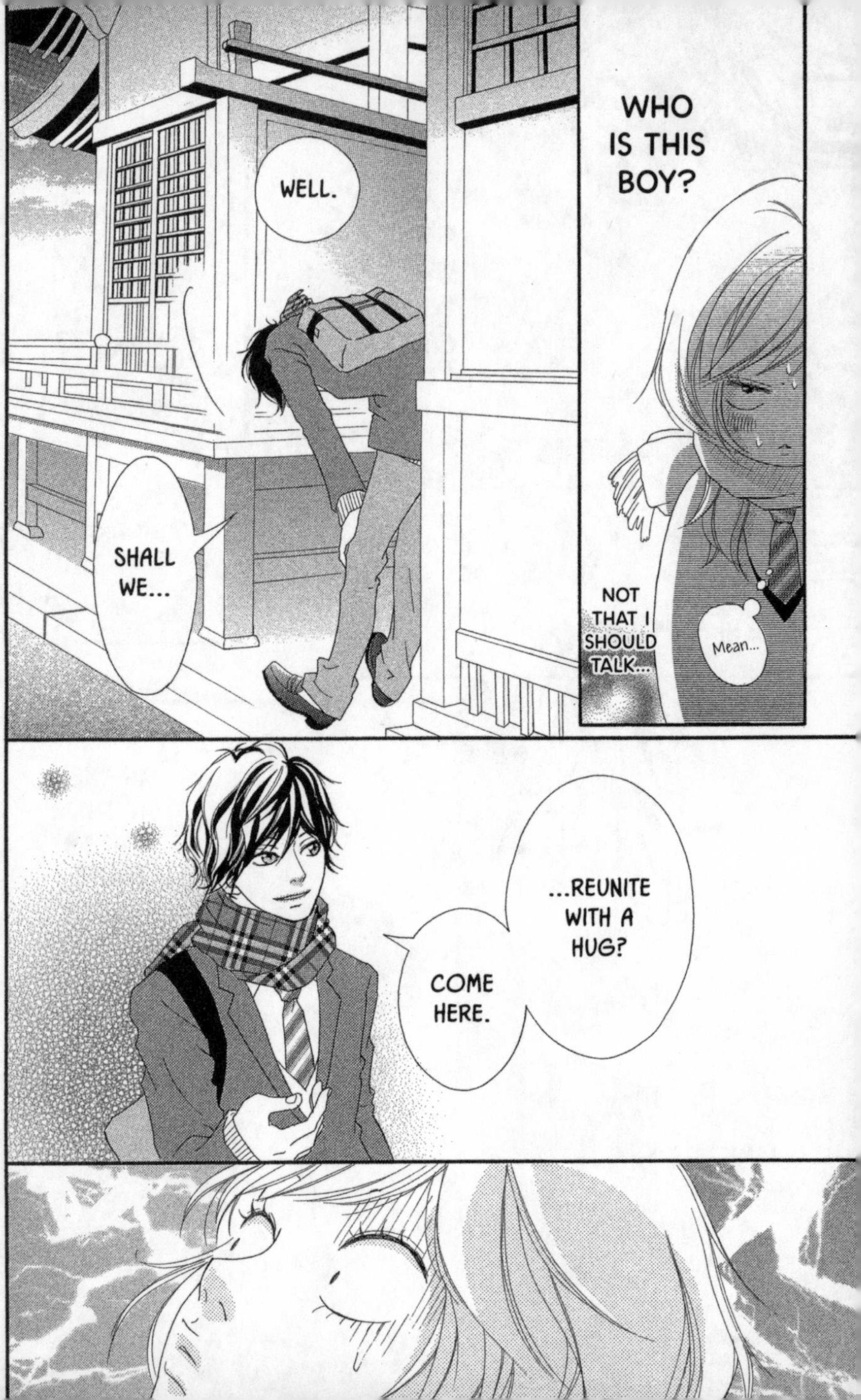
WHO IS THIS BOY?
NOT THAT I SHOULD TALK...
Mean...
WELL.
SHALL WE...
...REUNITE WITH A HUG?
COME HERE.

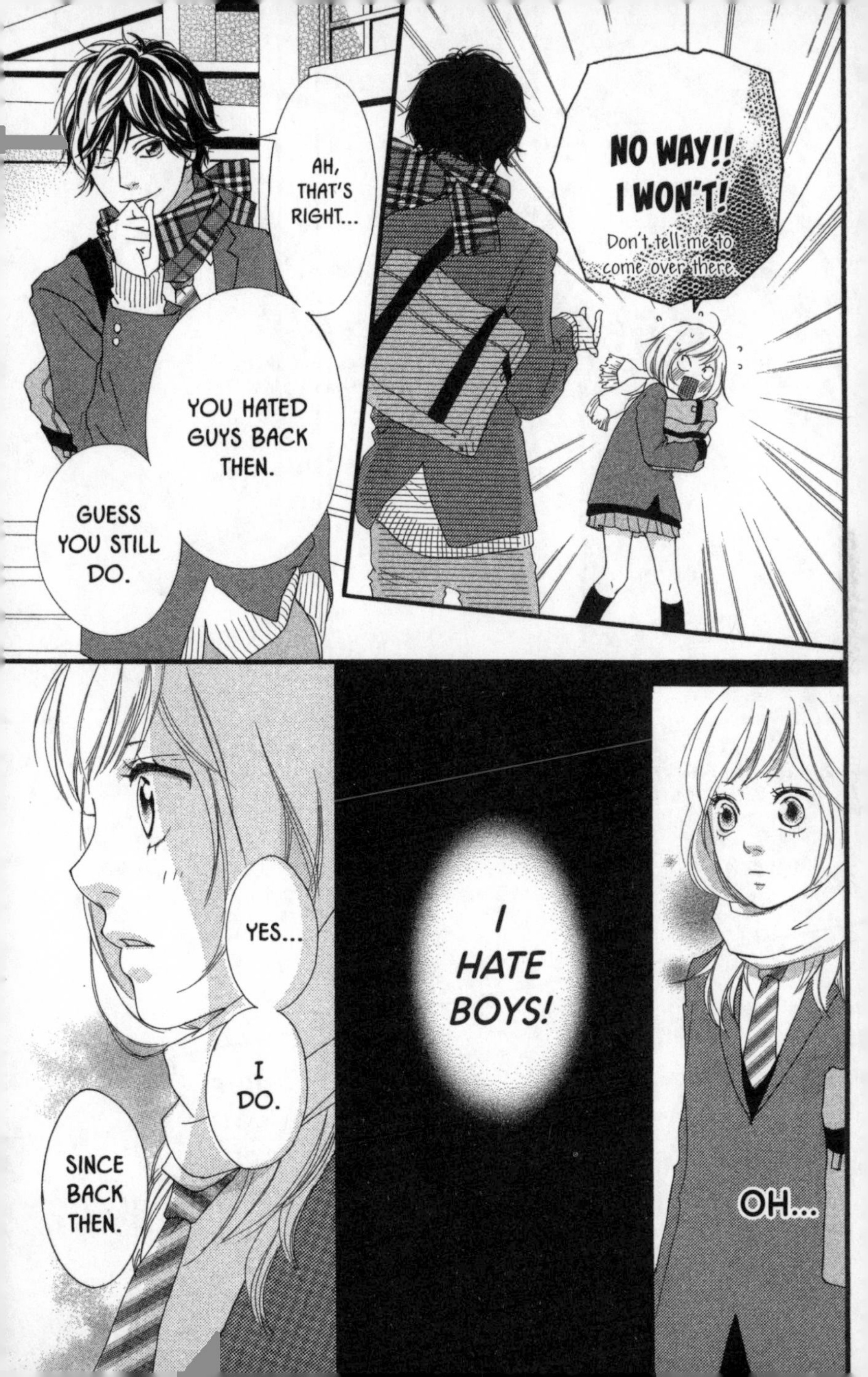
NO WAY!! I WON'T!
Don't tell me to come over there.
AH, THAT'S RIGHT...
YOU HATED GUYS BACK THEN.
GUESS YOU STILL DO.
OH...
I HATE BOYS!
YES...
I DO.
SINCE BACK THEN.

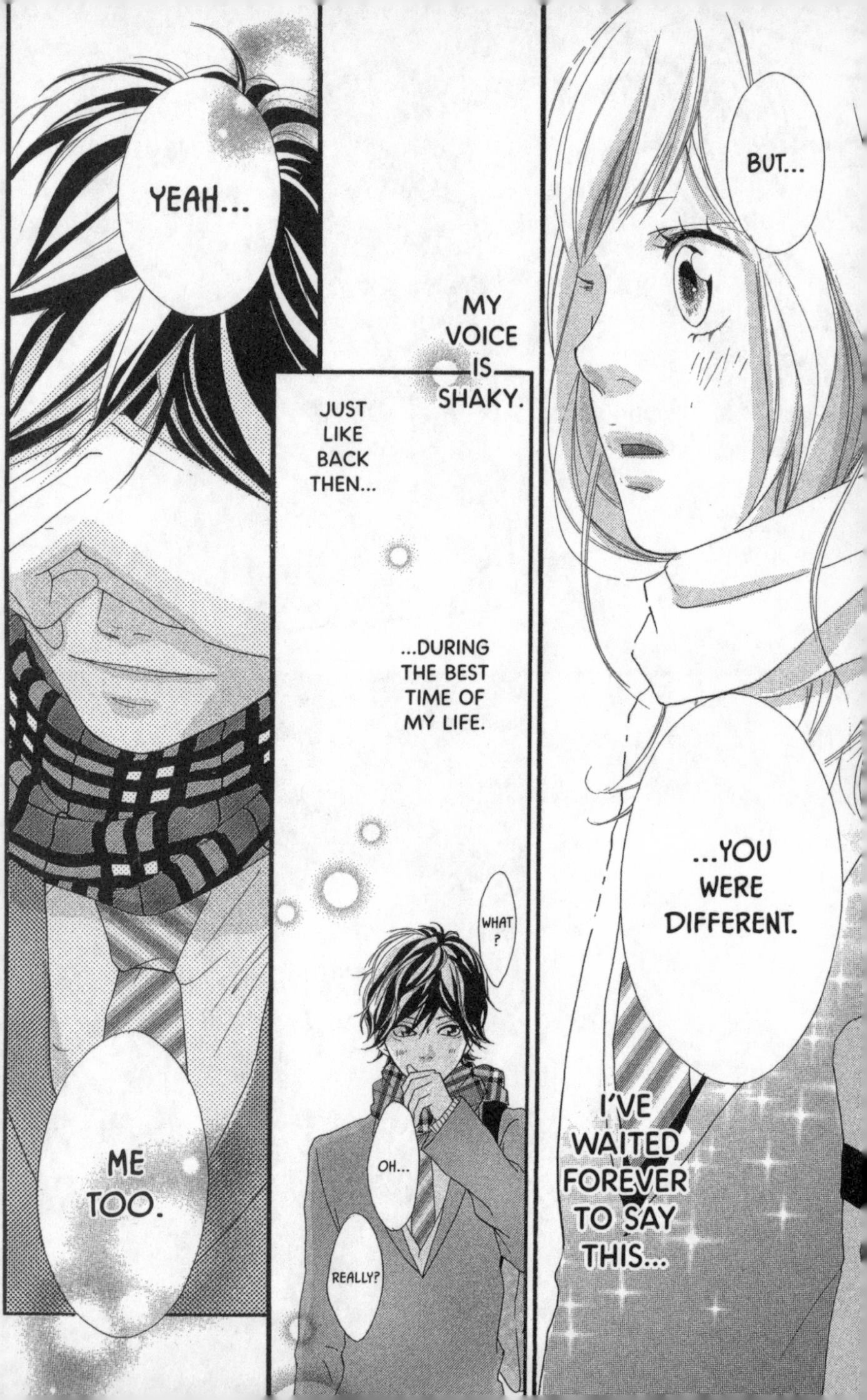
BUT...
...YOU WERE DIFFERENT.
I'VE WAITED FOREVER TO SAY THIS...
MY VOICE IS SHAKY.
JUST LIKE BACK THEN...
...DURING THE BEST TIME OF MY LIFE.
WHAT?
OH...
REALLY?
YEAH...
ME TOO.

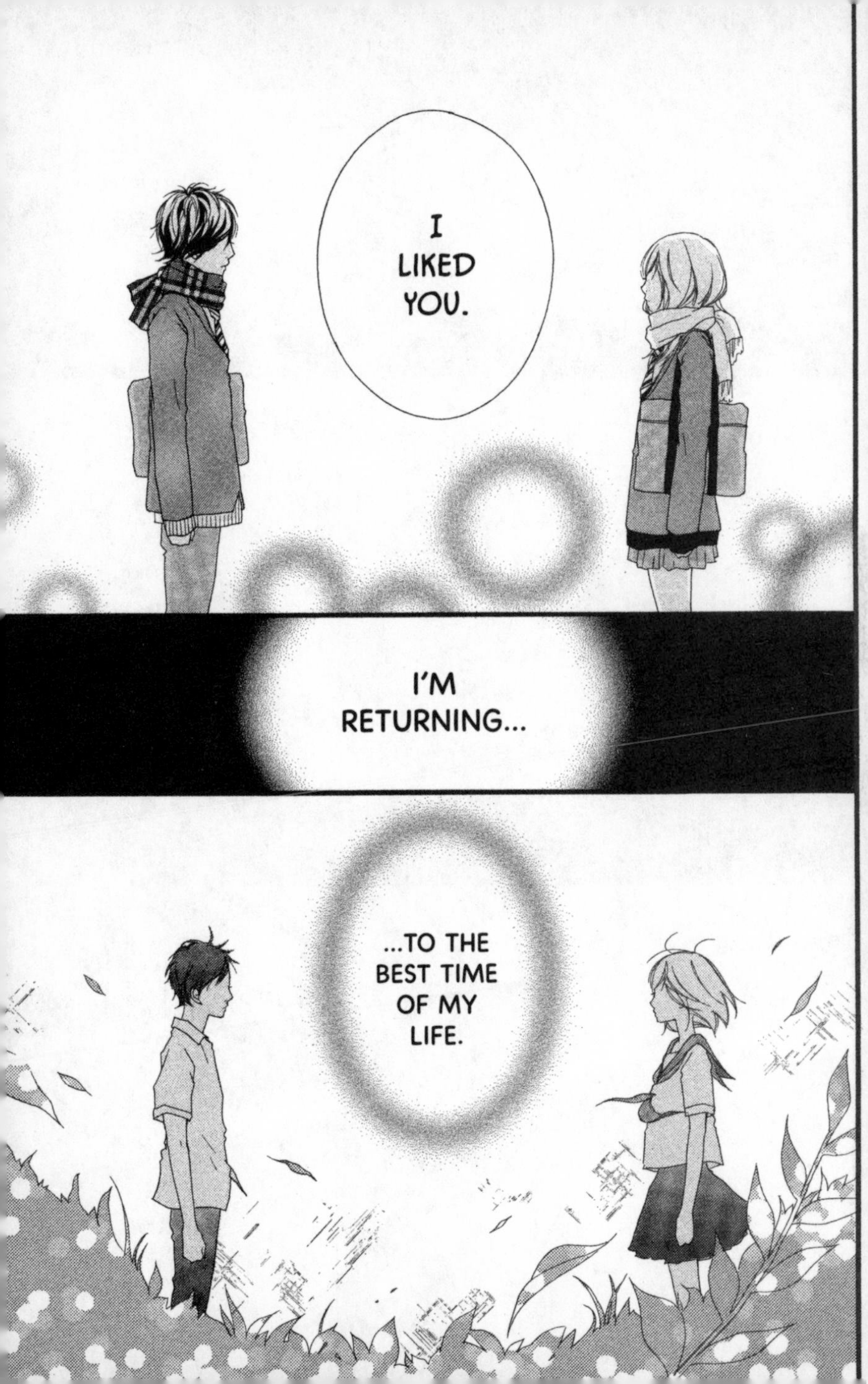
I LIKED YOU.
I'M RETURNING...
...TO THE BEST TIME OF MY LIFE.

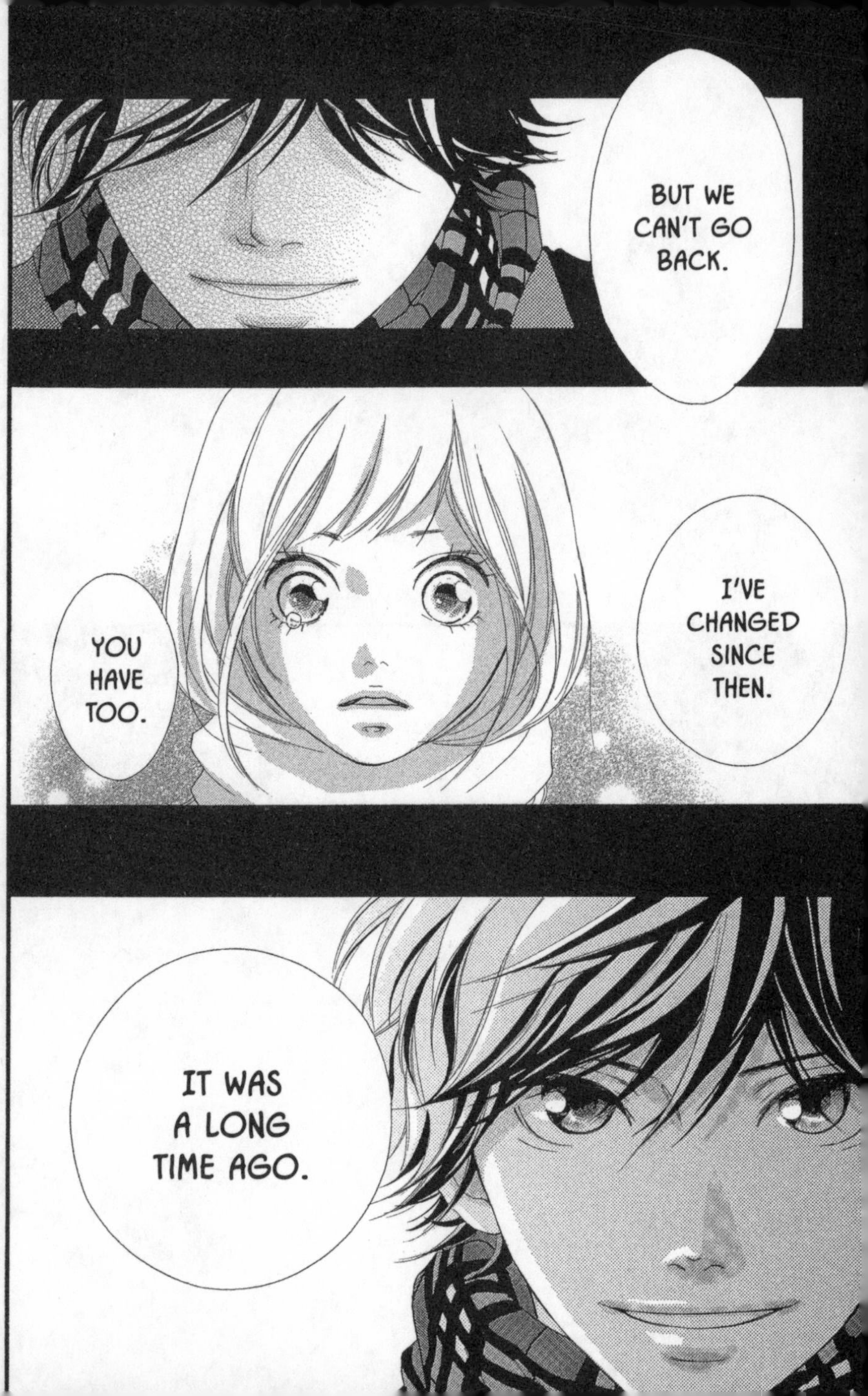
BUT WE CAN'T GO BACK.
I'VE CHANGED SINCE THEN.
YOU HAVE TOO.
IT WAS A LONG TIME AGO.

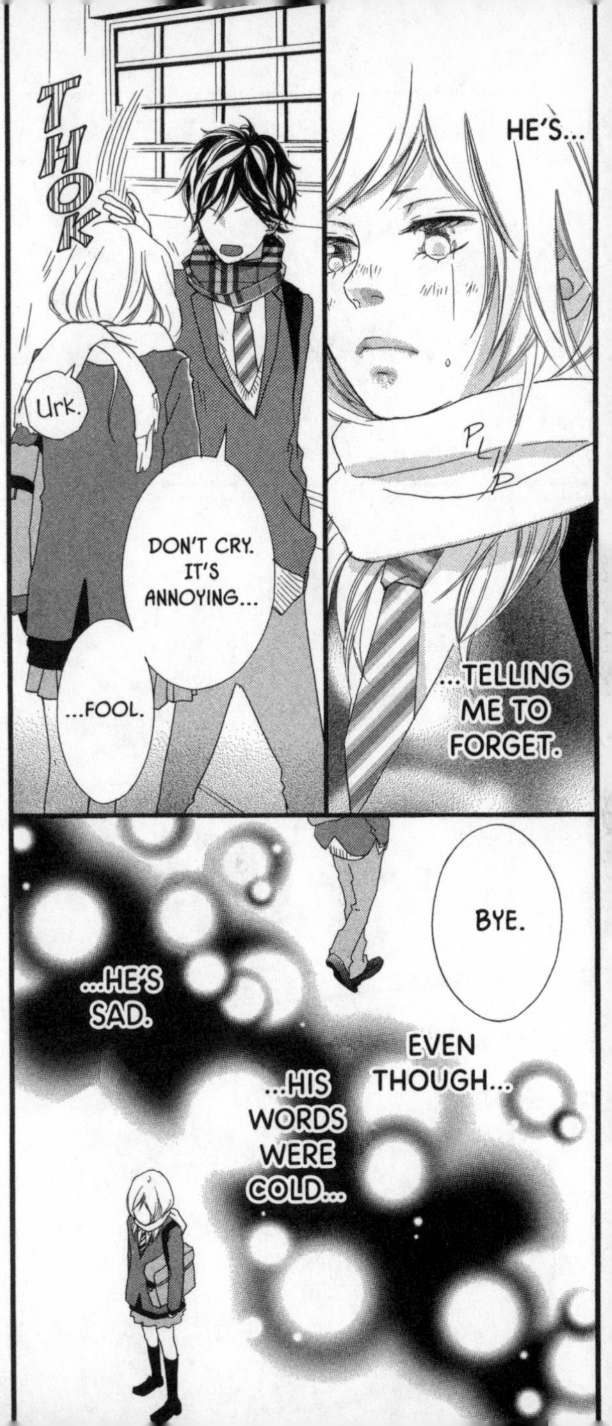
HE'S...
PLIP
...TELLING ME TO FORGET.
THOK
Urk.
DON'T CRY. IT'S ANNOYING...
...FOOL.
BYE.
EVEN THOUGH...
...HIS WORDS WERE COLD...
...HE'S SAD.

New Characters

Though volume 1 is coming out now, I'm still not used to drawing the characters. It really takes a while. And when my deadlines get close, I panic...and resentment starts to build. It's a constant battle because I know that I need to build a friendship with these kids.

It's unusual for me, but several characters in this story have colored hair. Shiny hair takes a long time to draw—I resent it. And they are resentful in turn. They steal my time!!! They require so much time and effort... So at the very least I need you readers to love them. I hope you enjoy them!

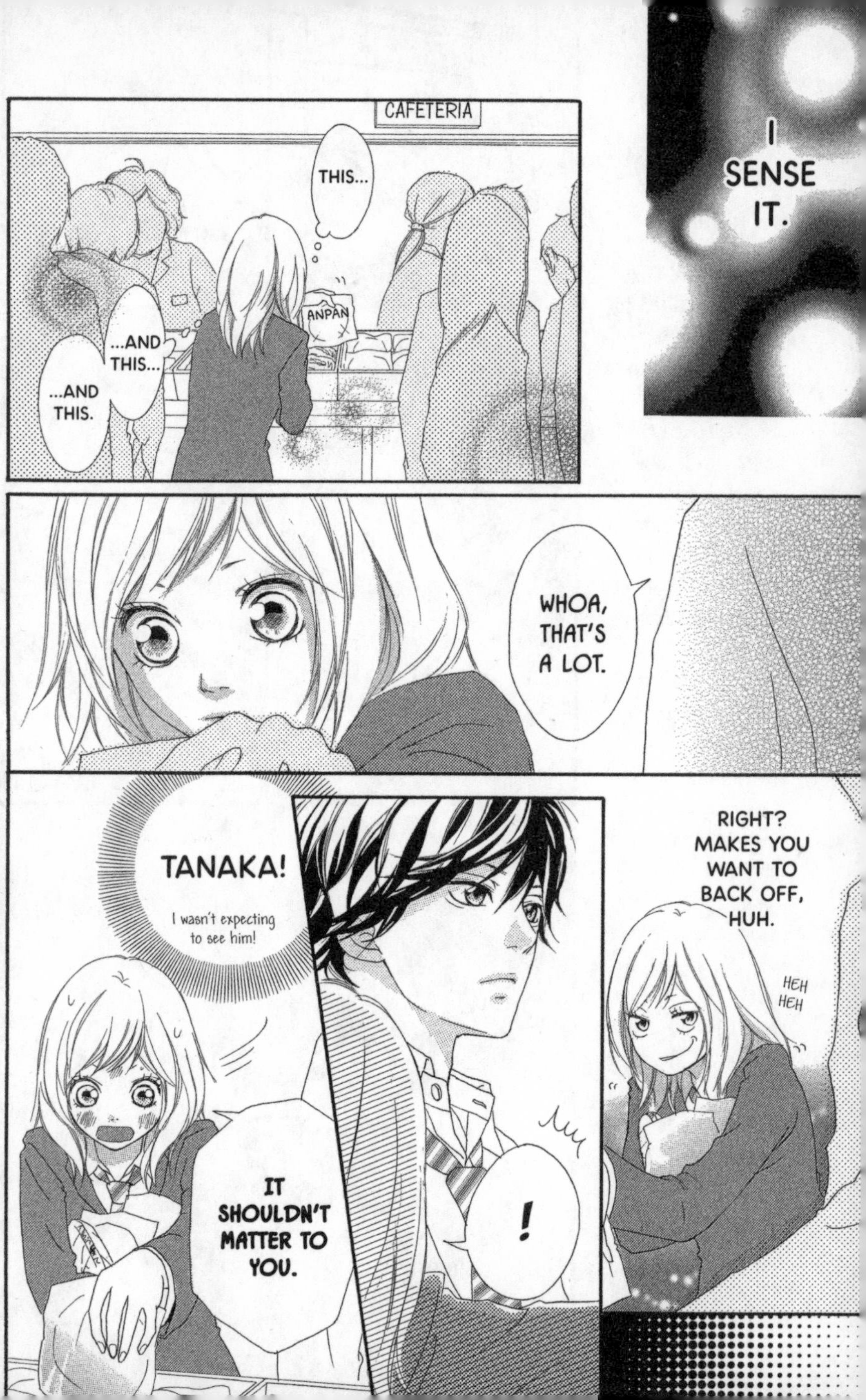
I SENSE IT.
CAFETERIA
THIS...
ANPAN
...AND THIS...
...AND THIS.
WHOA, THAT'S A LOT.
RIGHT? MAKES YOU WANT TO BACK OFF, HUH.
HEH HEH
!
TANAKA!
I wasn't expecting to see him!
IT SHOULDN'T MATTER TO YOU.

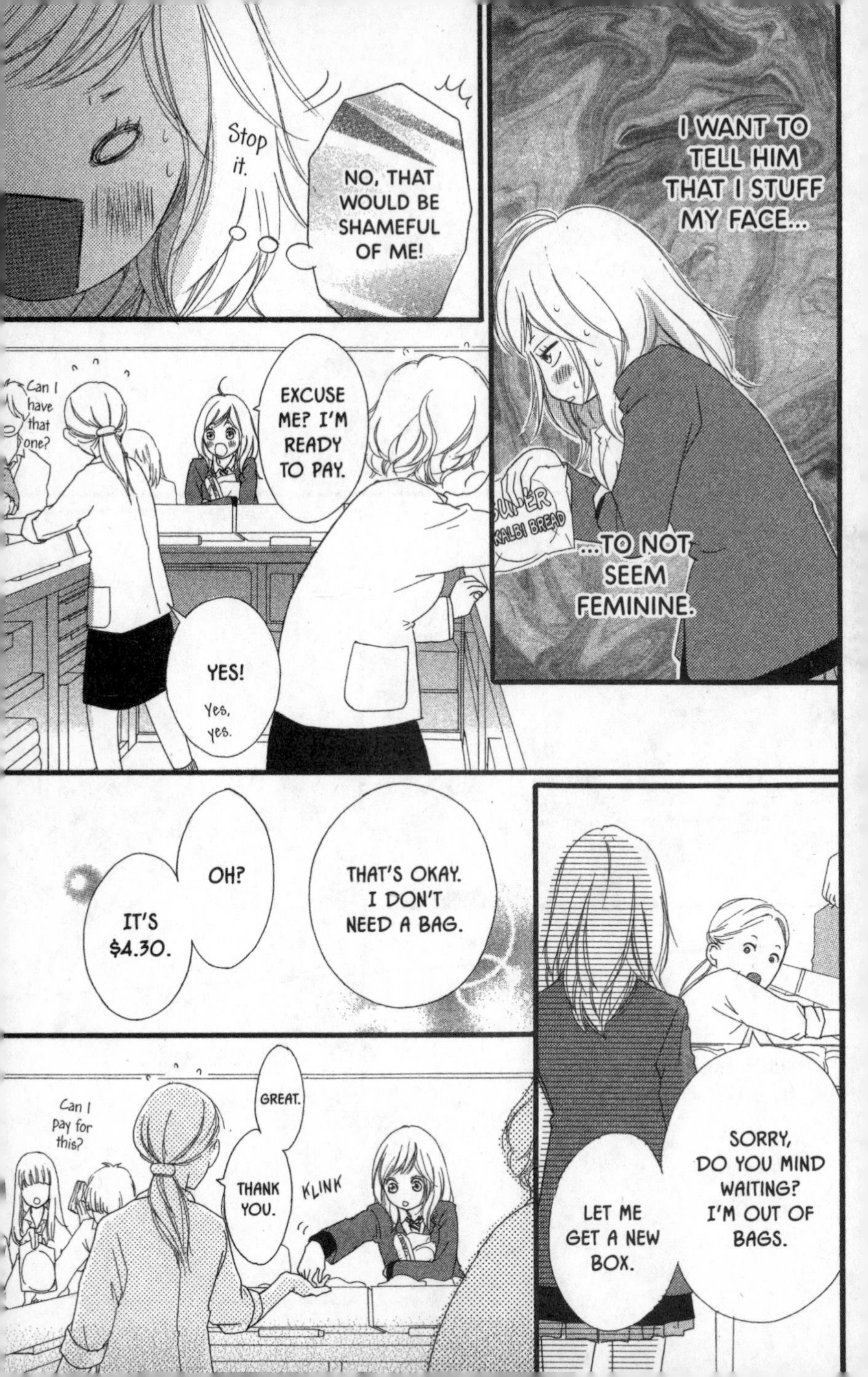
I WANT TO TELL HIM THAT I STUFF MY FACE...
SUPER KALBI BREAD
...TO NOT SEEM FEMININE.
NO, THAT WOULD BE SHAMEFUL OF ME!
Stop it.
EXCUSE ME? I'M READY TO PAY.
Can I have that one?
YES!
Yes, yes.
SORRY, DO YOU MIND WAITING? I'M OUT OF BAGS.
LET ME GET A NEW BOX.
THAT'S OKAY. I DON'T NEED A BAG.
OH?
IT'S $4.30.
GREAT.
THANK YOU.
KLINK
Can I pay for this?

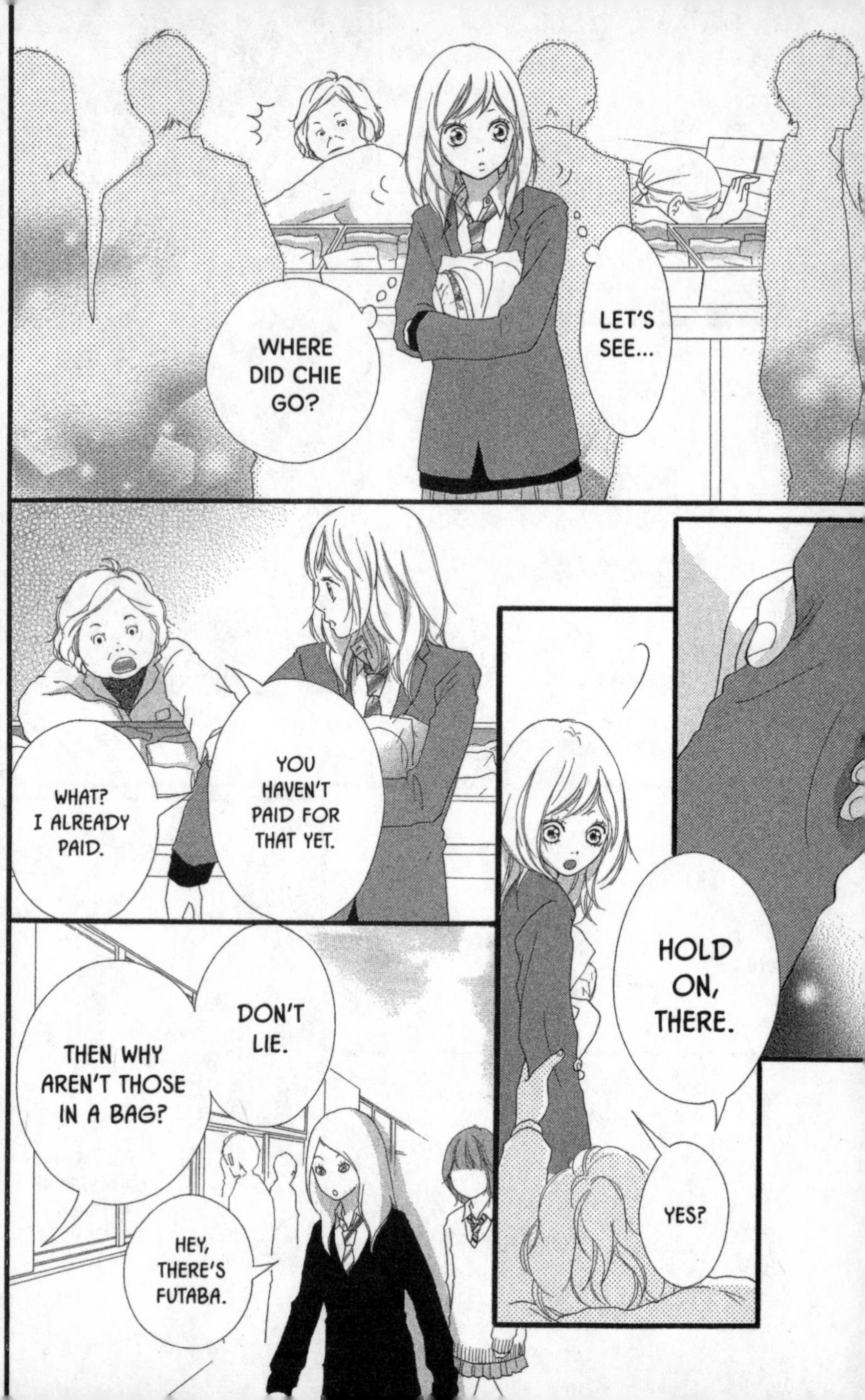
LET'S SEE...
WHERE DID CHIE GO?
HOLD ON, THERE.
YES?
YOU HAVEN'T PAID FOR THAT YET.
WHAT? I ALREADY PAID.
DON'T LIE.
THEN WHY AREN'T THOSE IN A BAG?
HEY, THERE'S FUTABA.

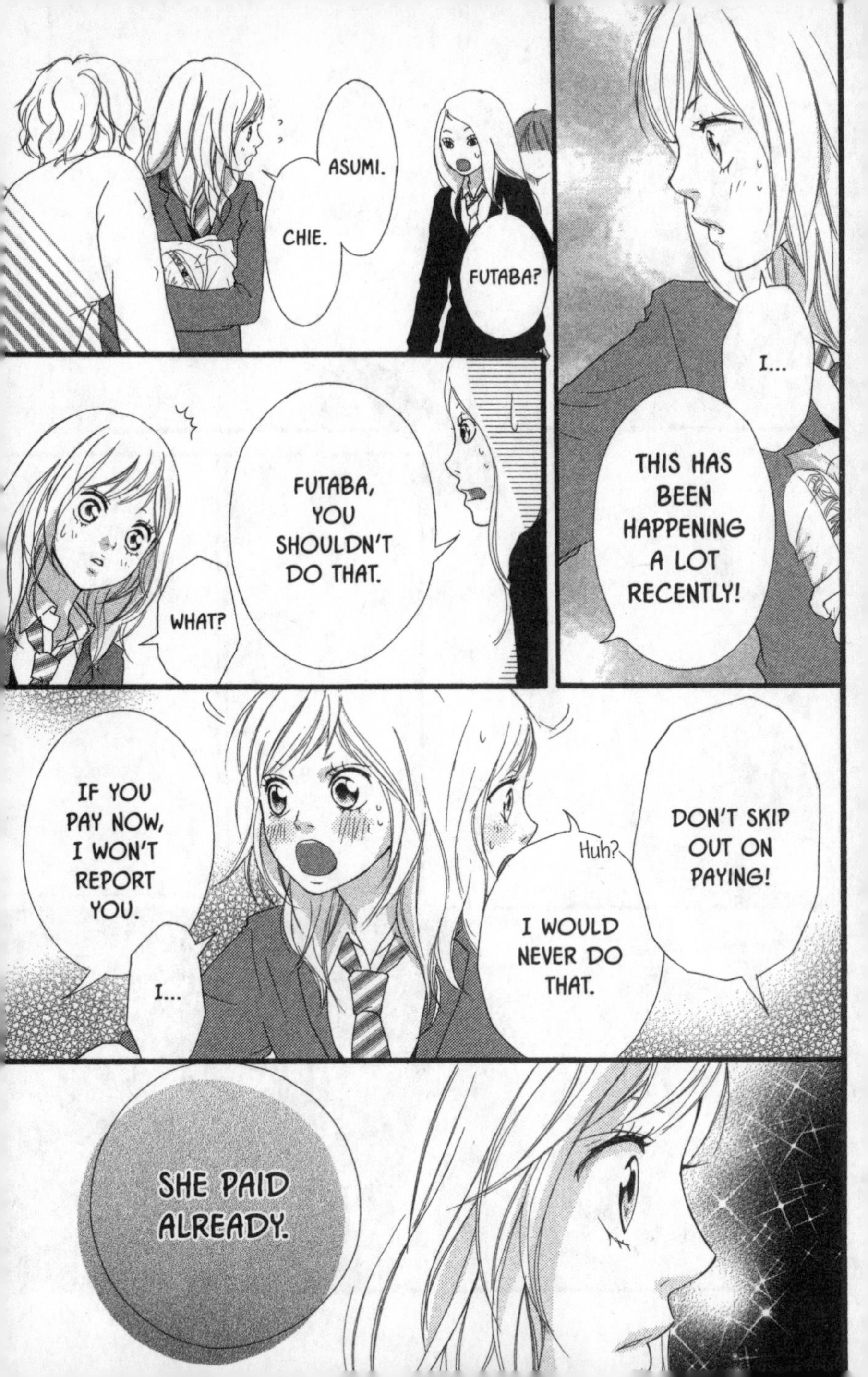
I...
THIS HAS BEEN HAPPENING A LOT RECENTLY!
FUTABA?
ASUMI.
CHIE.
FUTABA, YOU SHOULDN'T DO THAT.
WHAT?
DON'T SKIP OUT ON PAYING!
Huh?
I WOULD NEVER DO THAT.
IF YOU PAY NOW, I WON'T REPORT YOU.
I...
SHE PAID ALREADY.

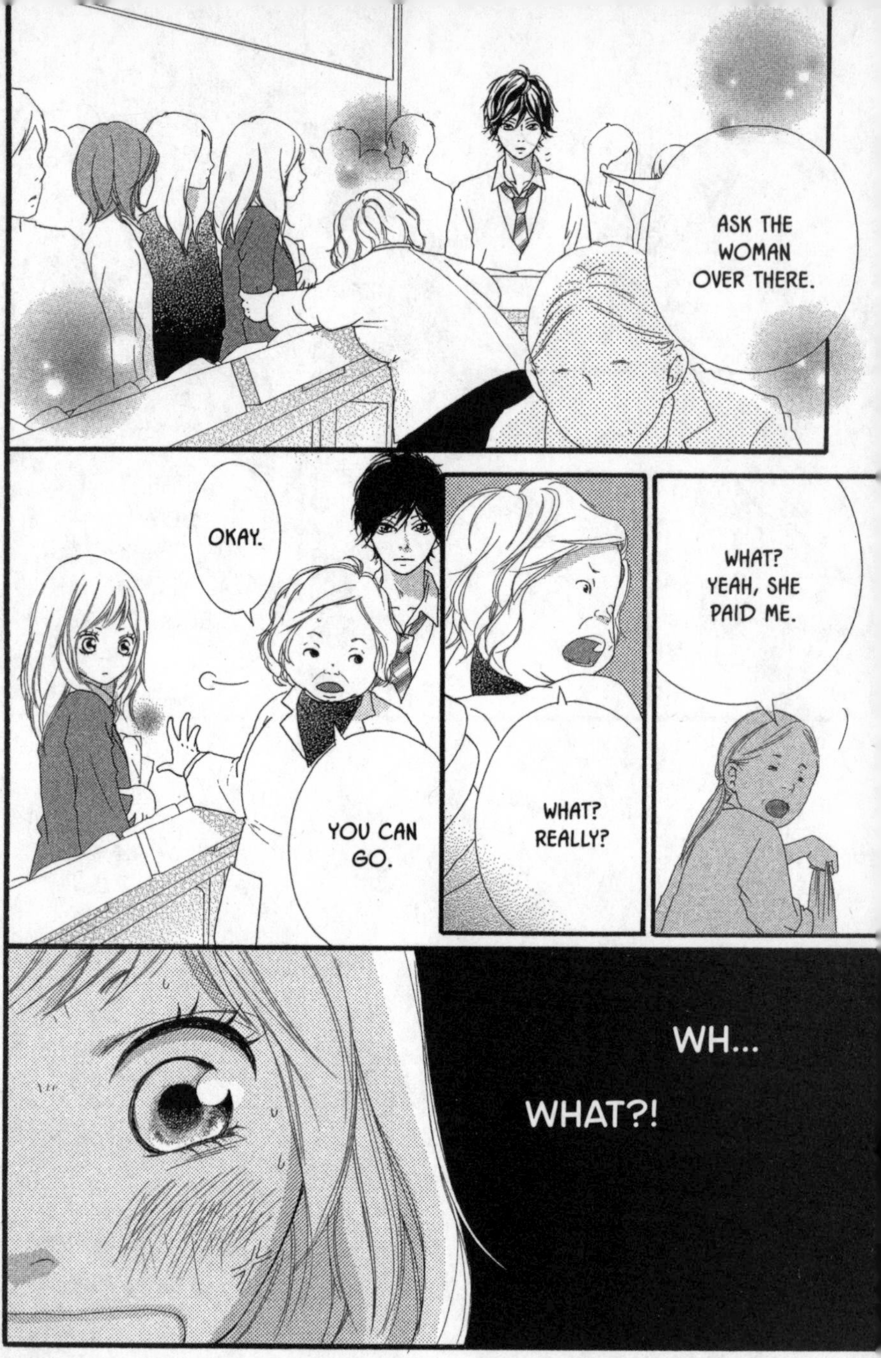
ASK THE WOMAN OVER THERE.
WHAT? YEAH, SHE PAID ME.
WHAT? REALLY?
OKAY.
YOU CAN GO.
WH...
WHAT?!

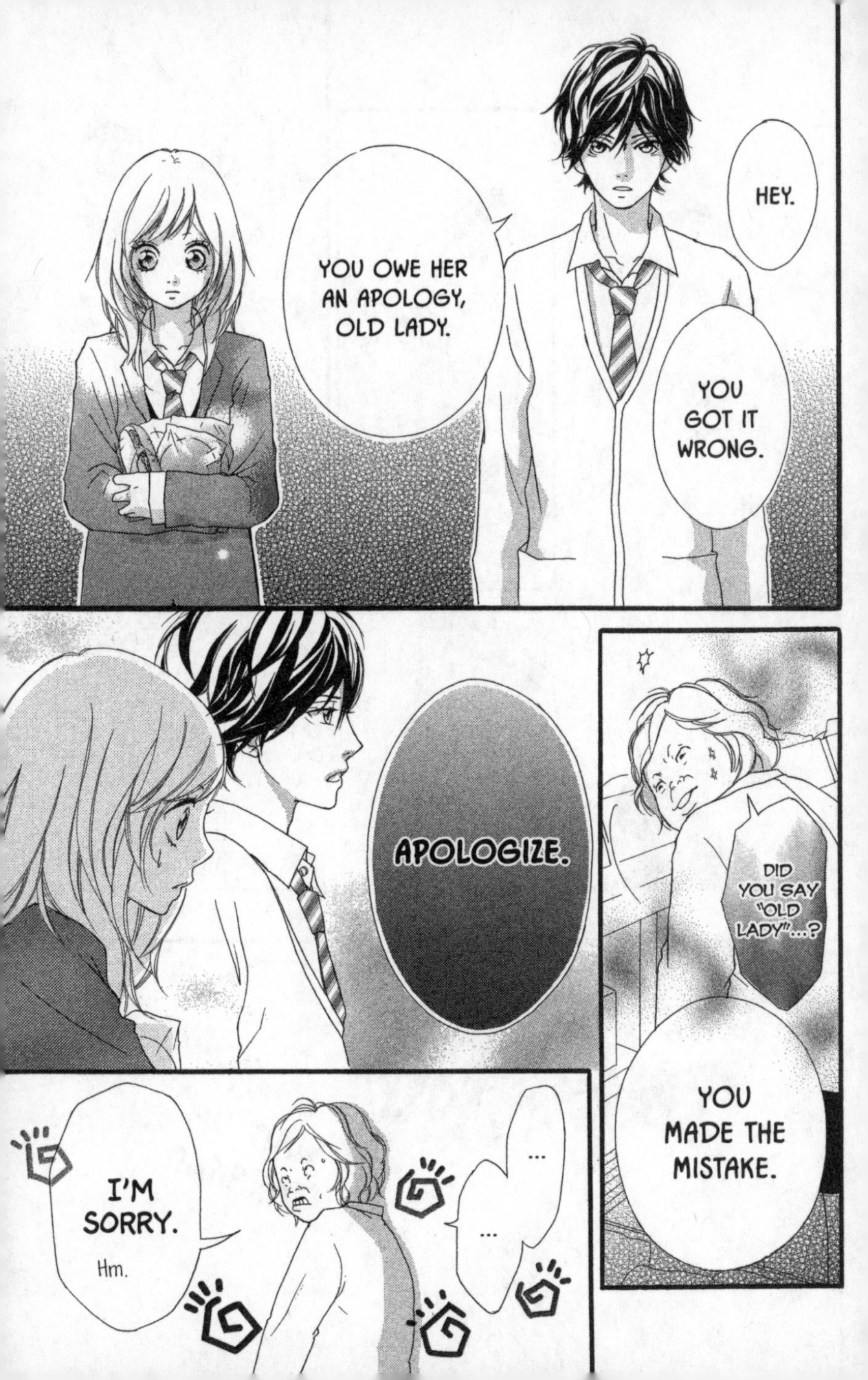
HEY.
YOU GOT IT WRONG.
YOU OWE HER AN APOLOGY, OLD LADY.
DID YOU SAY "OLD LADY"...?
YOU MADE THE MISTAKE.
APOLOGIZE.
...
...
I'M SORRY.
Hm.

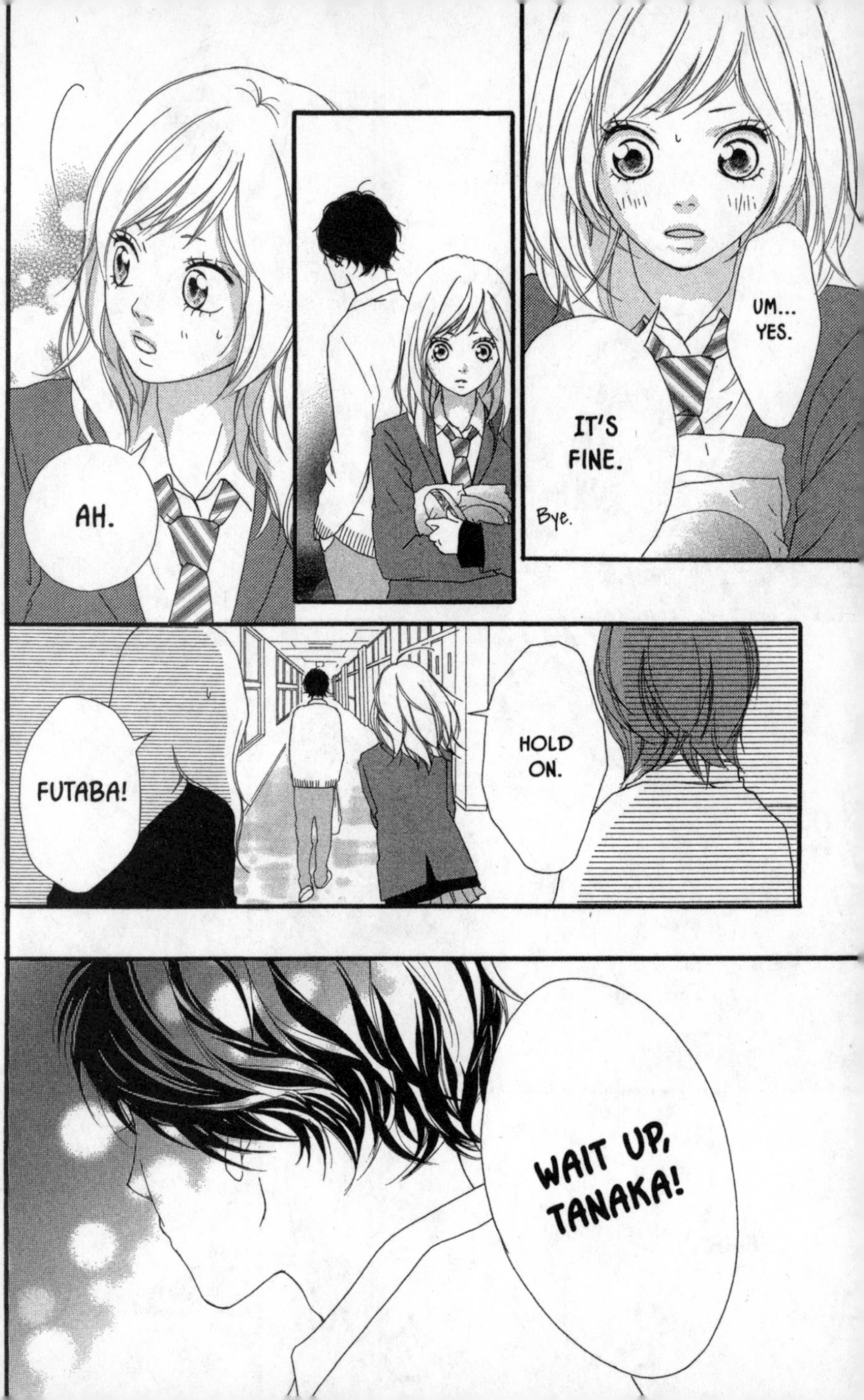
UM... YES.
IT'S FINE.
Bye.
AH.
HOLD ON.
FUTABA!
WAIT UP, TANAKA!

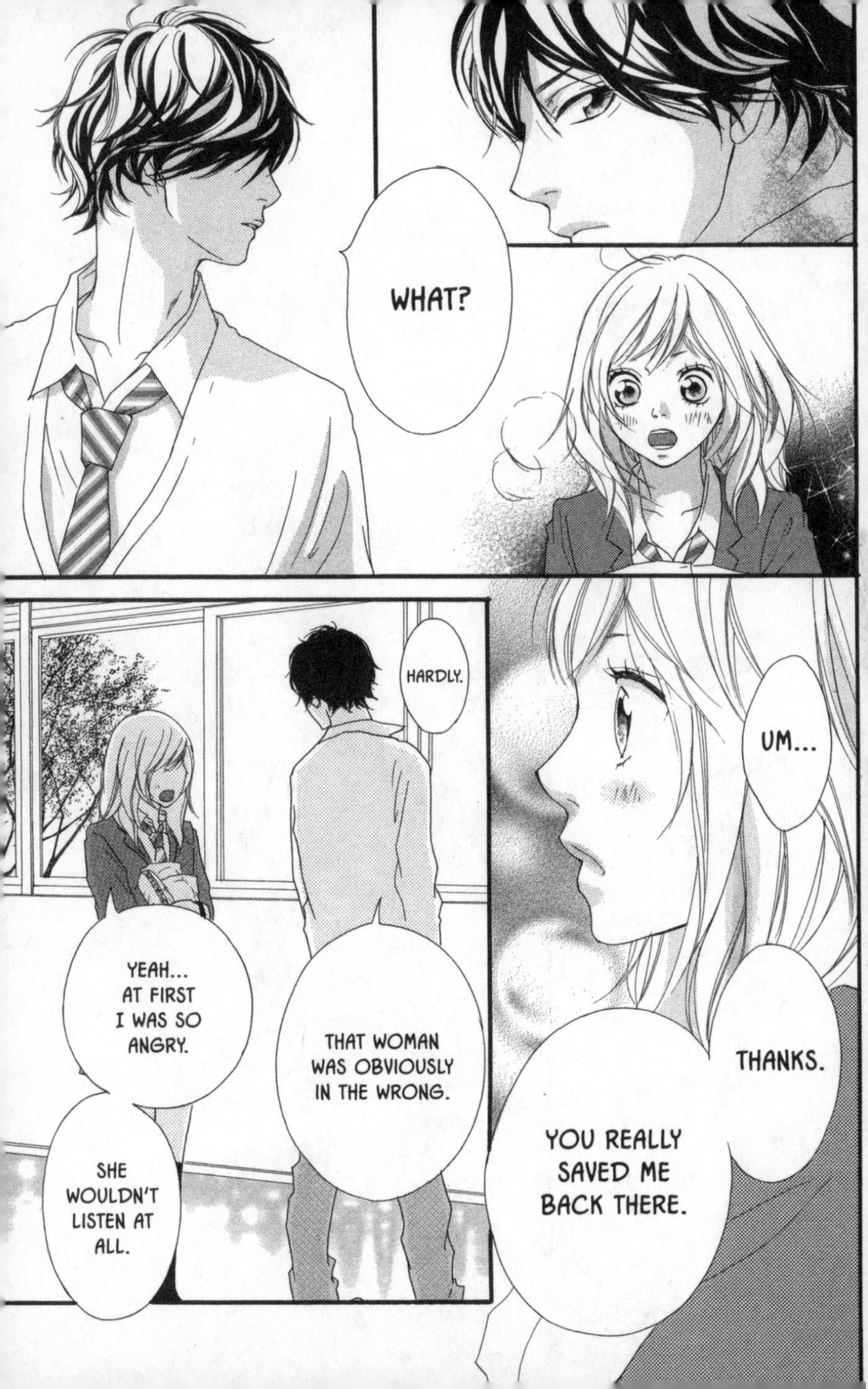
WHAT?
UM...
THANKS.
YOU REALLY SAVED ME BACK THERE.
HARDLY.
THAT WOMAN WAS OBVIOUSLY IN THE WRONG.
YEAH... AT FIRST I WAS SO ANGRY.
SHE WOULDN'T LISTEN AT ALL.

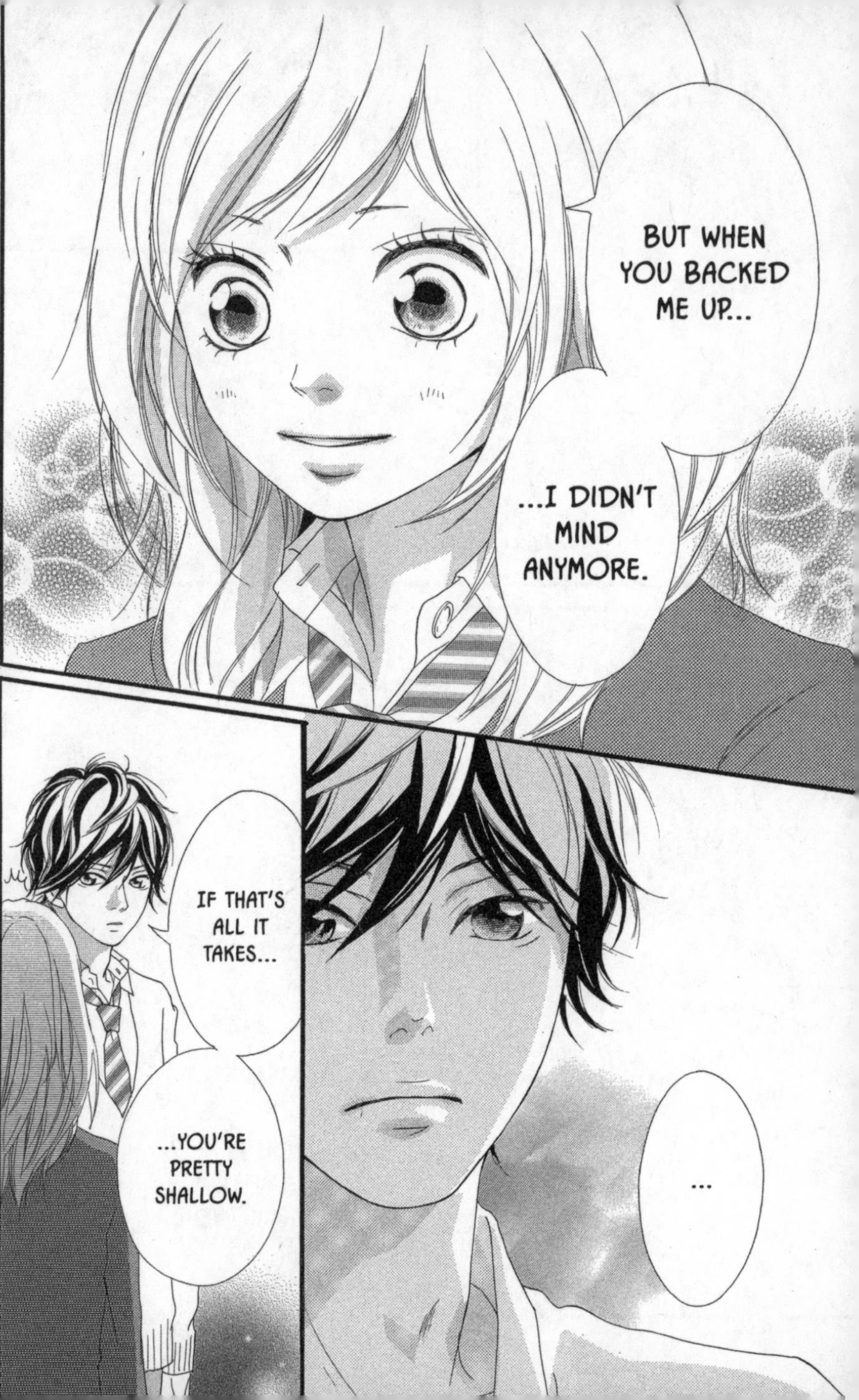
BUT WHEN YOU BACKED ME UP...
...I DIDN'T MIND ANYMORE.
...
IF THAT'S ALL IT TAKES...
...YOU'RE PRETTY SHALLOW.

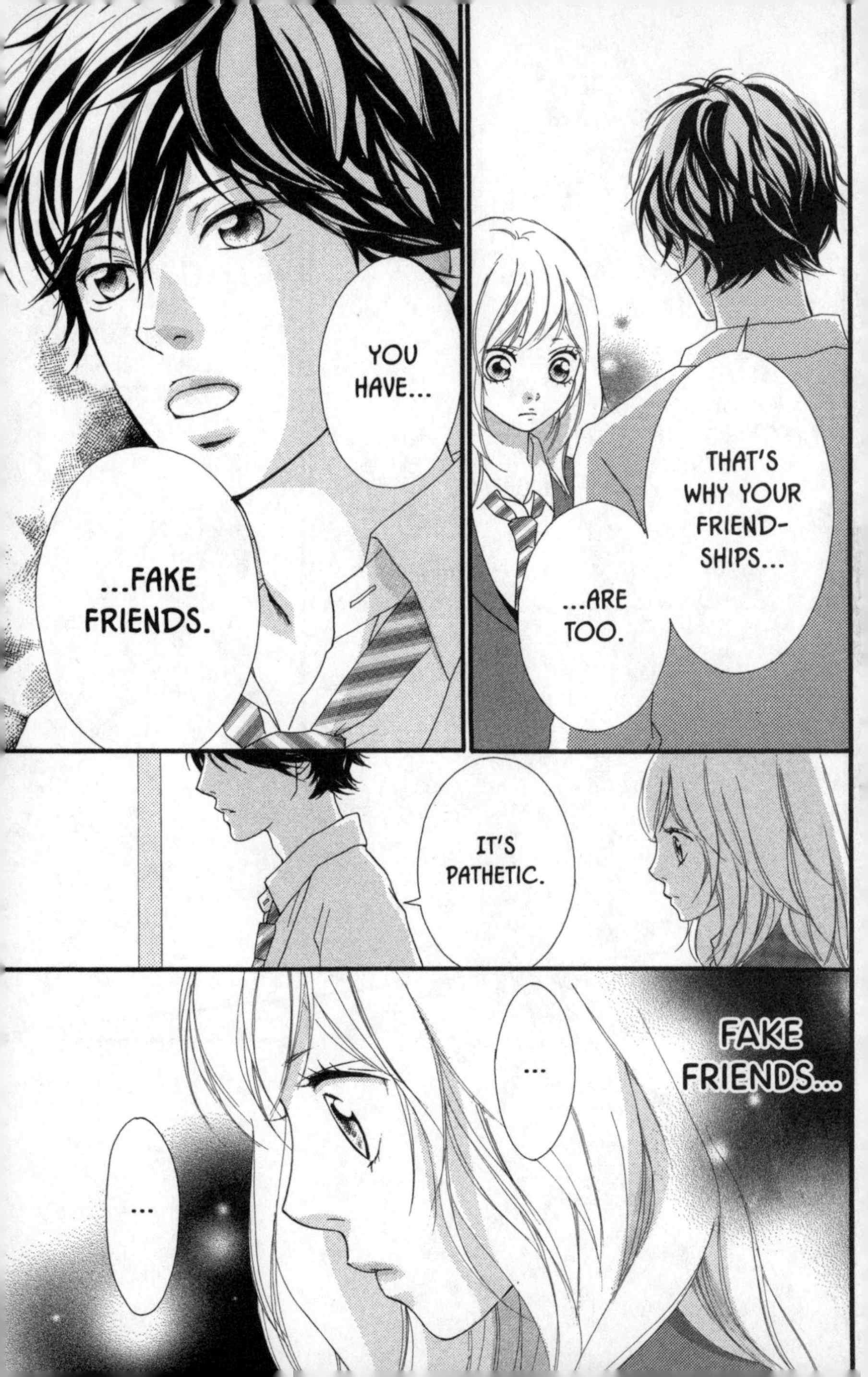
THAT'S WHY YOUR FRIEND-SHIPS...
...ARE TOO.
YOU HAVE...
...FAKE FRIENDS.
IT'S PATHETIC.
FAKE FRIENDS...
...
...

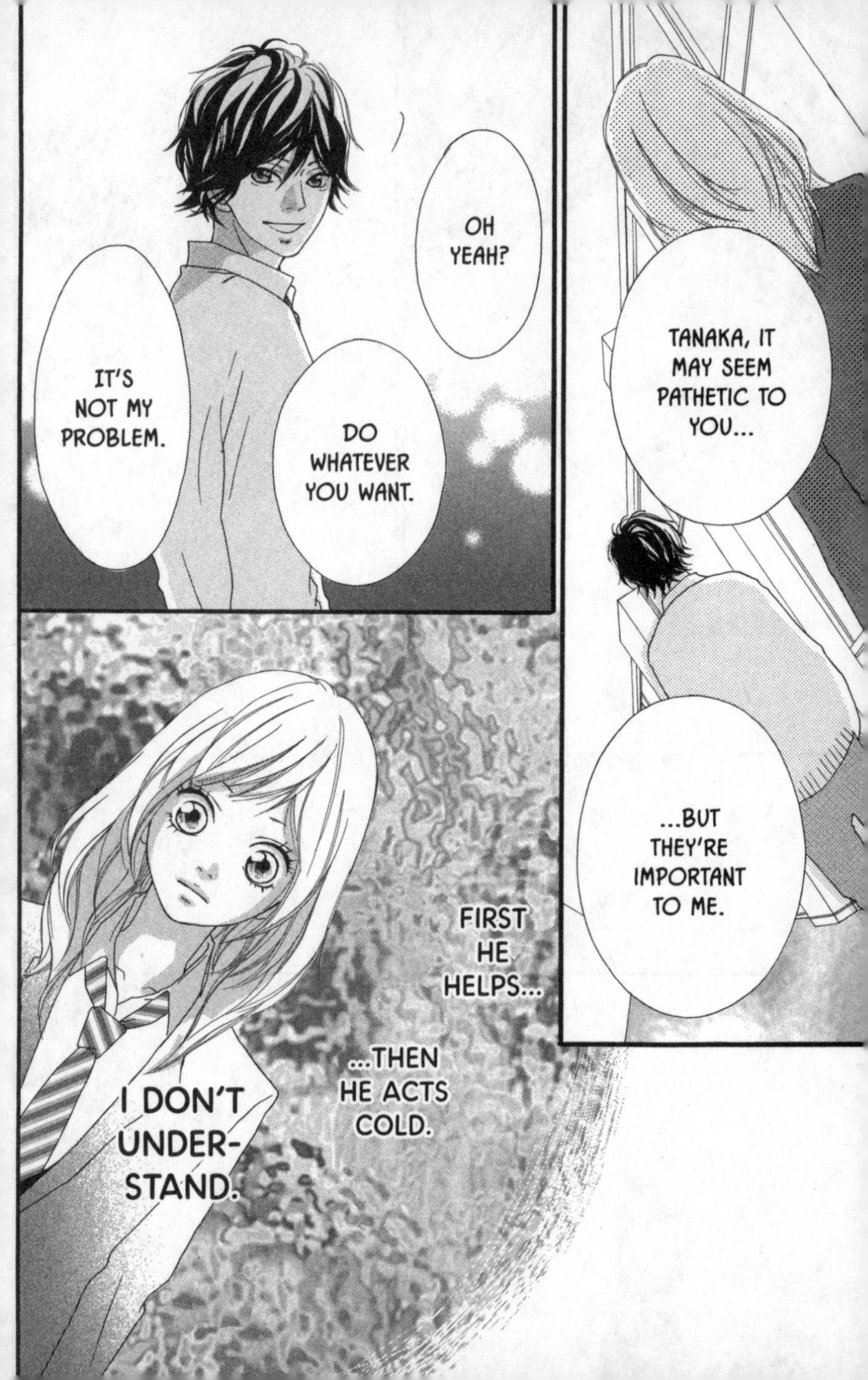
TANAKA, IT MAY SEEM PATHETIC TO YOU...
...BUT THEY'RE IMPORTANT TO ME.
OH YEAH?
DO WHATEVER YOU WANT.
IT'S NOT MY PROBLEM.
FIRST HE HELPS...
...THEN HE ACTS COLD.
I DON'T UNDER-STAND.

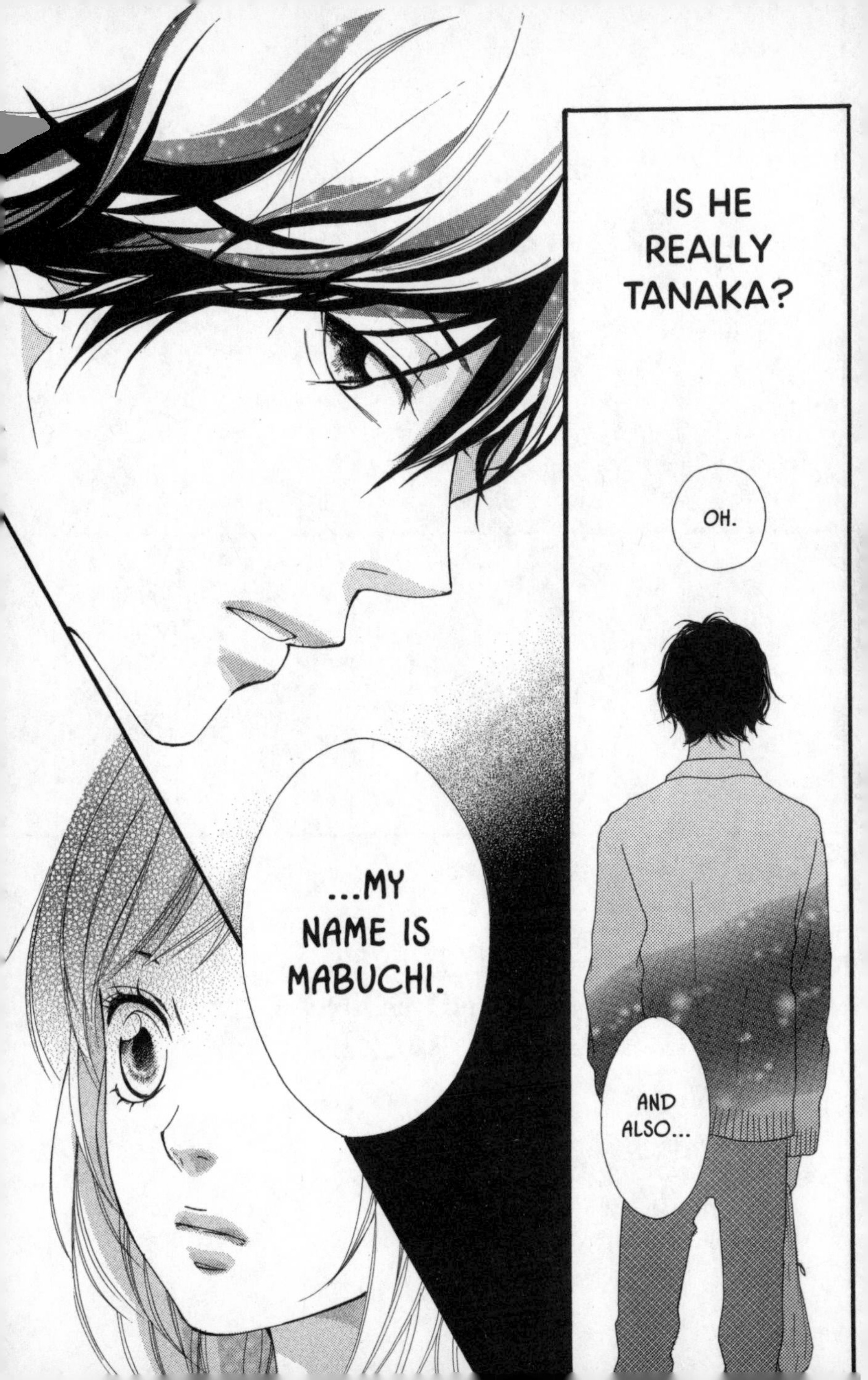
IS HE REALLY TANAKA?
OH.
AND ALSO...
...MY NAME IS MABUCHI.

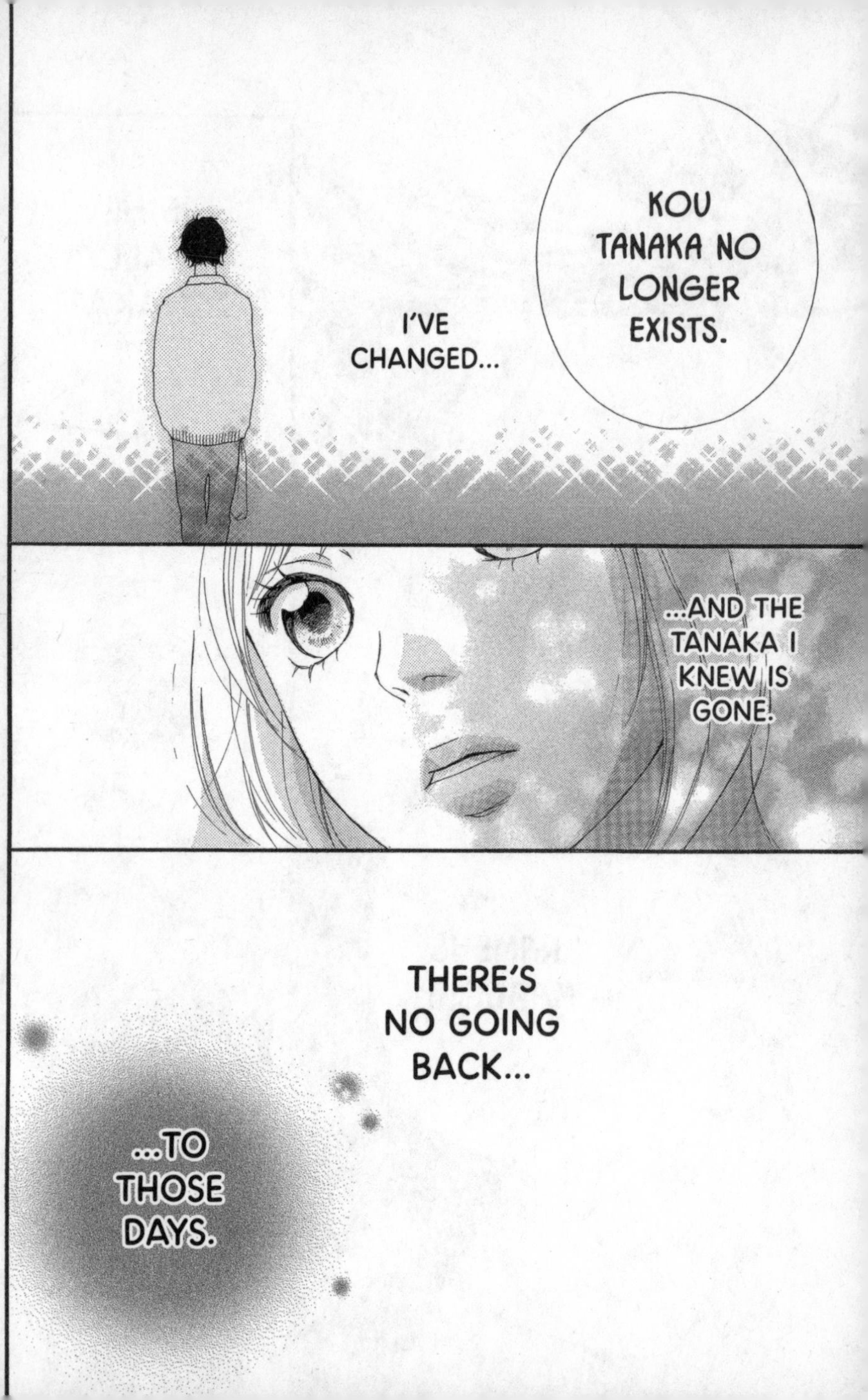
KOU TANAKA NO LONGER EXISTS.
I'VE CHANGED...
...AND THE TANAKA I KNEW IS GONE.
THERE'S NO GOING BACK...
...TO THOSE DAYS.

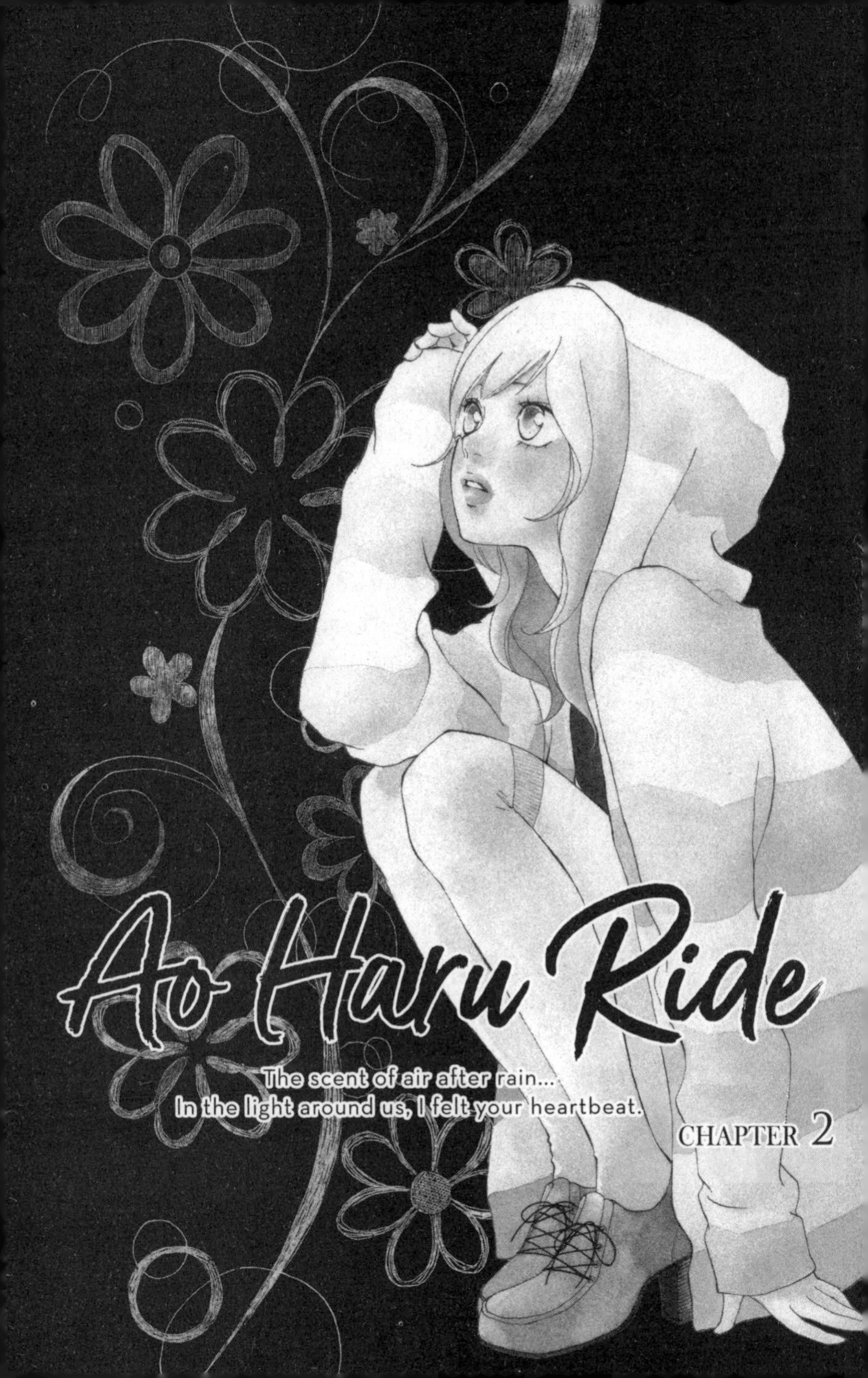
Ao Haru Ride
The scent of air after rain...
In the light around us, I felt your heartbeat.
CHAPTER 2

When I create manga, I periodically feel anxious about my work. When that happens, I always go to others for their opinions and advice, but everyone has a different opinion. And when I hear their thoughts, I always think the same thing: "This is how it always goes." What I mean is that there is no perfect solution. I know this, but I still get anxious and repeat the process over and over, though their advice only makes me more confused. There's really no point in doing this. It may be important to hear the opinions of many people, but once I try out those ideas and they don't work, I end up thinking, "Why don't these work for me?!" and I get discouraged. When really I should acknowledge they're not right for me and change my perspective. Also, if I get anxious, I should just talk to my editor. Yes, that's what I'll do. (It will be more work for my editor, but if you would mostly just lend an ear, then that will probably be enough for me. Thanks in advance for your help!) And so, together with Futaba and the others, I'd like to become stronger! Despite what I've written here, I think I'm generally strong, so please don't be too worried about me. This is who I am, so thank you in advance for your support.

★ Saki ★

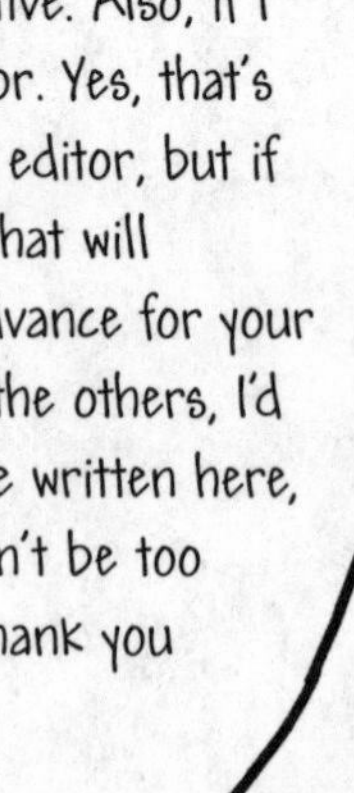

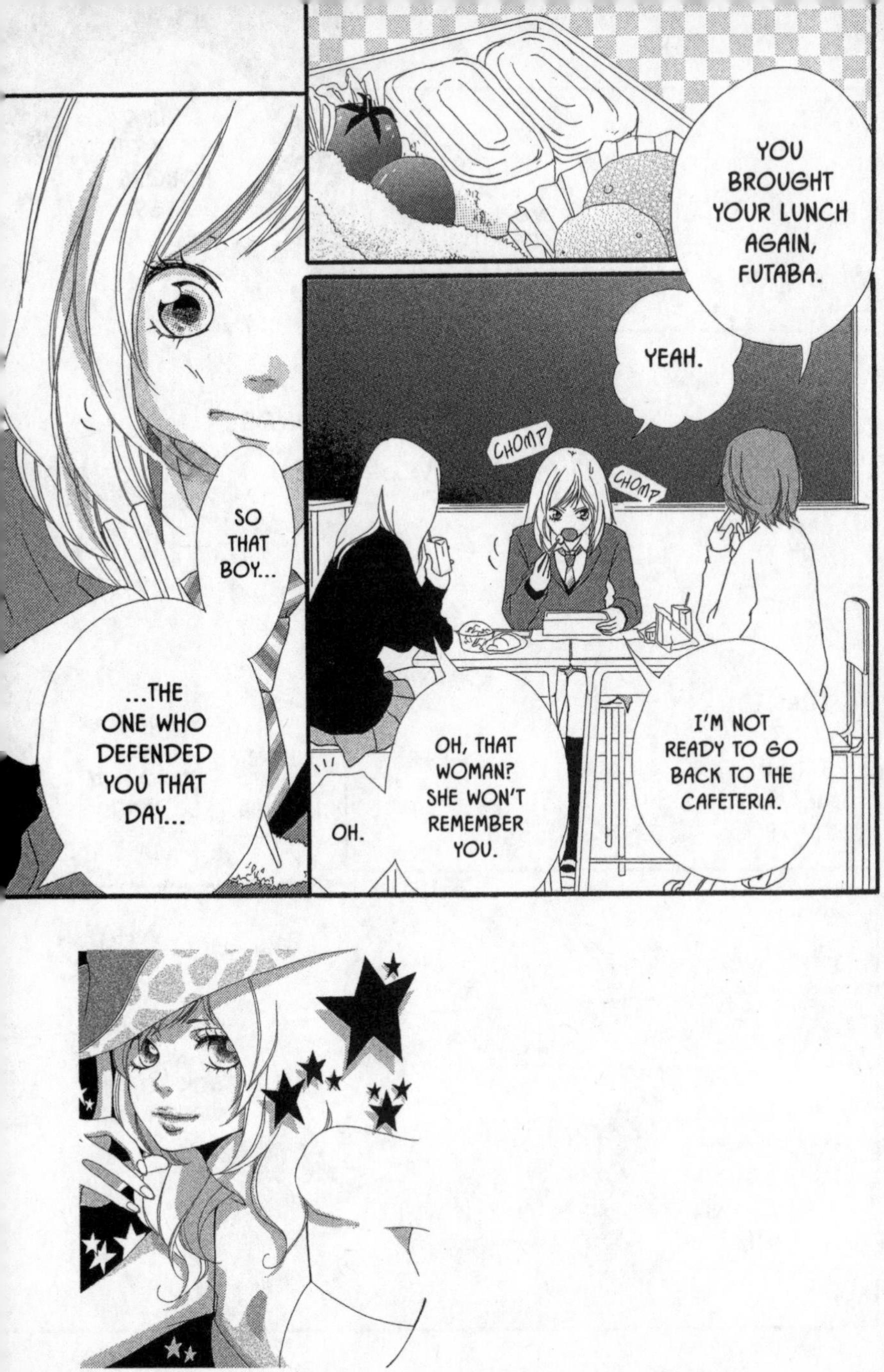
YOU BROUGHT YOUR LUNCH AGAIN, FUTABA.
YEAH.
CHOMP
CHOMP
I'M NOT READY TO GO BACK TO THE CAFETERIA.
OH, THAT WOMAN? SHE WON'T REMEMBER YOU.
OH.
SO THAT BOY...
...THE ONE WHO DEFENDED YOU THAT DAY...

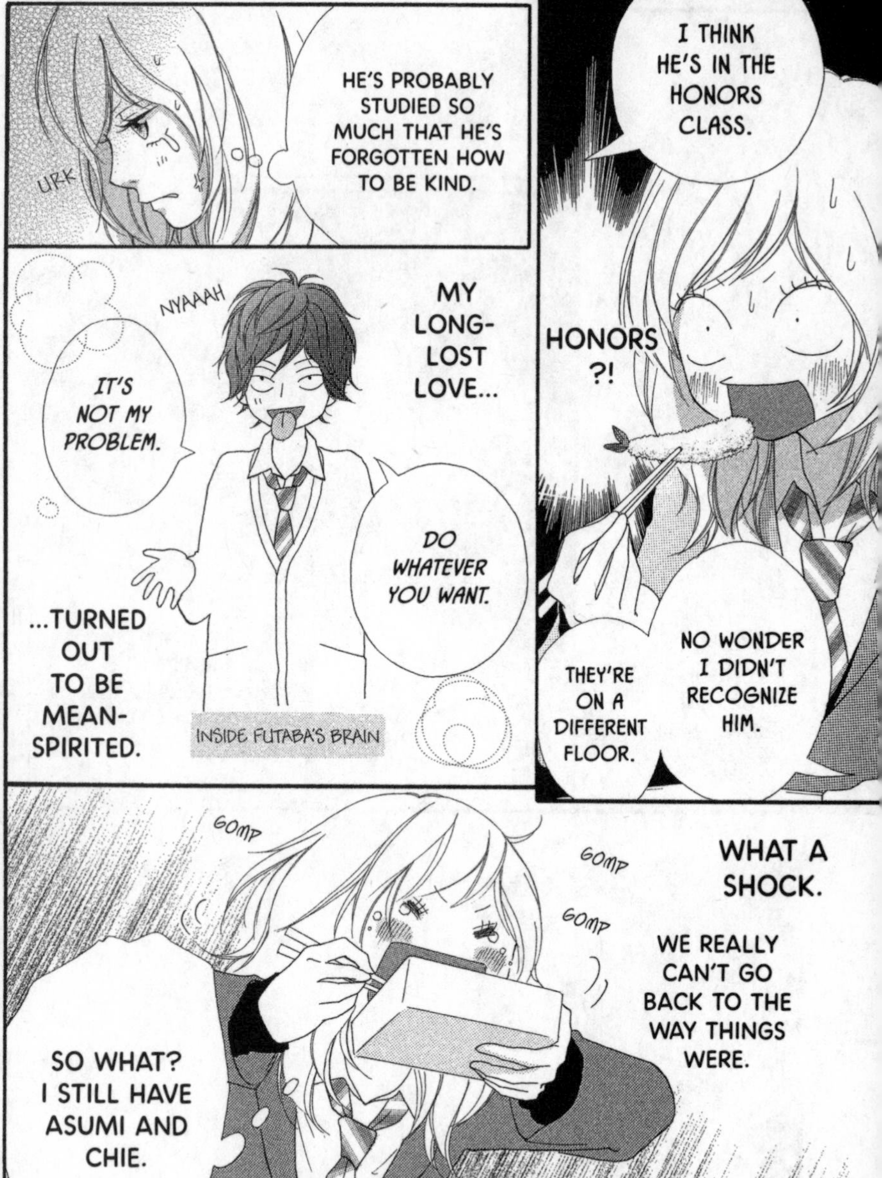
I THINK HE'S IN THE HONORS CLASS.
HONORS ?!
NO WONDER I DIDN'T RECOGNIZE HIM.
THEY'RE ON A DIFFERENT FLOOR.
HE'S PROBABLY STUDIED SO MUCH THAT HE'S FORGOTTEN HOW TO BE KIND.
URK
MY LONG-LOST LOVE...
NYAAAH
DO WHATEVER YOU WANT.
IT'S NOT MY PROBLEM.
...TURNED OUT TO BE MEAN-SPIRITED.
INSIDE FUTABA'S BRAIN
WHAT A SHOCK.
GOMP
GOMP
GOMP
WE REALLY CAN'T GO BACK TO THE WAY THINGS WERE.
SO WHAT? I STILL HAVE ASUMI AND CHIE.

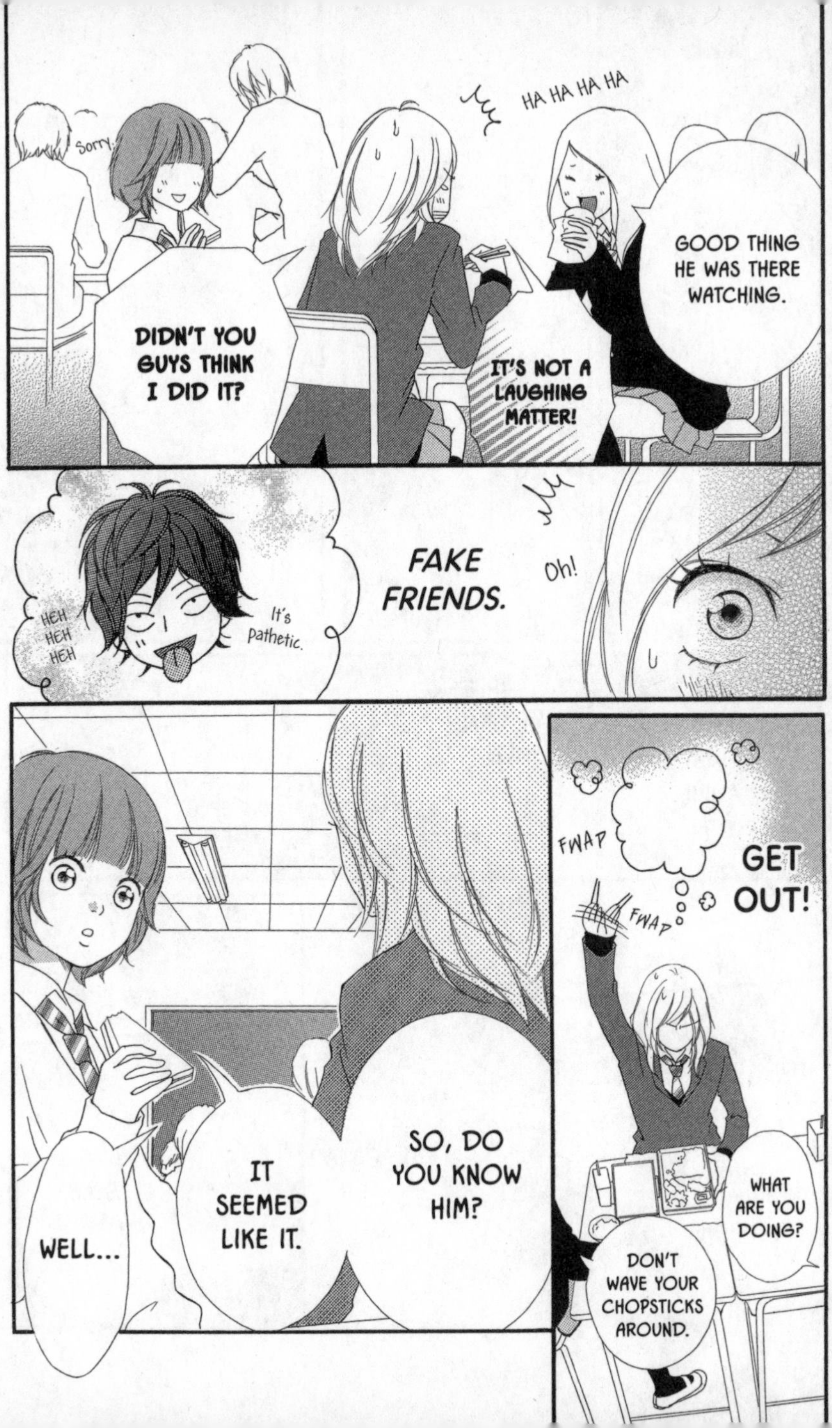
HA HA HA HA
GOOD THING HE WAS THERE WATCHING.
IT'S NOT A LAUGHING MATTER!
DIDN'T YOU GUYS THINK I DID IT?
Sorry.
Oh!
FAKE FRIENDS.
It's pathetic.
HEH HEH HEH
GET OUT!
FWAP
FWAP
WHAT ARE YOU DOING?
DON'T WAVE YOUR CHOPSTICKS AROUND.
SO, DO YOU KNOW HIM?
IT SEEMED LIKE IT.
WELL...

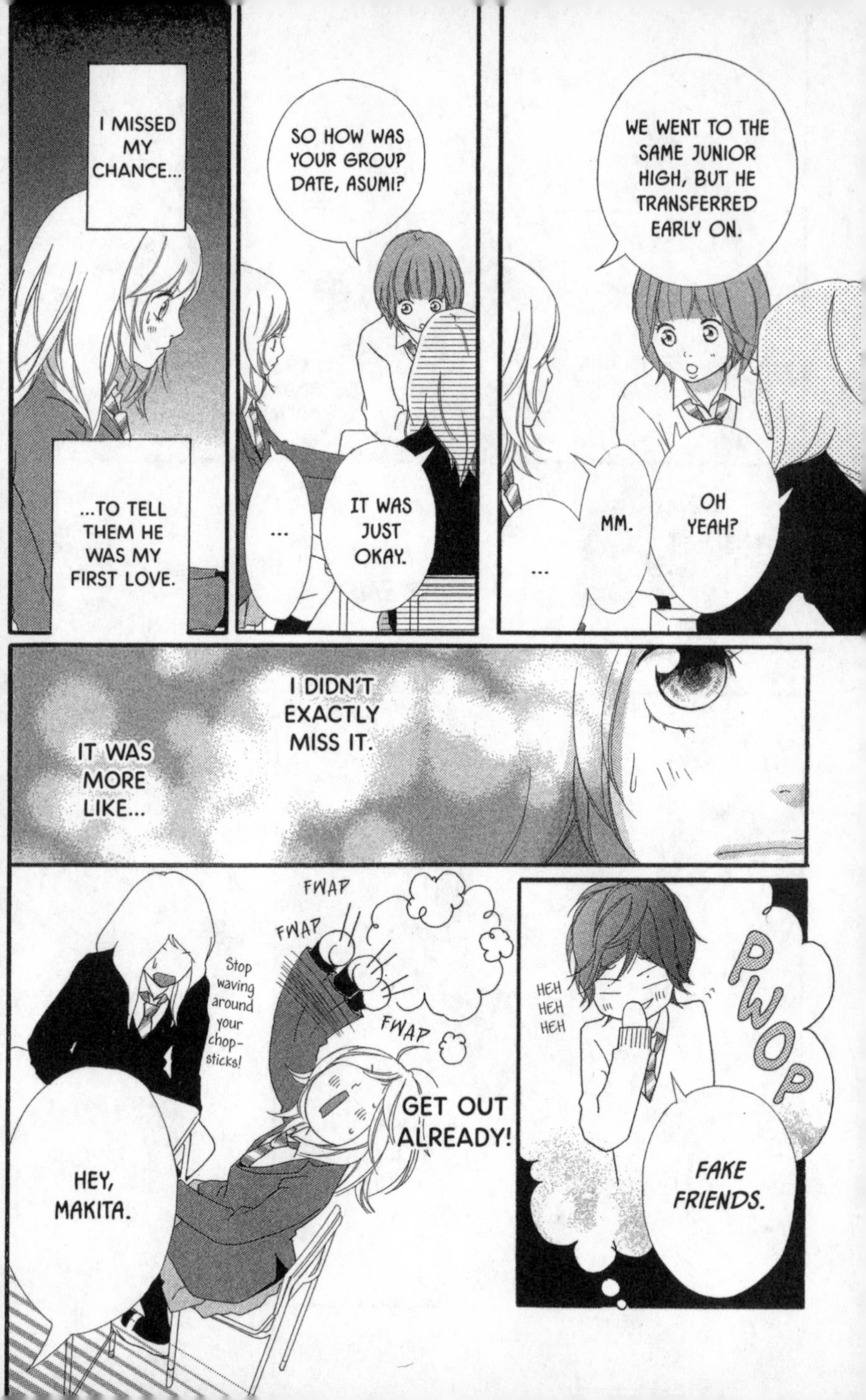
WE WENT TO THE SAME JUNIOR HIGH, BUT HE TRANSFERRED EARLY ON.
OH YEAH?
MM.
...
SO HOW WAS YOUR GROUP DATE, ASUMI?
IT WAS JUST OKAY.
...
I MISSED MY CHANCE...
...TO TELL THEM HE WAS MY FIRST LOVE.
I DIDN'T EXACTLY MISS IT.
IT WAS MORE LIKE...
PWOP
HEH HEH HEH
FAKE FRIENDS.
FWAP
FWAP
FWAP
GET OUT ALREADY!
Stop waving around your chop-sticks!
HEY, MAKITA.

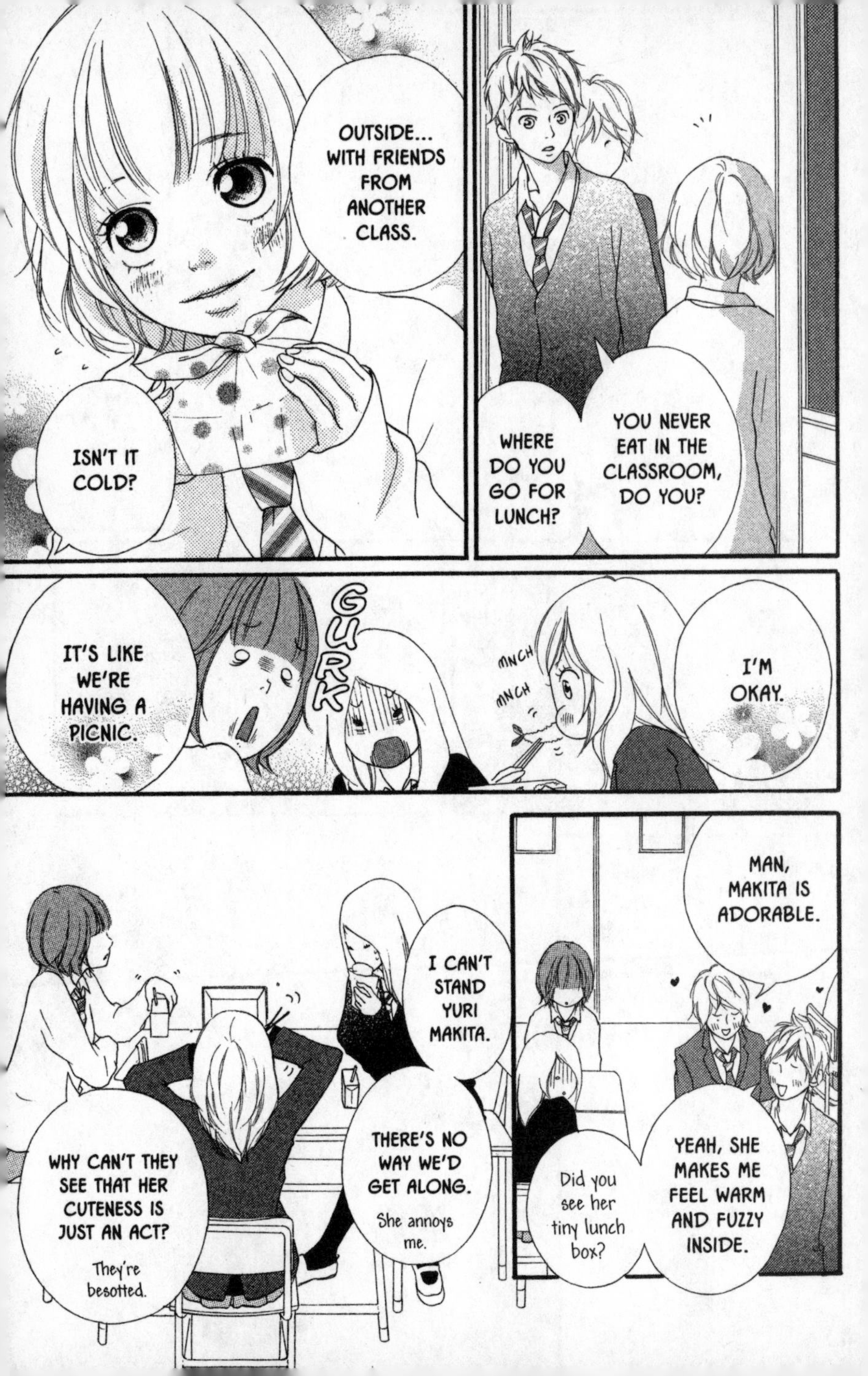
YOU NEVER EAT IN THE CLASSROOM, DO YOU?
WHERE DO YOU GO FOR LUNCH?
OUTSIDE... WITH FRIENDS FROM ANOTHER CLASS.
ISN'T IT COLD?
I'M OKAY.
MNCH
MNCH
GURK
IT'S LIKE WE'RE HAVING A PICNIC.
MAN, MAKITA IS ADORABLE.
YEAH, SHE MAKES ME FEEL WARM AND FUZZY INSIDE.
Did you see her tiny lunch box?
I CAN'T STAND YURI MAKITA.
THERE'S NO WAY WE'D GET ALONG.
She annoys me.
WHY CAN'T THEY SEE THAT HER CUTENESS IS JUST AN ACT?
They're besotted.

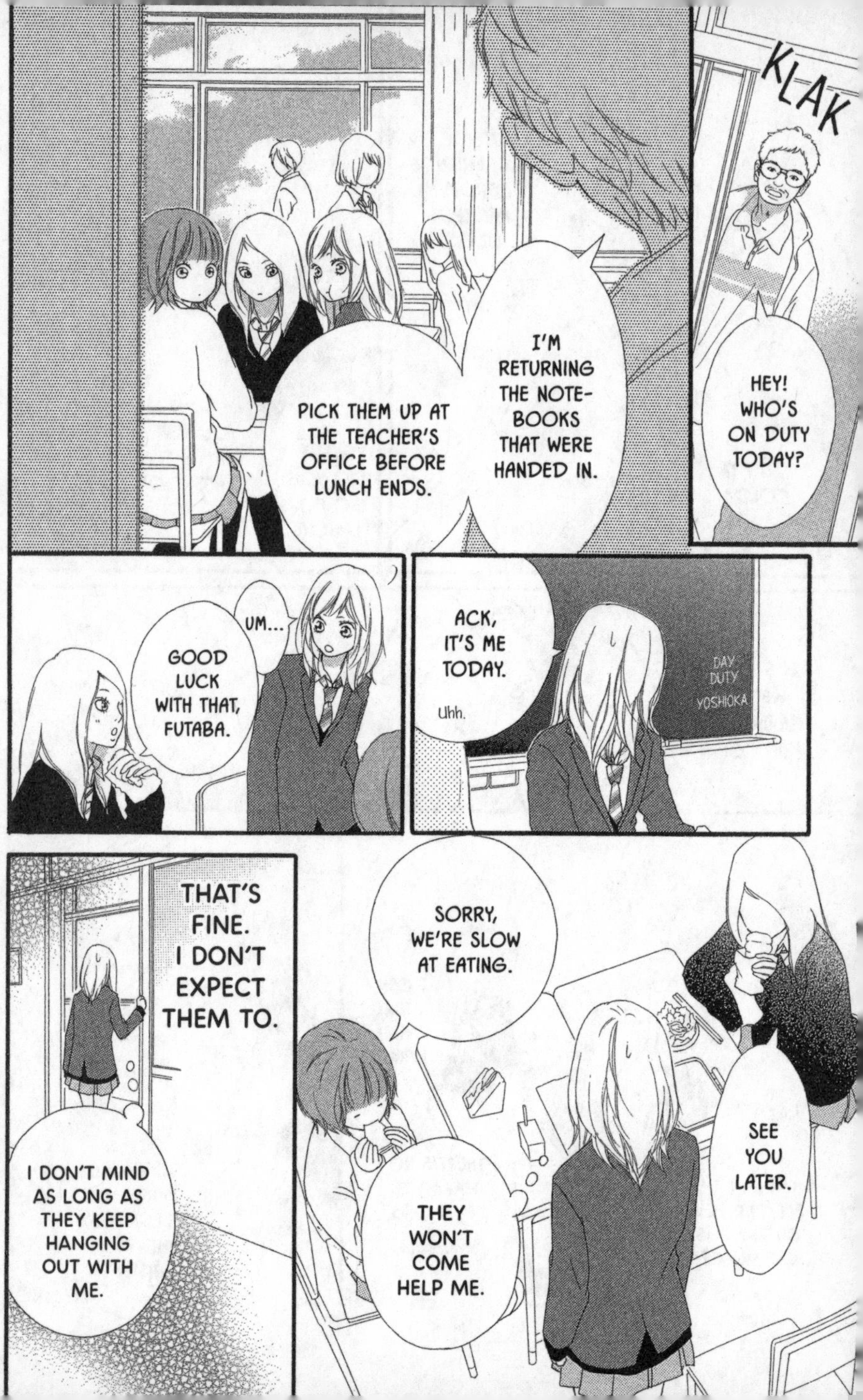
KLAK
HEY! WHO'S ON DUTY TODAY?
I'M RETURNING THE NOTE-BOOKS THAT WERE HANDED IN.
PICK THEM UP AT THE TEACHER'S OFFICE BEFORE LUNCH ENDS.
ACK, IT'S ME TODAY.
Uhh.
DAY DUTY
YOSHIOKA
UM...
GOOD LUCK WITH THAT, FUTABA.
SEE YOU LATER.
SORRY, WE'RE SLOW AT EATING.
THEY WON'T COME HELP ME.
THAT'S FINE. I DON'T EXPECT THEM TO.
I DON'T MIND AS LONG AS THEY KEEP HANGING OUT WITH ME.

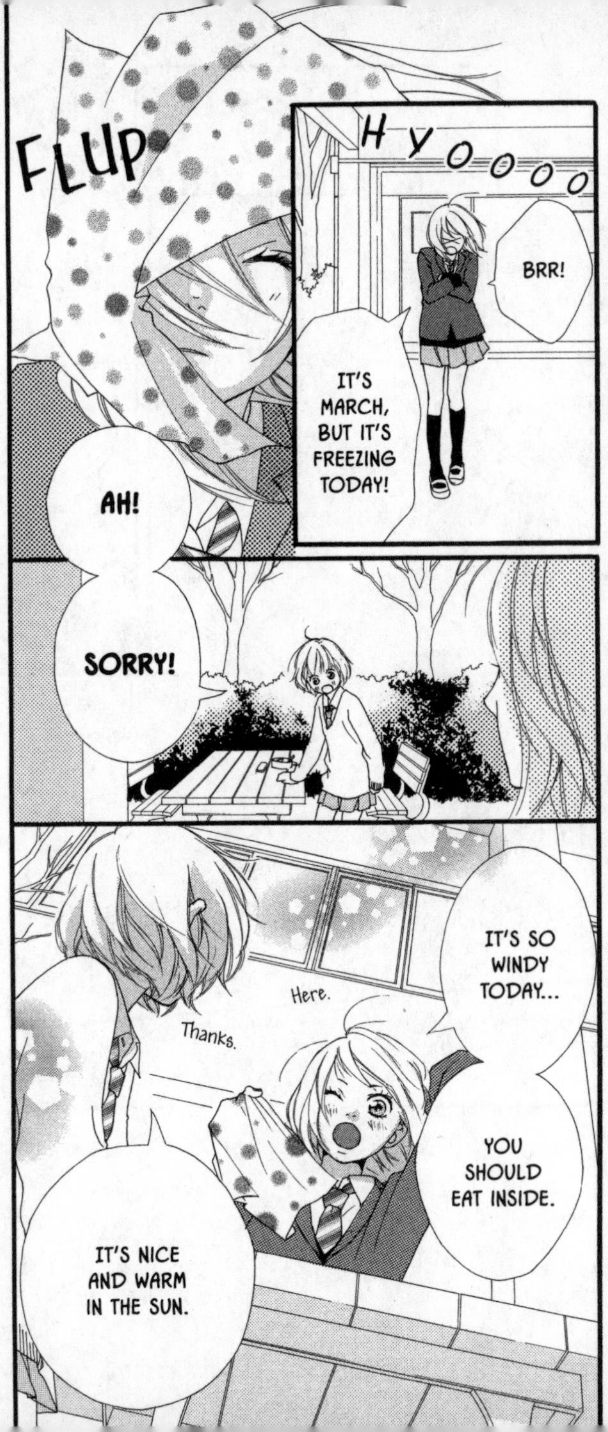
HYOOOO
BRR!
IT'S MARCH, BUT IT'S FREEZING TODAY!
FLUP
AH!
SORRY!
IT'S SO WINDY TODAY...
YOU SHOULD EAT INSIDE.
Here.
Thanks.
IT'S NICE AND WARM IN THE SUN.

Until recently I couldn't draft out stories while listening to music, but suddenly I can. And I do it while wearing headphones. When I'm focused, I don't hear anything at all. But when I get stuck, I hear the music. And when I get really stuck, I start to think the music is too loud and annoying. It's so interesting. It feels like I'm moving between two worlds, and it's rather fascinating. Focus is really interesting.

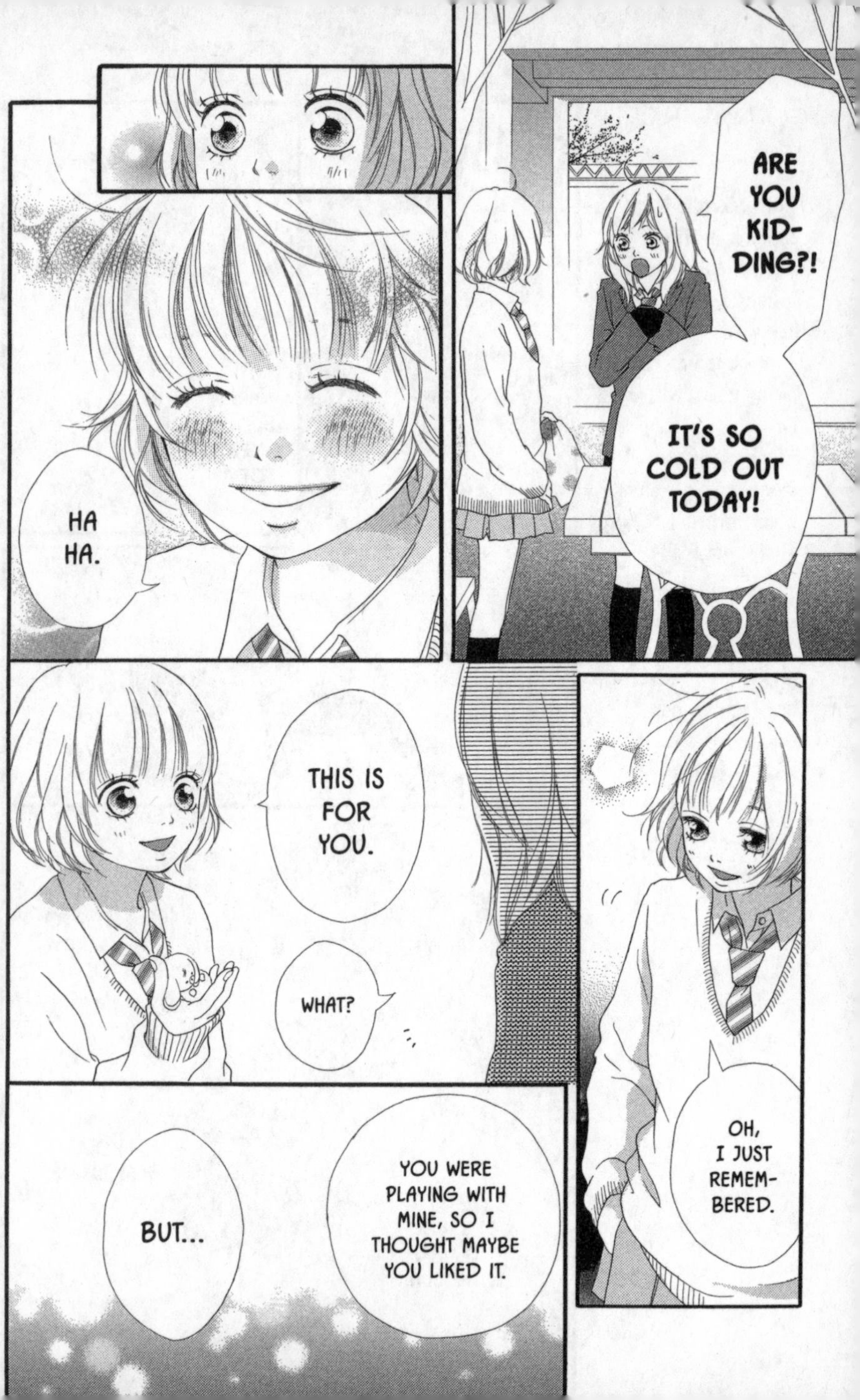
ARE YOU KID-DING?!
IT'S SO COLD OUT TODAY!
HA HA.
OH, I JUST REMEM-BERED.
THIS IS FOR YOU.
WHAT?
YOU WERE PLAYING WITH MINE, SO I THOUGHT MAYBE YOU LIKED IT.
BUT...

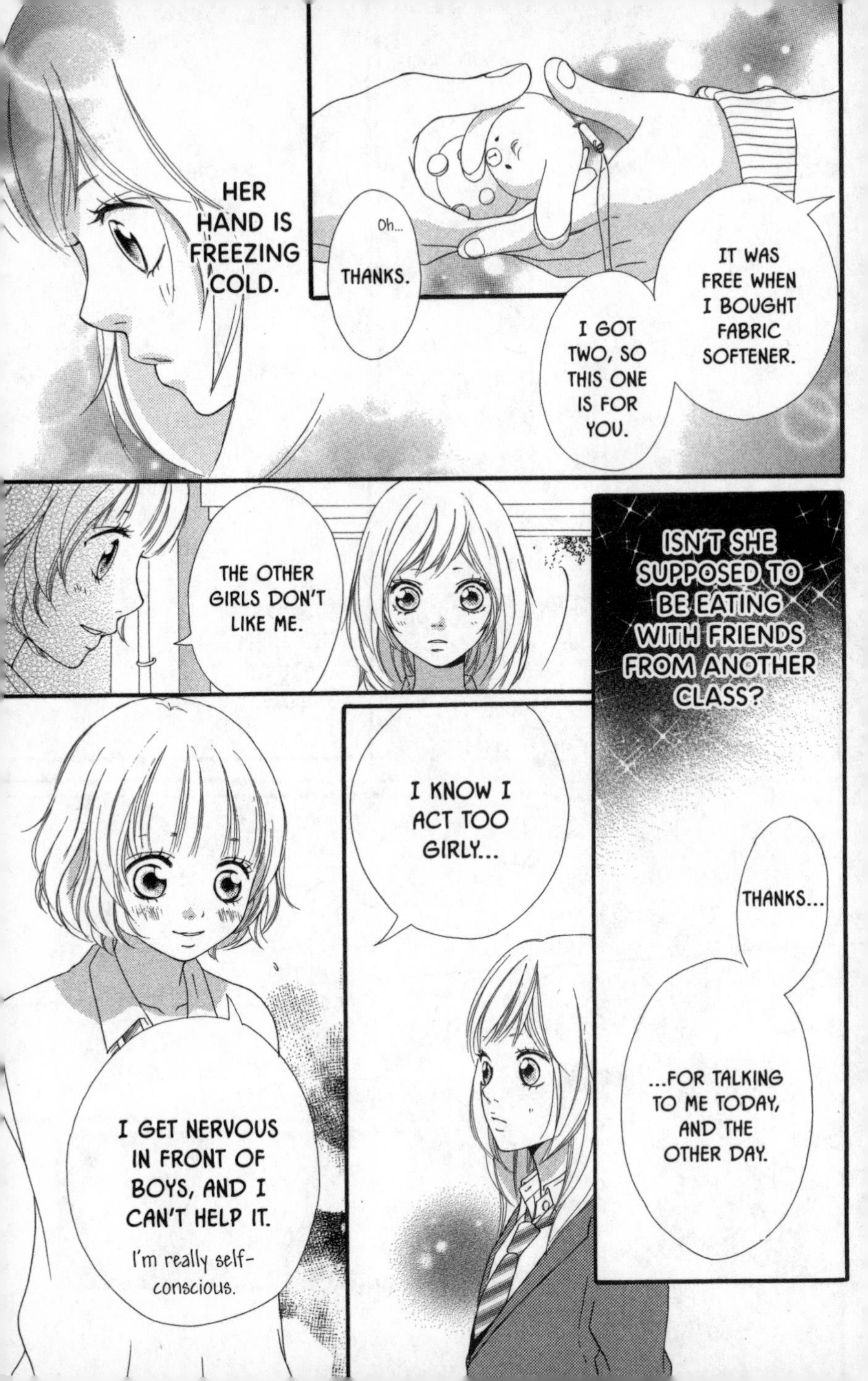
IT WAS FREE WHEN I BOUGHT FABRIC SOFTENER.
I GOT TWO, SO THIS ONE IS FOR YOU.
Oh... THANKS.
HER HAND IS FREEZING COLD.
ISN'T SHE SUPPOSED TO BE EATING WITH FRIENDS FROM ANOTHER CLASS?
THE OTHER GIRLS DON'T LIKE ME.
I KNOW I ACT TOO GIRLY...
I GET NERVOUS IN FRONT OF BOYS, AND I CAN'T HELP IT.
I'm really self-conscious.
THANKS...
...FOR TALKING TO ME TODAY, AND THE OTHER DAY.

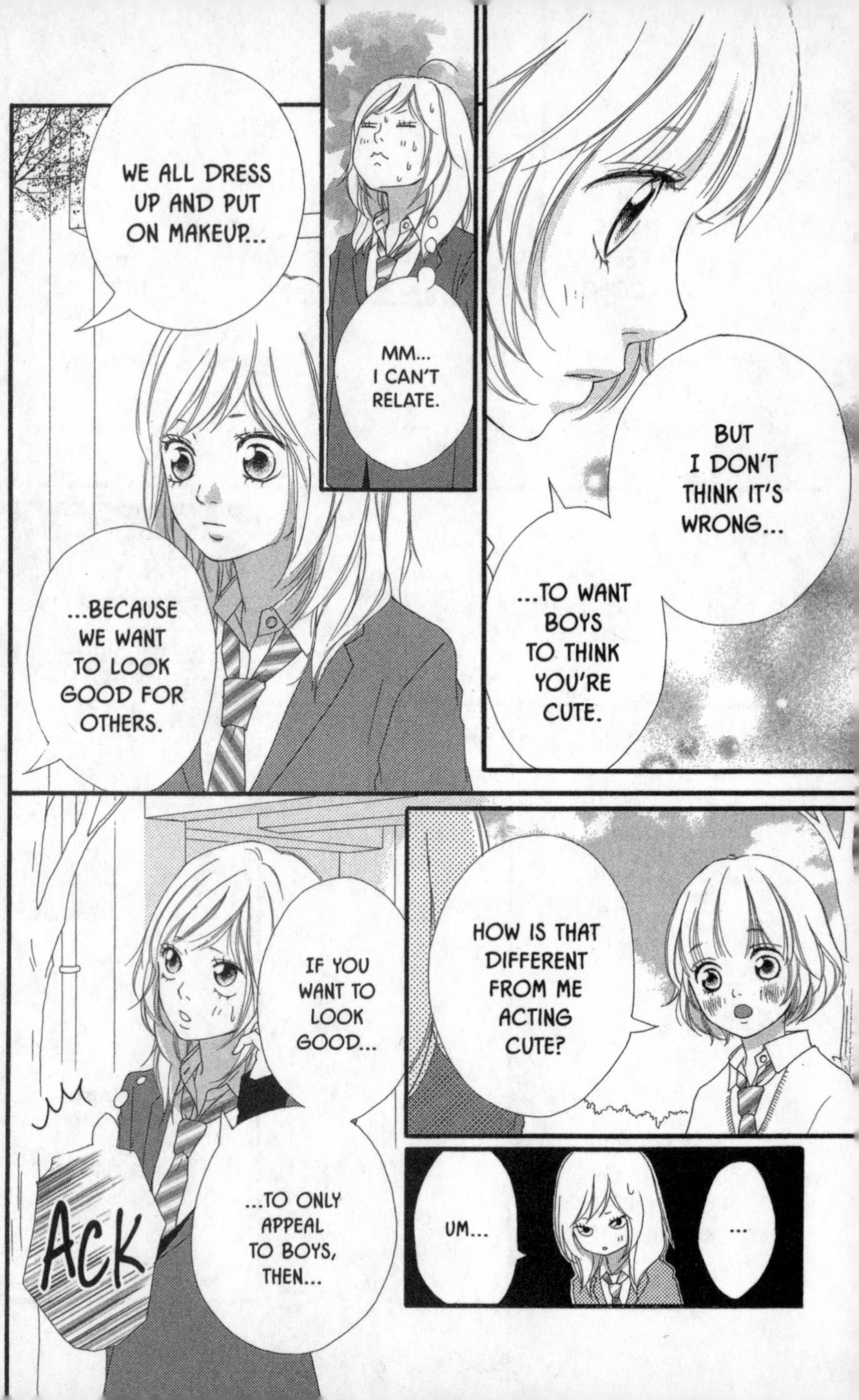
BUT I DON'T THINK IT'S WRONG...
...TO WANT BOYS TO THINK YOU'RE CUTE.
MM... I CAN'T RELATE.
WE ALL DRESS UP AND PUT ON MAKEUP...
...BECAUSE WE WANT TO LOOK GOOD FOR OTHERS.
HOW IS THAT DIFFERENT FROM ME ACTING CUTE?
...
UM...
IF YOU WANT TO LOOK GOOD...
...TO ONLY APPEAL TO BOYS, THEN...
ACK

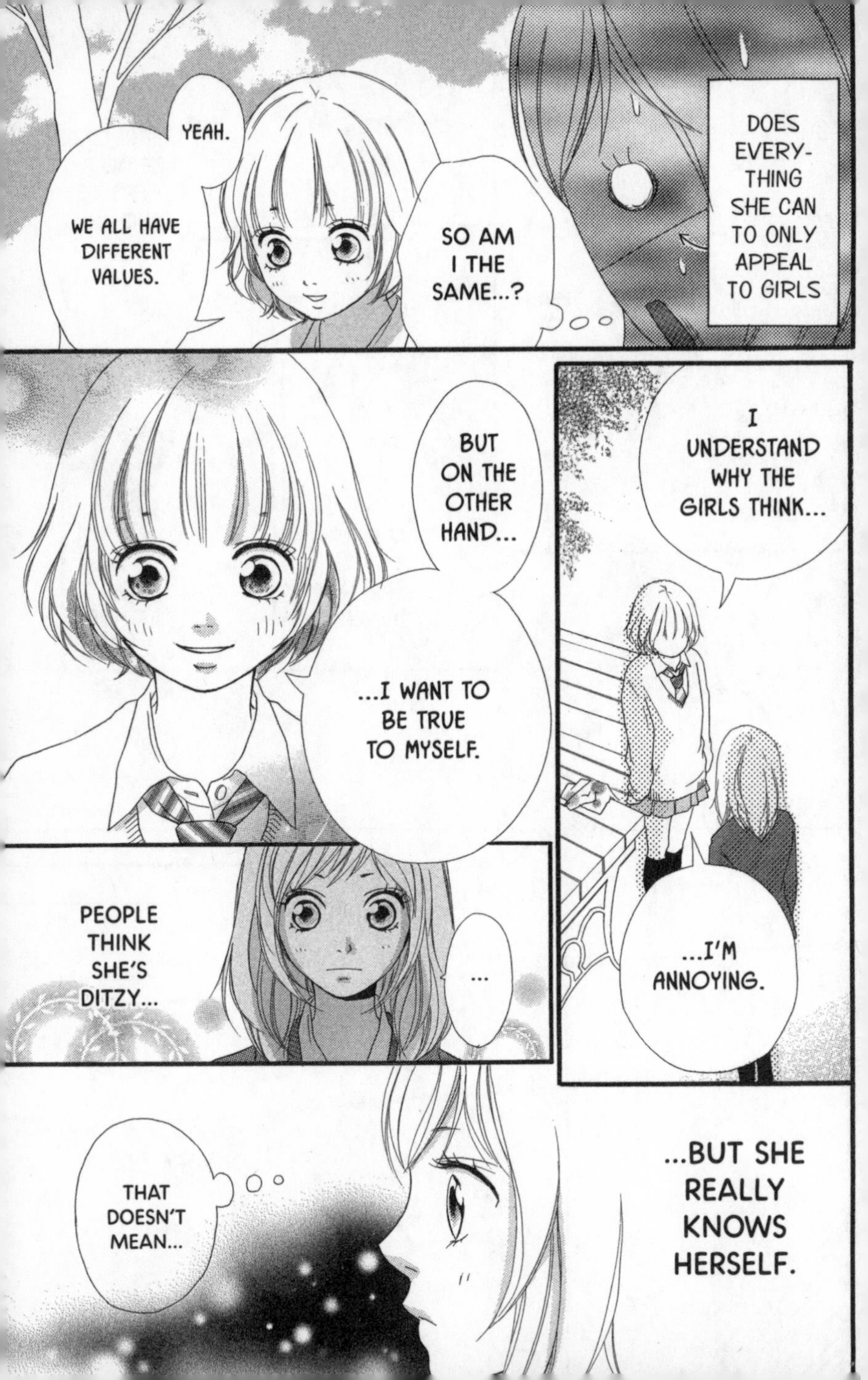

DOES EVERY-THING SHE CAN TO ONLY APPEAL TO GIRLS
SO AM I THE SAME...?
YEAH.
WE ALL HAVE DIFFERENT VALUES.
I UNDERSTAND WHY THE GIRLS THINK...
...I'M ANNOYING.
BUT ON THE OTHER HAND...
...I WANT TO BE TRUE TO MYSELF.
...
PEOPLE THINK SHE'S DITZY...
...BUT SHE REALLY KNOWS HERSELF.
THAT DOESN'T MEAN...

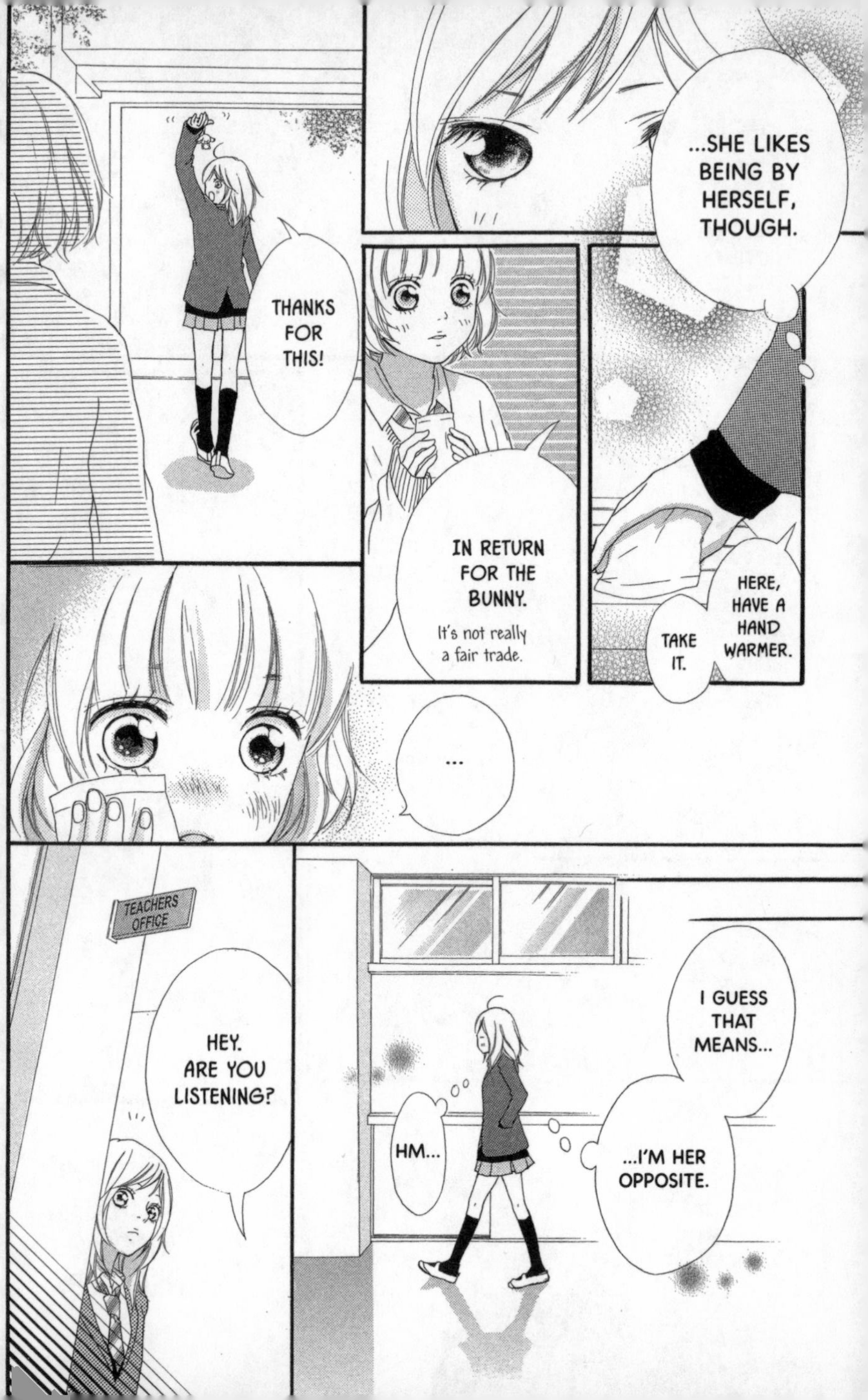
...SHE LIKES BEING BY HERSELF, THOUGH.
HERE, HAVE A HAND WARMER.
TAKE IT.
IN RETURN FOR THE BUNNY.
It's not really a fair trade.
THANKS FOR THIS!
...
I GUESS THAT MEANS...
...I'M HER OPPOSITE.
HM...
TEACHERS OFFICE
HEY. ARE YOU LISTENING?

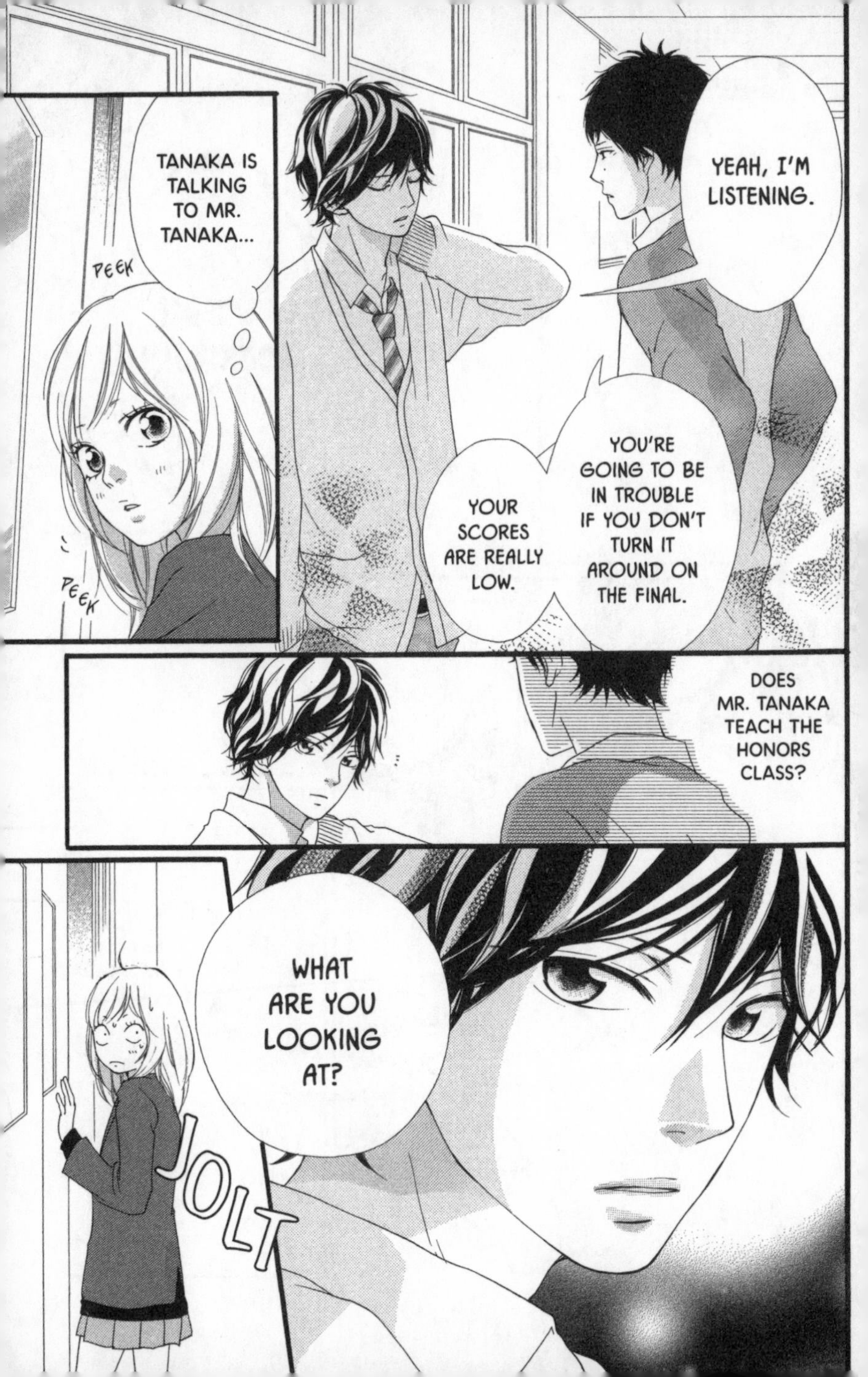
YEAH, I'M LISTENING.
YOU'RE GOING TO BE IN TROUBLE IF YOU DON'T TURN IT AROUND ON THE FINAL.
YOUR SCORES ARE REALLY LOW.
TANAKA IS TALKING TO MR. TANAKA...
PEEK
PEEK
DOES MR. TANAKA TEACH THE HONORS CLASS?
WHAT ARE YOU LOOKING AT?
JOLT

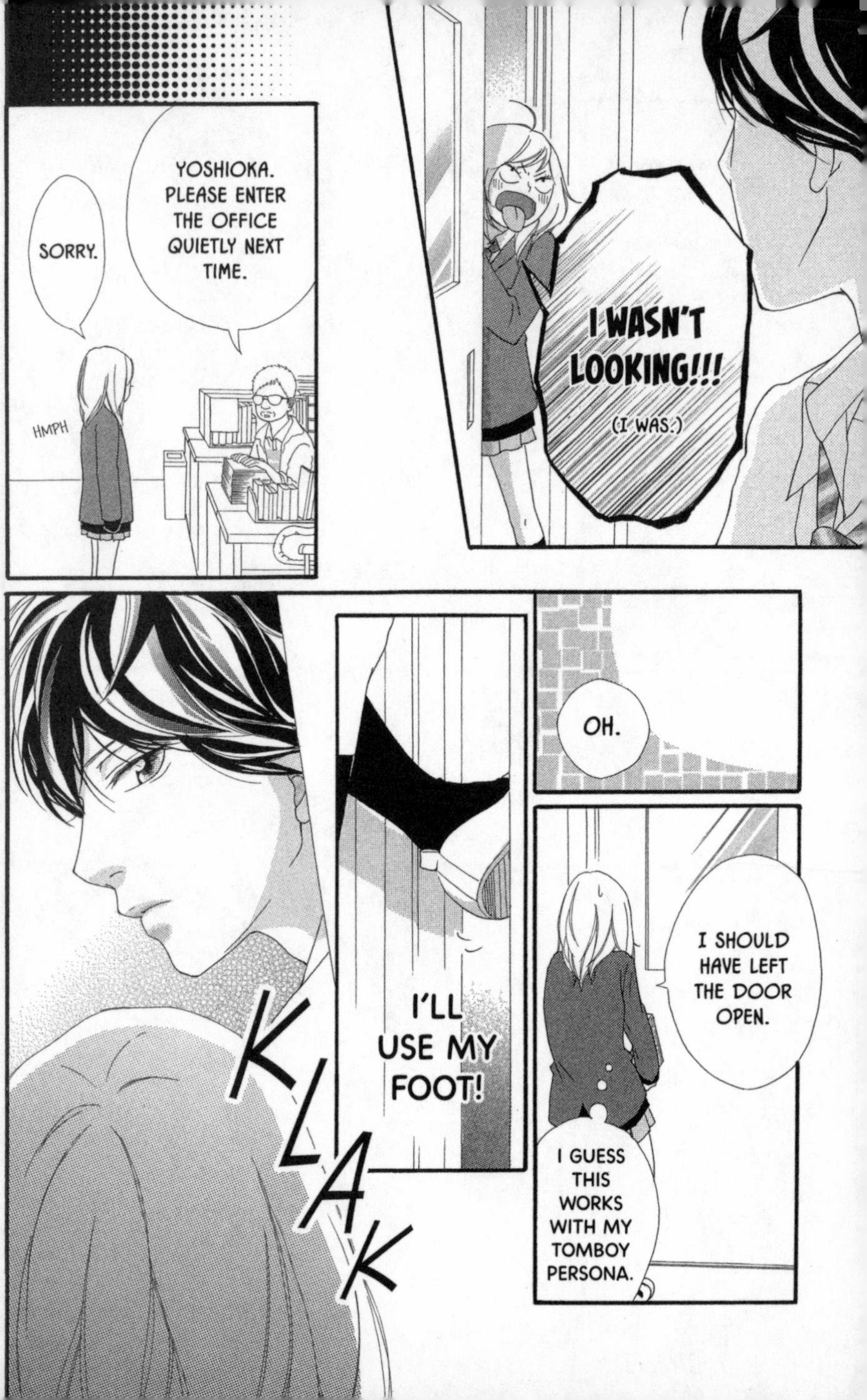
I WASN'T LOOKING!!!
(I WAS.)
YOSHIOKA. PLEASE ENTER THE OFFICE QUIETLY NEXT TIME.
SORRY.
HMPH
OH.
I SHOULD HAVE LEFT THE DOOR OPEN.
I GUESS THIS WORKS WITH MY TOMBOY PERSONA.
I'LL USE MY FOOT!
KLAK

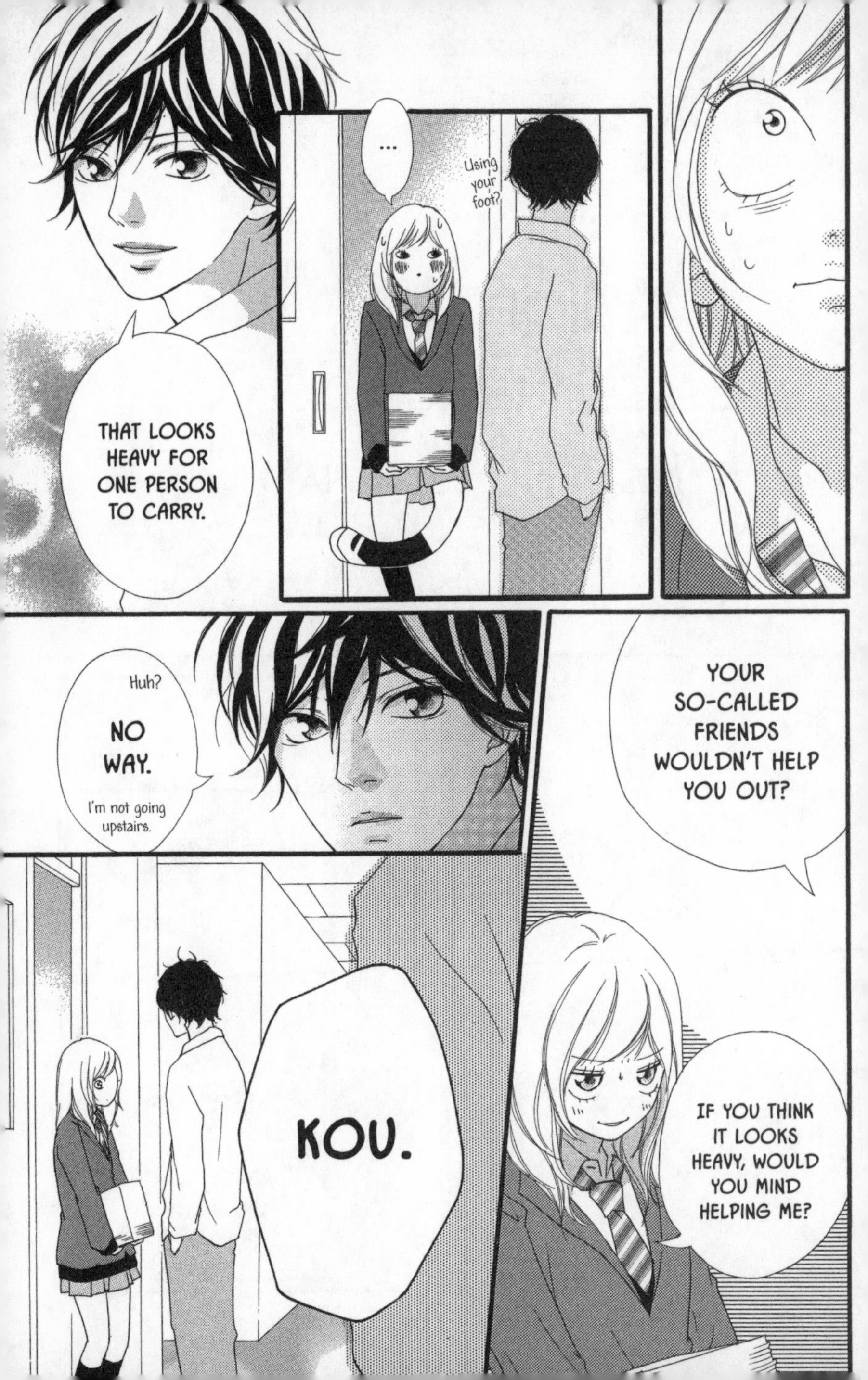
Using your foot?
...
THAT LOOKS HEAVY FOR ONE PERSON TO CARRY.
YOUR SO-CALLED FRIENDS WOULDN'T HELP YOU OUT?
IF YOU THINK IT LOOKS HEAVY, WOULD YOU MIND HELPING ME?
Huh?
NO WAY.
I'm not going upstairs.
KOU.

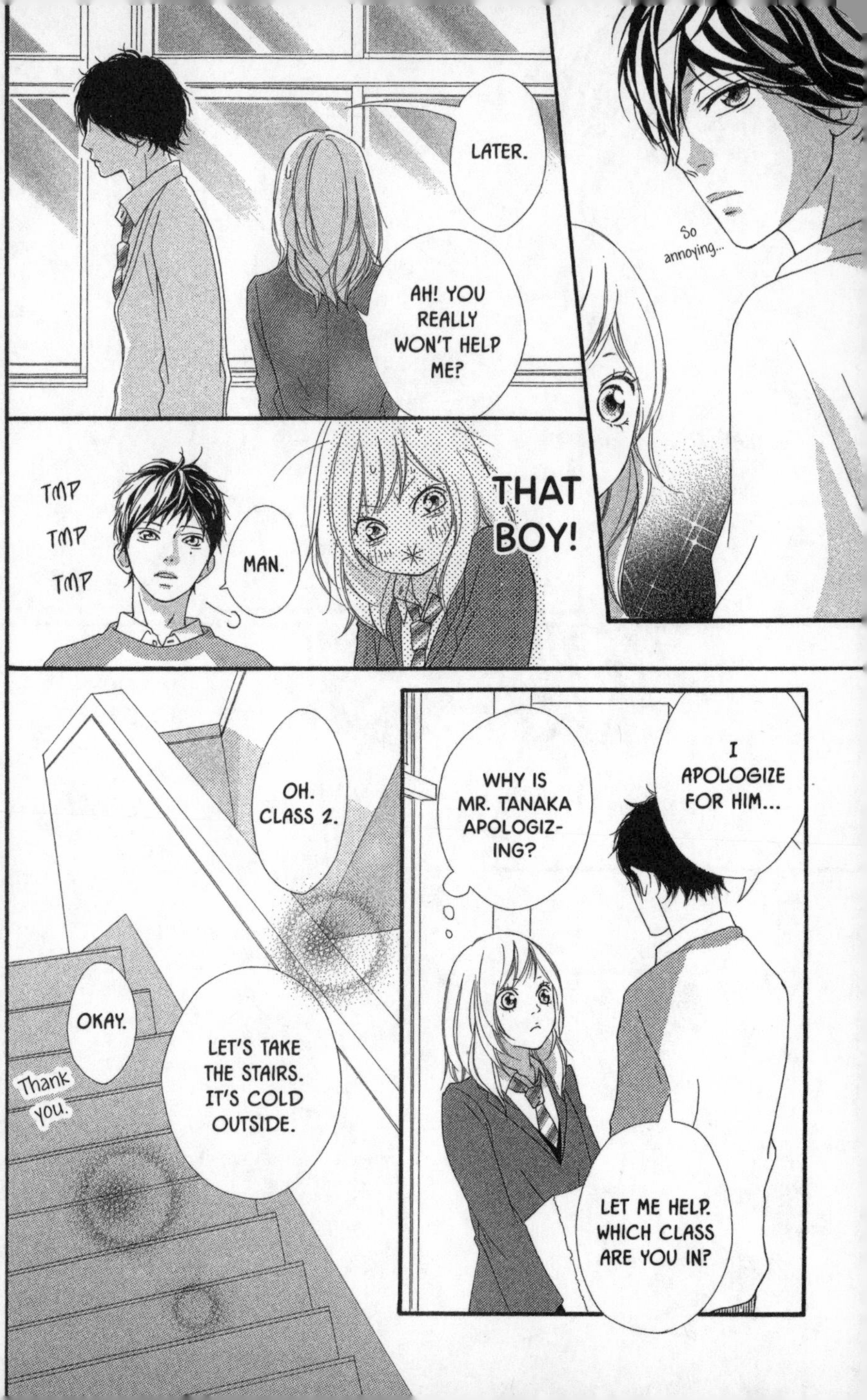

So annoying...
LATER.
AH! YOU REALLY WON'T HELP ME?
THAT BOY!
MAN.
TMP TMP TMP
I APOLOGIZE FOR HIM...
WHY IS MR. TANAKA APOLOGIZ-ING?
LET ME HELP. WHICH CLASS ARE YOU IN?
OH. CLASS 2.
LET'S TAKE THE STAIRS. IT'S COLD OUTSIDE.
OKAY.
Thank you.

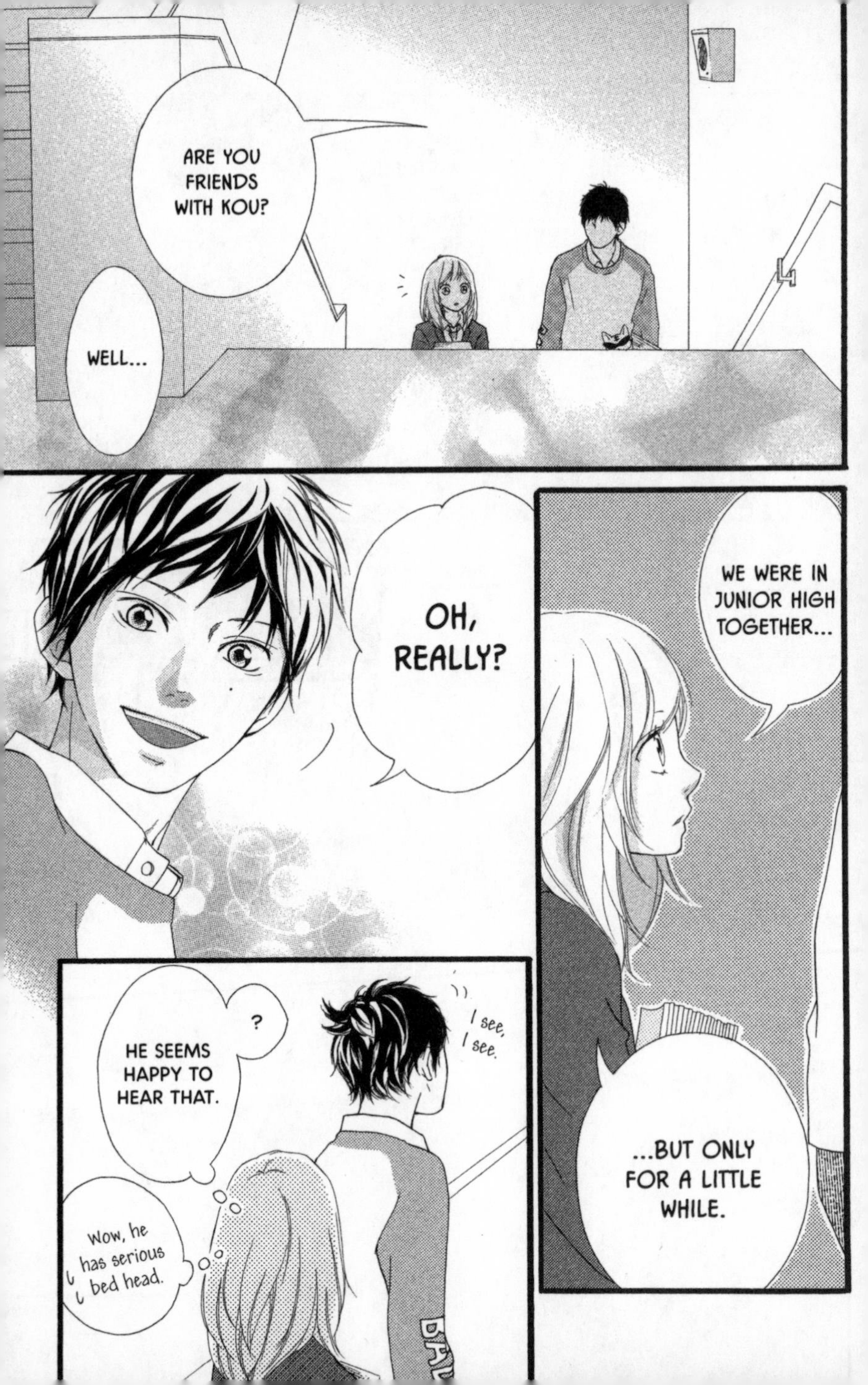
ARE YOU FRIENDS WITH KOU?
WELL...
WE WERE IN JUNIOR HIGH TOGETHER...
...BUT ONLY FOR A LITTLE WHILE.
OH, REALLY?
I see, I see.
?
HE SEEMS HAPPY TO HEAR THAT.
Wow, he has serious bed head.

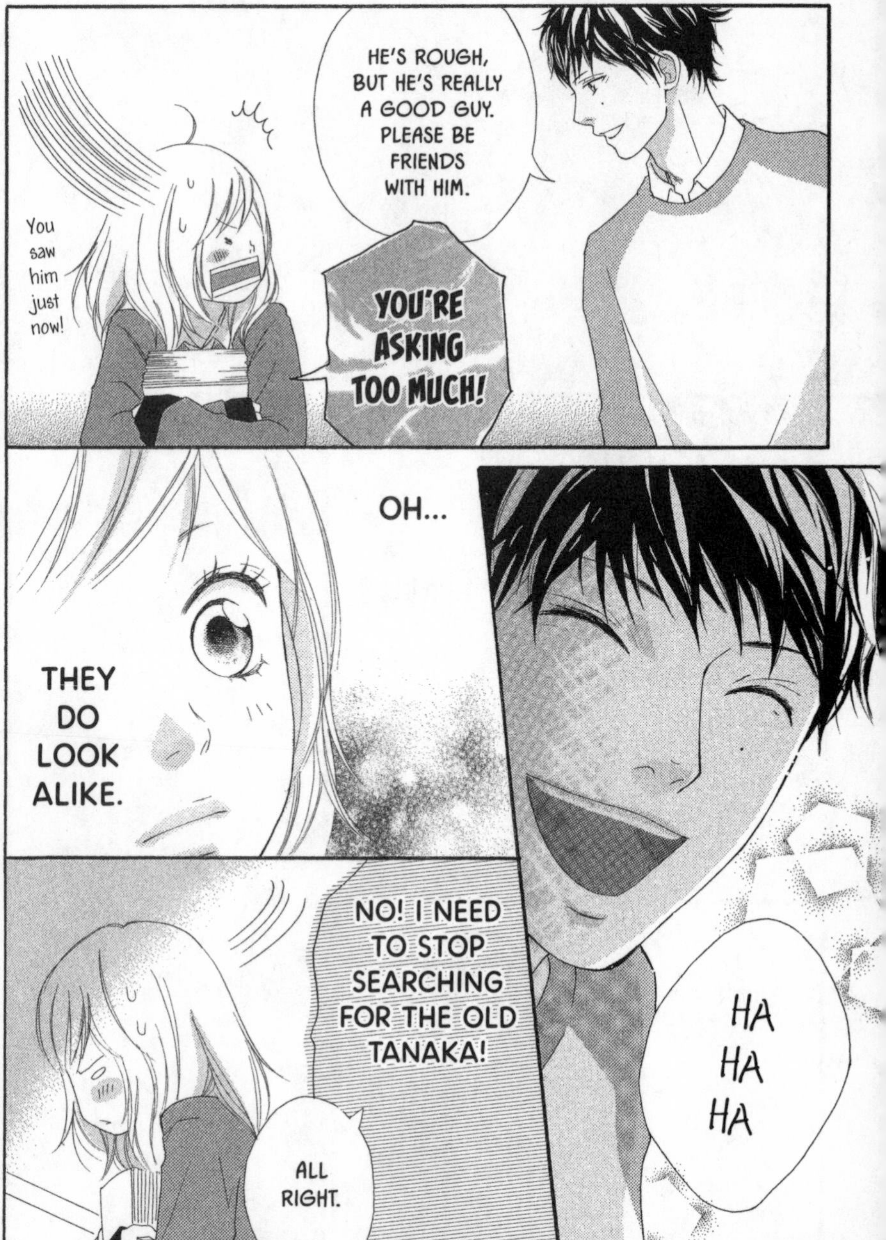
HE'S ROUGH, BUT HE'S REALLY A GOOD GUY. PLEASE BE FRIENDS WITH HIM.
YOU'RE ASKING TOO MUCH!
You saw him just now!
HA HA HA
OH...
THEY DO LOOK ALIKE.
NO! I NEED TO STOP SEARCHING FOR THE OLD TANAKA!
ALL RIGHT.

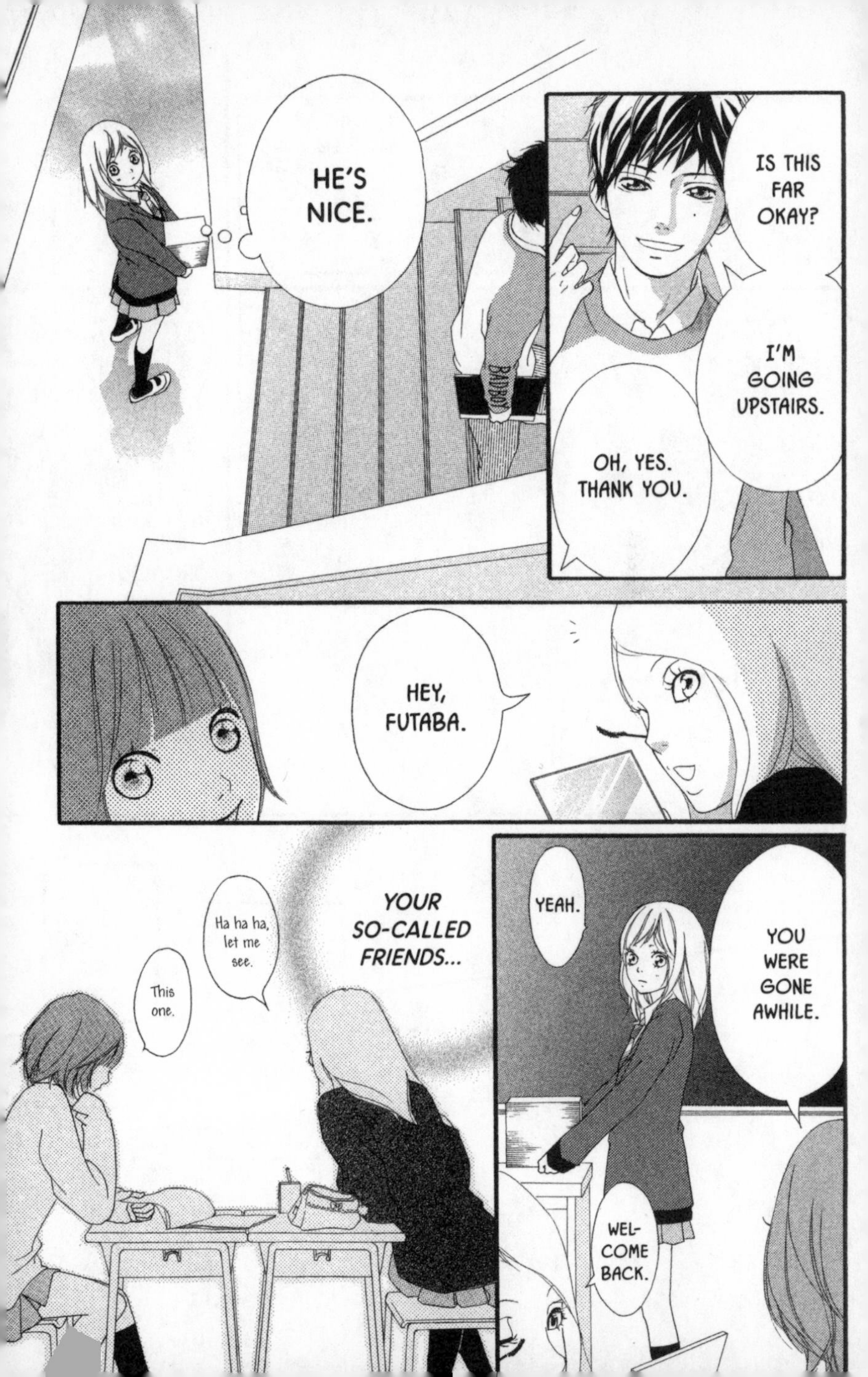
IS THIS FAR OKAY?
I'M GOING UPSTAIRS.
OH, YES. THANK YOU.
HE'S NICE.
HEY, FUTABA.
YOU WERE GONE AWHILE.
YEAH.
WEL-COME BACK.
YOUR SO-CALLED FRIENDS...
Ha ha ha, let me see.
This one.

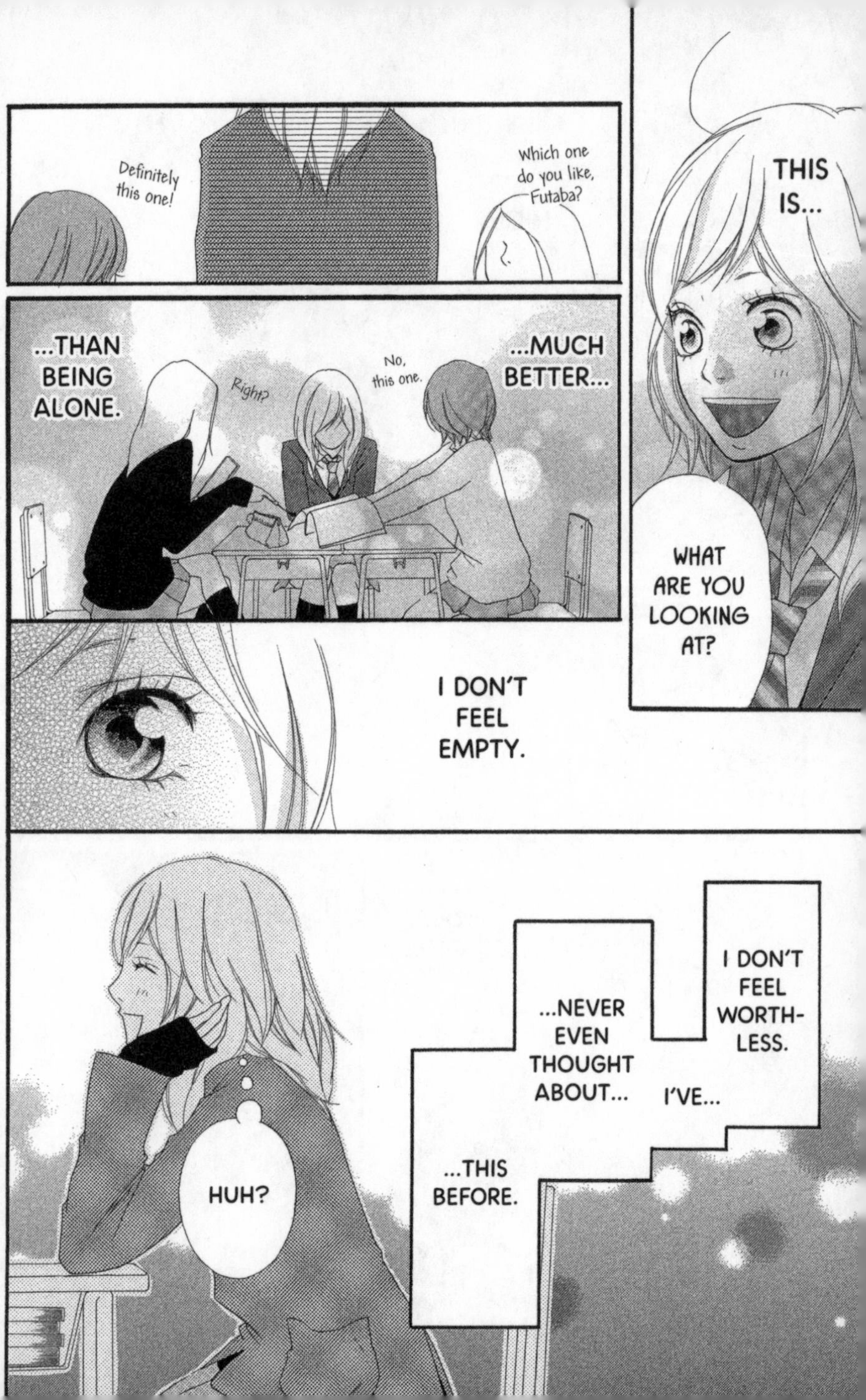
THIS IS...
WHAT ARE YOU LOOKING AT?
Which one do you like, Futaba?
Definitely this one!
...MUCH BETTER...
No, this one.
Right?
...THAN BEING ALONE.
I DON'T FEEL EMPTY.
I DON'T FEEL WORTH-LESS.
I'VE...
...NEVER EVEN THOUGHT ABOUT...
...THIS BEFORE.
HUH?

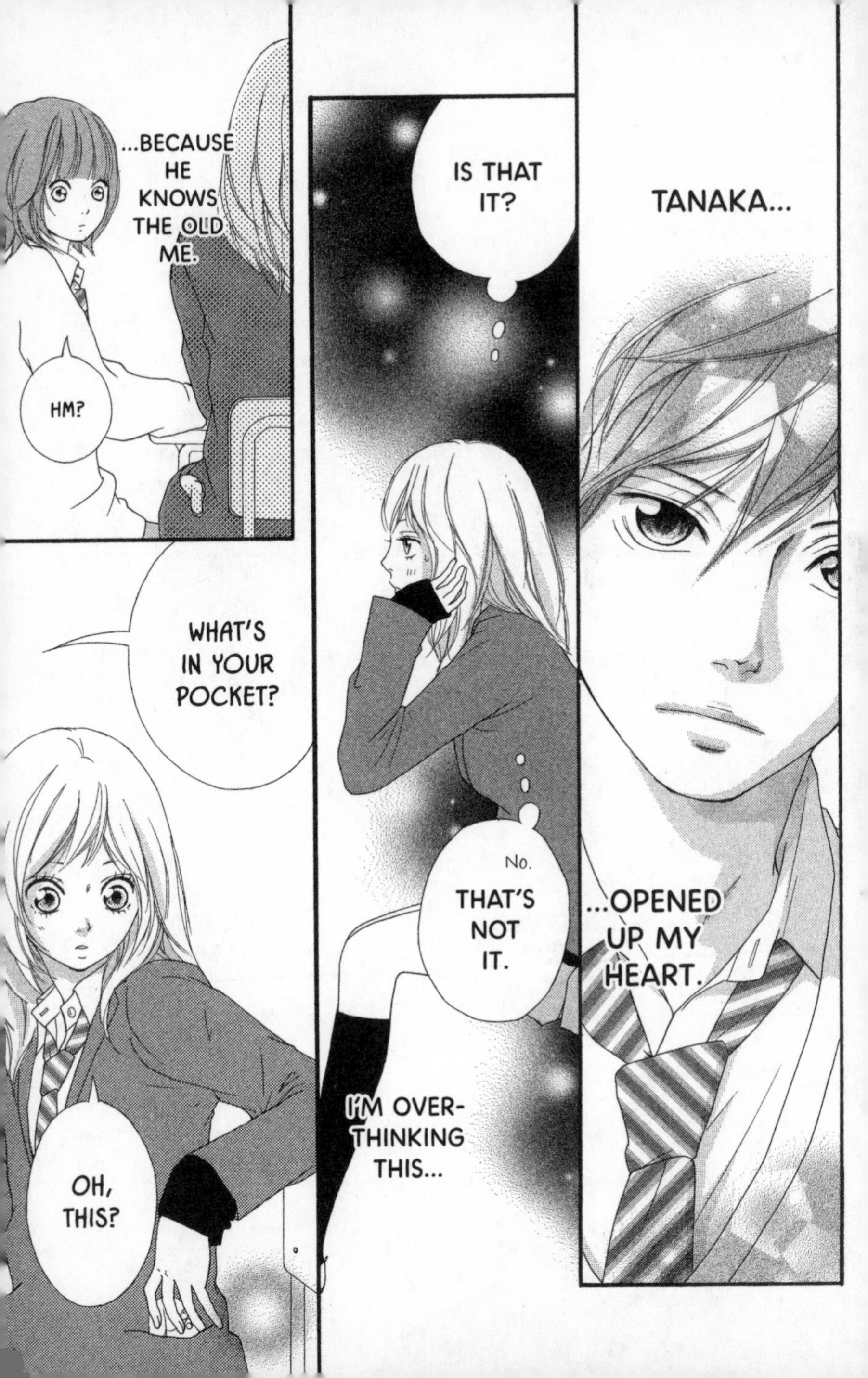
TANAKA...
...OPENED UP MY HEART.
IS THAT IT?
No.
THAT'S NOT IT.
I'M OVER-THINKING THIS...
...BECAUSE HE KNOWS THE OLD ME.
HM?
WHAT'S IN YOUR POCKET?
OH, THIS?

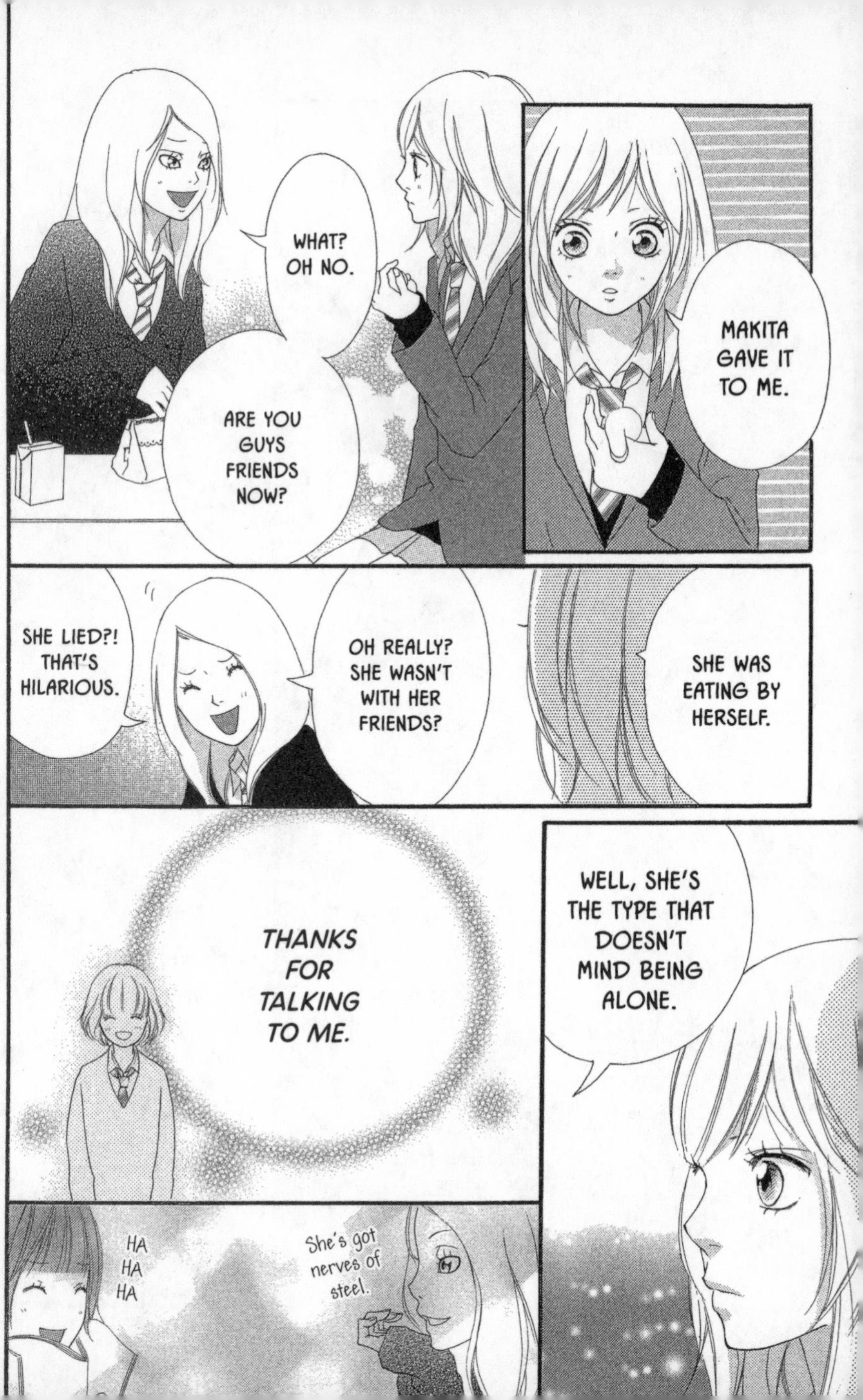
ARE YOU GUYS FRIENDS NOW?
WHAT? OH NO.
MAKITA GAVE IT TO ME.
SHE WAS EATING BY HERSELF.
OH REALLY? SHE WASN'T WITH HER FRIENDS?
SHE LIED?! THAT'S HILARIOUS.
WELL, SHE'S THE TYPE THAT DOESN'T MIND BEING ALONE.
THANKS FOR TALKING TO ME.
She's got nerves of steel.
HA HA HA

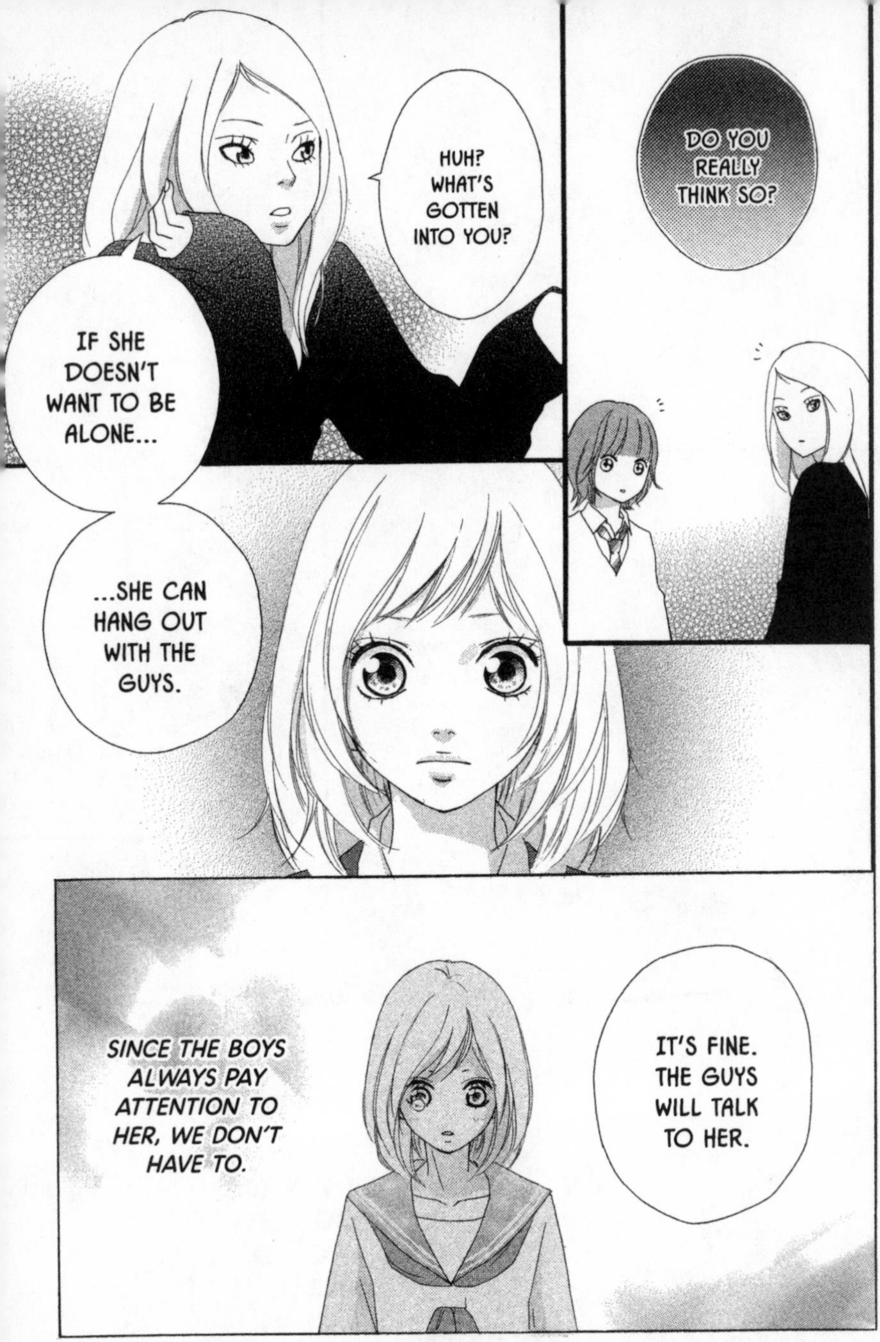
DO YOU REALLY THINK SO?
HUH? WHAT'S GOTTEN INTO YOU?
IF SHE DOESN'T WANT TO BE ALONE...
...SHE CAN HANG OUT WITH THE GUYS.
IT'S FINE. THE GUYS WILL TALK TO HER.
SINCE THE BOYS ALWAYS PAY ATTENTION TO HER, WE DON'T HAVE TO.

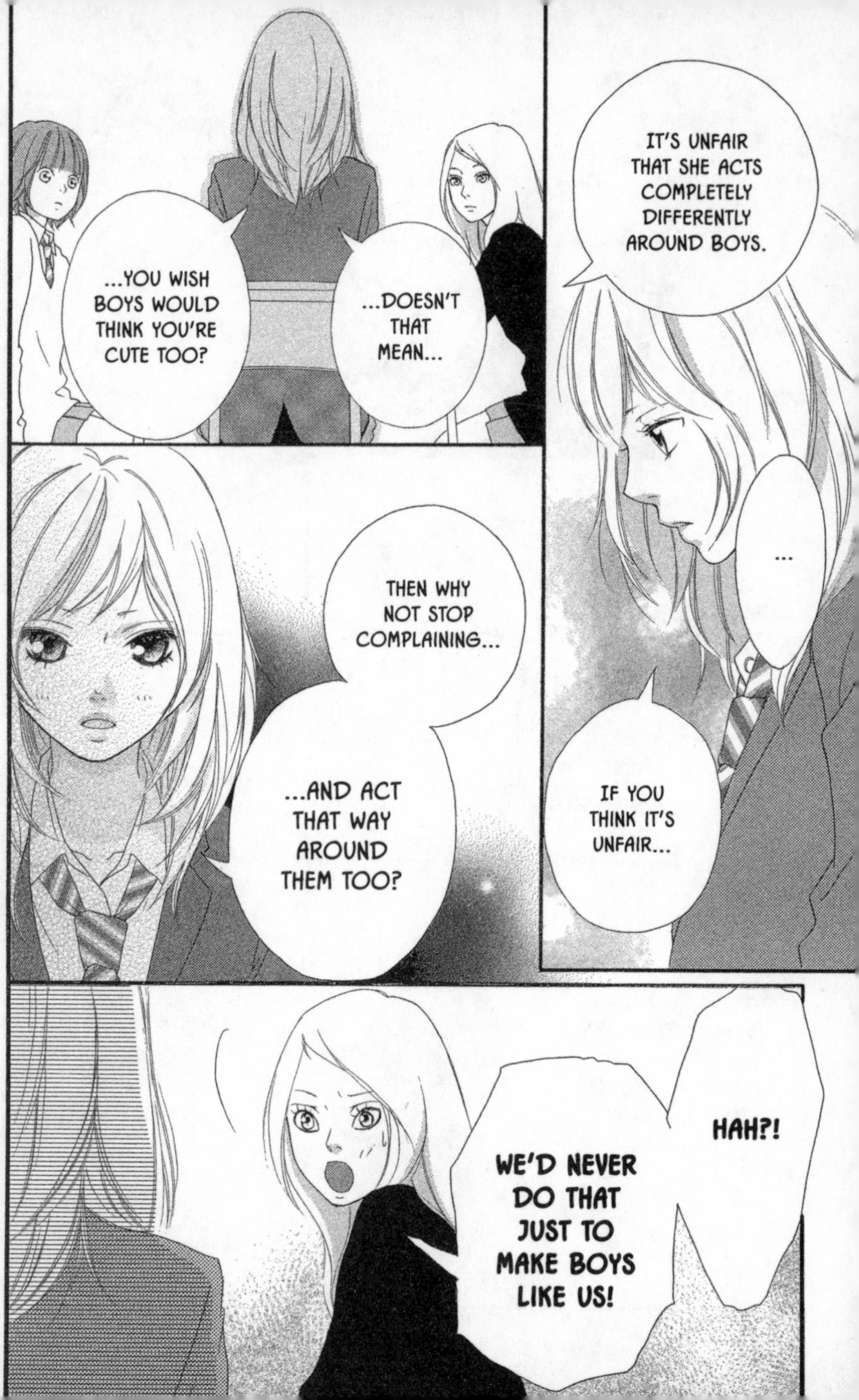
IT'S UNFAIR THAT SHE ACTS COMPLETELY DIFFERENTLY AROUND BOYS.
...
IF YOU THINK IT'S UNFAIR...
...DOESN'T THAT MEAN...
...YOU WISH BOYS WOULD THINK YOU'RE CUTE TOO?
THEN WHY NOT STOP COMPLAINING...
...AND ACT THAT WAY AROUND THEM TOO?
HAH?!
WE'D NEVER DO THAT JUST TO MAKE BOYS LIKE US!

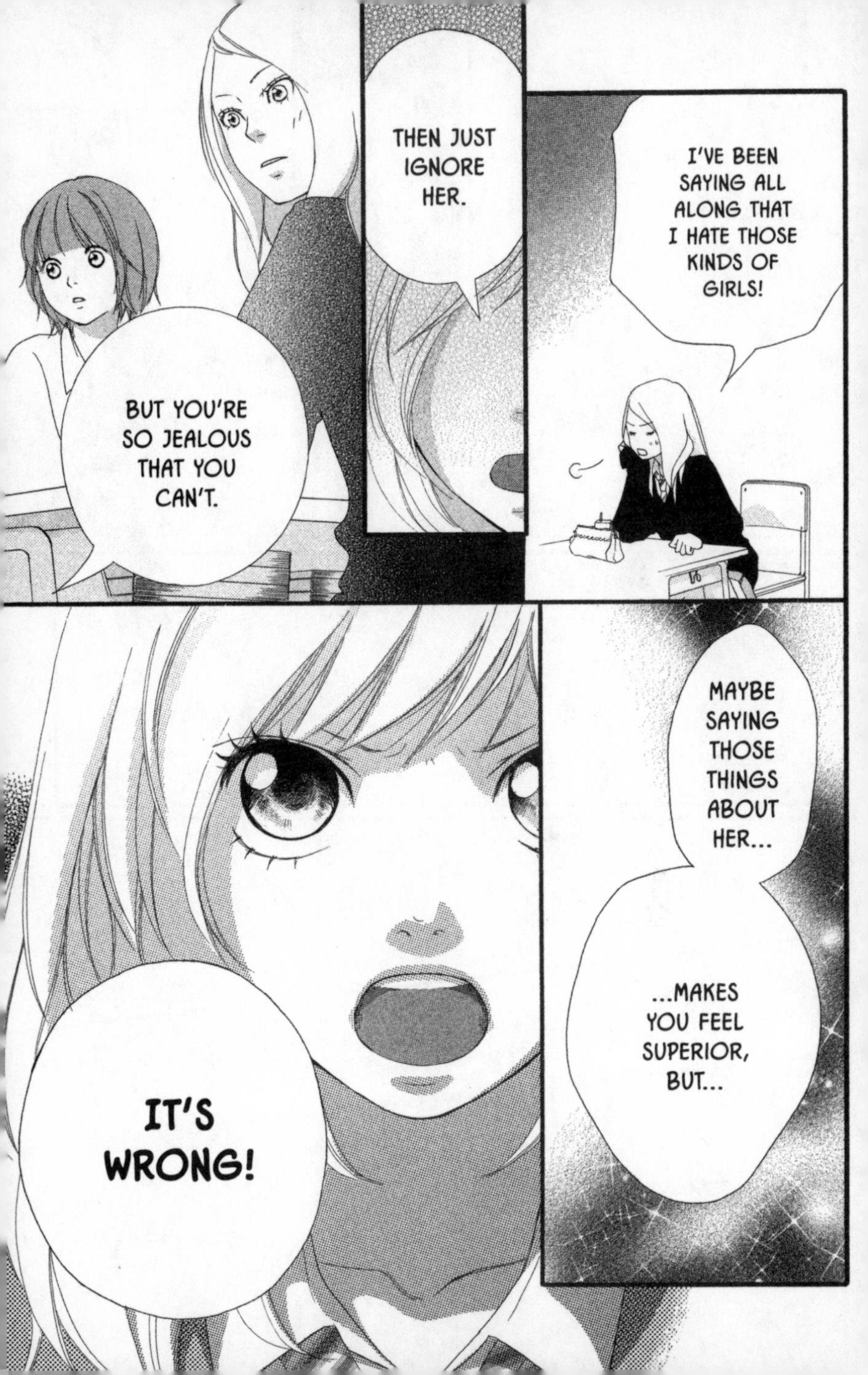
I'VE BEEN SAYING ALL ALONG THAT I HATE THOSE KINDS OF GIRLS!
THEN JUST IGNORE HER.
BUT YOU'RE SO JEALOUS THAT YOU CAN'T.
MAYBE SAYING THOSE THINGS ABOUT HER...
...MAKES YOU FEEL SUPERIOR, BUT...
IT'S WRONG!

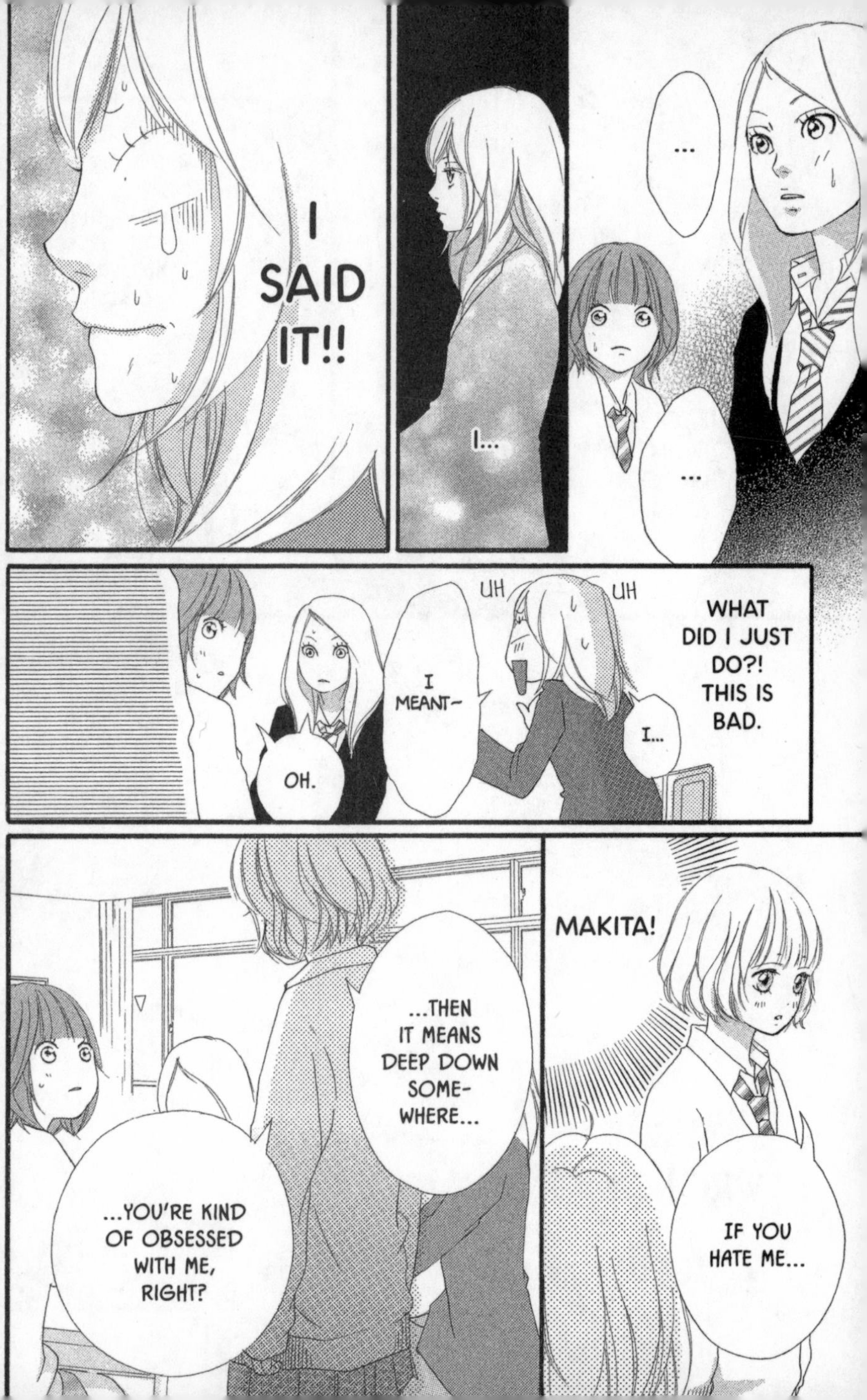
...
...
I...
I SAID IT!!
WHAT DID I JUST DO?! THIS IS BAD.
UH
UH
I...
I MEANT–
OH.
MAKITA!
IF YOU HATE ME...
...THEN IT MEANS DEEP DOWN SOME-WHERE...
...YOU'RE KIND OF OBSESSED WITH ME, RIGHT?

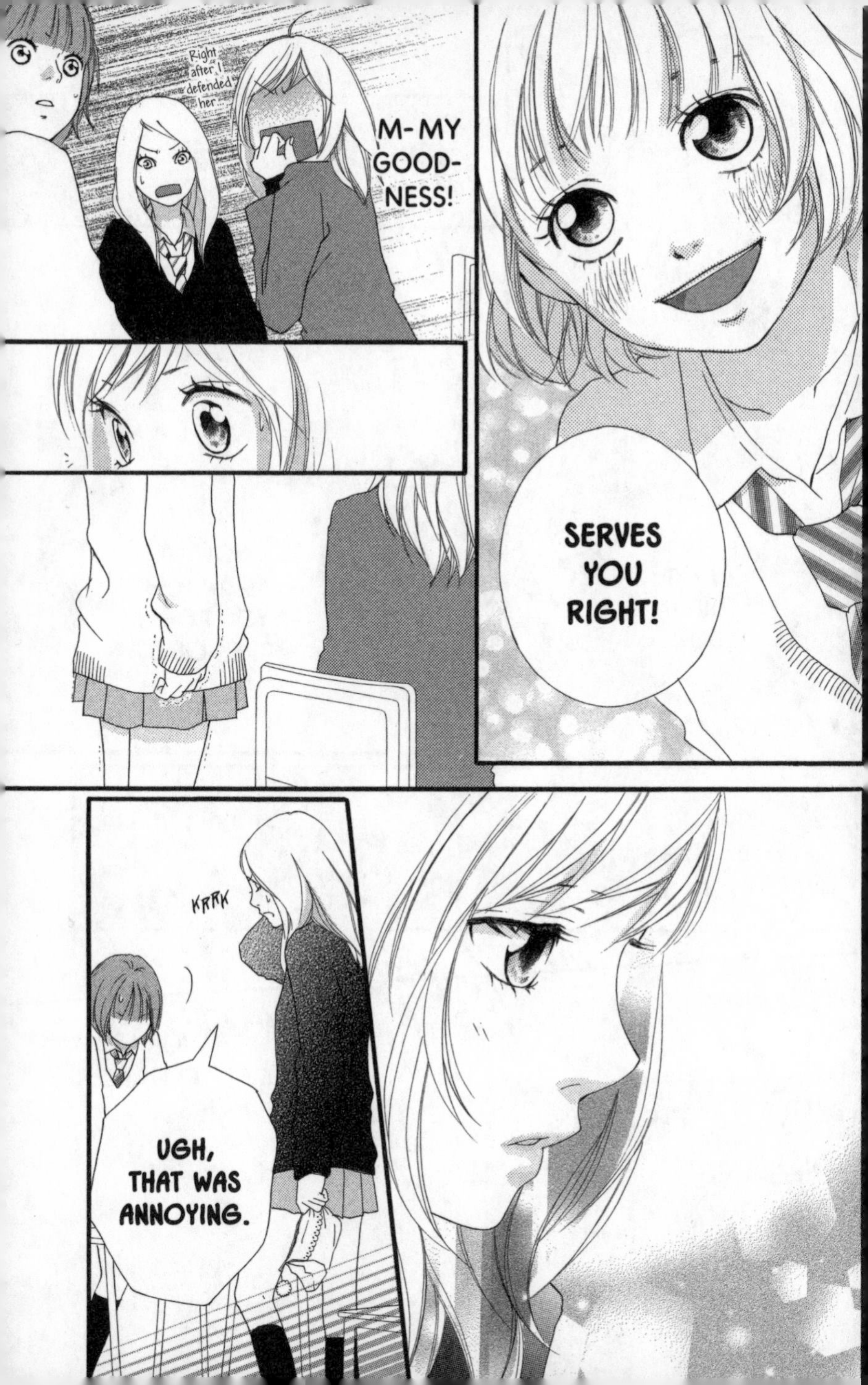
SERVES YOU RIGHT!
M-MY GOODNESS!
Right after I defended her...
KRRK
UGH, THAT WAS ANNOYING.

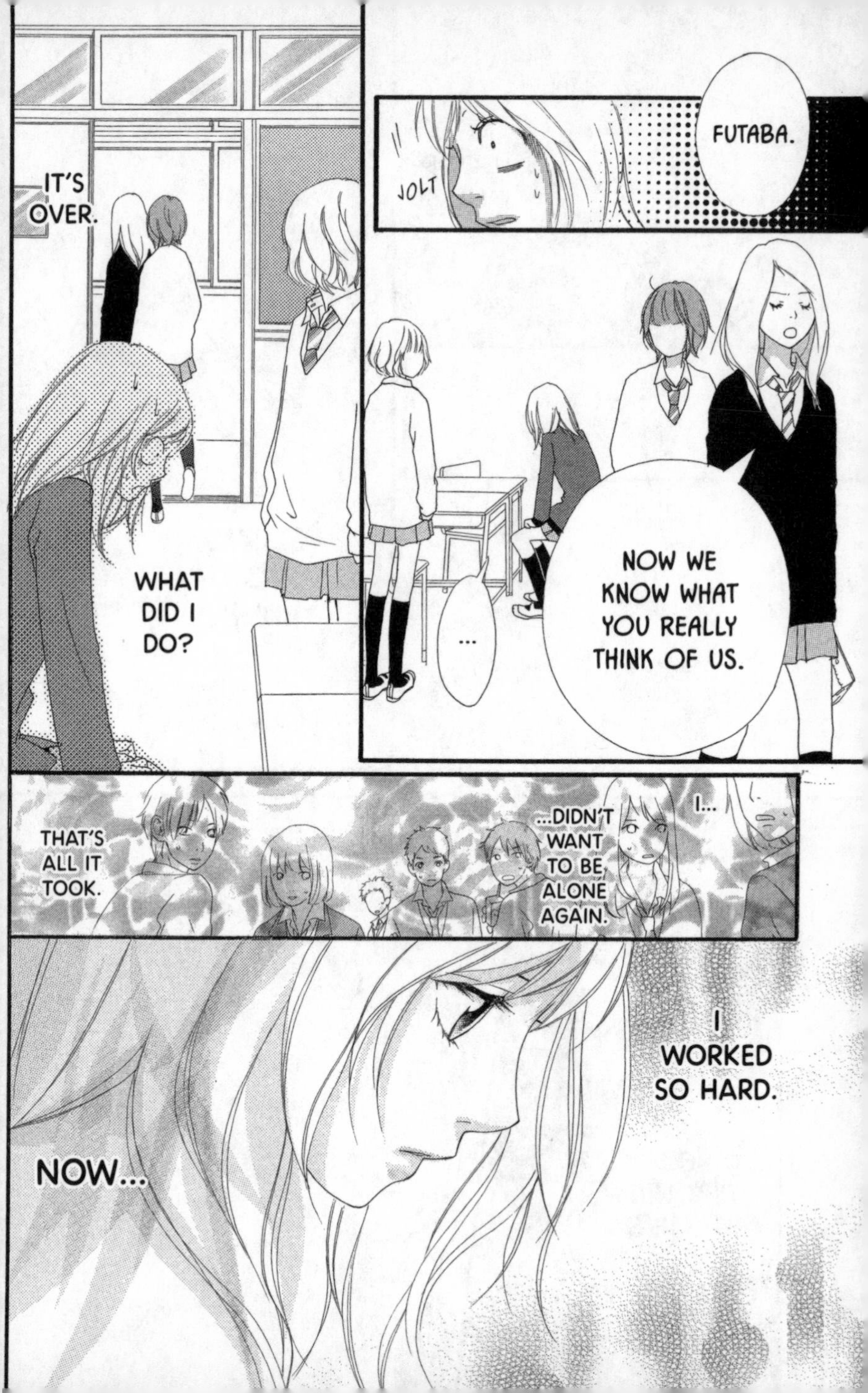
FUTABA.
JOLT
NOW WE KNOW WHAT YOU REALLY THINK OF US.
...
IT'S OVER.
WHAT DID I DO?
I...
...DIDN'T WANT TO BE ALONE AGAIN.
THAT'S ALL IT TOOK.
I WORKED SO HARD.
NOW...

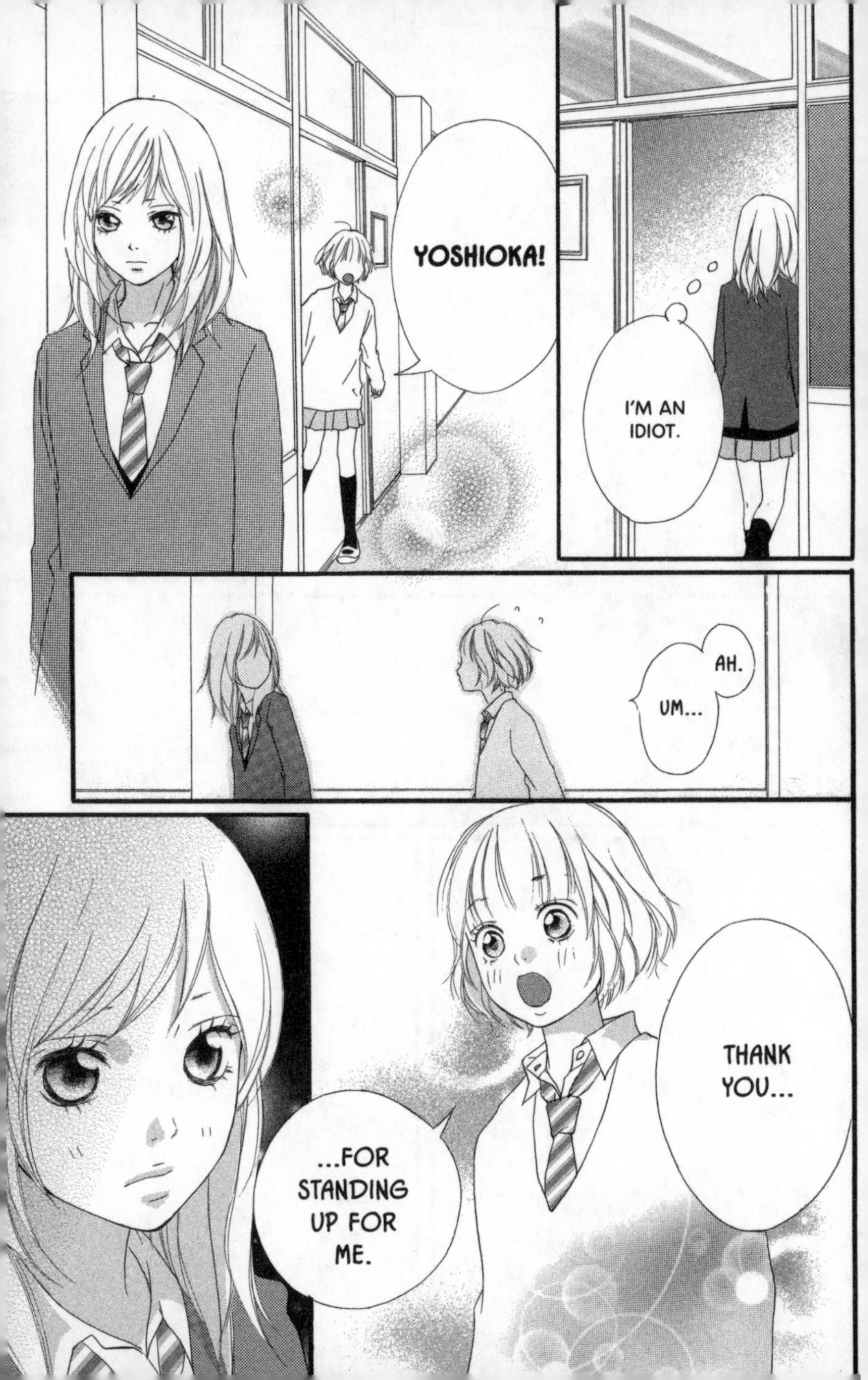
I'M AN IDIOT.
YOSHIOKA!
AH.
UM...
THANK YOU...
...FOR STANDING UP FOR ME.

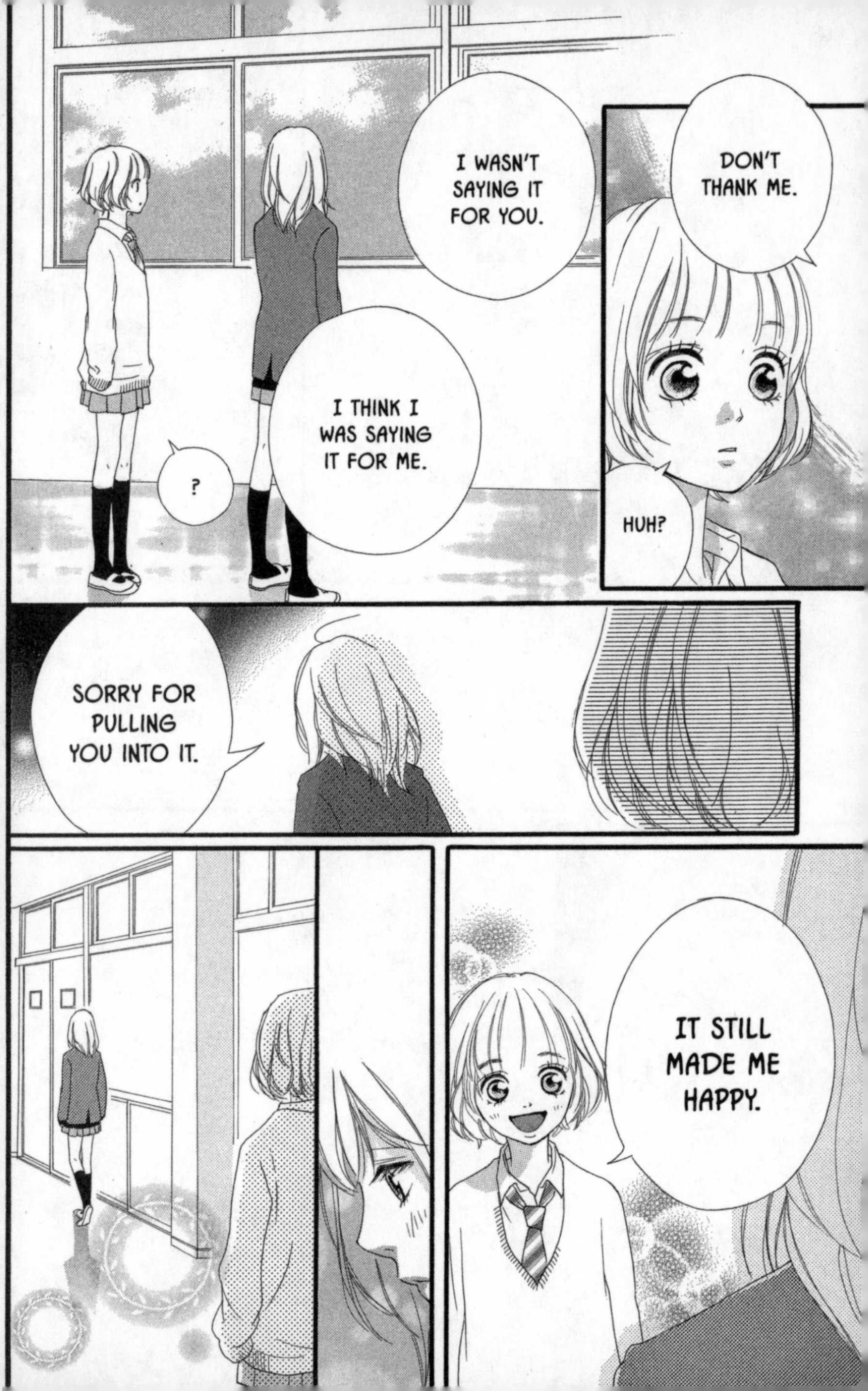
DON'T THANK ME.
HUH?
I WASN'T SAYING IT FOR YOU.
I THINK I WAS SAYING IT FOR ME.
?
SORRY FOR PULLING YOU INTO IT.
IT STILL MADE ME HAPPY.

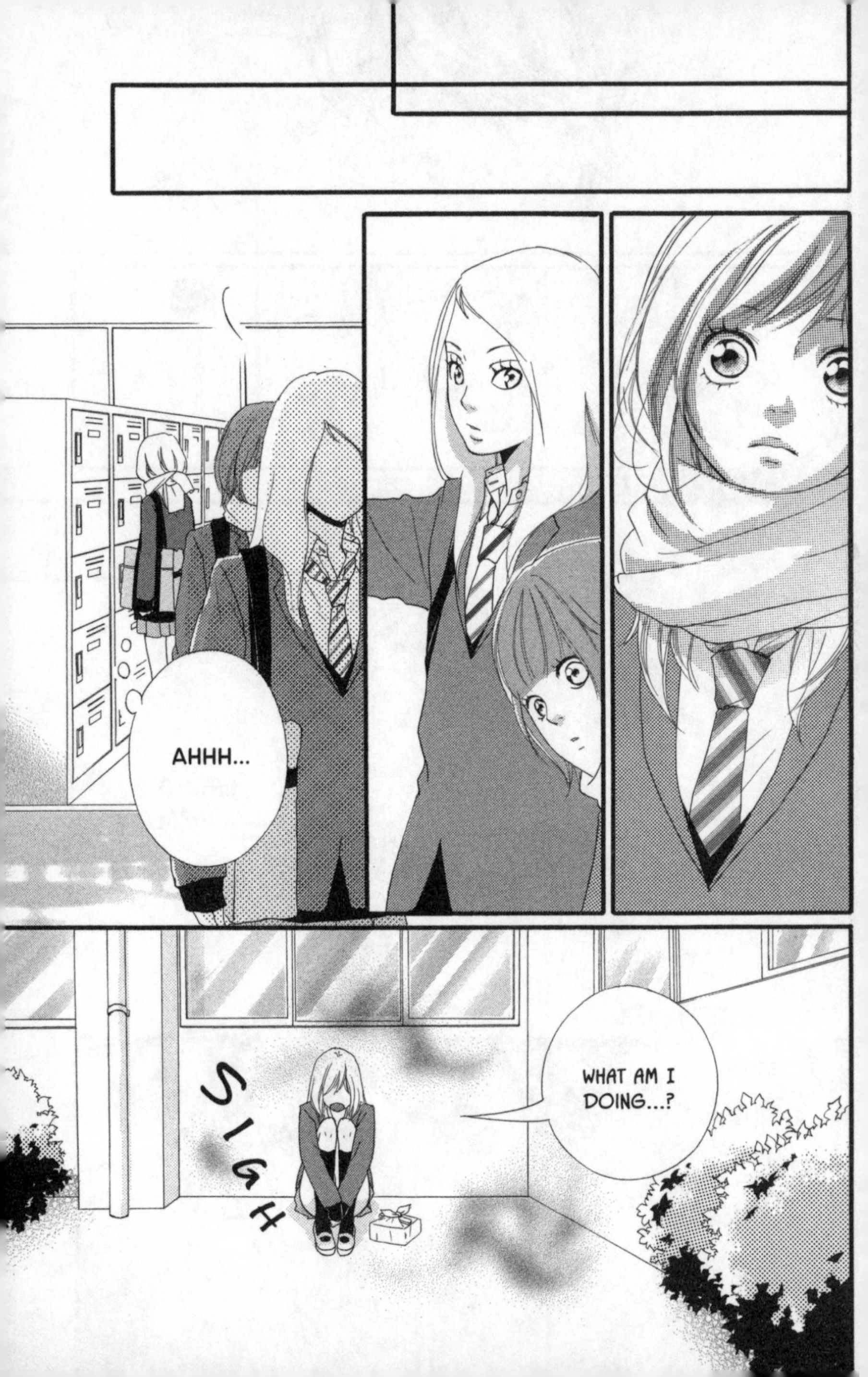
AHHH...
WHAT AM I DOING...?
SIGH

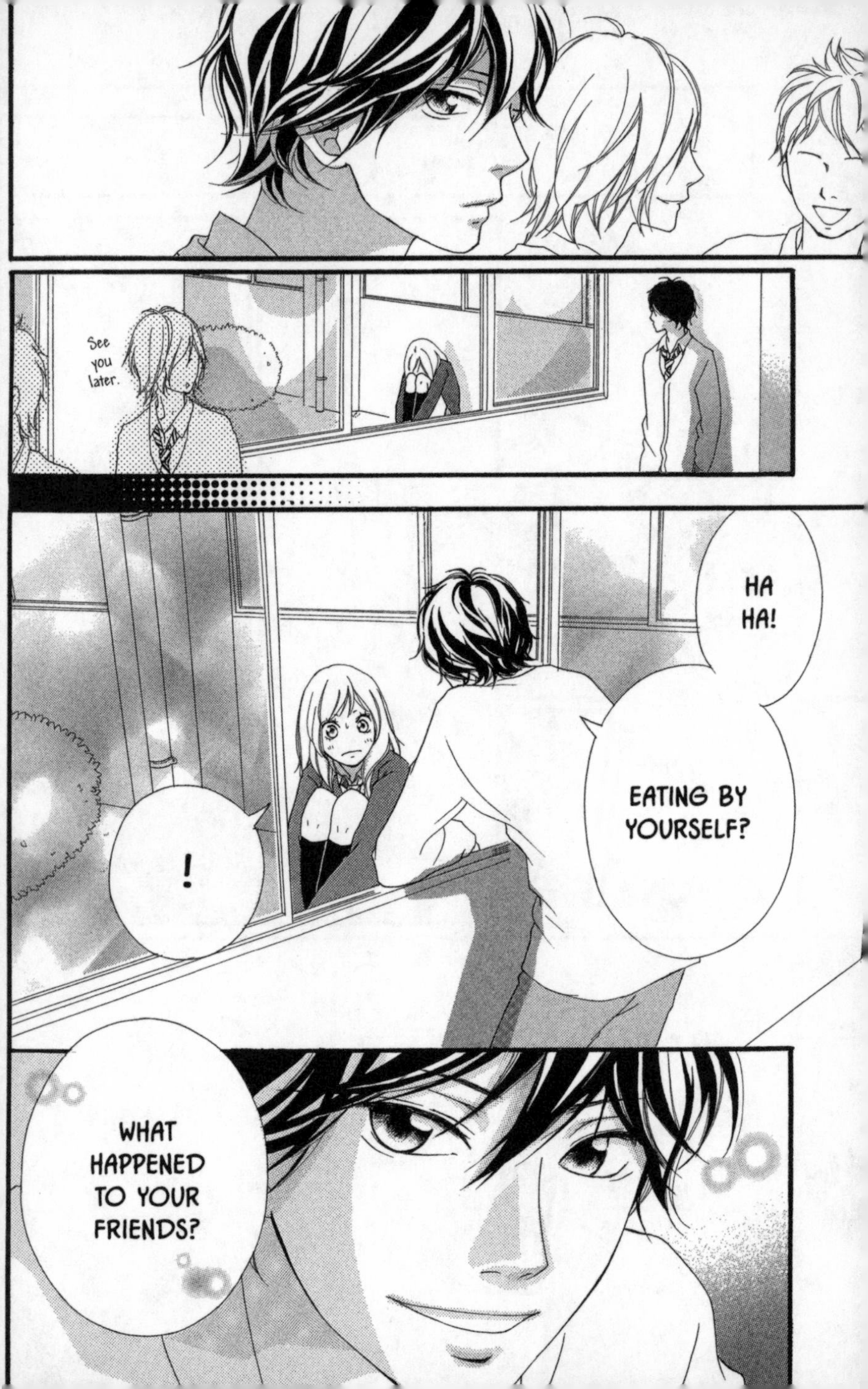
See you later.
HA HA!
EATING BY YOURSELF?
!
WHAT HAPPENED TO YOUR FRIENDS?

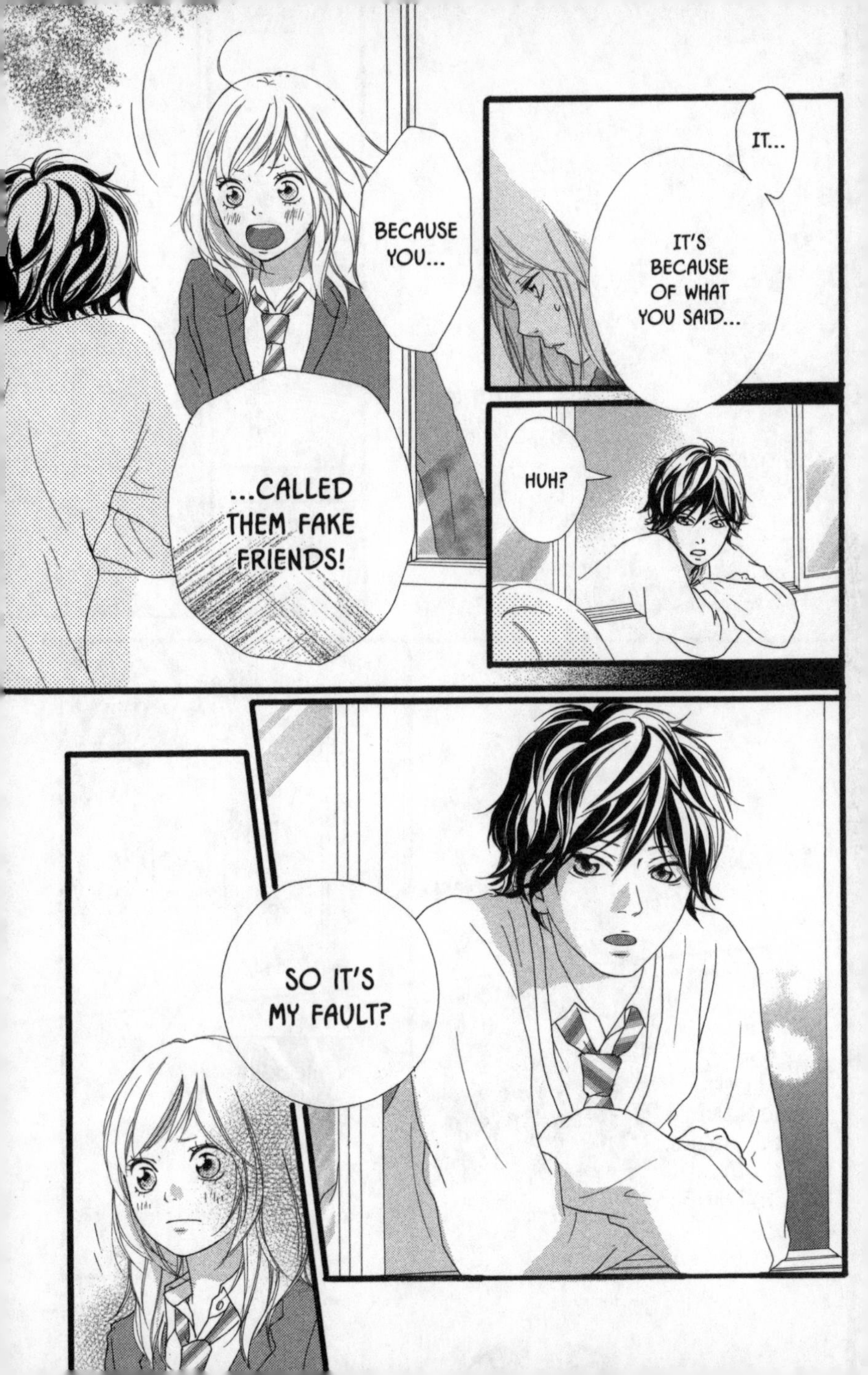
IT...
IT'S BECAUSE OF WHAT YOU SAID...
HUH?
BECAUSE YOU...
...CALLED THEM FAKE FRIENDS!
SO IT'S MY FAULT?

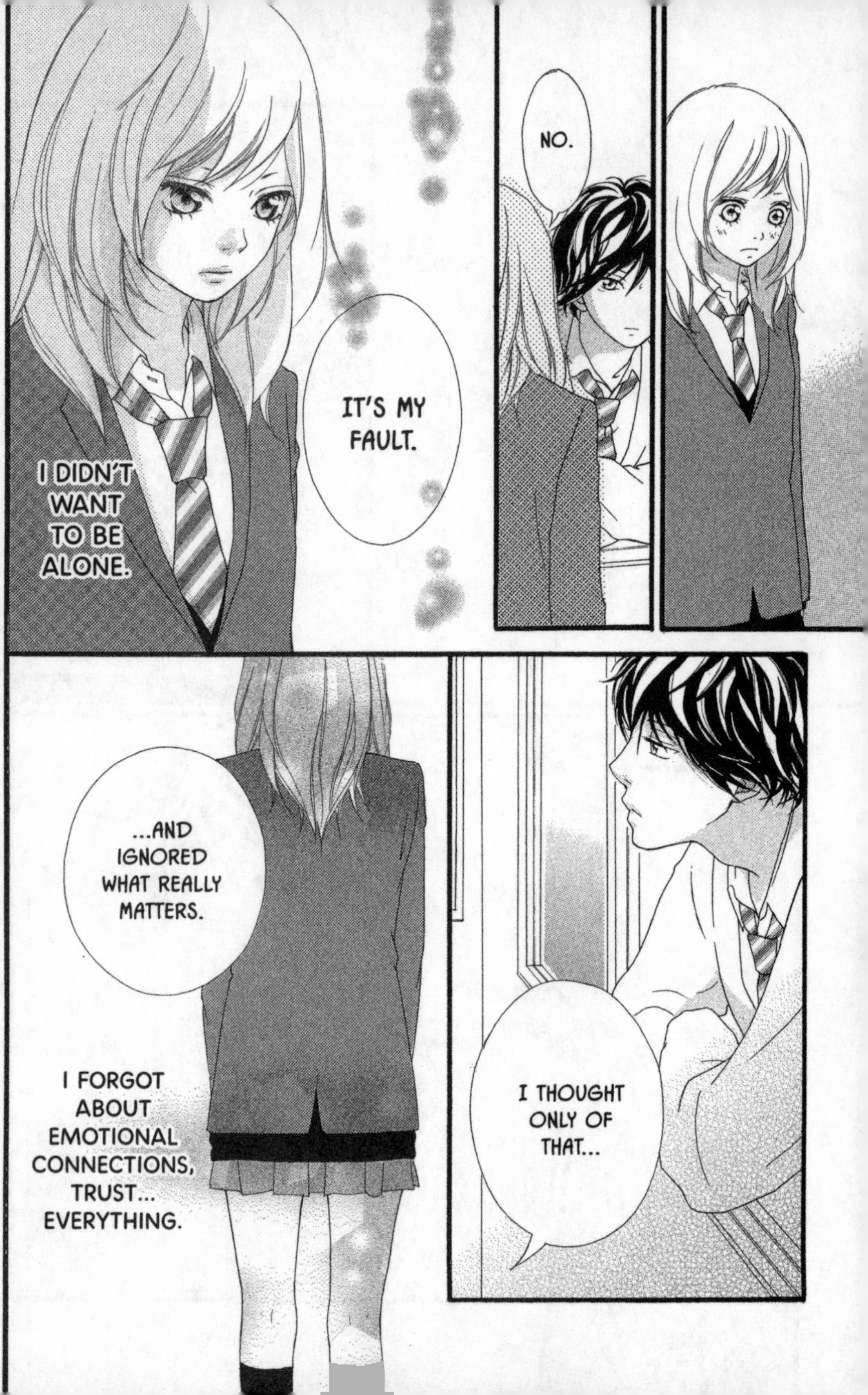
NO.
IT'S MY FAULT.
I DIDN'T WANT TO BE ALONE.
I THOUGHT ONLY OF THAT...
...AND IGNORED WHAT REALLY MATTERS.
I FORGOT ABOUT EMOTIONAL CONNECTIONS, TRUST... EVERYTHING.

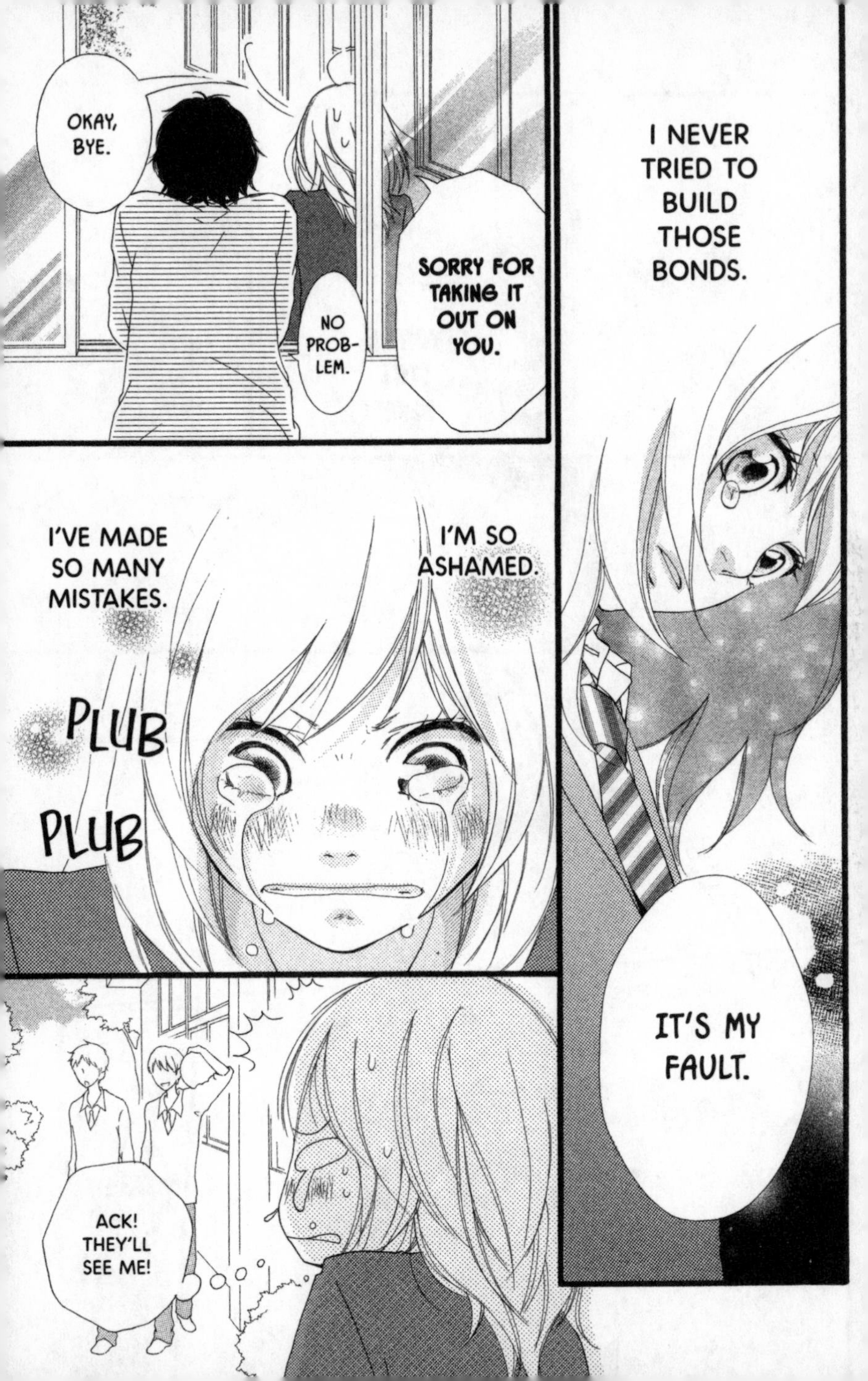
I NEVER TRIED TO BUILD THOSE BONDS.
IT'S MY FAULT.
SORRY FOR TAKING IT OUT ON YOU.
NO PROB-LEM.
OKAY, BYE.
I'M SO ASHAMED.
I'VE MADE SO MANY MISTAKES.
PLUB
PLUB
ACK! THEY'LL SEE ME!

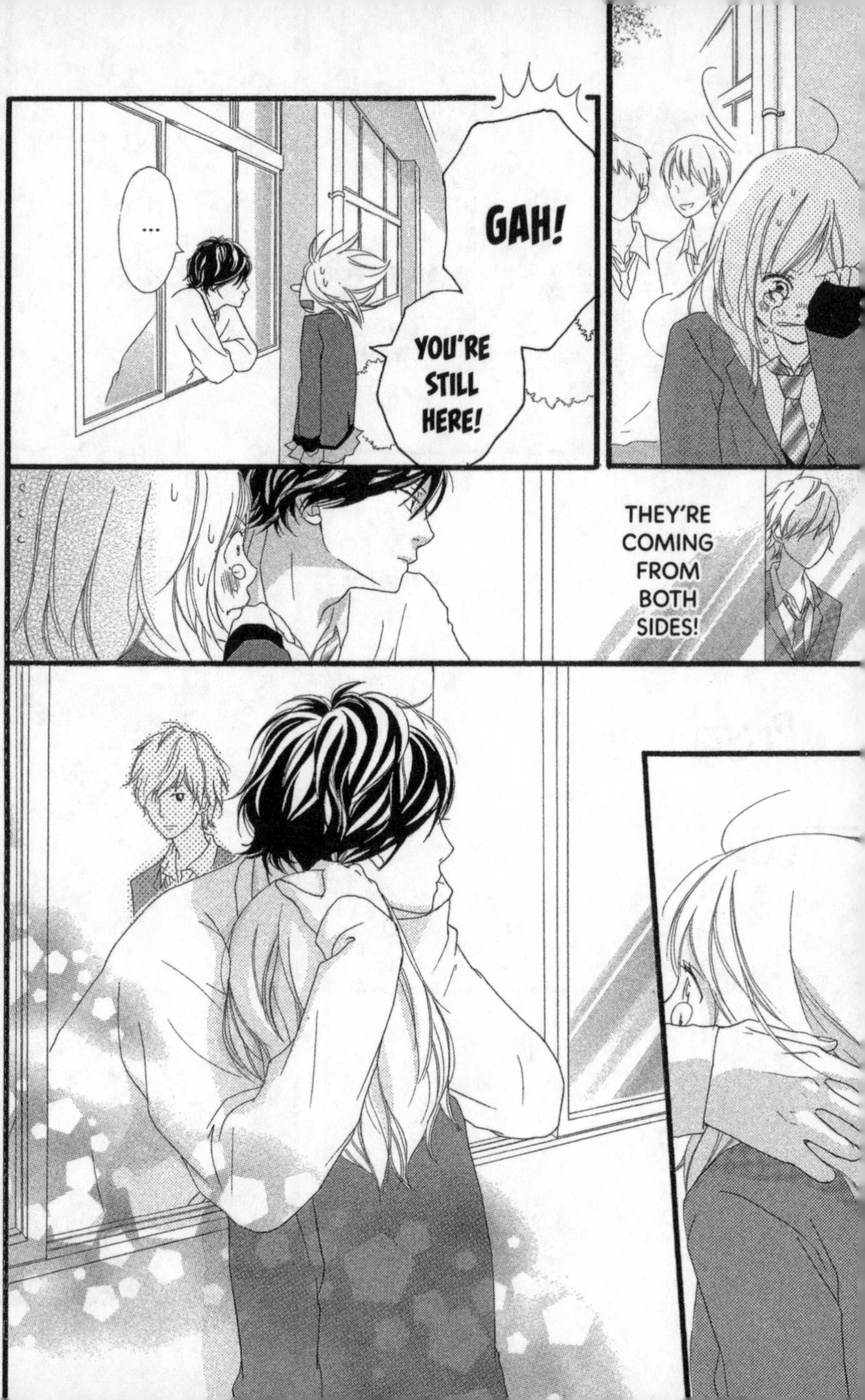
GAH!
YOU'RE STILL HERE!
...
THEY'RE COMING FROM BOTH SIDES!

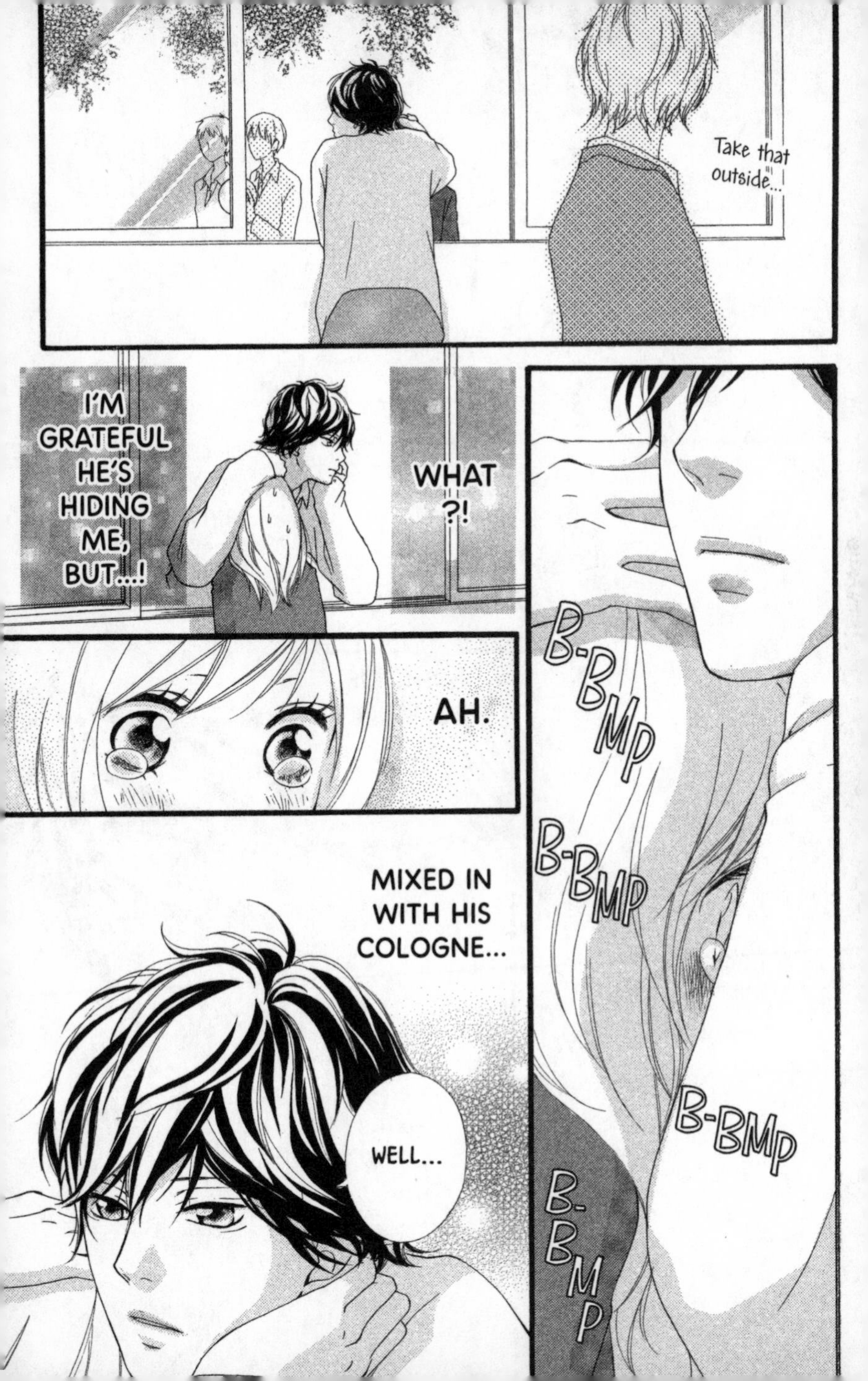
Take that outside...
B-BMP
B-BMP
B-BMP
B-BMP
WHAT?!
I'M GRATEFUL HE'S HIDING ME, BUT...!
AH.
MIXED IN WITH HIS COLOGNE...
WELL...

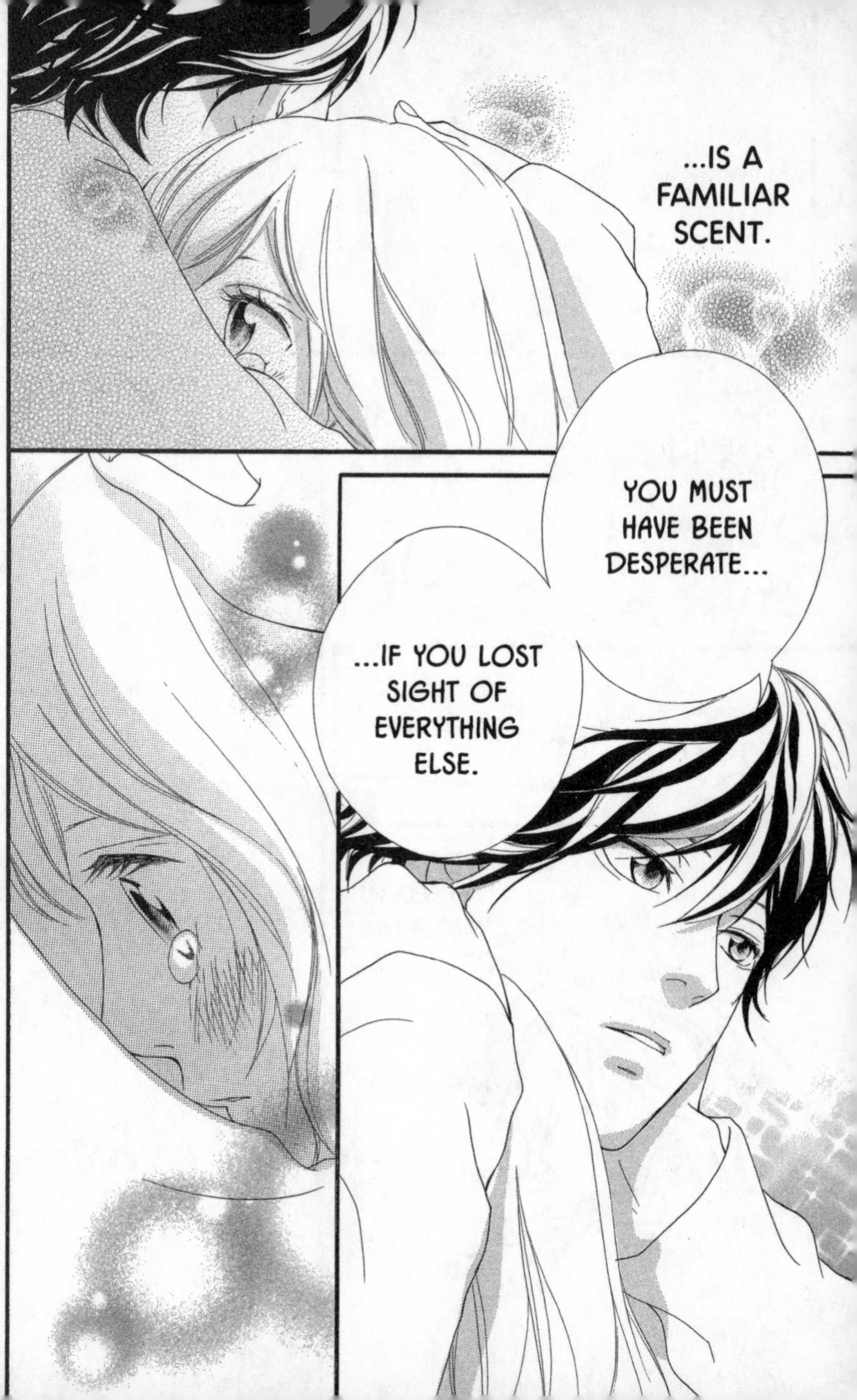
...IS A FAMILIAR SCENT.
YOU MUST HAVE BEEN DESPERATE...
...IF YOU LOST SIGHT OF EVERYTHING ELSE.

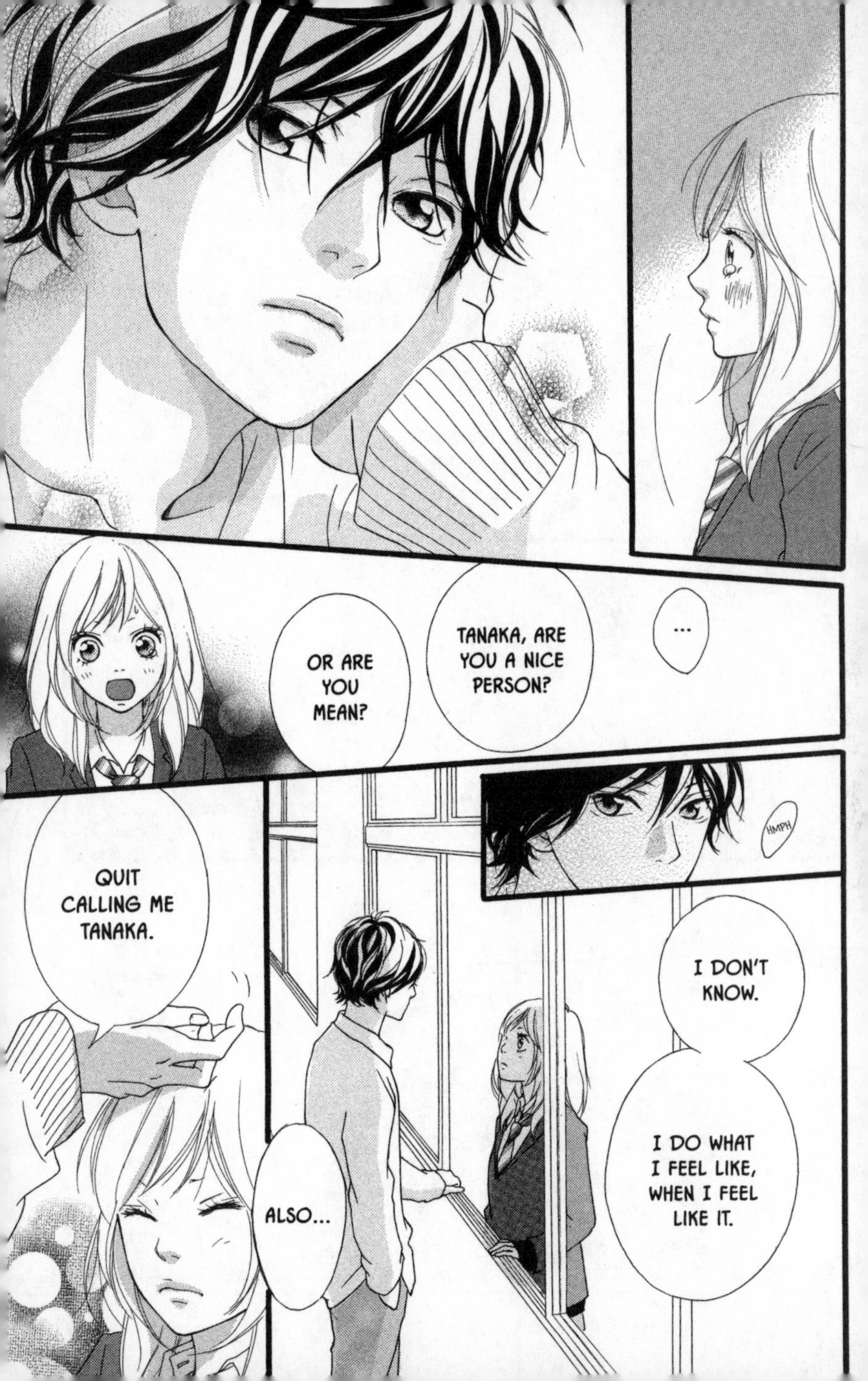
...
TANAKA, ARE YOU A NICE PERSON?
OR ARE YOU MEAN?
HMPH
I DON'T KNOW.
I DO WHAT I FEEL LIKE, WHEN I FEEL LIKE IT.
ALSO...
QUIT CALLING ME TANAKA.

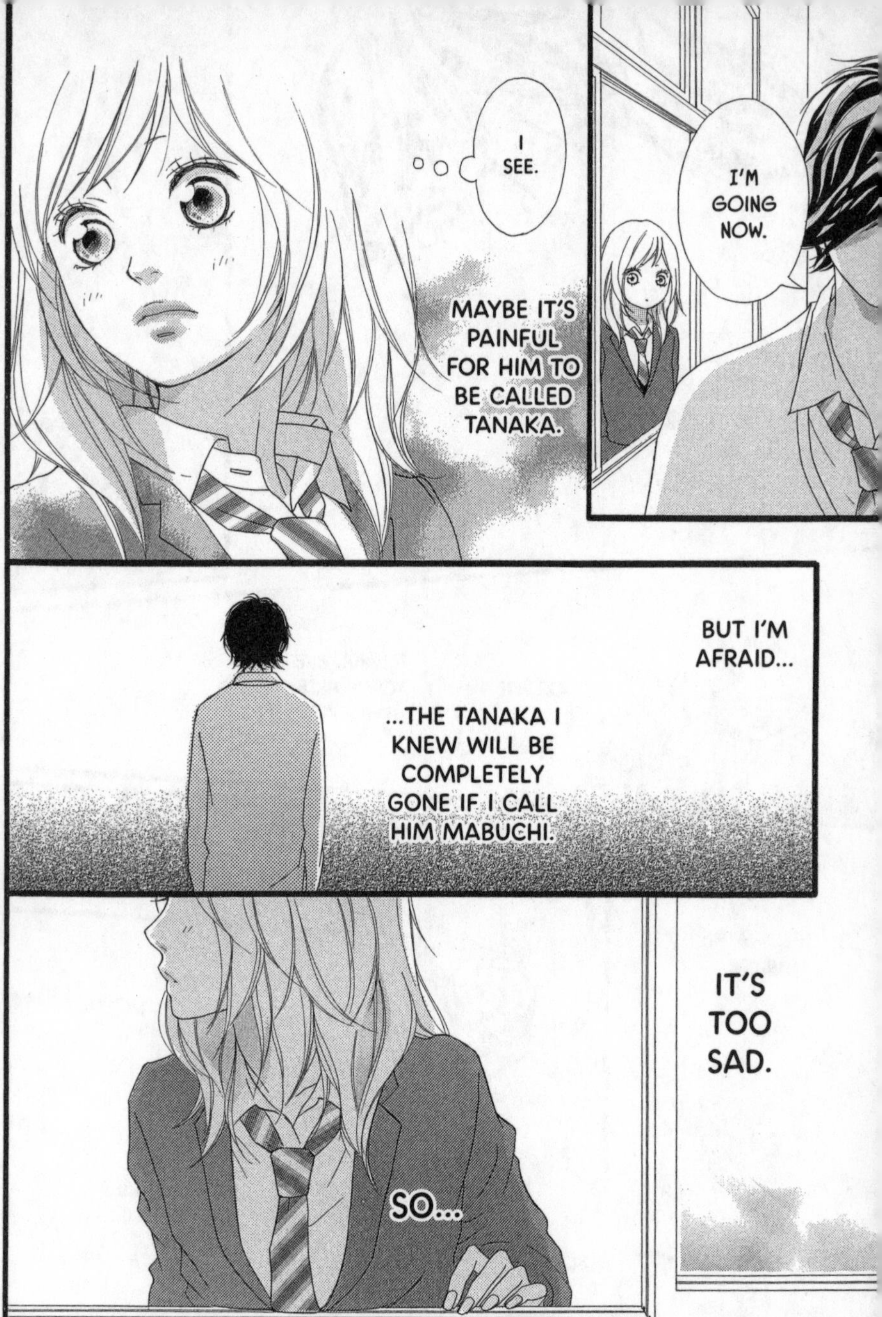
I'M GOING NOW.
I SEE.
MAYBE IT'S PAINFUL FOR HIM TO BE CALLED TANAKA.
BUT I'M AFRAID...
...THE TANAKA I KNEW WILL BE COMPLETELY GONE IF I CALL HIM MABUCHI.
IT'S TOO SAD.
SO...

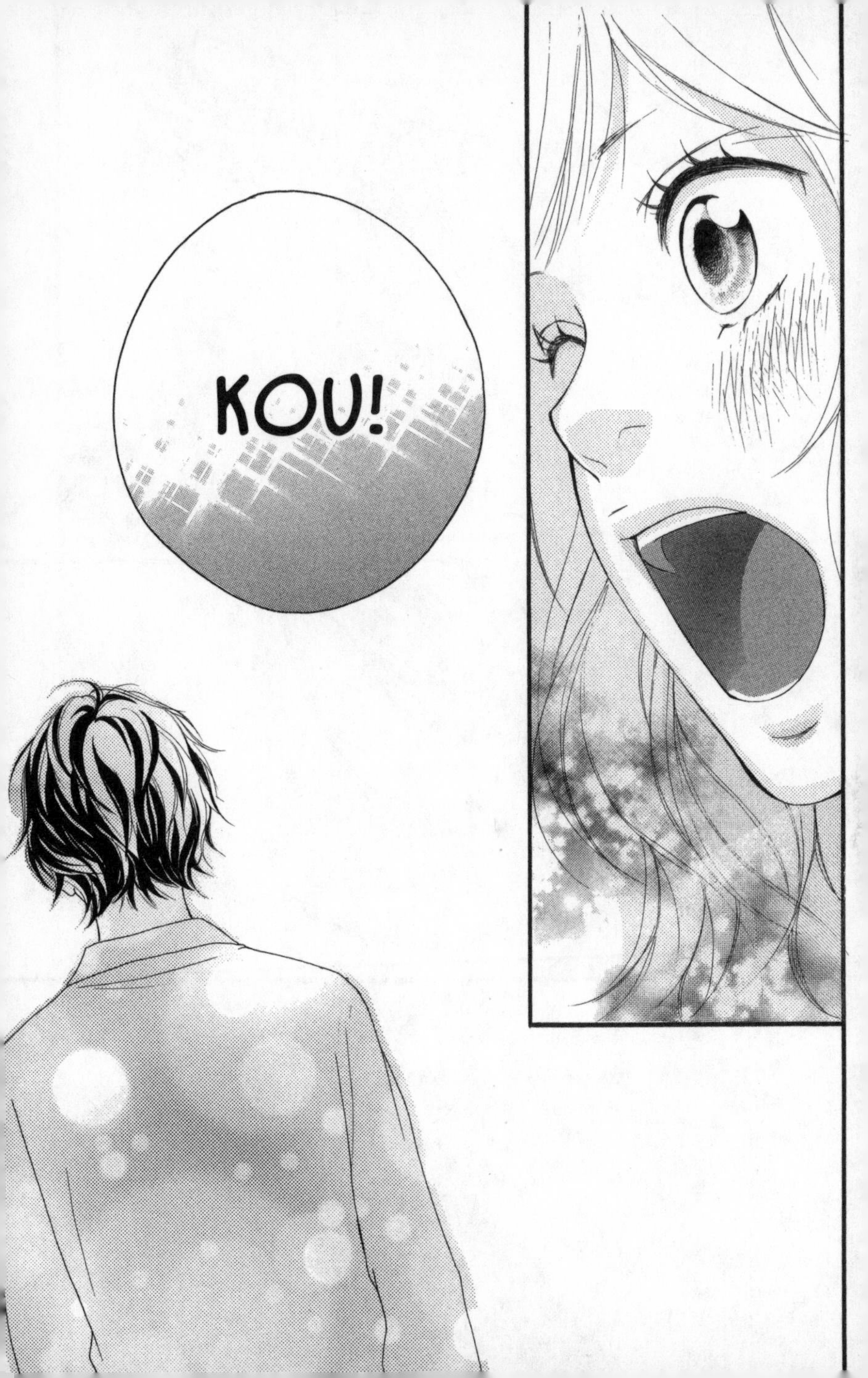
KOU!

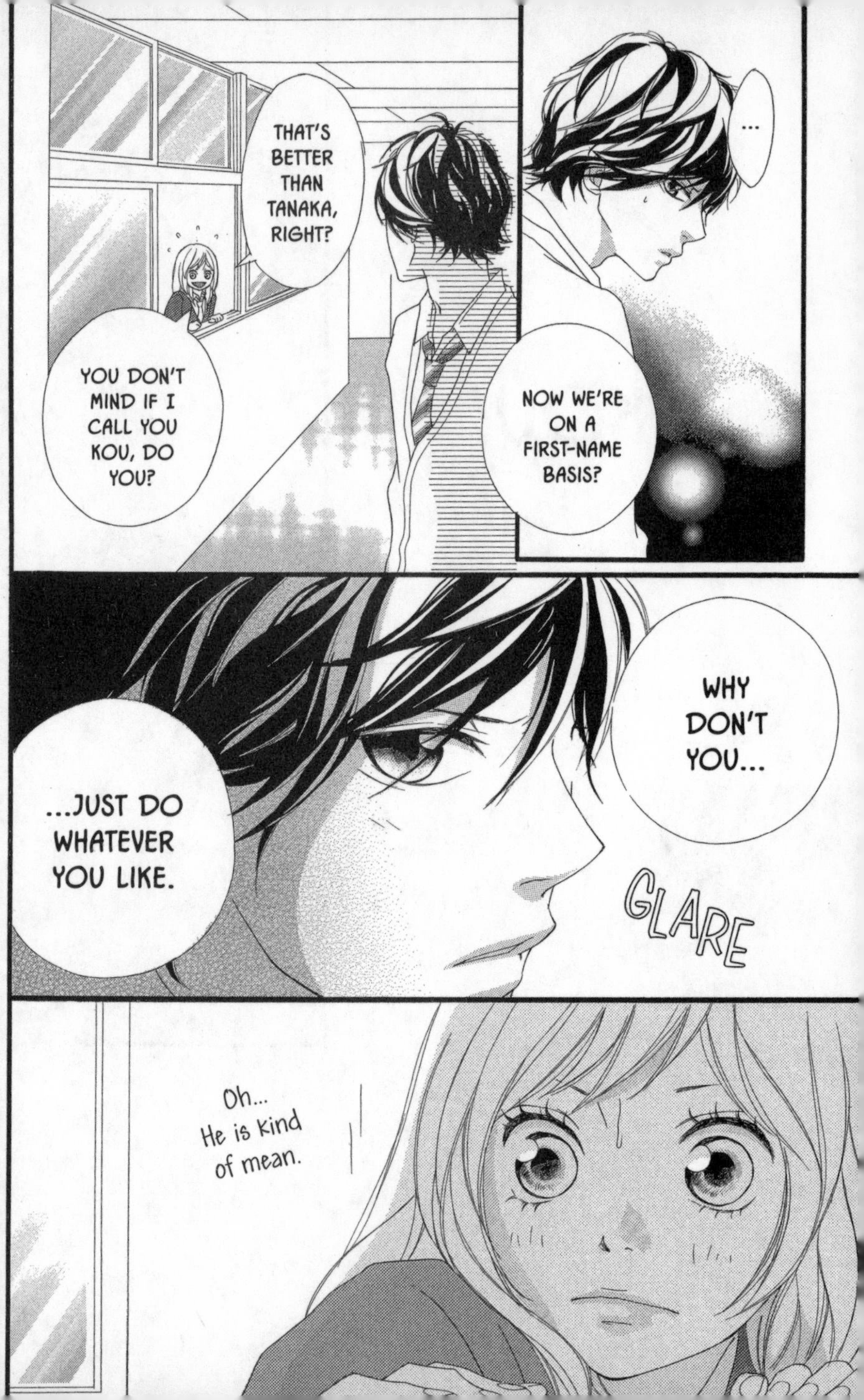
...
NOW WE'RE ON A FIRST-NAME BASIS?
THAT'S BETTER THAN TANAKA, RIGHT?
YOU DON'T MIND IF I CALL YOU KOU, DO YOU?
WHY DON'T YOU...
GLARE
...JUST DO WHATEVER YOU LIKE.
Oh... He is kind of mean.

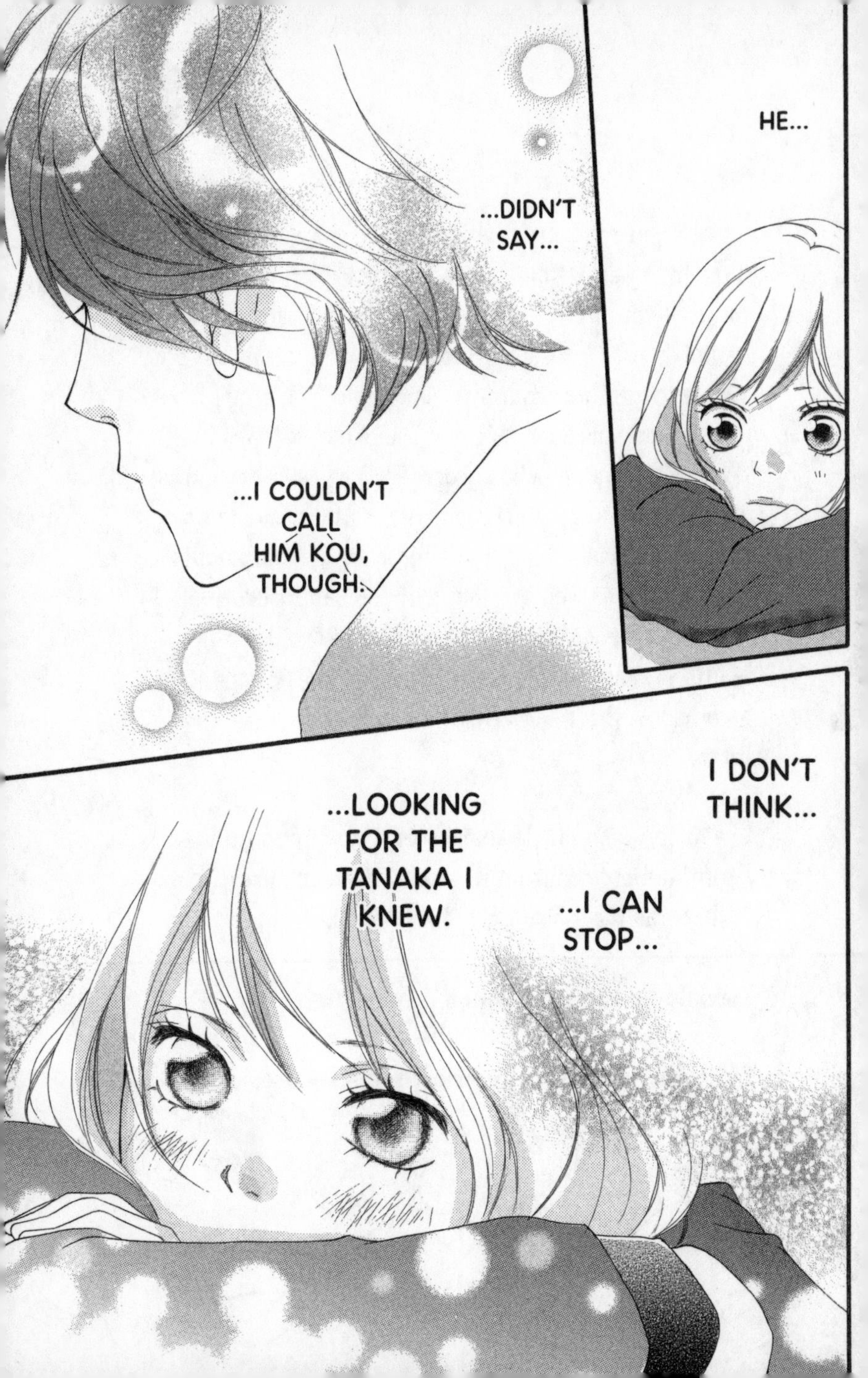
HE...
...DIDN'T SAY...
...I COULDN'T CALL HIM KOU, THOUGH.
I DON'T THINK...
...I CAN STOP...
...LOOKING FOR THE TANAKA I KNEW.

Now, if you read the drama between the girls and thought it was a typical girls' quarrel, then I must tell you that you are mistaken. The truth is I came up with Asumi's and Chie's lines based on a conversation I overheard between two men. They said, "That guy does well at work because he's good-looking. If that's all it takes, I'll go get plastic surgery." (They went on and on about it.) In our society, women are often said to be catty, but I don't think that's the case. It's not about gender. People who are like that are simply like that. I also think age doesn't play a role either. There are adults who are like this too. When I used to work for a company, there were many disingenuous older men there.

I need to watch out to make sure I don't end up like Asumi without realizing it. Maybe it's more likely that I'll become more like Chie than Asumi.

I should be careful. I will be careful. Yes.

I wish the world would overflow with nice people!

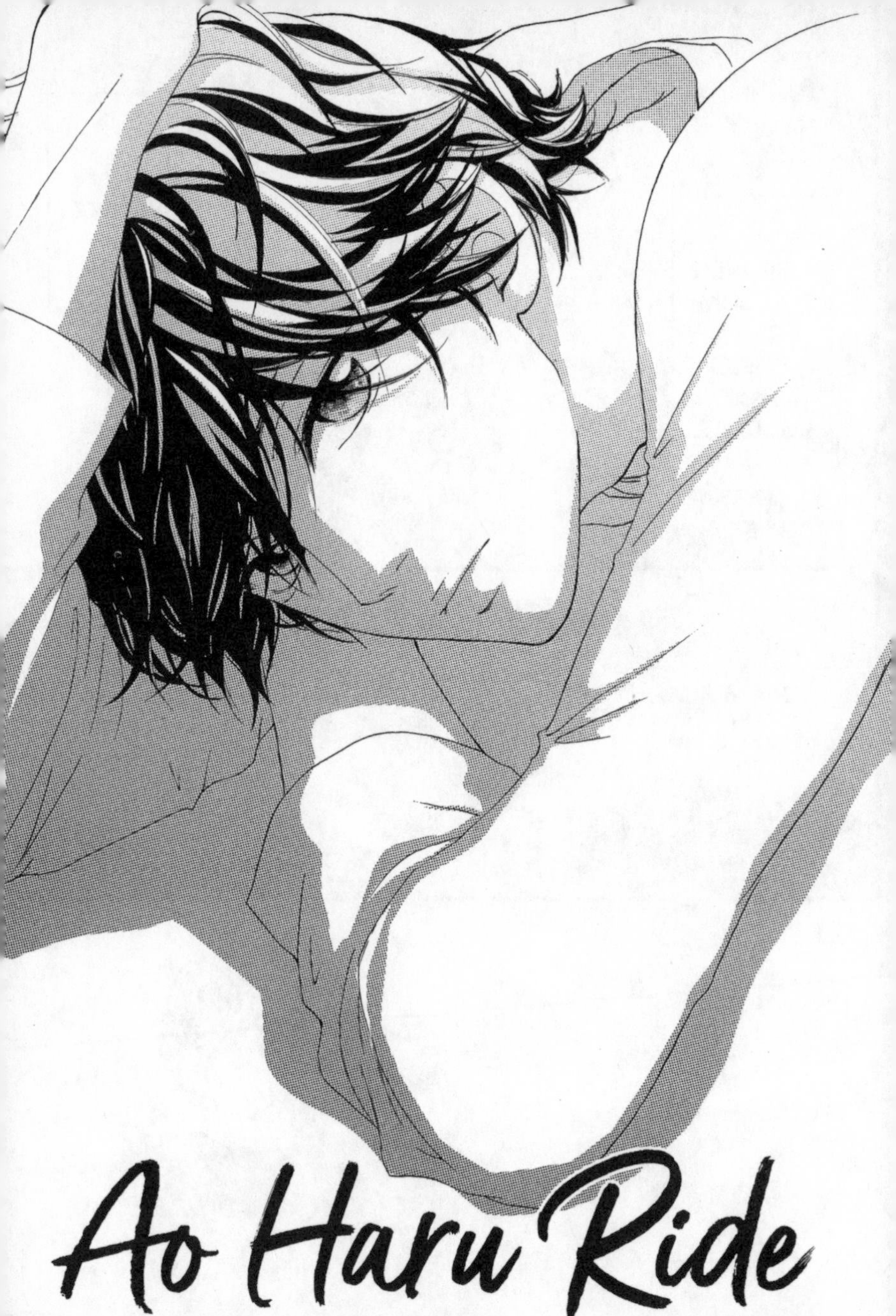

Ao Haru Ride

The scent of air after rain...
In the light around us, I felt your heartbeat.

CHAPTER 3

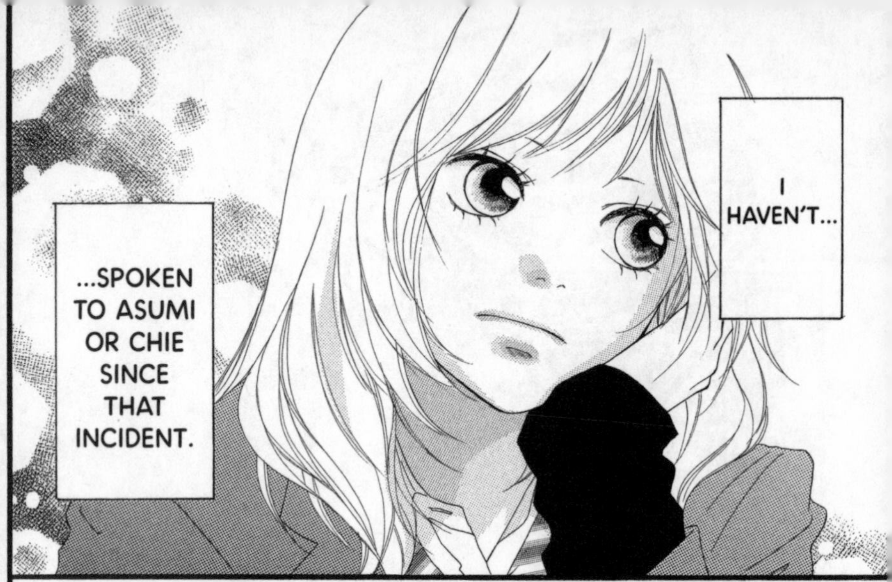
I HAVEN'T...
...SPOKEN TO ASUMI OR CHIE SINCE THAT INCIDENT.

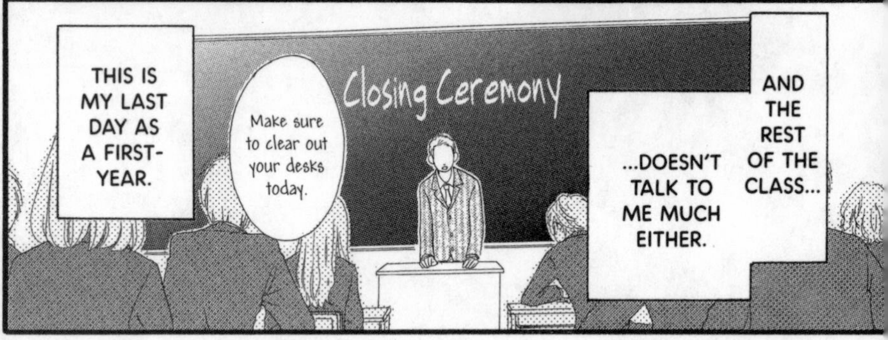
AND THE REST OF THE CLASS...
...DOESN'T TALK TO ME MUCH EITHER.
Closing Ceremony
Make sure to clear out your desks today.
THIS IS MY LAST DAY AS A FIRST-YEAR.

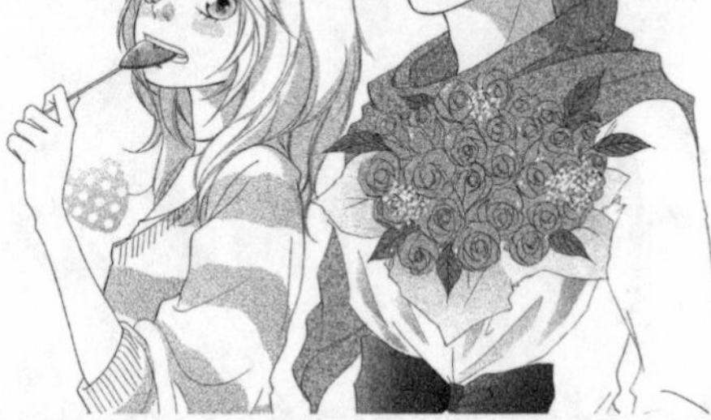

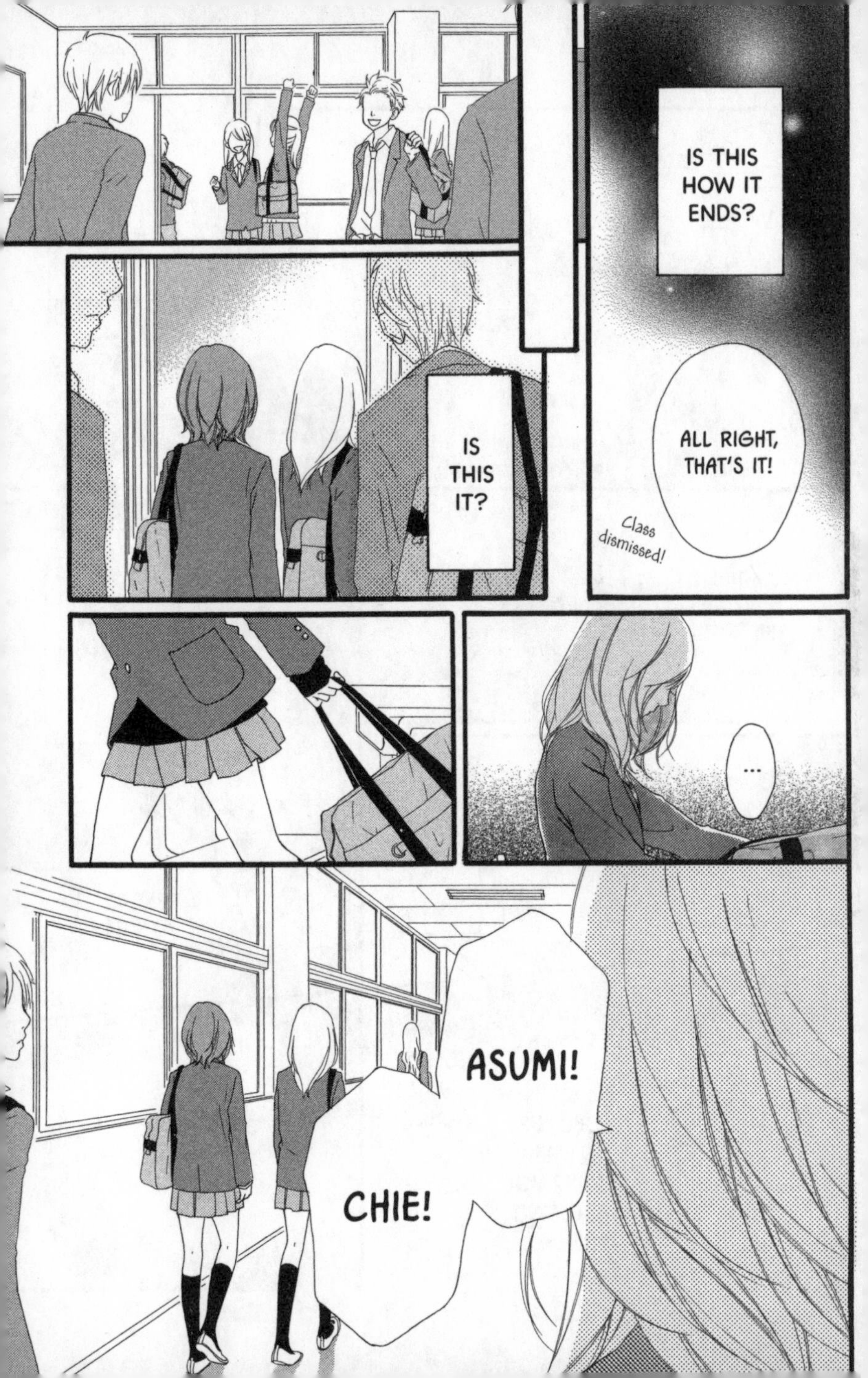

IS THIS HOW IT ENDS?
ALL RIGHT, THAT'S IT!
Class dismissed!
IS THIS IT?
...
ASUMI!
CHIE!

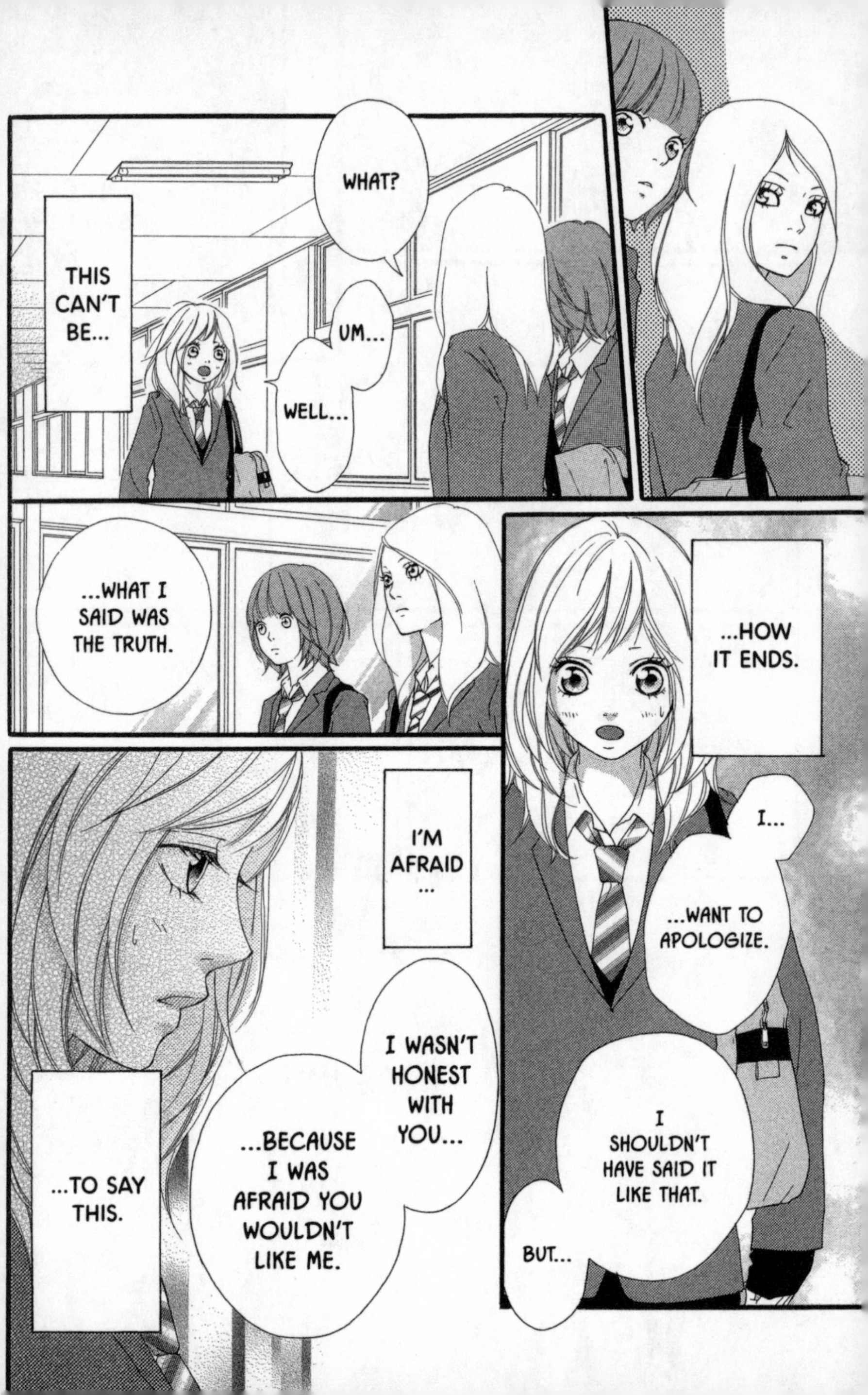
WHAT?
UM...
WELL...
THIS CAN'T BE...
...HOW IT ENDS.
I...
...WANT TO APOLOGIZE.
I SHOULDN'T HAVE SAID IT LIKE THAT.
BUT...
...WHAT I SAID WAS THE TRUTH.
I'M AFRAID...
I WASN'T HONEST WITH YOU...
...BECAUSE I WAS AFRAID YOU WOULDN'T LIKE ME.
...TO SAY THIS.

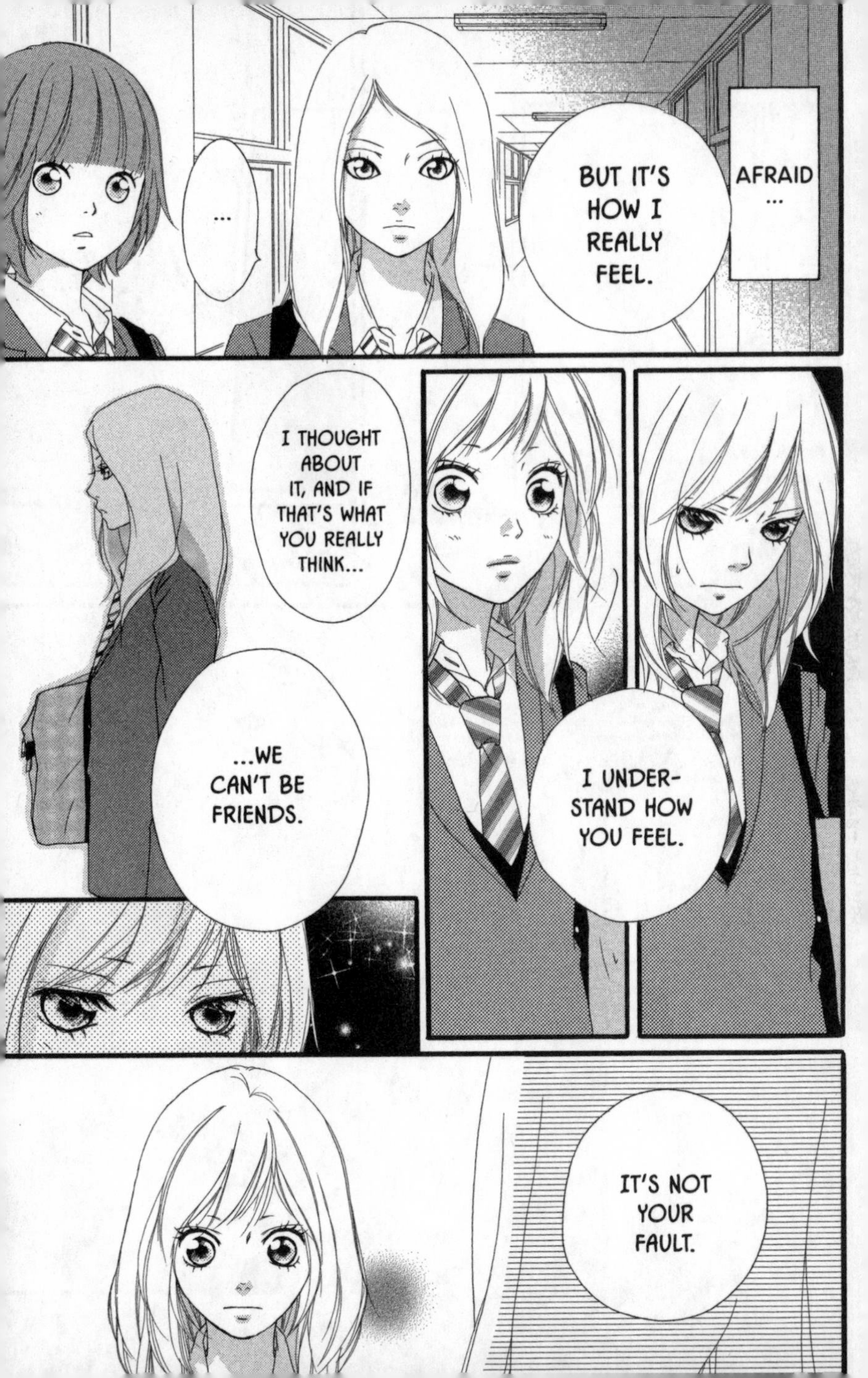
AFRAID ...
BUT IT'S HOW I REALLY FEEL.
...
I UNDER-STAND HOW YOU FEEL.
I THOUGHT ABOUT IT, AND IF THAT'S WHAT YOU REALLY THINK...
...WE CAN'T BE FRIENDS.
IT'S NOT YOUR FAULT.

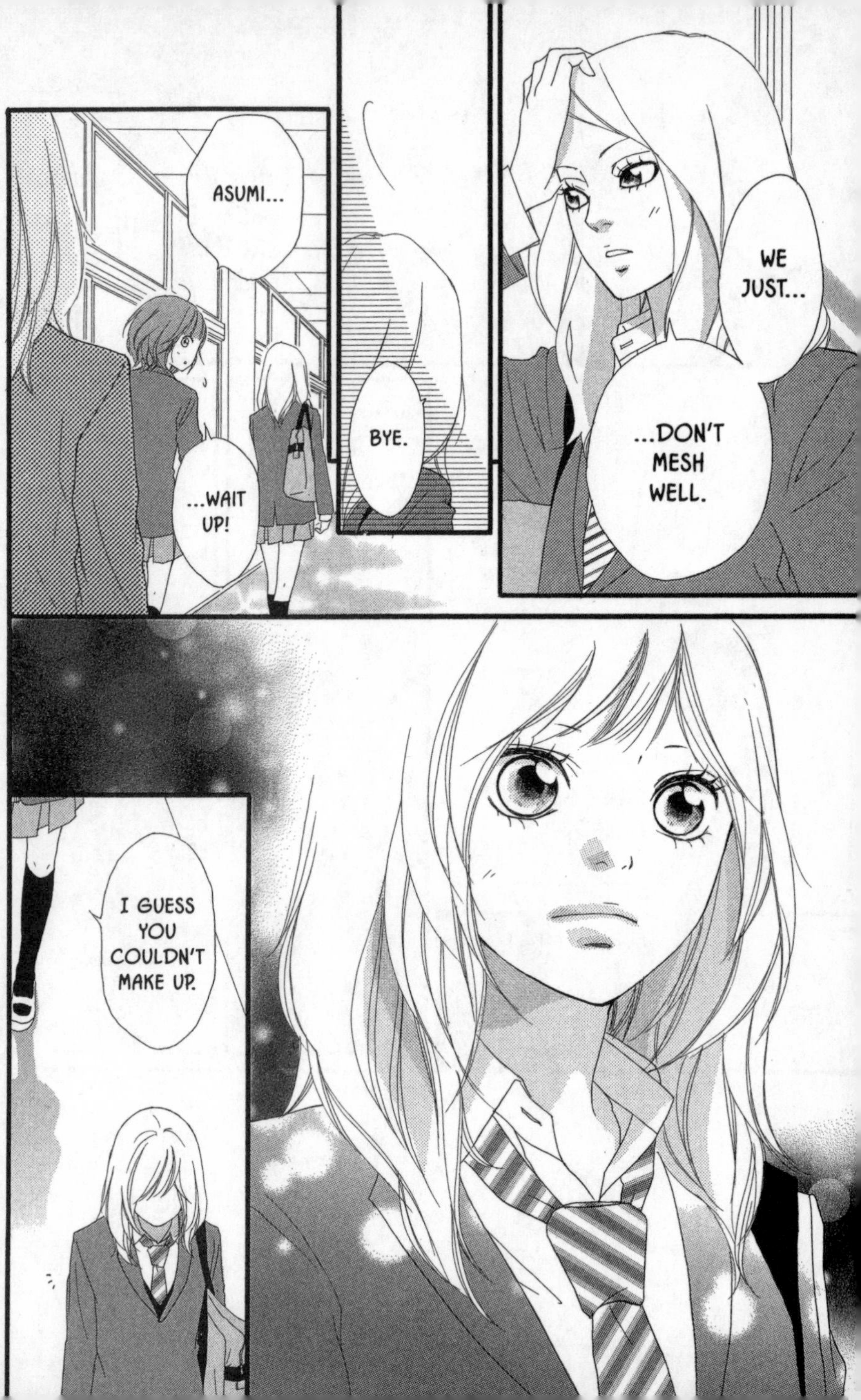
WE JUST...
...DON'T MESH WELL.
BYE.
ASUMI...
...WAIT UP!
I GUESS YOU COULDN'T MAKE UP.

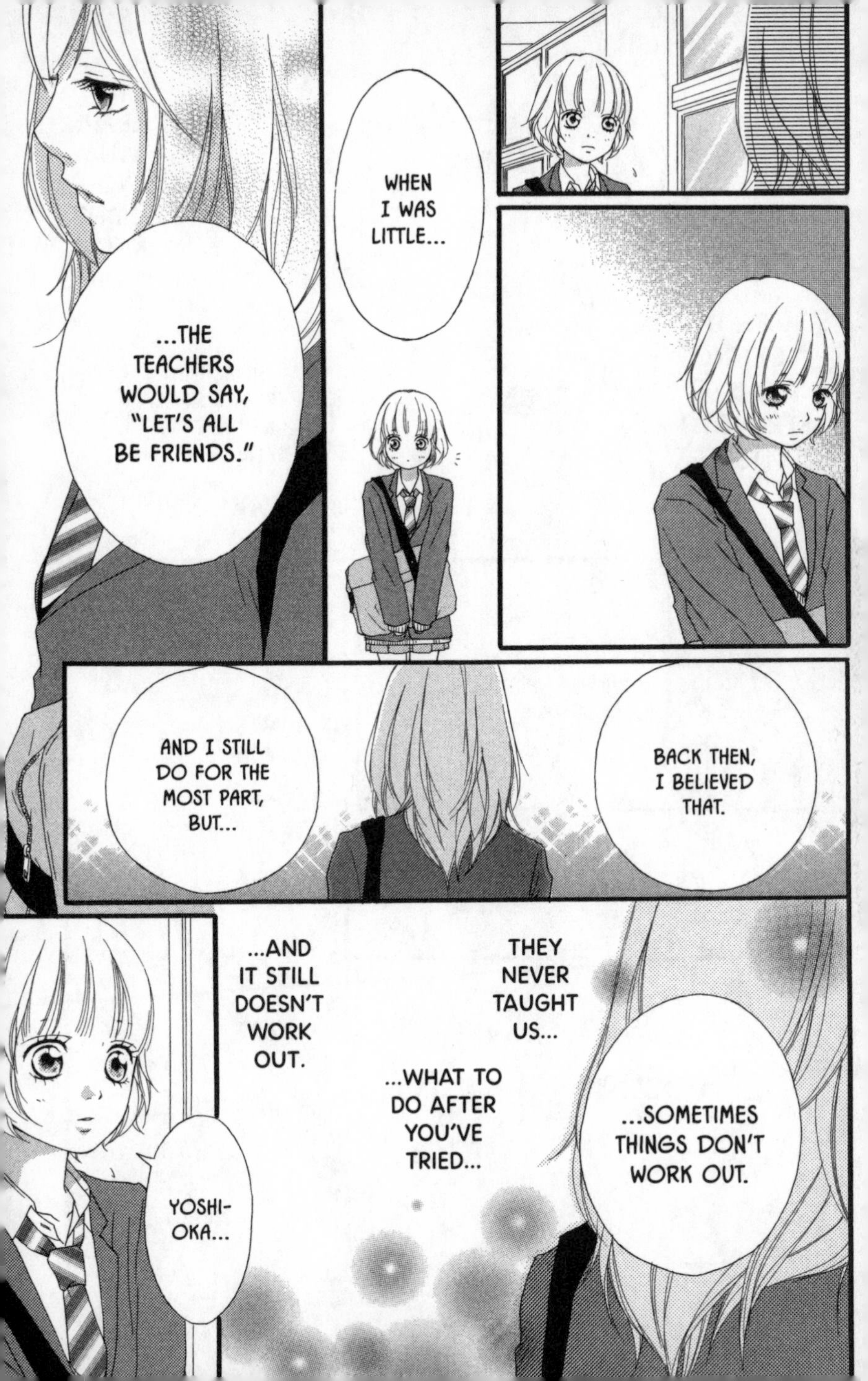
WHEN I WAS LITTLE...
...THE TEACHERS WOULD SAY, "LET'S ALL BE FRIENDS."
BACK THEN, I BELIEVED THAT.
AND I STILL DO FOR THE MOST PART, BUT...
...SOMETIMES THINGS DON'T WORK OUT.
THEY NEVER TAUGHT US...
...WHAT TO DO AFTER YOU'VE TRIED...
...AND IT STILL DOESN'T WORK OUT.
YOSHI-OKA...

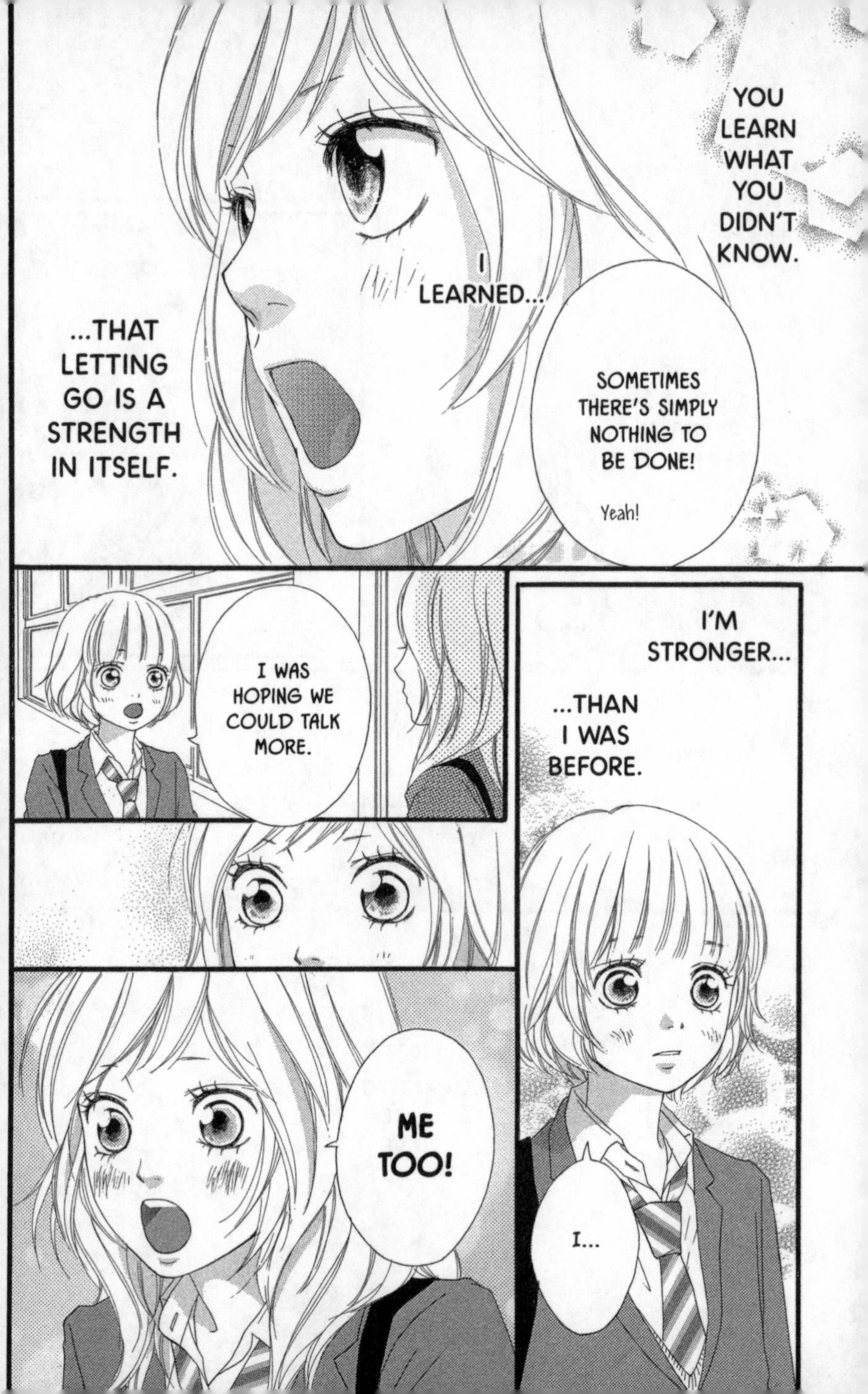
YOU LEARN WHAT YOU DIDN'T KNOW.
I LEARNED...
SOMETIMES THERE'S SIMPLY NOTHING TO BE DONE!
Yeah!
...THAT LETTING GO IS A STRENGTH IN ITSELF.
I'M STRONGER...
...THAN I WAS BEFORE.
I...
I WAS HOPING WE COULD TALK MORE.
ME TOO!

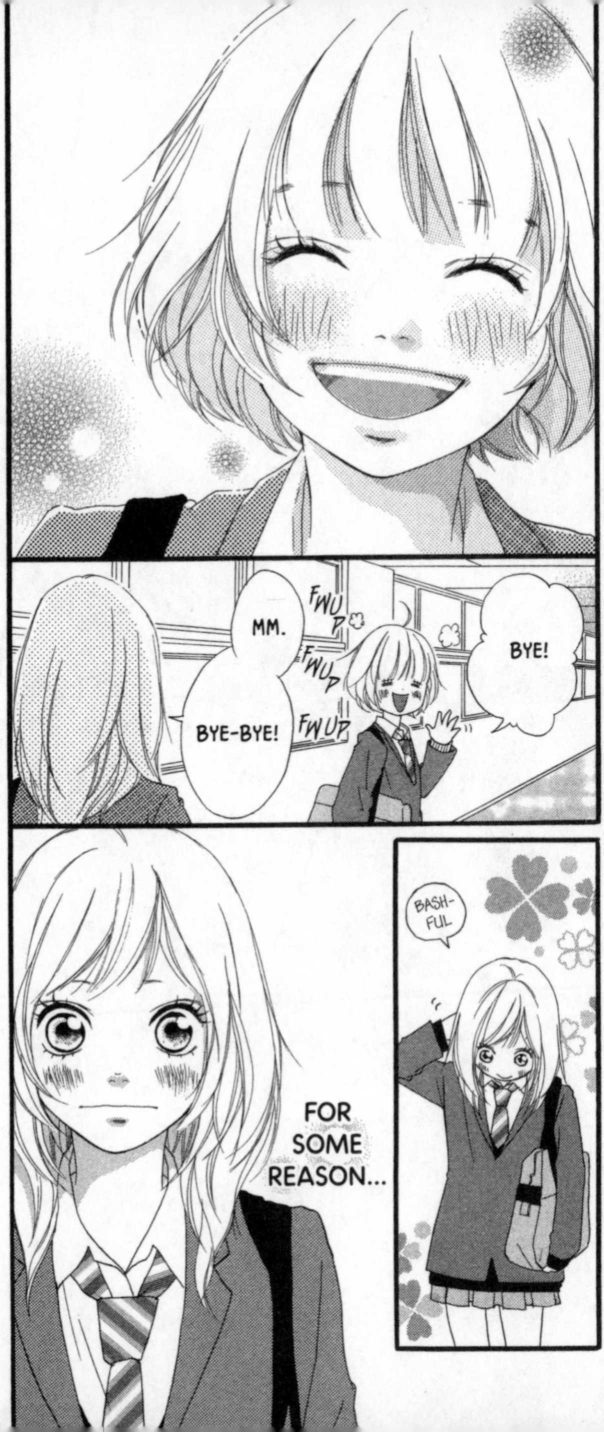
BYE!
FWUP
FWUP
FWUP
MM.
BYE-BYE!
BASH-FUL
FOR SOME REASON...

I solicited requests from the readers for these sidebars in *Ao Haru Ride*! It's my hope that I can make these fun for you.

I also wanted to mention something. In the magazine we often give gifts or prizes to readers. If you don't get selected for a prize—or if you didn't enter before the deadline—please understand that even if you ask our editorial department, they can't give the goods to you. ♡ But it would make me happy if you picked up the magazine from time to time to increase your chances of getting the gifts!!

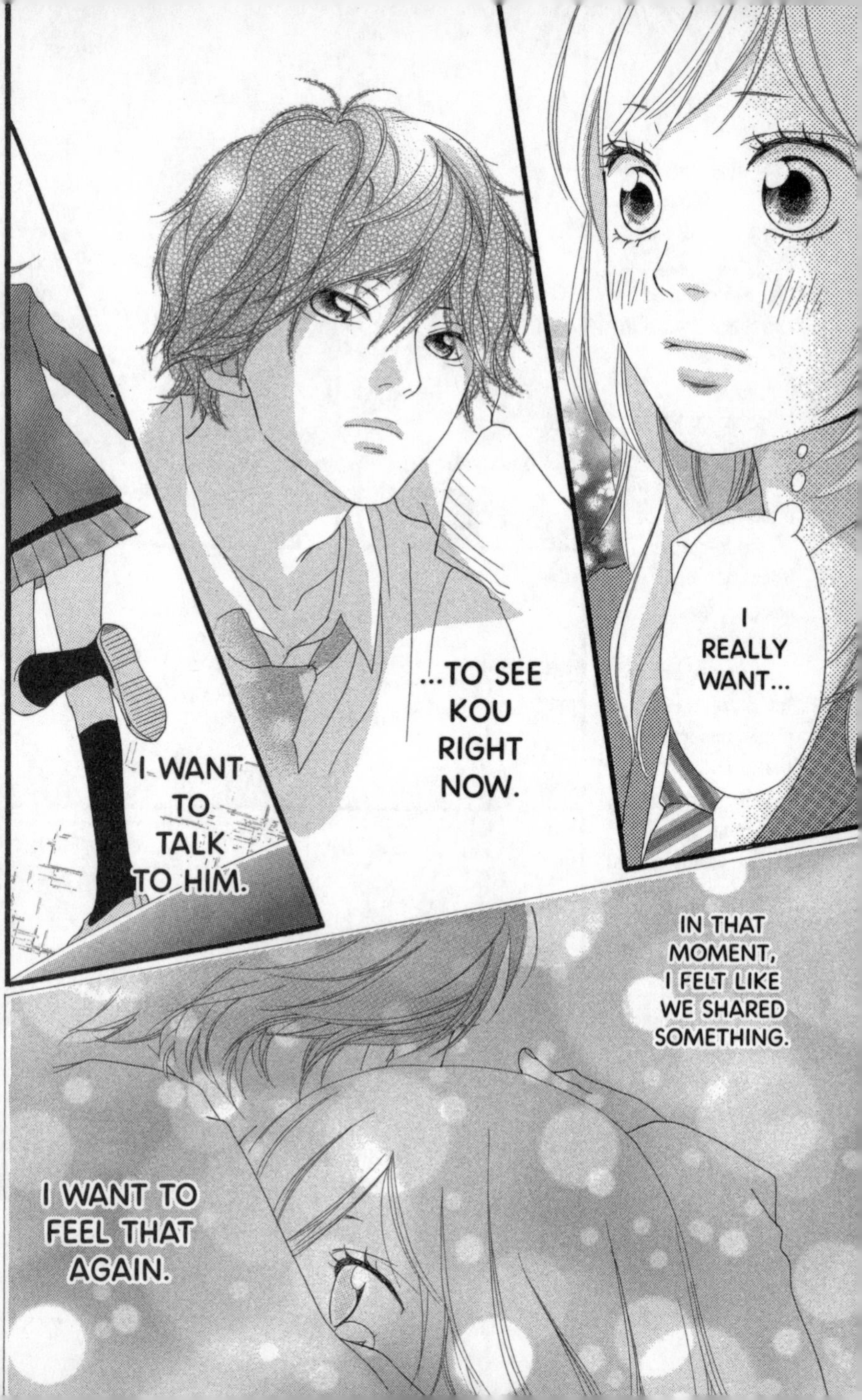
I REALLY WANT...
...TO SEE KOU RIGHT NOW.
I WANT TO TALK TO HIM.
IN THAT MOMENT, I FELT LIKE WE SHARED SOMETHING.
I WANT TO FEEL THAT AGAIN.

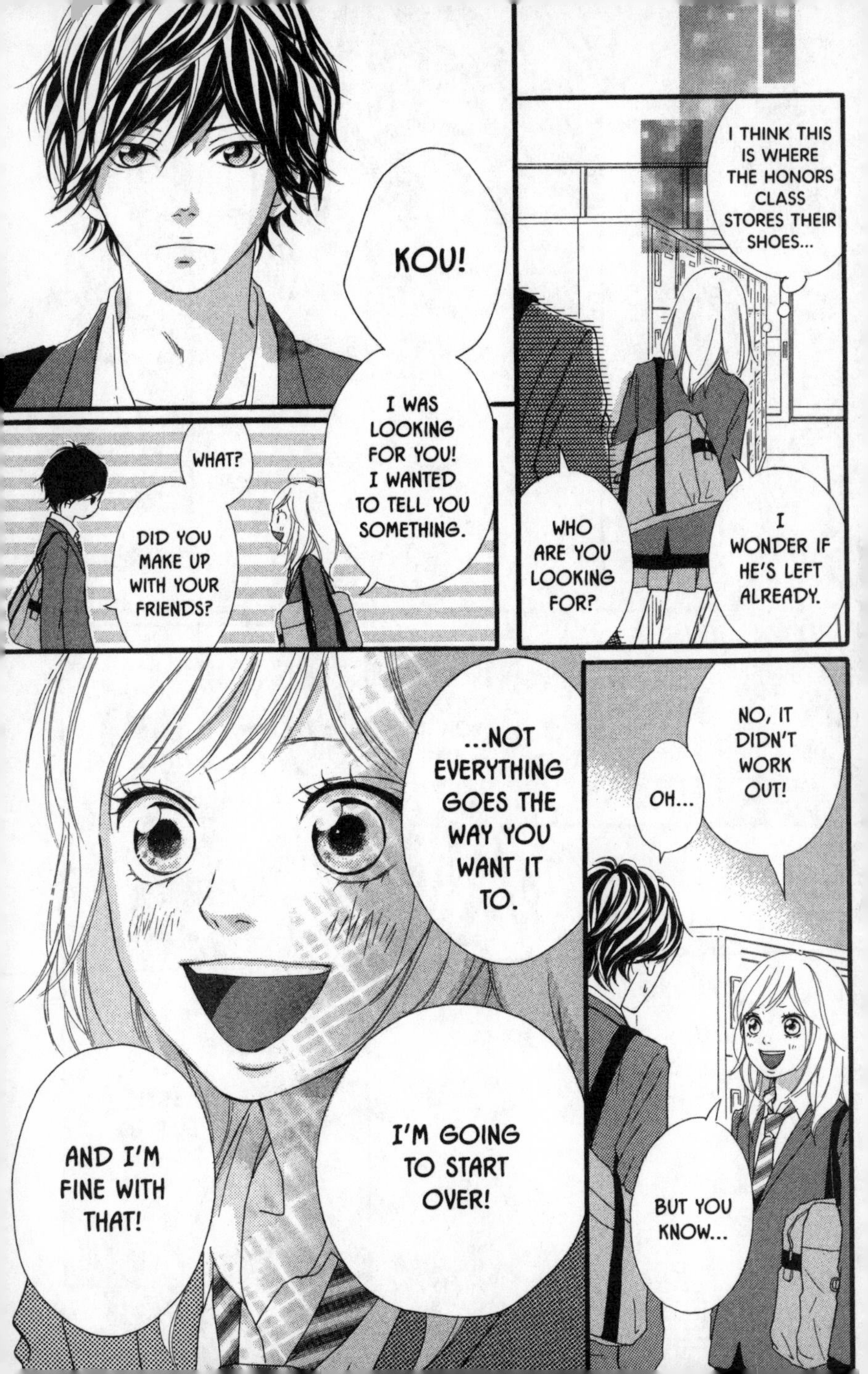
I THINK THIS IS WHERE THE HONORS CLASS STORES THEIR SHOES...
I WONDER IF HE'S LEFT ALREADY.
WHO ARE YOU LOOKING FOR?
KOU!
I WAS LOOKING FOR YOU! I WANTED TO TELL YOU SOMETHING.
WHAT?
DID YOU MAKE UP WITH YOUR FRIENDS?
NO, IT DIDN'T WORK OUT!
OH...
BUT YOU KNOW...
...NOT EVERYTHING GOES THE WAY YOU WANT IT TO.
I'M GOING TO START OVER!
AND I'M FINE WITH THAT!

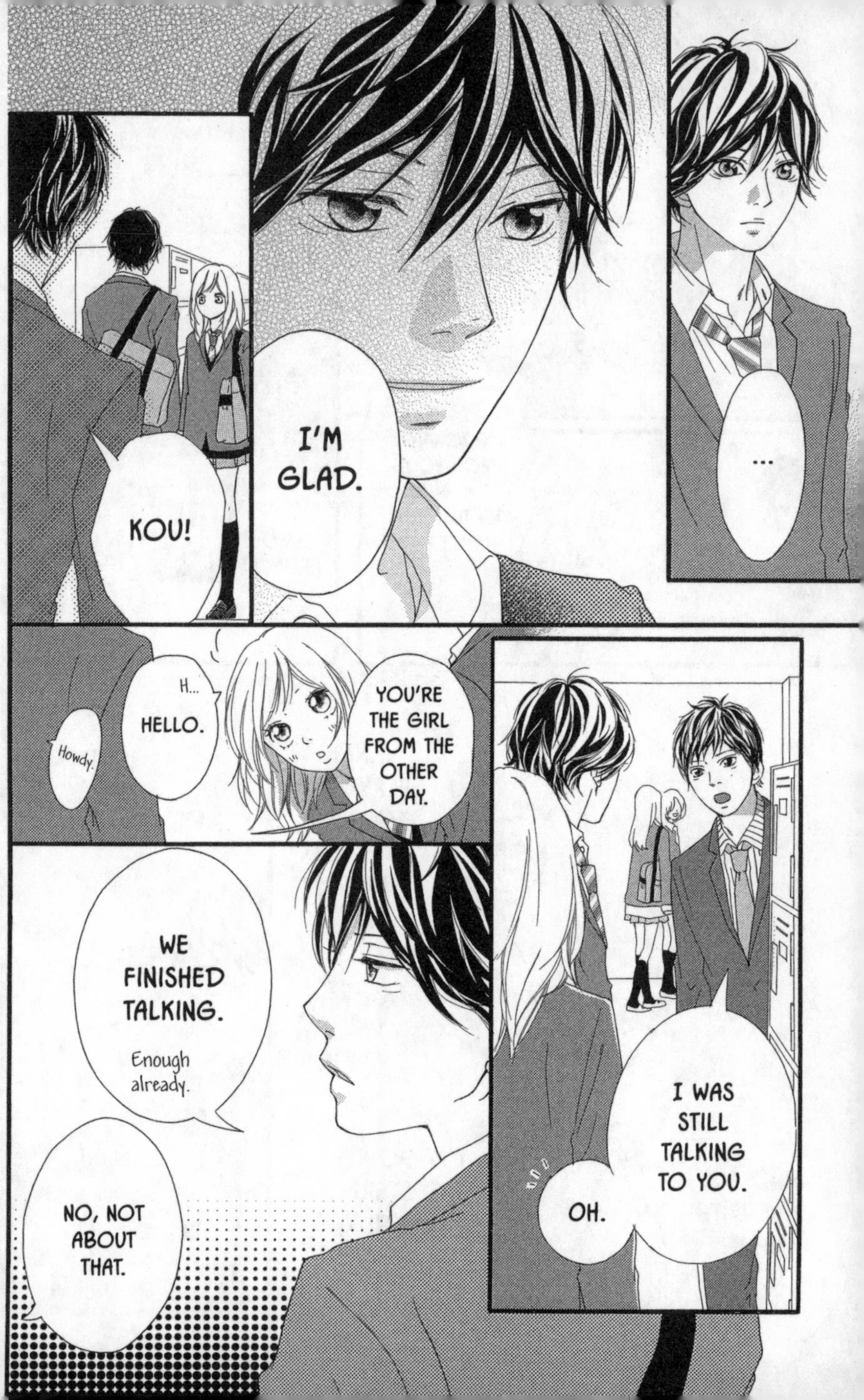
...
I'M GLAD.
KOU!
I WAS STILL TALKING TO YOU.
OH.
YOU'RE THE GIRL FROM THE OTHER DAY.
H... HELLO.
Howdy.
WE FINISHED TALKING.
Enough already.
NO, NOT ABOUT THAT.

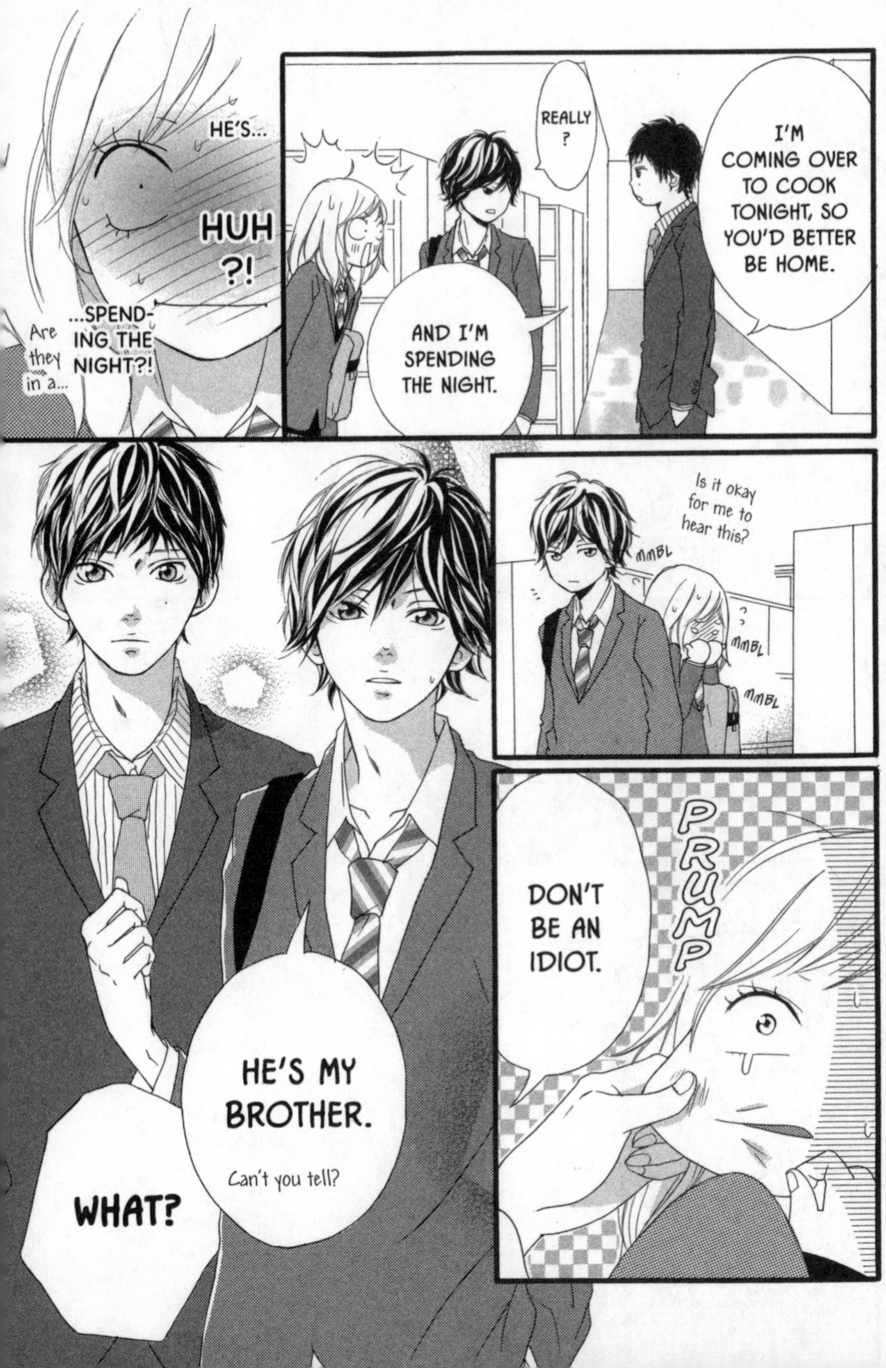
I'M COMING OVER TO COOK TONIGHT, SO YOU'D BETTER BE HOME.
REALLY ?
AND I'M SPENDING THE NIGHT.
HE'S...
HUH ?!
...SPEND-ING THE NIGHT?!
Are they in a...
Is it okay for me to hear this?
MMBL
MMBL
MMBL
PRUMP
DON'T BE AN IDIOT.
HE'S MY BROTHER.
Can't you tell?
WHAT?

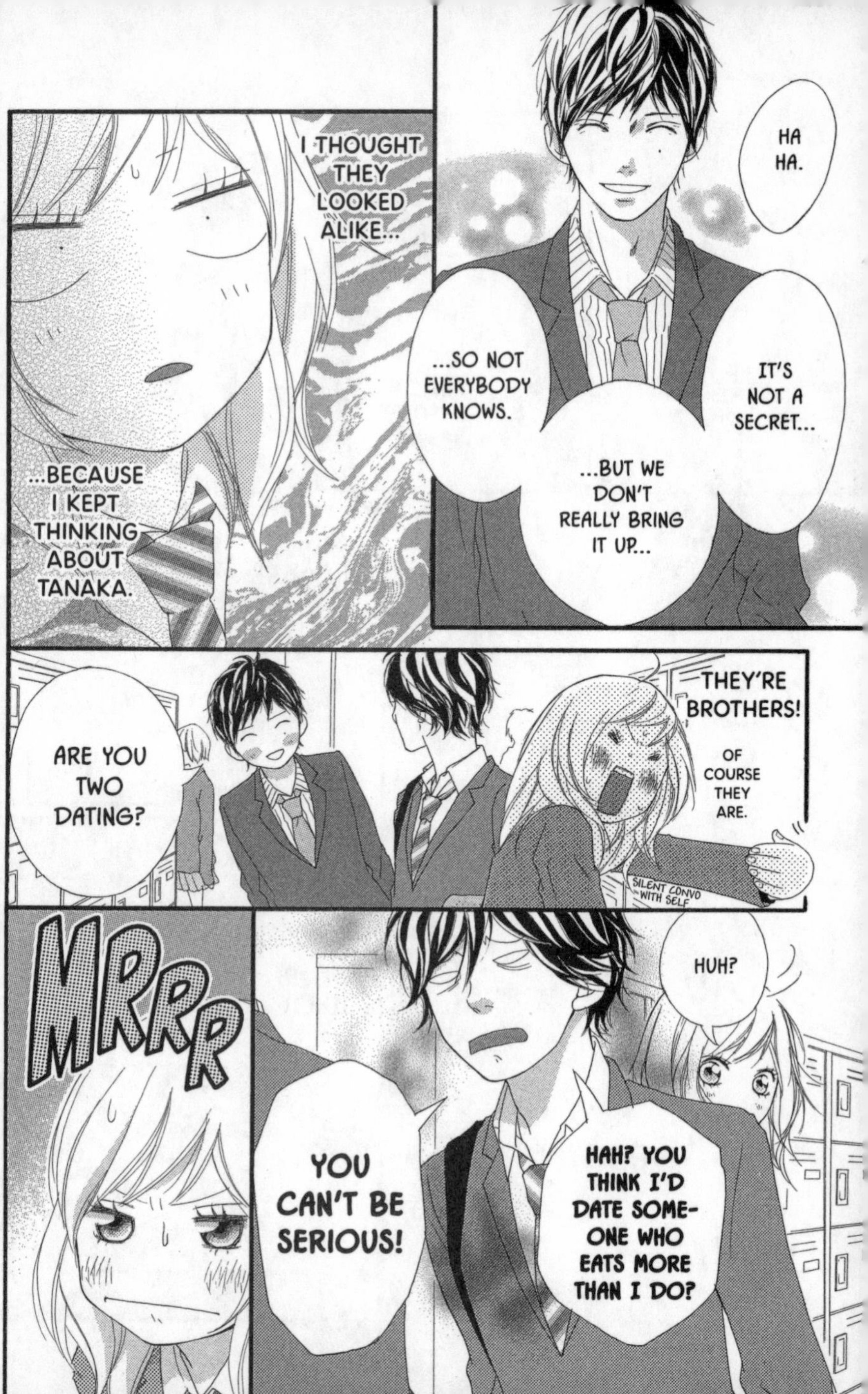
HA HA.
IT'S NOT A SECRET...
...BUT WE DON'T REALLY BRING IT UP...
...SO NOT EVERYBODY KNOWS.
I THOUGHT THEY LOOKED ALIKE...
...BECAUSE I KEPT THINKING ABOUT TANAKA.
THEY'RE BROTHERS!
OF COURSE THEY ARE.
SILENT CONVO WITH SELF
ARE YOU TWO DATING?
HUH?
HAH? YOU THINK I'D DATE SOME-ONE WHO EATS MORE THAN I DO?
YOU CAN'T BE SERIOUS!
MRRR

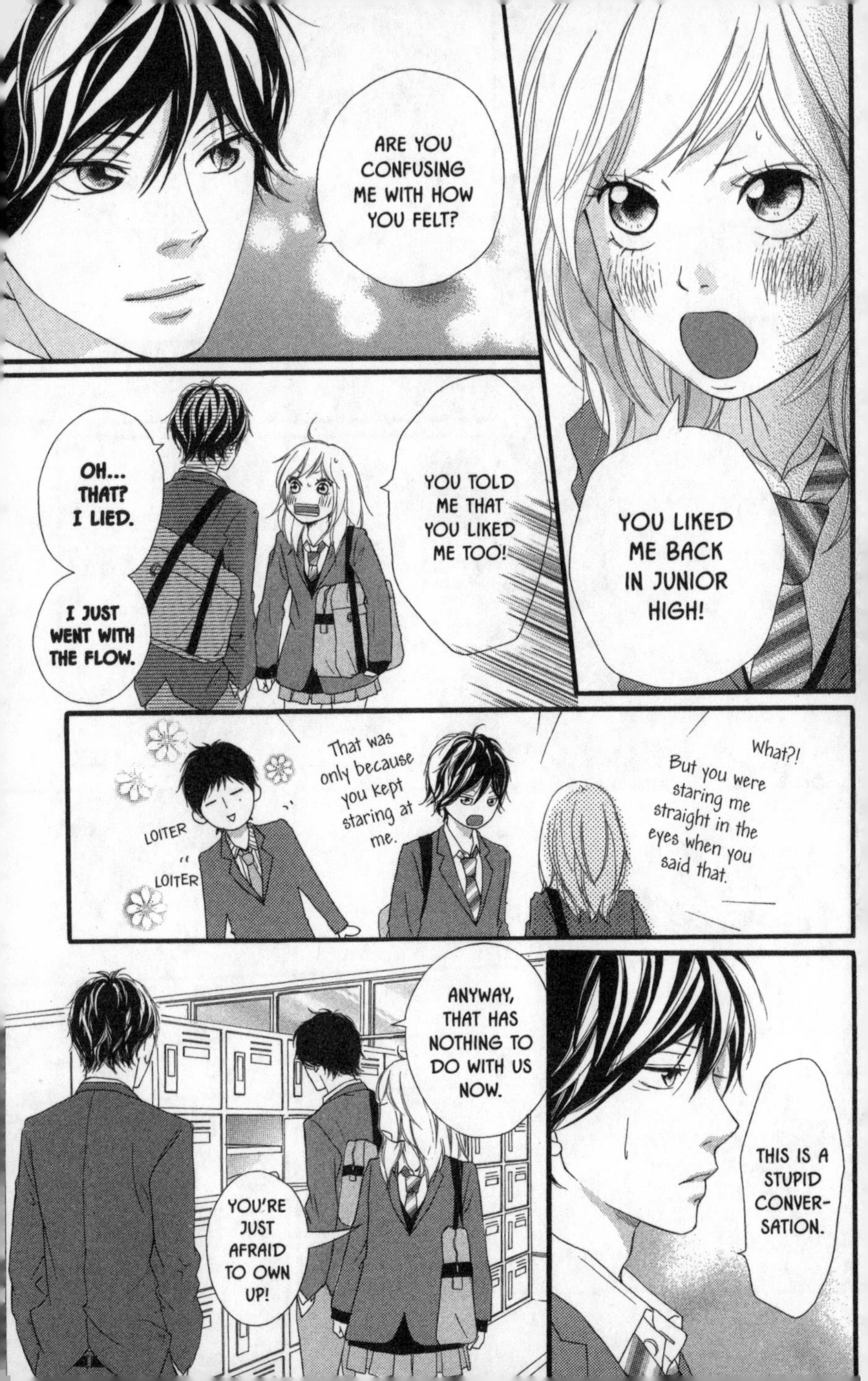
YOU LIKED ME BACK IN JUNIOR HIGH!
ARE YOU CONFUSING ME WITH HOW YOU FELT?
YOU TOLD ME THAT YOU LIKED ME TOO!
OH... THAT? I LIED.
I JUST WENT WITH THE FLOW.
What?!
But you were staring me straight in the eyes when you said that.
That was only because you kept staring at me.
LOITER
LOITER
THIS IS A STUPID CONVERSATION.
ANYWAY, THAT HAS NOTHING TO DO WITH US NOW.
YOU'RE JUST AFRAID TO OWN UP!

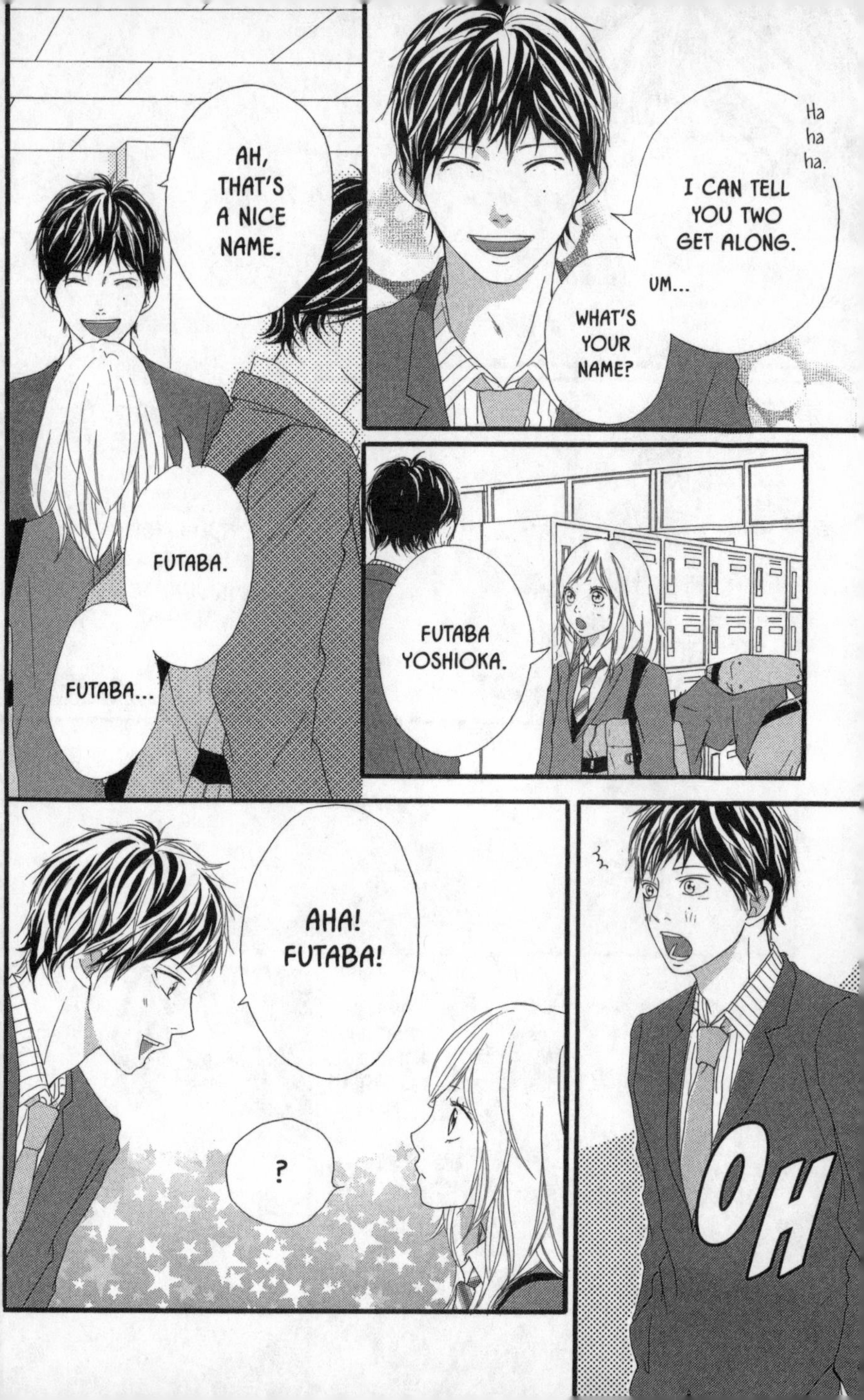
Ha ha ha.
I CAN TELL YOU TWO GET ALONG.
UM...
WHAT'S YOUR NAME?
FUTABA YOSHIOKA.
AH, THAT'S A NICE NAME.
FUTABA.
FUTABA...
OH
AHA! FUTABA!
?

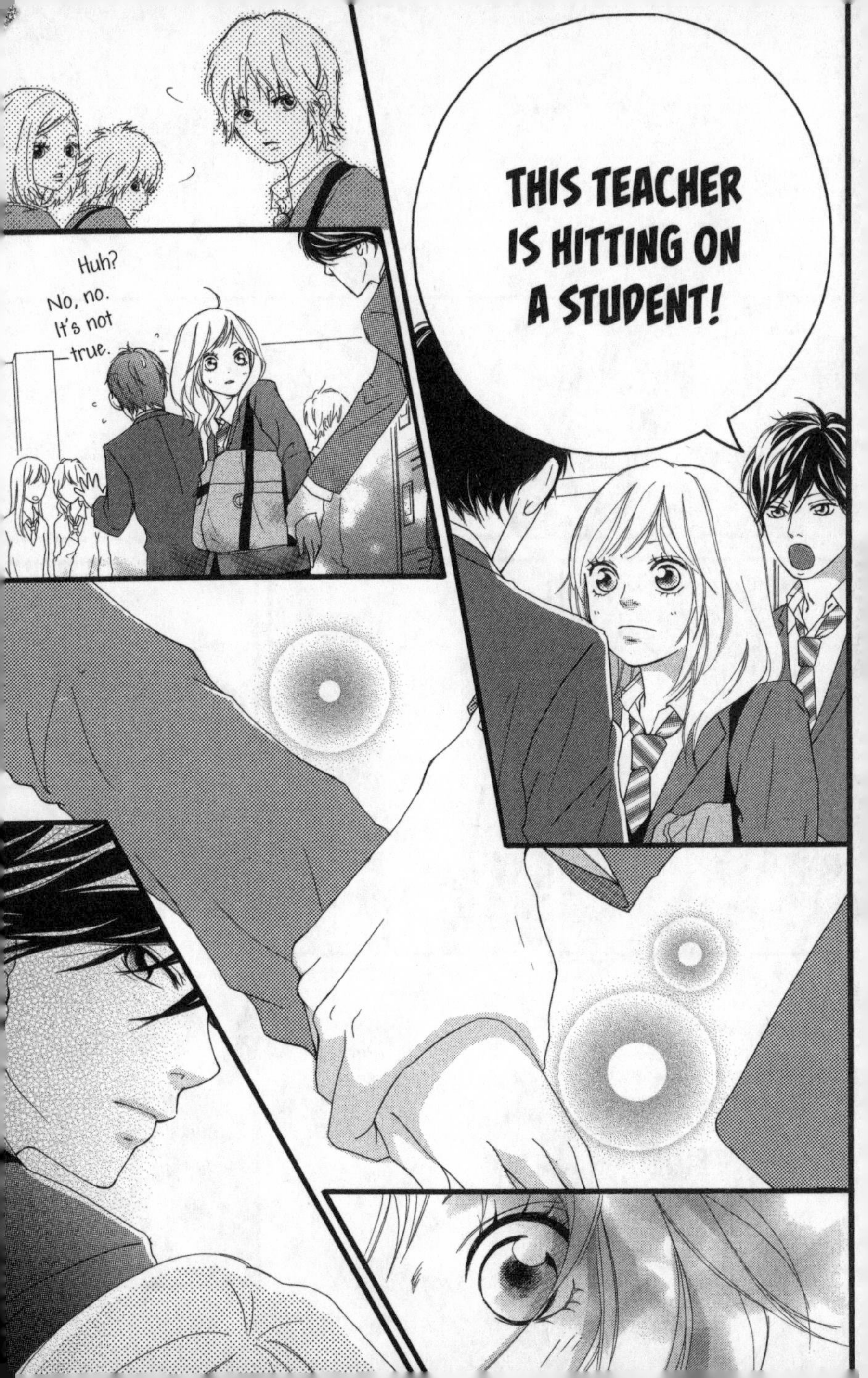
THIS TEACHER IS HITTING ON A STUDENT!
Huh?
No, no. It's not true.

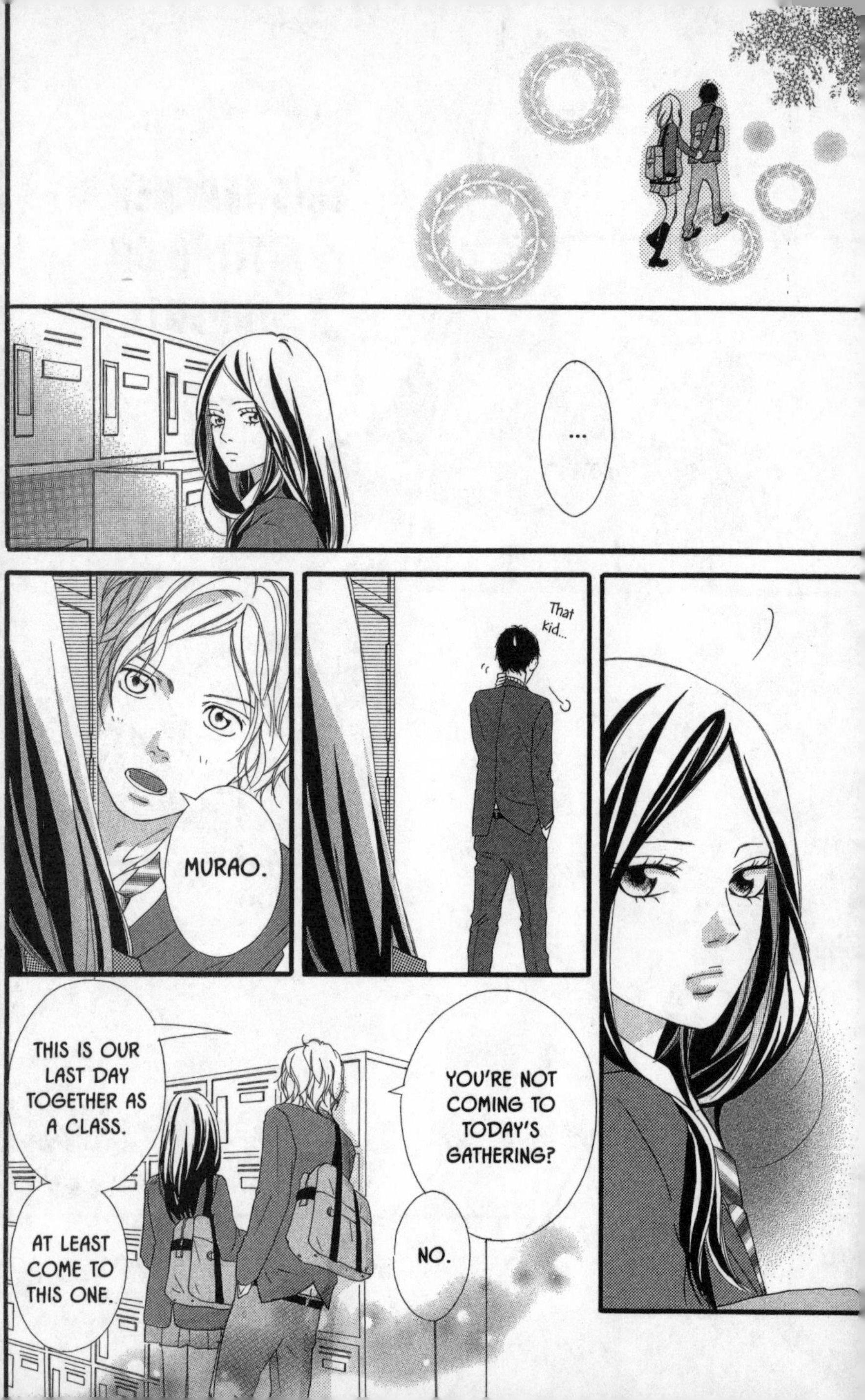
...
That kid...
MURAO.
YOU'RE NOT COMING TO TODAY'S GATHERING?
NO.
THIS IS OUR LAST DAY TOGETHER AS A CLASS.
AT LEAST COME TO THIS ONE.

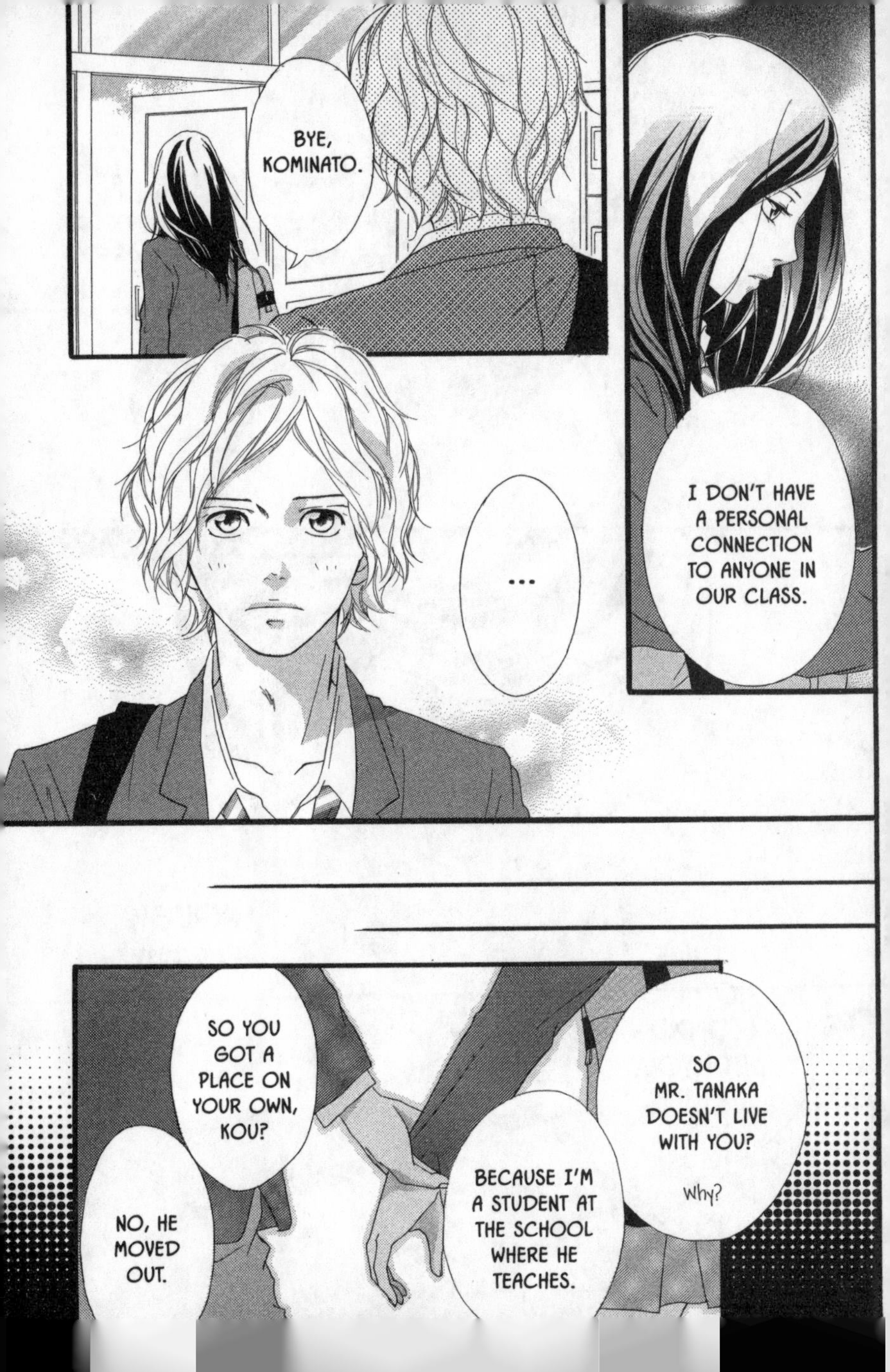
I DON'T HAVE A PERSONAL CONNECTION TO ANYONE IN OUR CLASS.
BYE, KOMINATO.
...
SO YOU GOT A PLACE ON YOUR OWN, KOU?
NO, HE MOVED OUT.
SO MR. TANAKA DOESN'T LIVE WITH YOU?
Why?
BECAUSE I'M A STUDENT AT THE SCHOOL WHERE HE TEACHES.

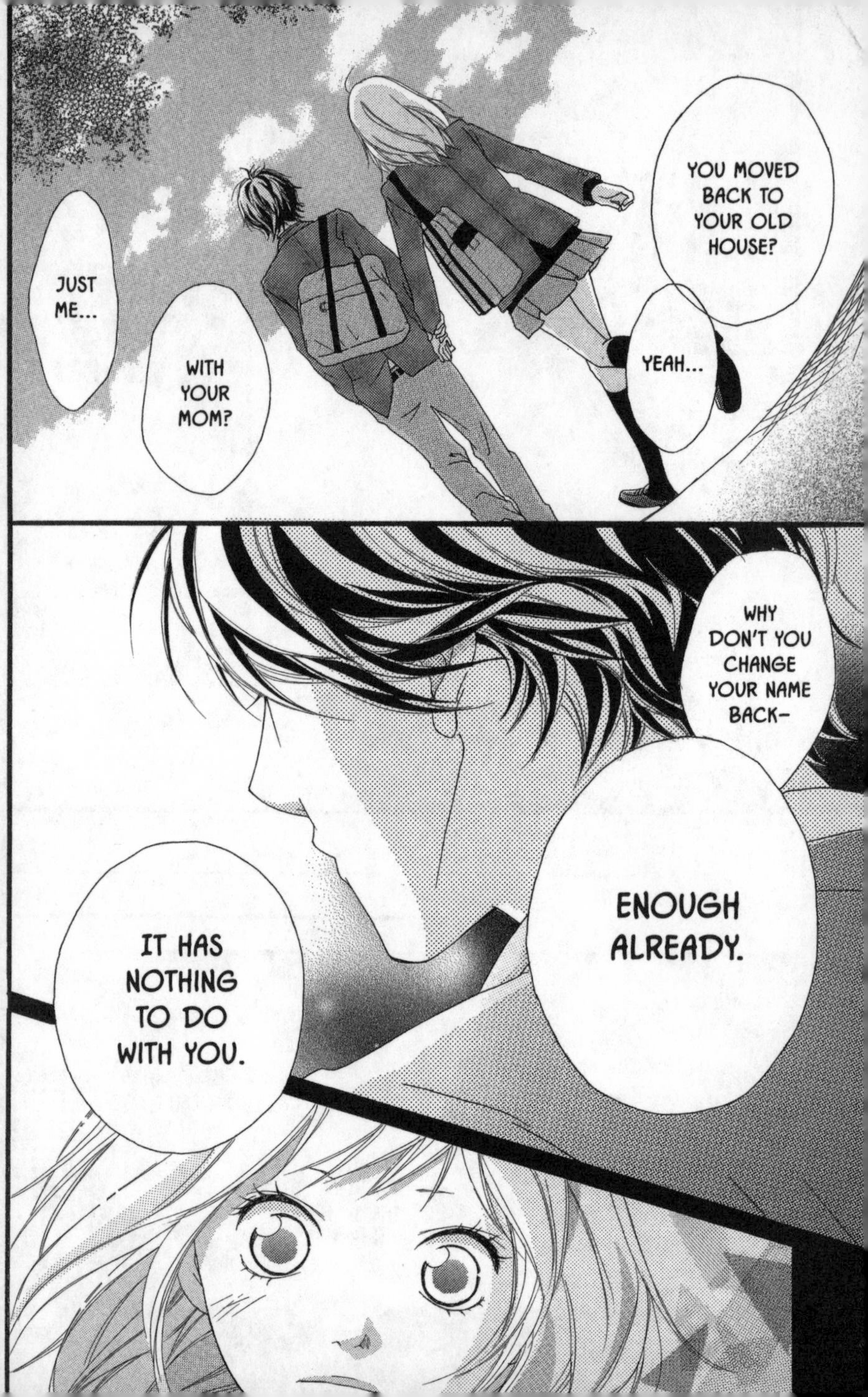
YOU MOVED BACK TO YOUR OLD HOUSE?
YEAH...
WITH YOUR MOM?
JUST ME...
WHY DON'T YOU CHANGE YOUR NAME BACK–
ENOUGH ALREADY.
IT HAS NOTHING TO DO WITH YOU.

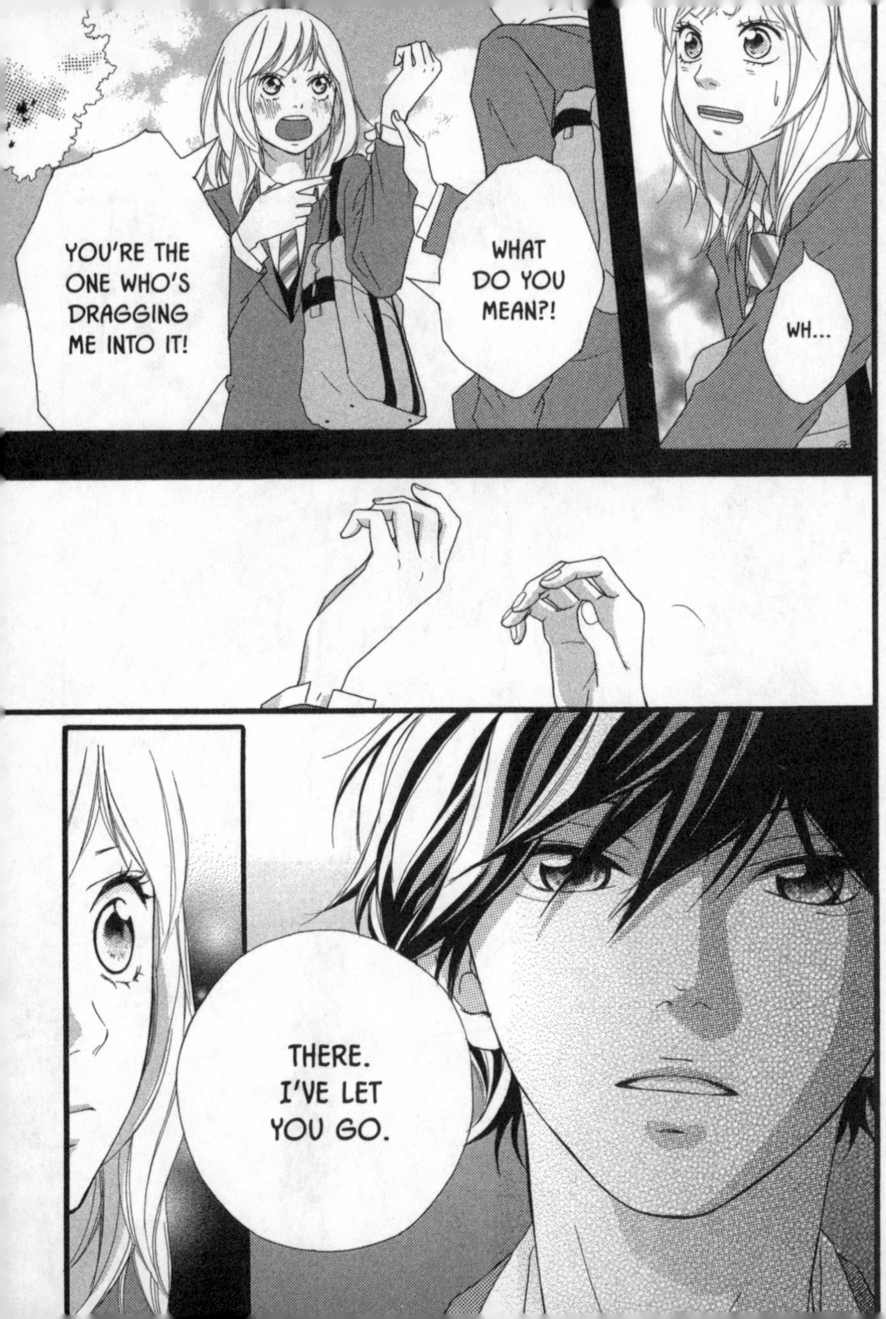
WH...
WHAT DO YOU MEAN?!
YOU'RE THE ONE WHO'S DRAGGING ME INTO IT!
THERE. I'VE LET YOU GO.

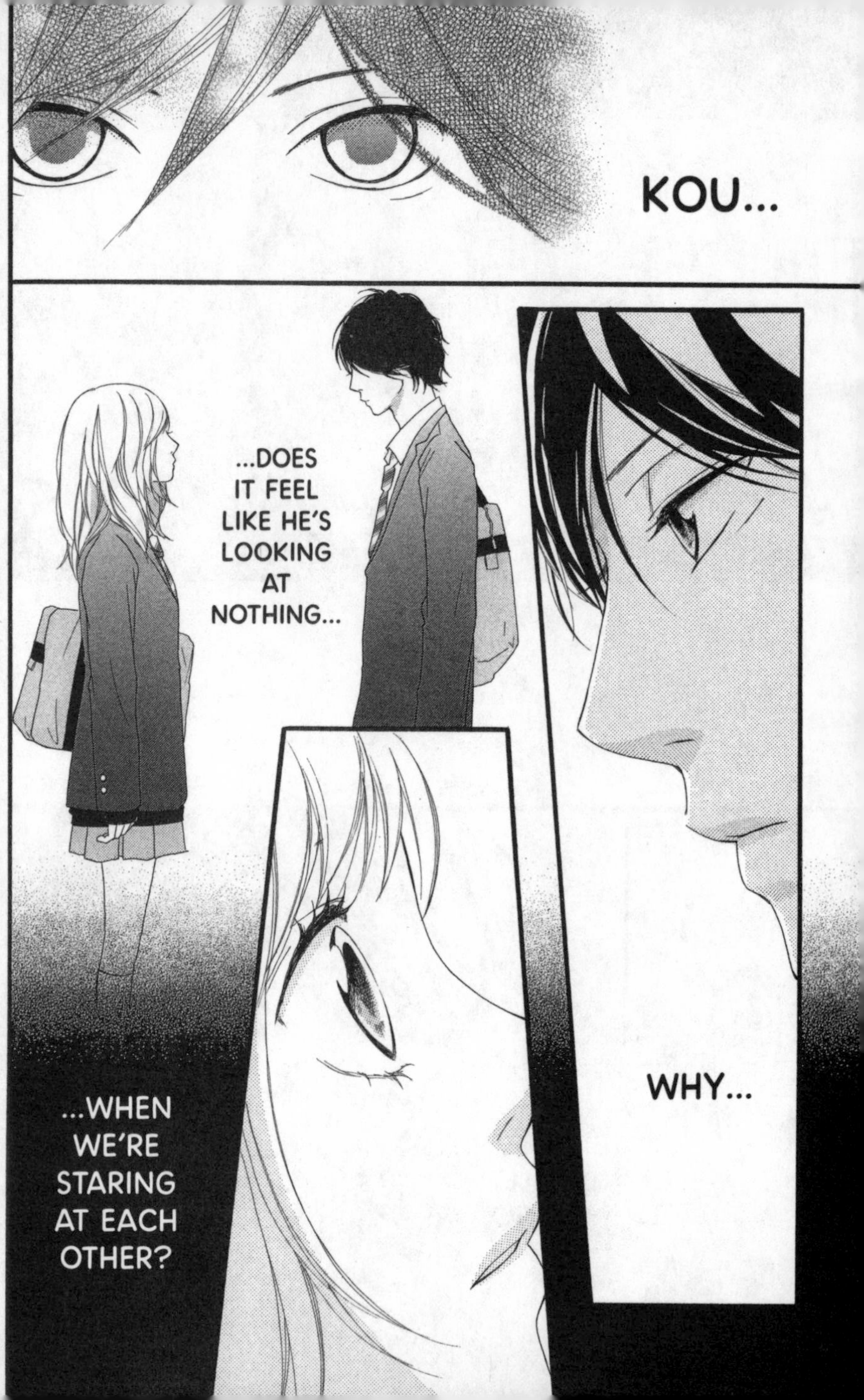
KOU...
WHY...
...DOES IT FEEL LIKE HE'S LOOKING AT NOTHING...
...WHEN WE'RE STARING AT EACH OTHER?

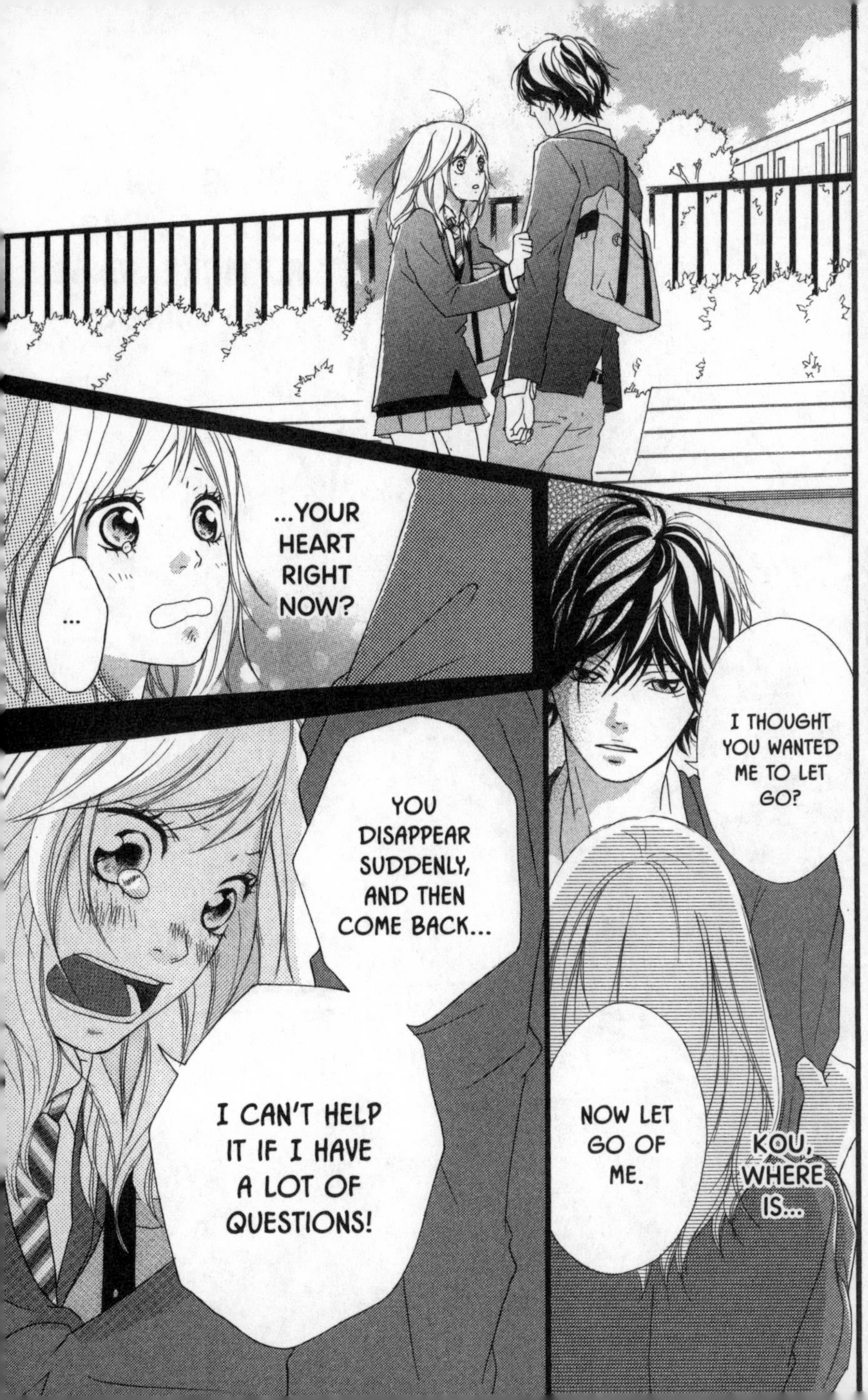
I THOUGHT YOU WANTED ME TO LET GO?
KOU, WHERE IS...
NOW LET GO OF ME.
...YOUR HEART RIGHT NOW?
...
YOU DISAPPEAR SUDDENLY, AND THEN COME BACK...
I CAN'T HELP IT IF I HAVE A LOT OF QUESTIONS!

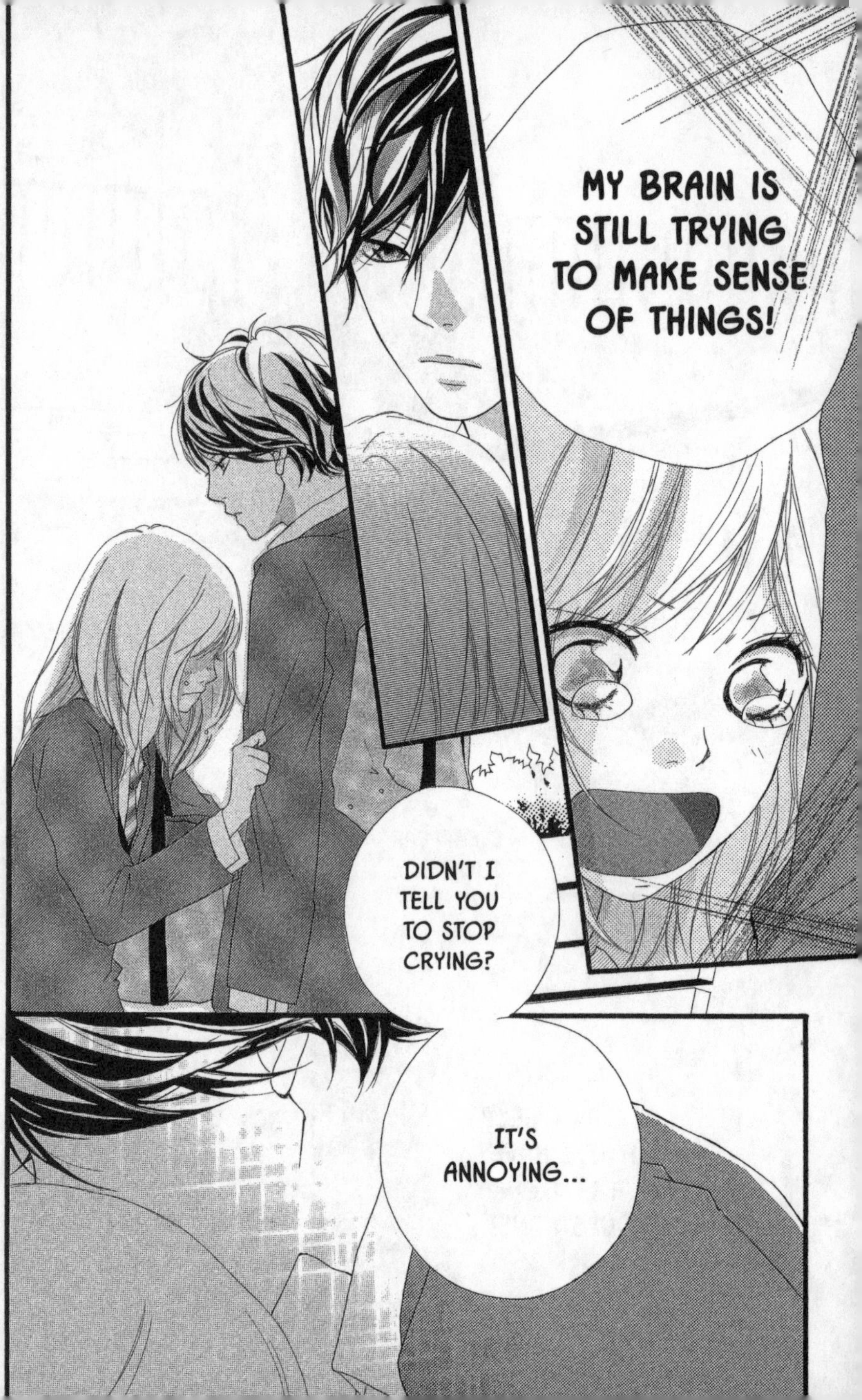
MY BRAIN IS STILL TRYING TO MAKE SENSE OF THINGS!
DIDN'T I TELL YOU TO STOP CRYING?
IT'S ANNOYING...

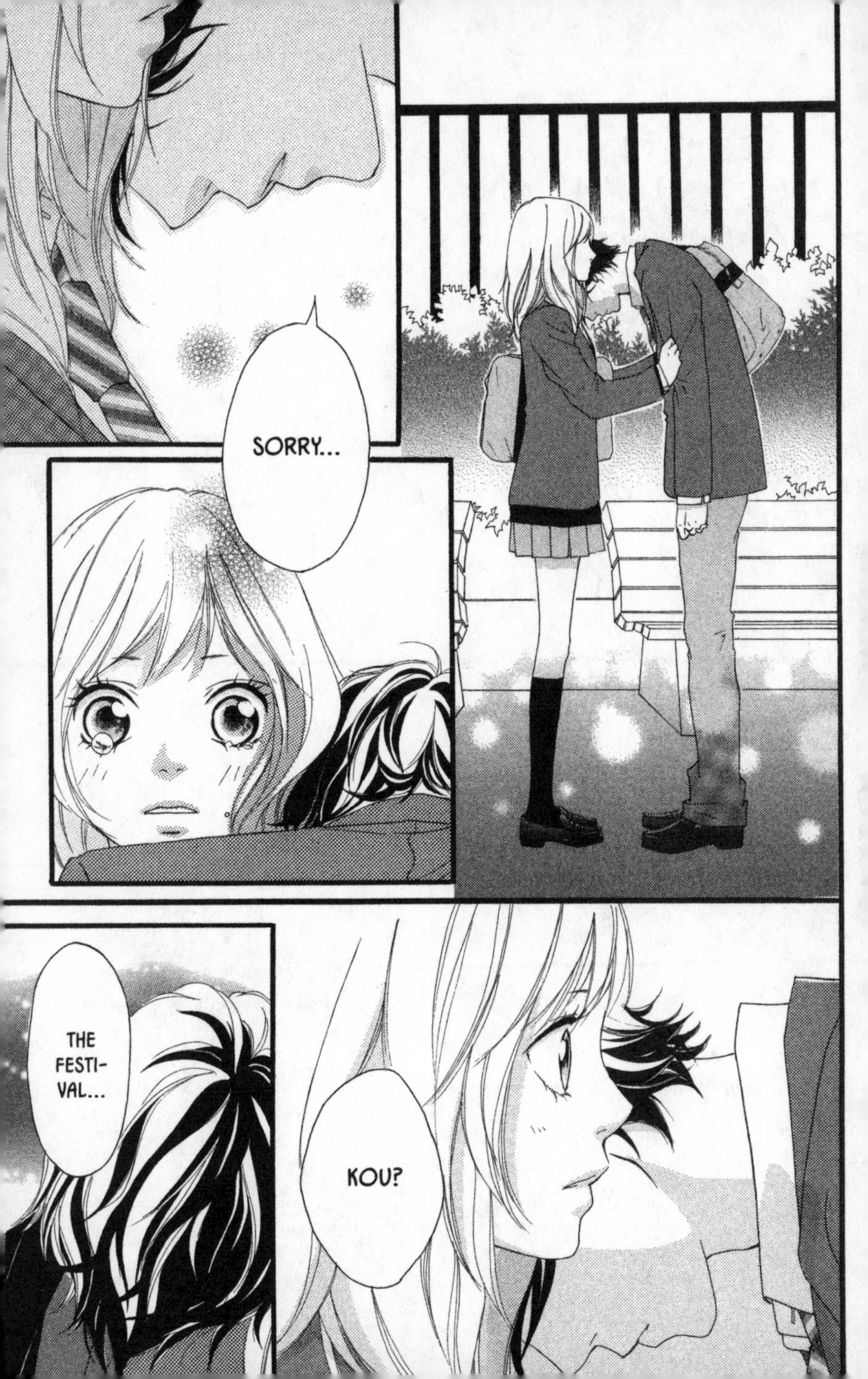
SORRY...
KOU?
THE FESTI-VAL...

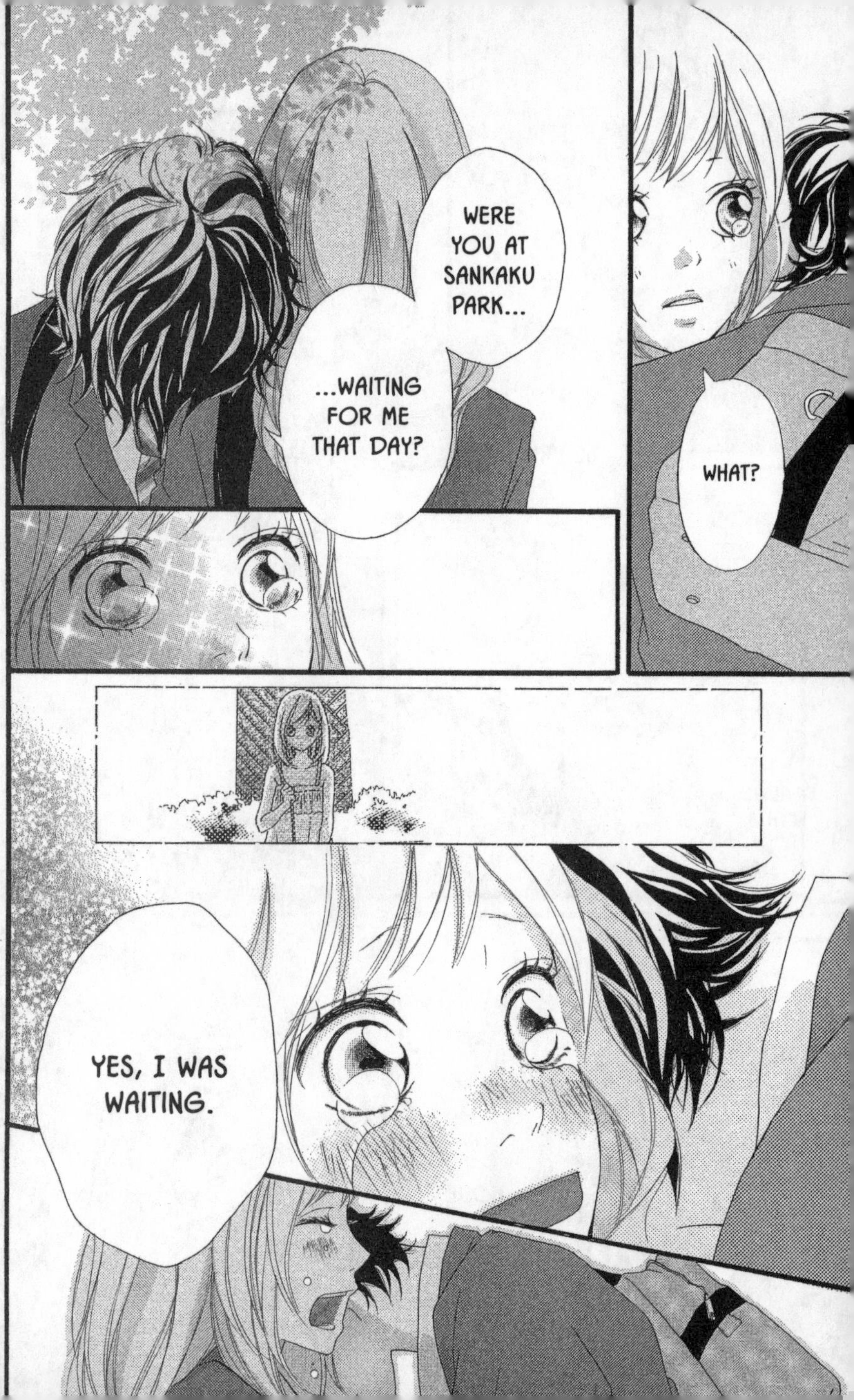
WHAT?
WERE YOU AT SANKAKU PARK...
...WAITING FOR ME THAT DAY?
YES, I WAS WAITING.

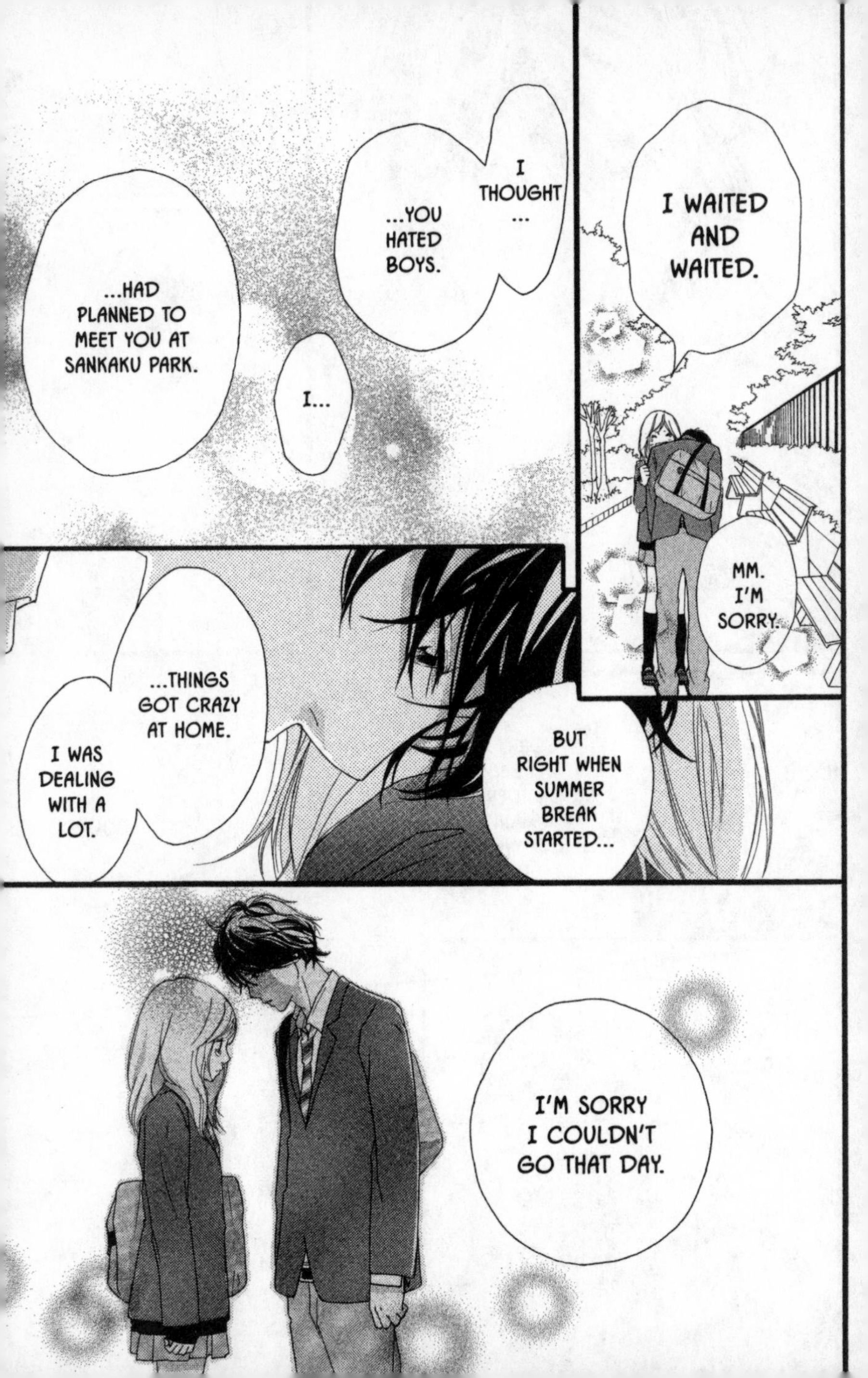
I WAITED AND WAITED.
MM. I'M SORRY.
I THOUGHT...
...YOU HATED BOYS.
I...
...HAD PLANNED TO MEET YOU AT SANKAKU PARK.
BUT RIGHT WHEN SUMMER BREAK STARTED...
...THINGS GOT CRAZY AT HOME.
I WAS DEALING WITH A LOT.
I'M SORRY I COULDN'T GO THAT DAY.

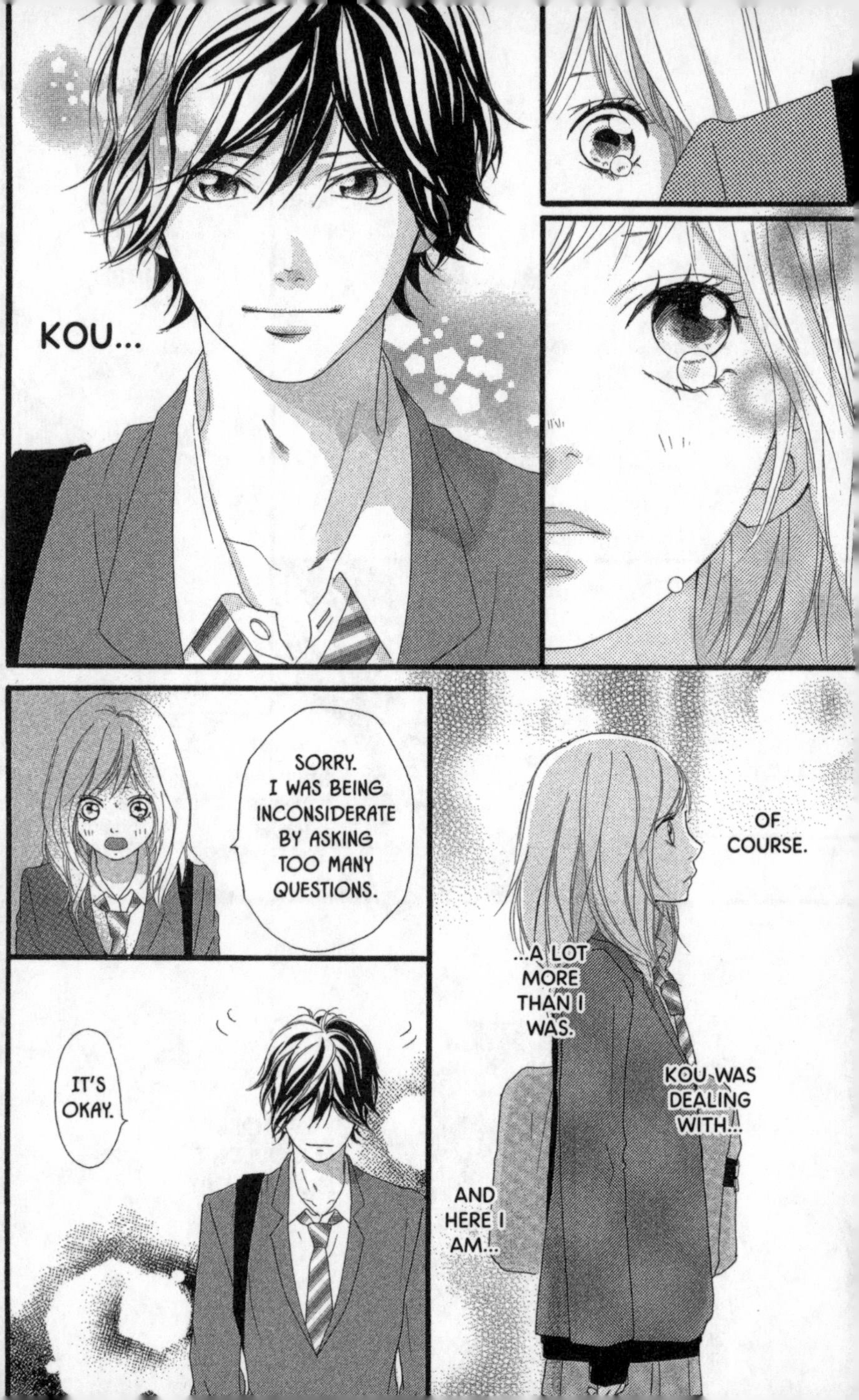
KOU...
OF COURSE.
KOU WAS DEALING WITH...
...A LOT MORE THAN I WAS.
AND HERE I AM...
SORRY. I WAS BEING INCONSIDERATE BY ASKING TOO MANY QUESTIONS.
IT'S OKAY.

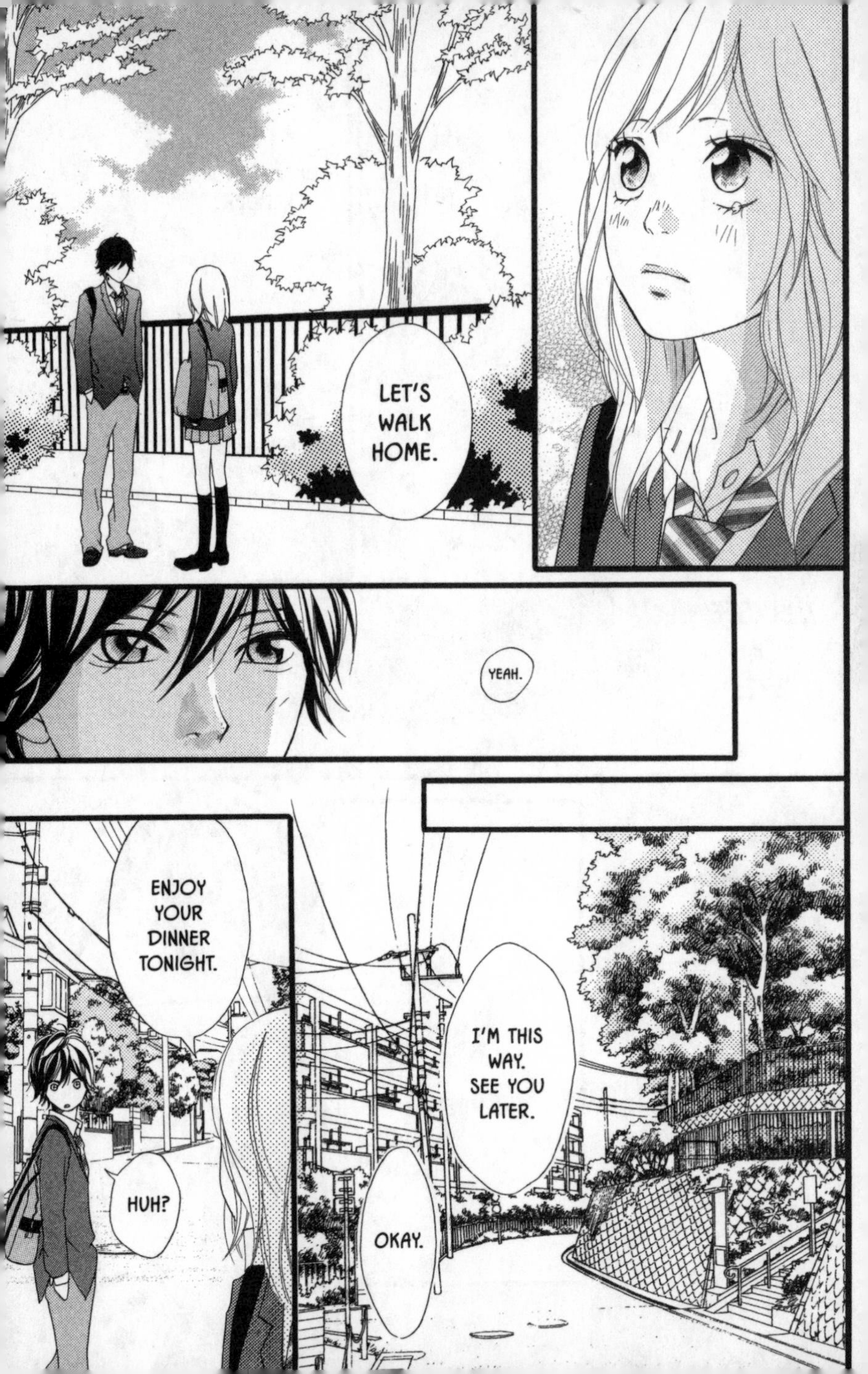
LET'S WALK HOME.
YEAH.
I'M THIS WAY. SEE YOU LATER.
OKAY.
ENJOY YOUR DINNER TONIGHT.
HUH?

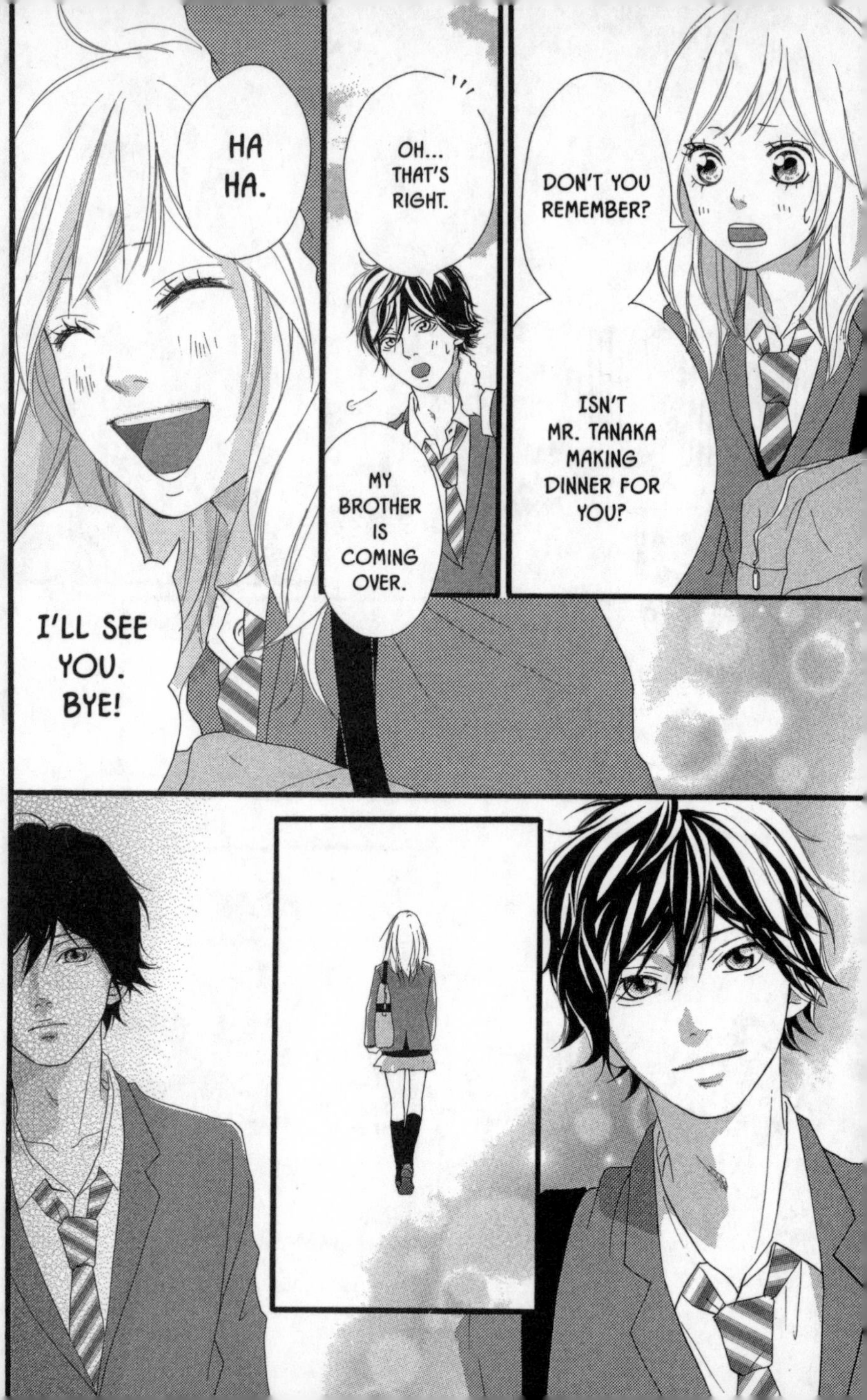
DON'T YOU REMEMBER?
ISN'T MR. TANAKA MAKING DINNER FOR YOU?
OH... THAT'S RIGHT.
MY BROTHER IS COMING OVER.
HA HA.
I'LL SEE YOU. BYE!

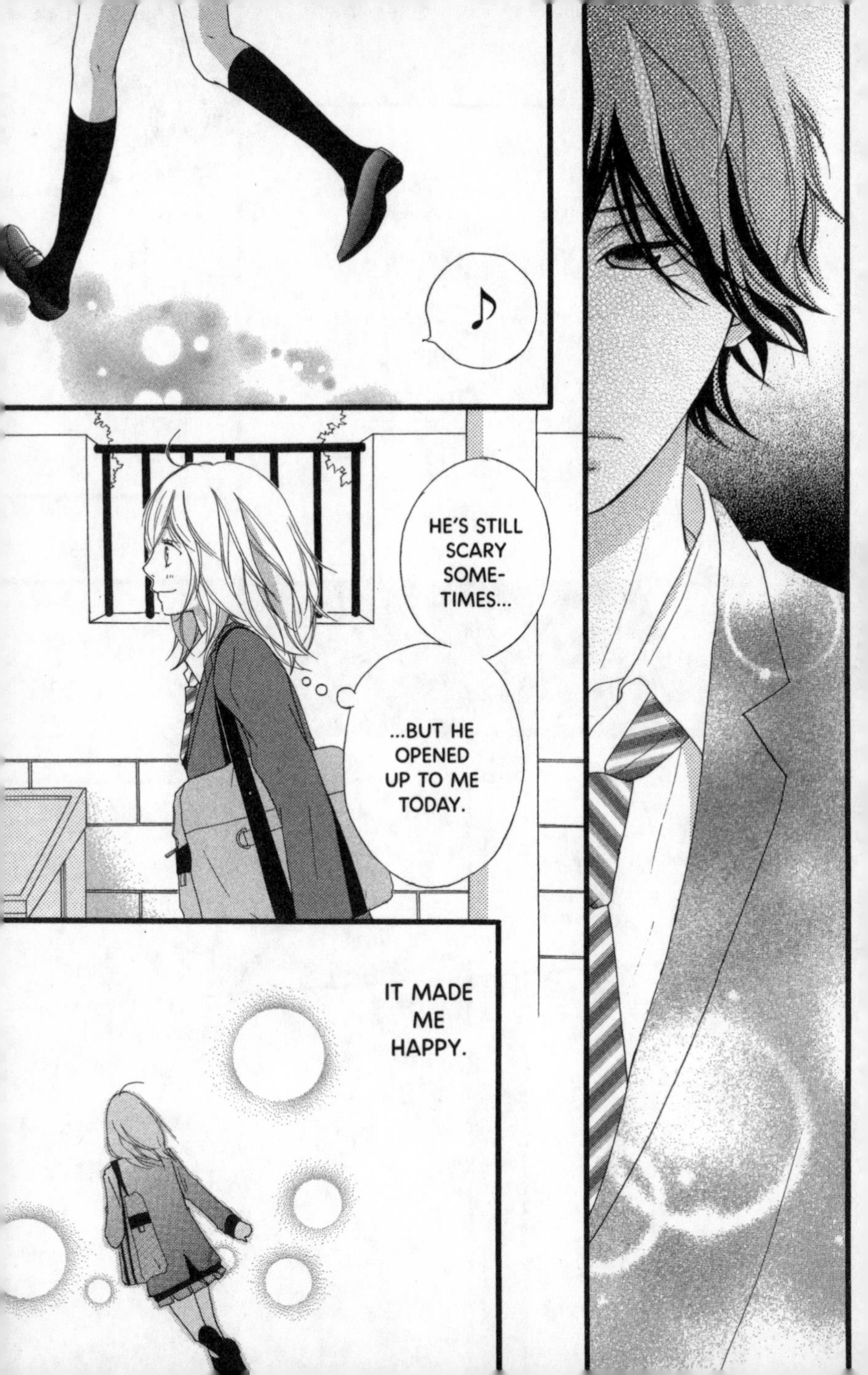
♪
HE'S STILL SCARY SOME-TIMES...
...BUT HE OPENED UP TO ME TODAY.
IT MADE ME HAPPY.

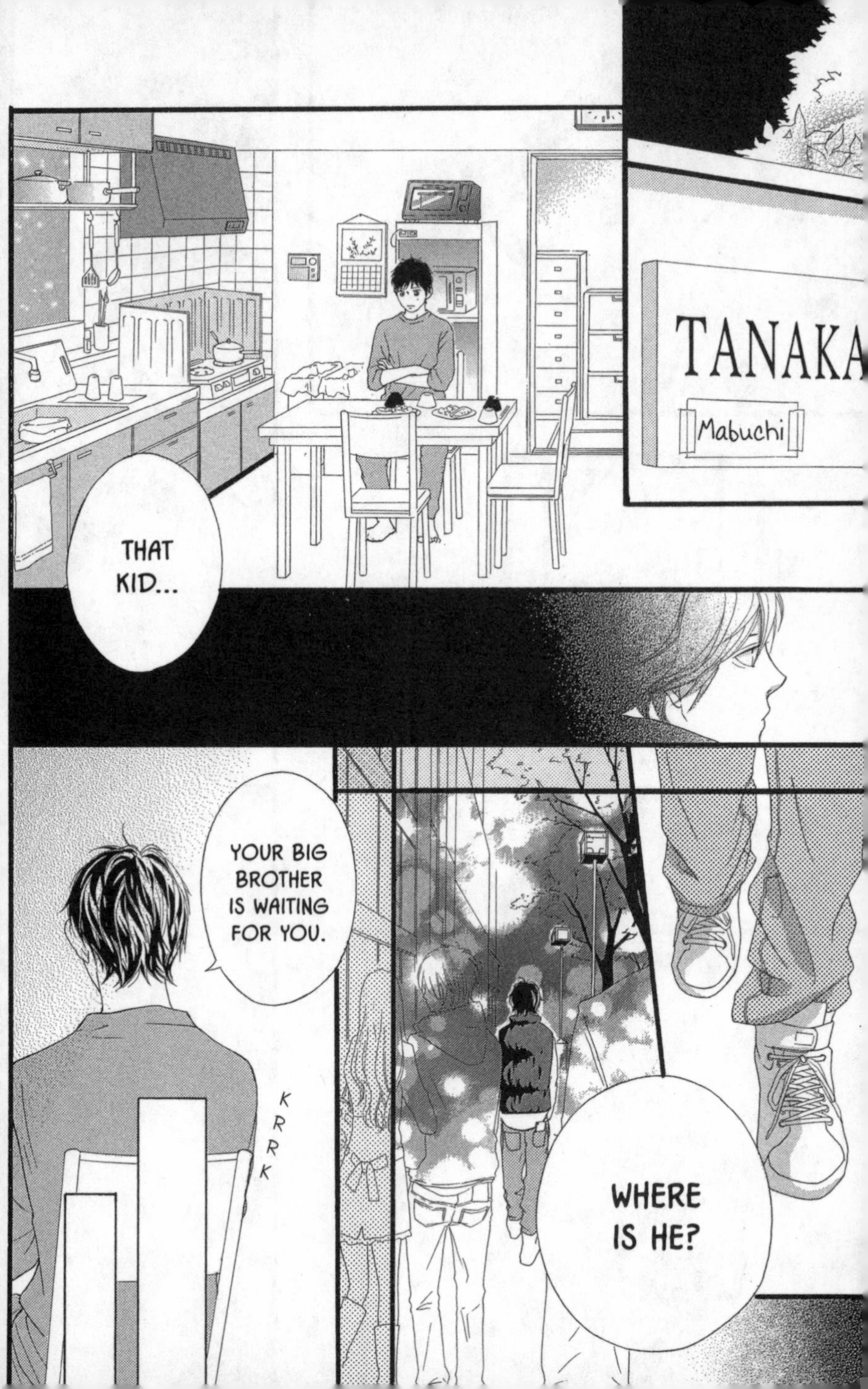
TANAKA
Mabuchi
THAT KID...
WHERE IS HE?
YOUR BIG BROTHER IS WAITING FOR YOU.
KRRK

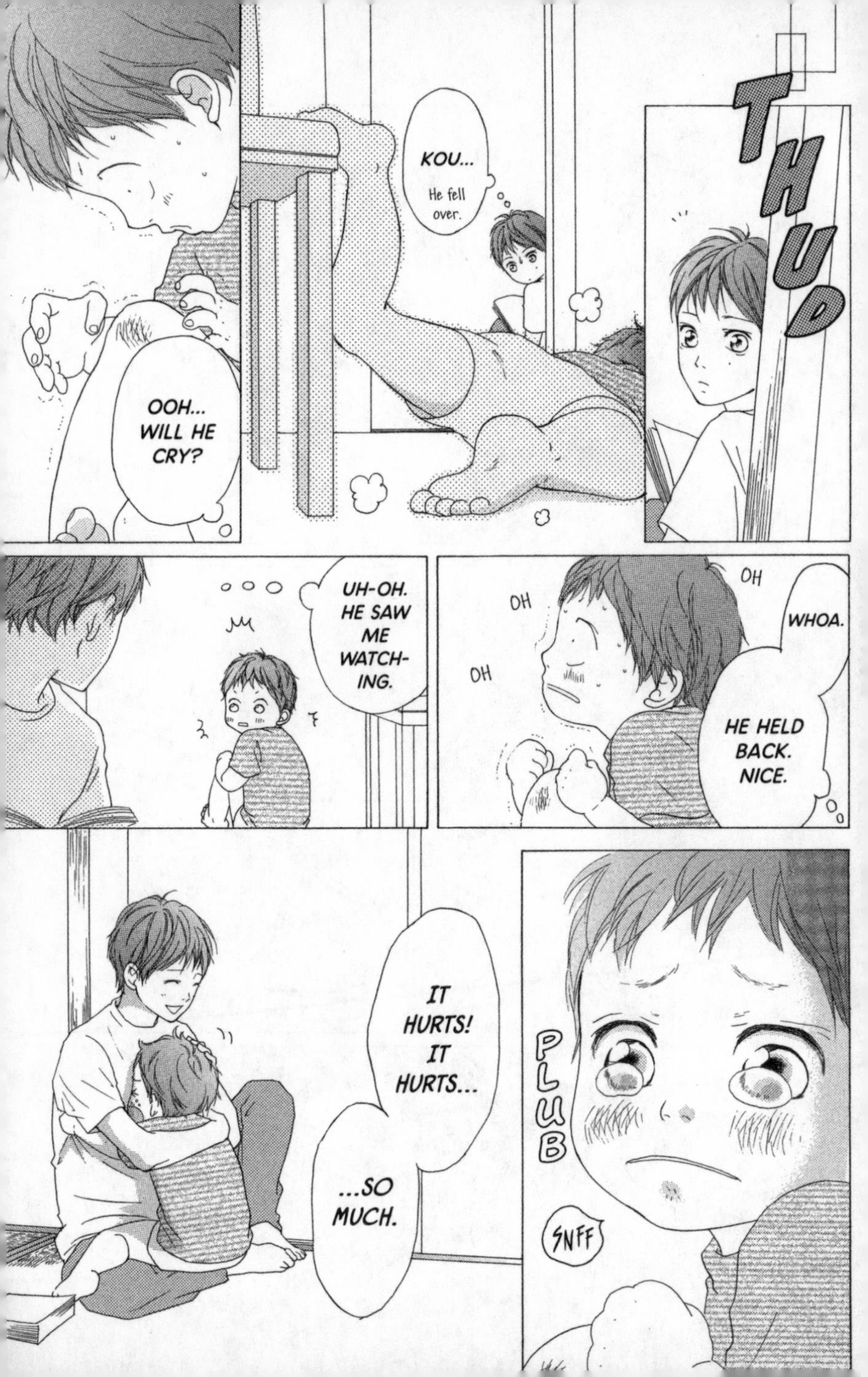
THUD
KOU...
He fell over.
OOH... WILL HE CRY?
OH
WHOA.
OH
OH
HE HELD BACK. NICE.
UH-OH. HE SAW ME WATCHING.
PLUB
SNFF
IT HURTS! IT HURTS...
...SO MUCH.

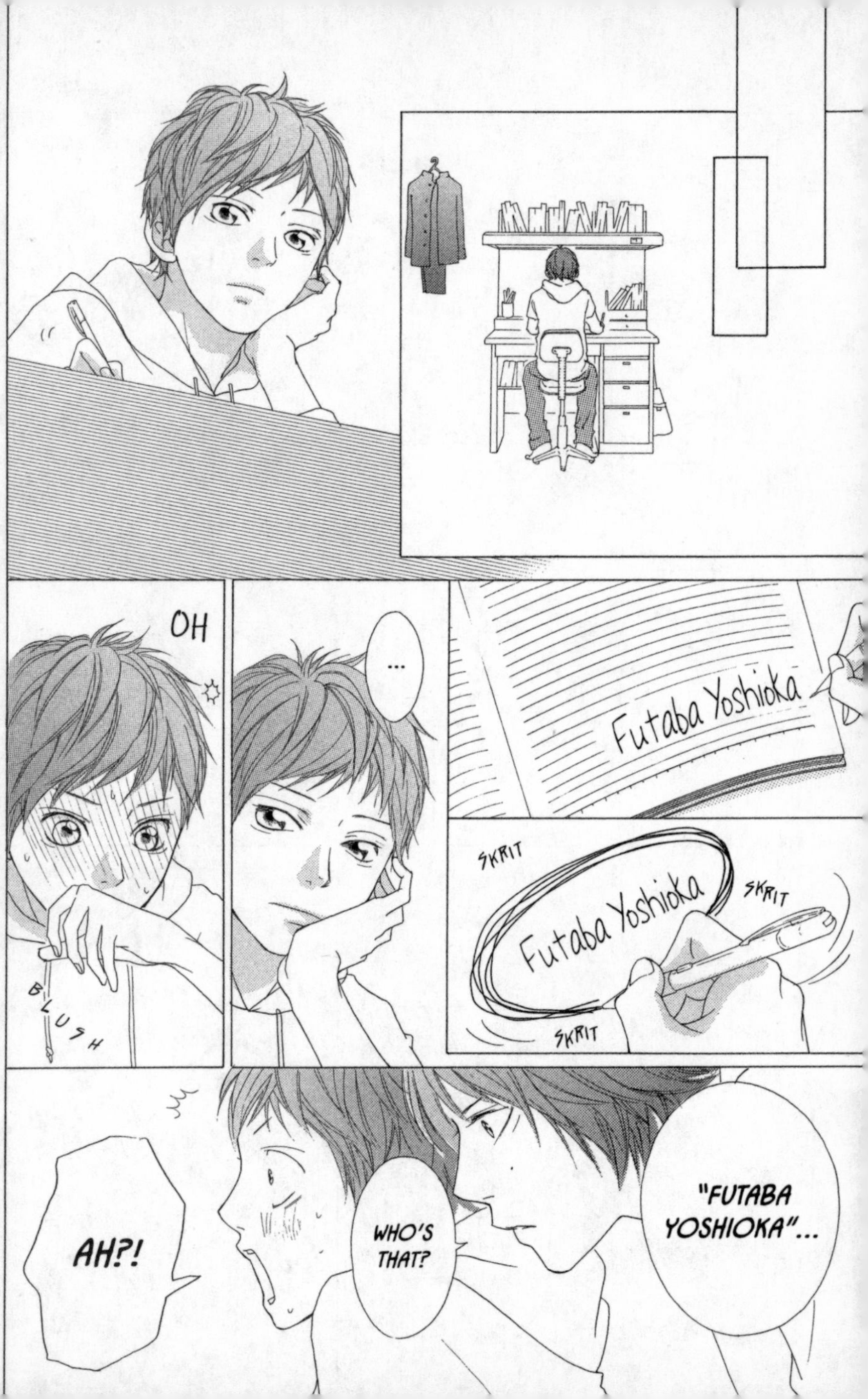
Futaba Yoshioka
SKRIT
Futaba Yoshioka
SKRIT
SKRIT
...
OH
BLUSH
"FUTABA YOSHIOKA"...
WHO'S THAT?
AH?!

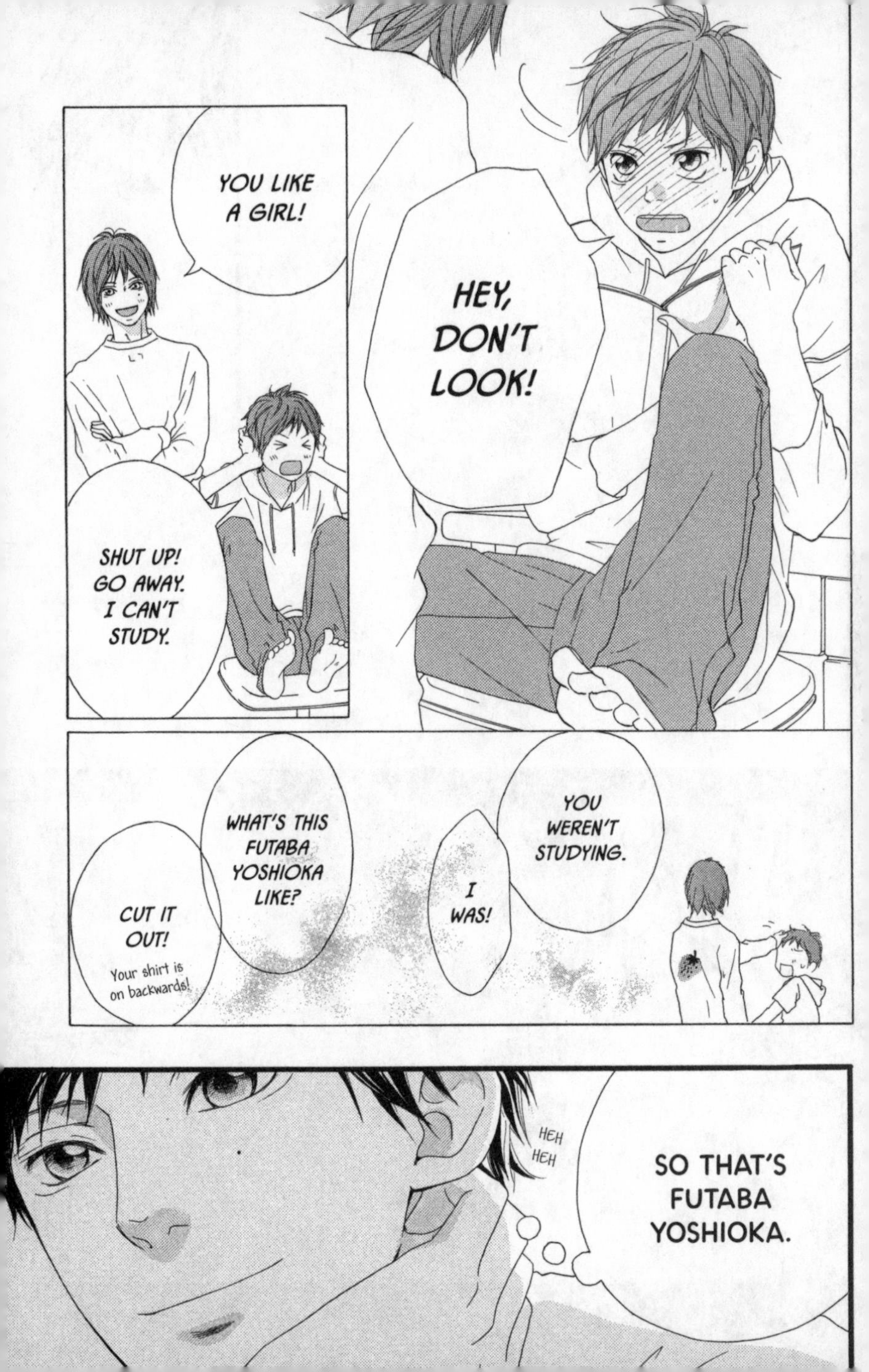

HEY, DON'T LOOK!
YOU LIKE A GIRL!
SHUT UP! GO AWAY. I CAN'T STUDY.
YOU WEREN'T STUDYING.
I WAS!
WHAT'S THIS FUTABA YOSHIOKA LIKE?
CUT IT OUT!
Your shirt is on backwards!
HEH HEH
SO THAT'S FUTABA YOSHIOKA.

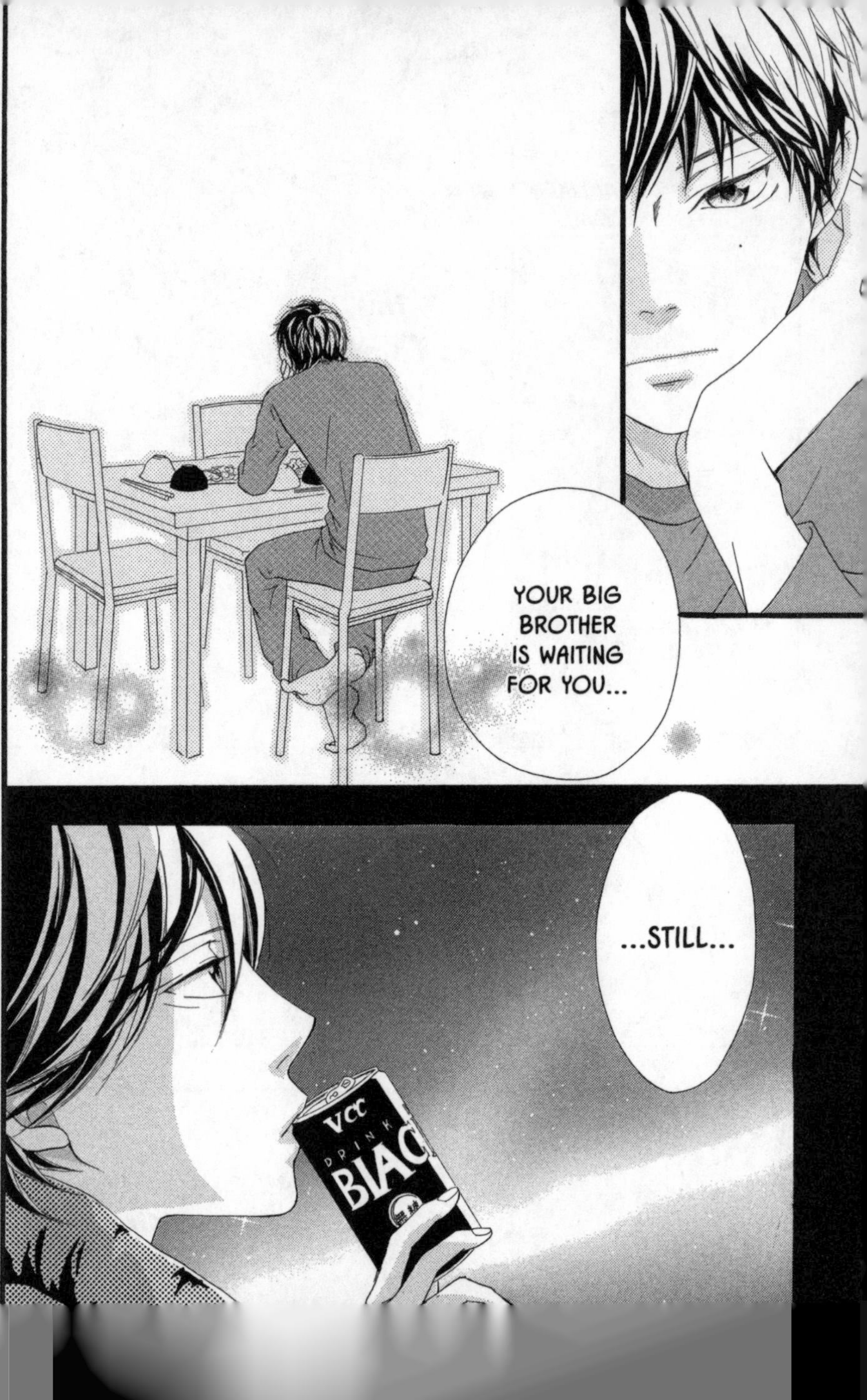
YOUR BIG BROTHER IS WAITING FOR YOU...
...STILL...
VCC
DRINK

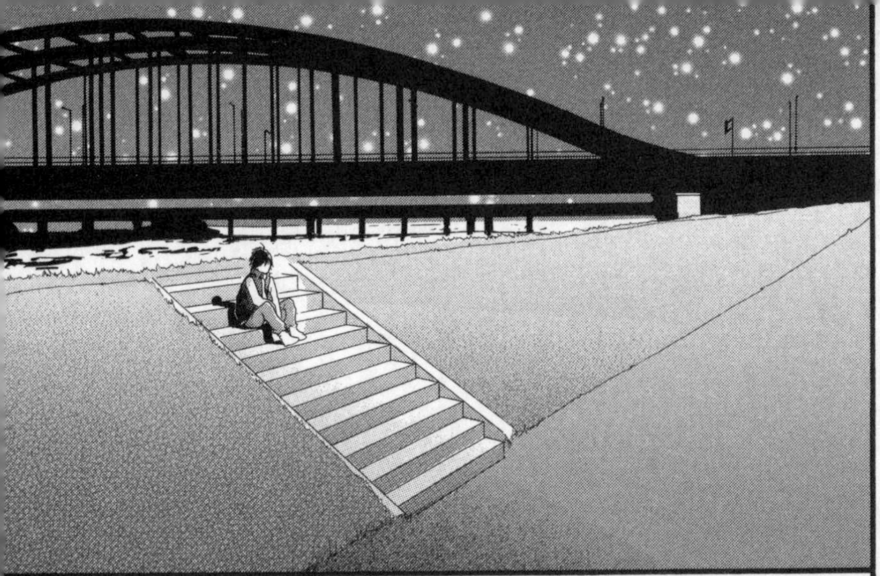

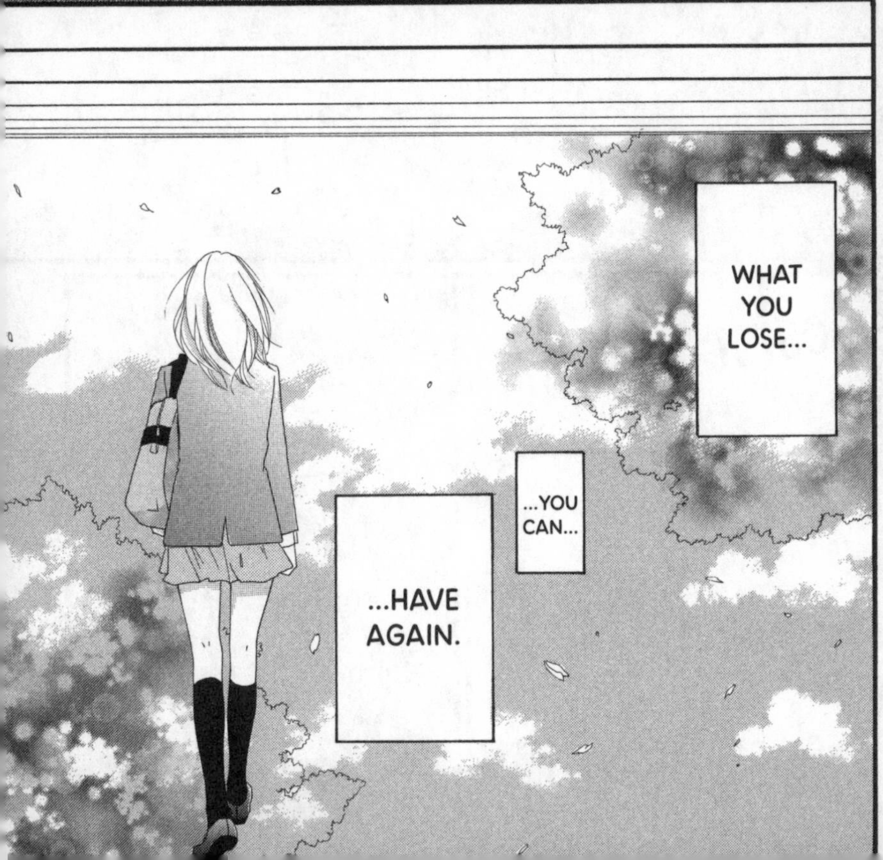
WHAT YOU LOSE...
...YOU CAN...
...HAVE AGAIN.

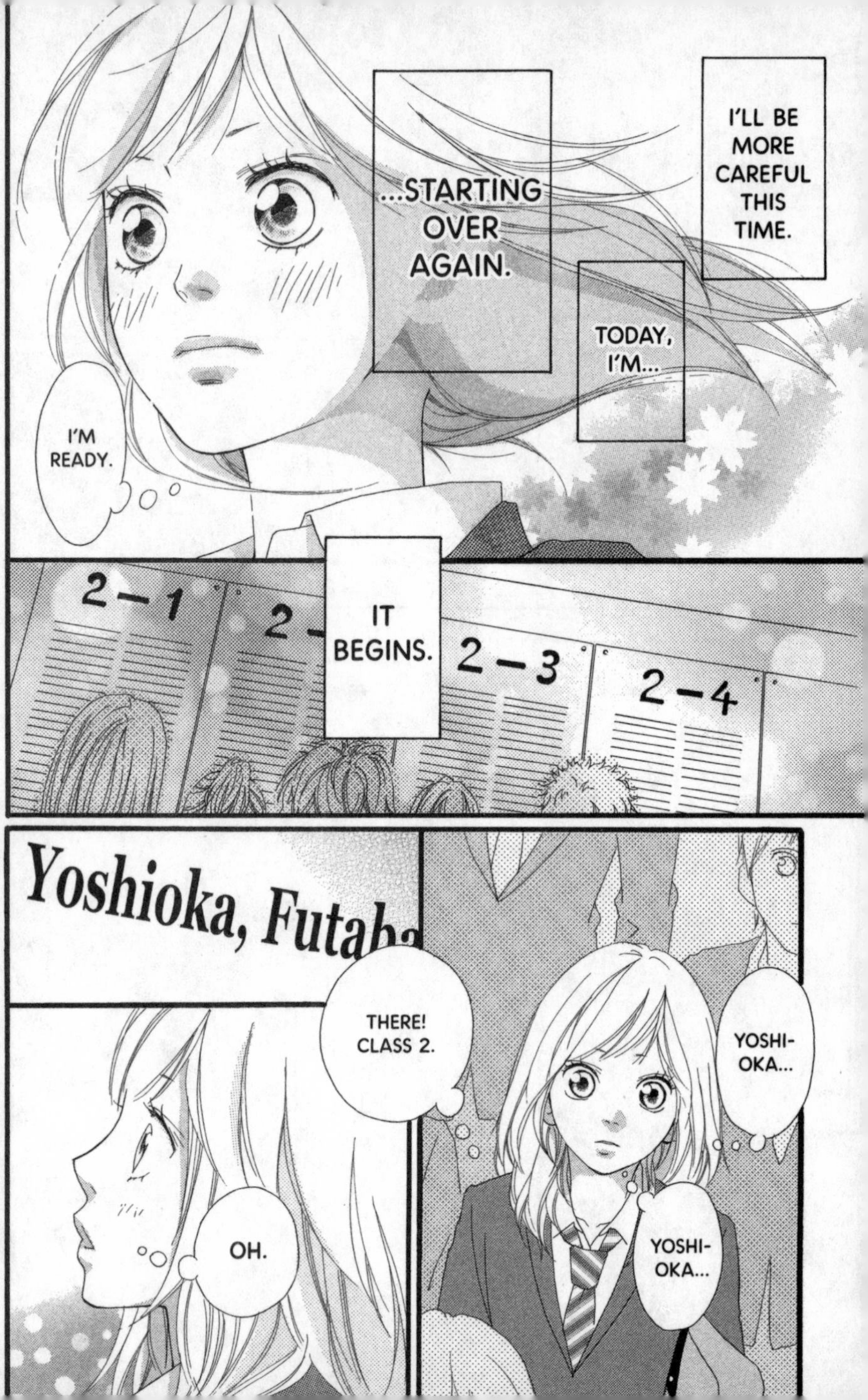
I'LL BE MORE CAREFUL THIS TIME.
TODAY, I'M...
...STARTING OVER AGAIN.
I'M READY.
2—4
2—3
IT BEGINS.
2—1
YOSHI-OKA...
THERE! CLASS 2.
YOSHI-OKA...
Yoshioka, Futab
OH.

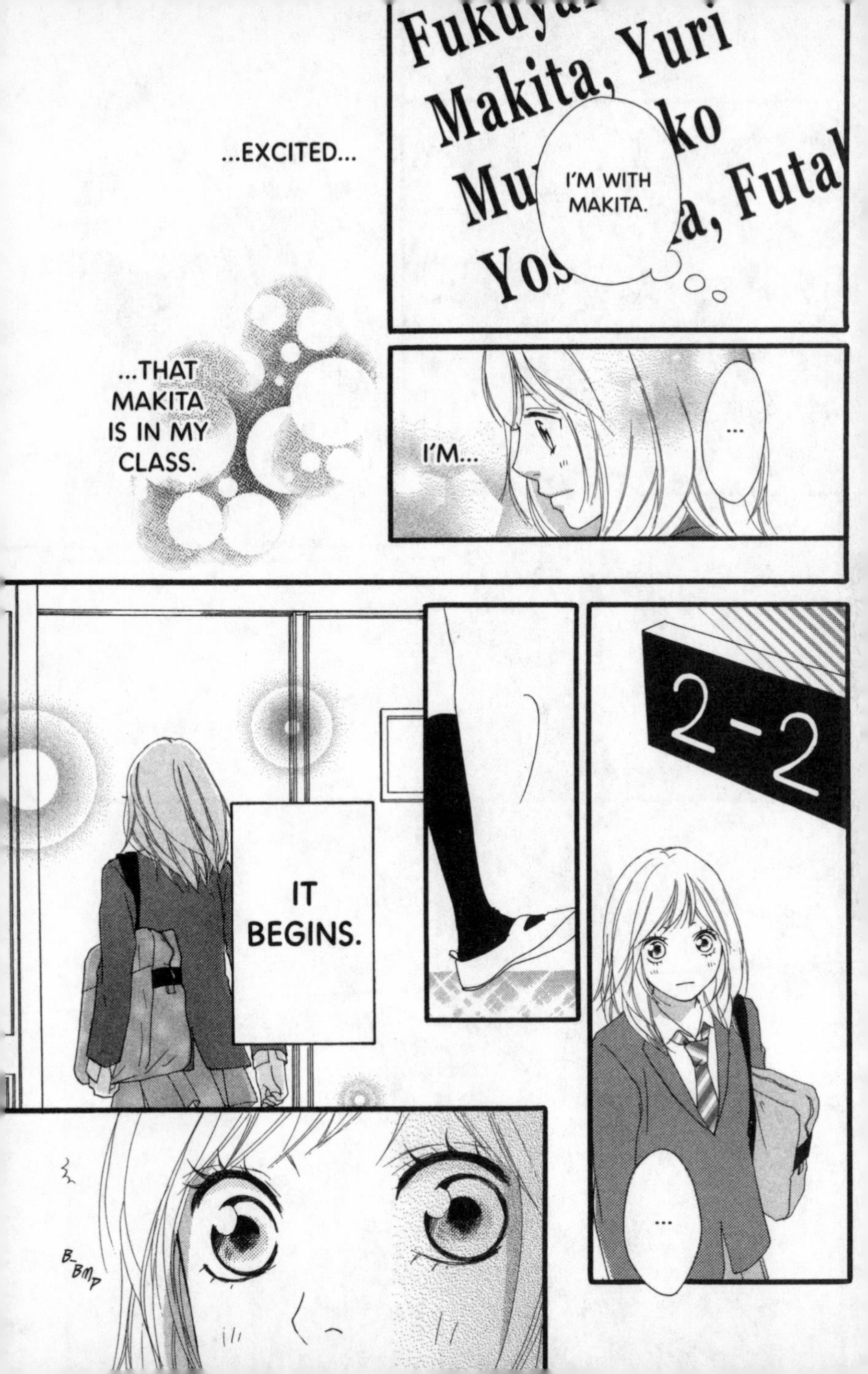
Fukuya
Makita, Yuri
Mu ko
Yos a, Futa
I'M WITH MAKITA.
...
I'M...
...EXCITED...
...THAT MAKITA IS IN MY CLASS.
2-2
...
IT BEGINS.
B-BMP

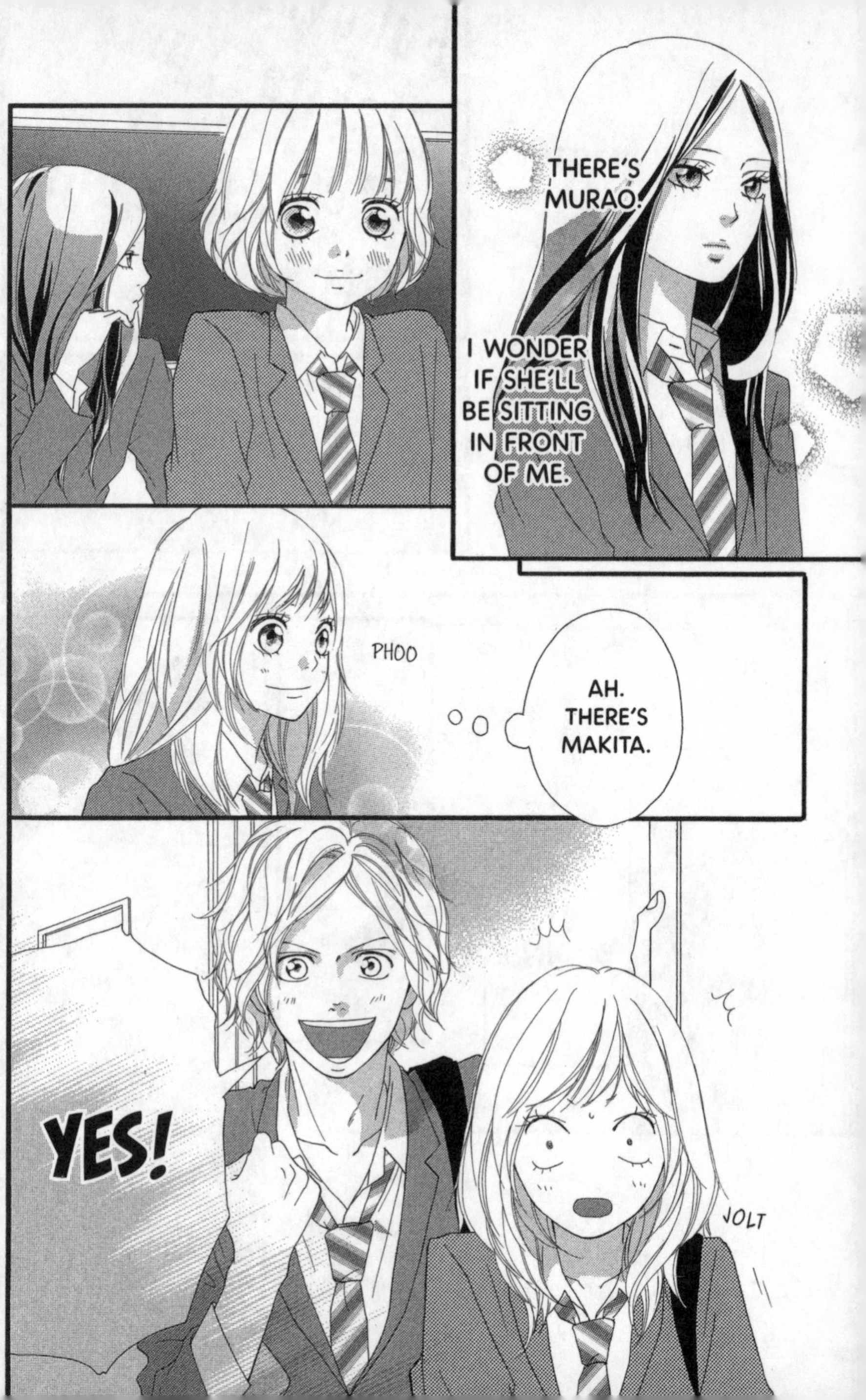
THERE'S MURAO!
I WONDER IF SHE'LL BE SITTING IN FRONT OF ME.
AH. THERE'S MAKITA.
PHOO
JOLT
YES!

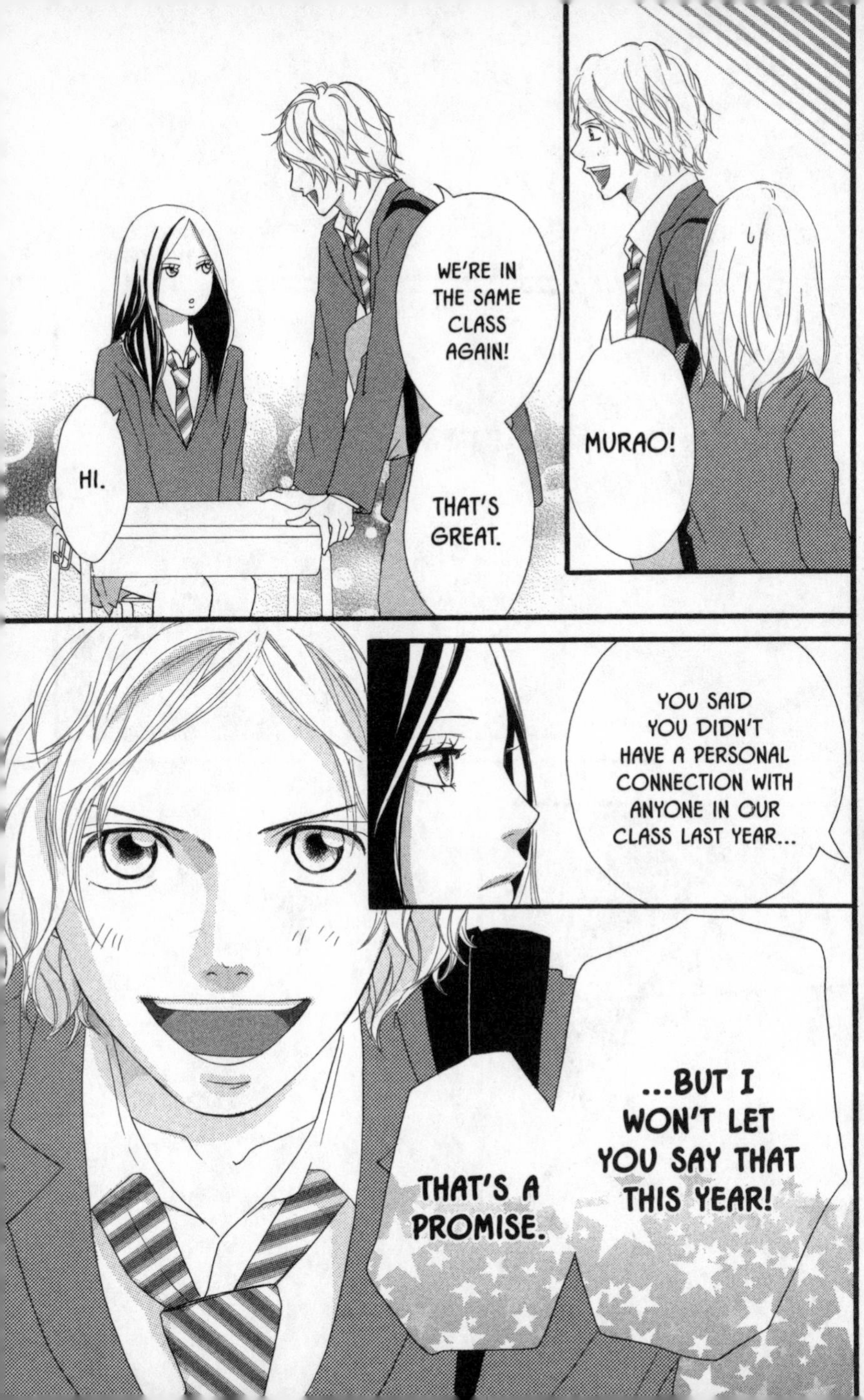
MURAO!
WE'RE IN THE SAME CLASS AGAIN!
THAT'S GREAT.
HI.
YOU SAID YOU DIDN'T HAVE A PERSONAL CONNECTION WITH ANYONE IN OUR CLASS LAST YEAR...
...BUT I WON'T LET YOU SAY THAT THIS YEAR!
THAT'S A PROMISE.

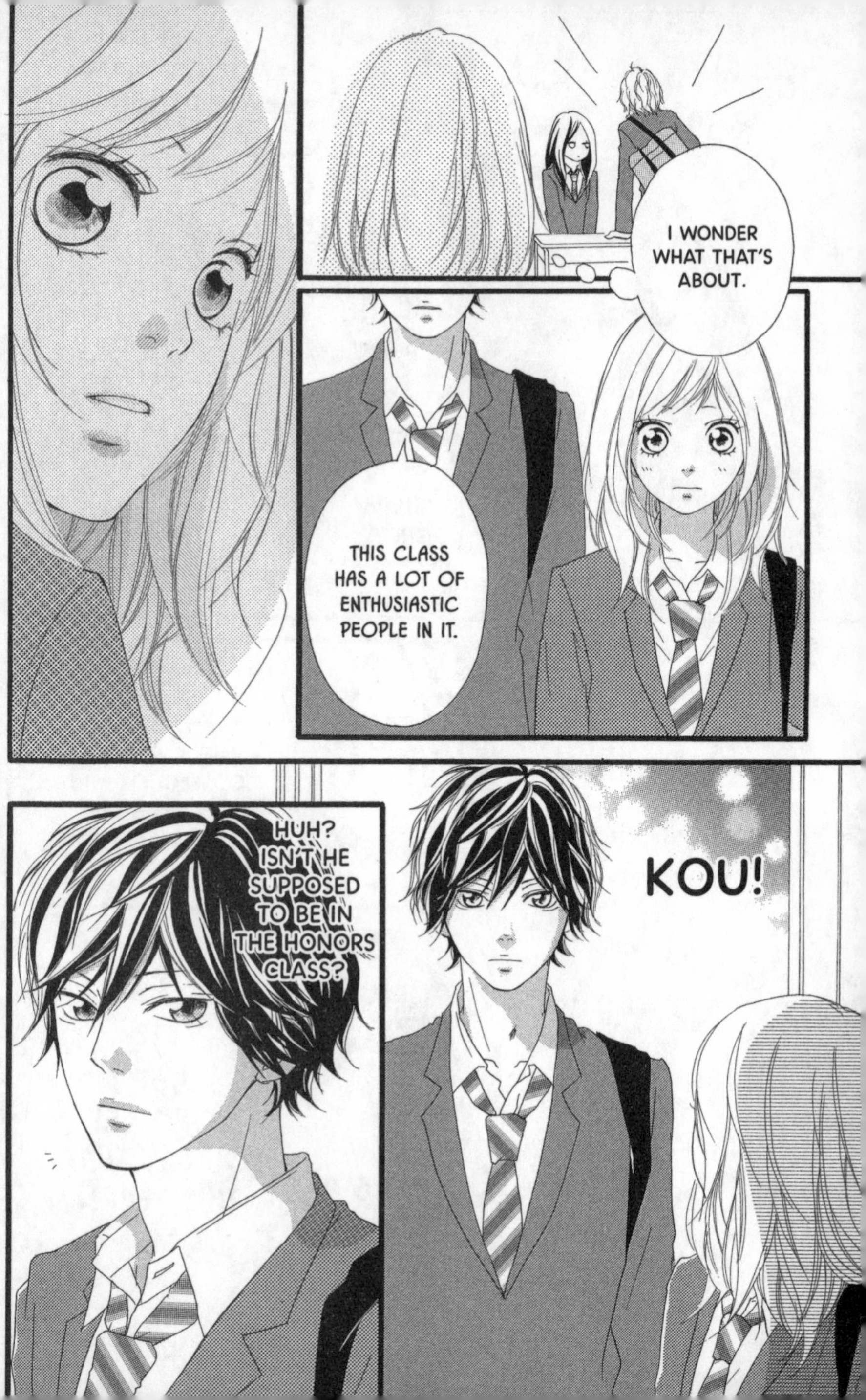
I WONDER WHAT THAT'S ABOUT.
THIS CLASS HAS A LOT OF ENTHUSIASTIC PEOPLE IN IT.
KOU!
HUH? ISN'T HE SUPPOSED TO BE IN THE HONORS CLASS?

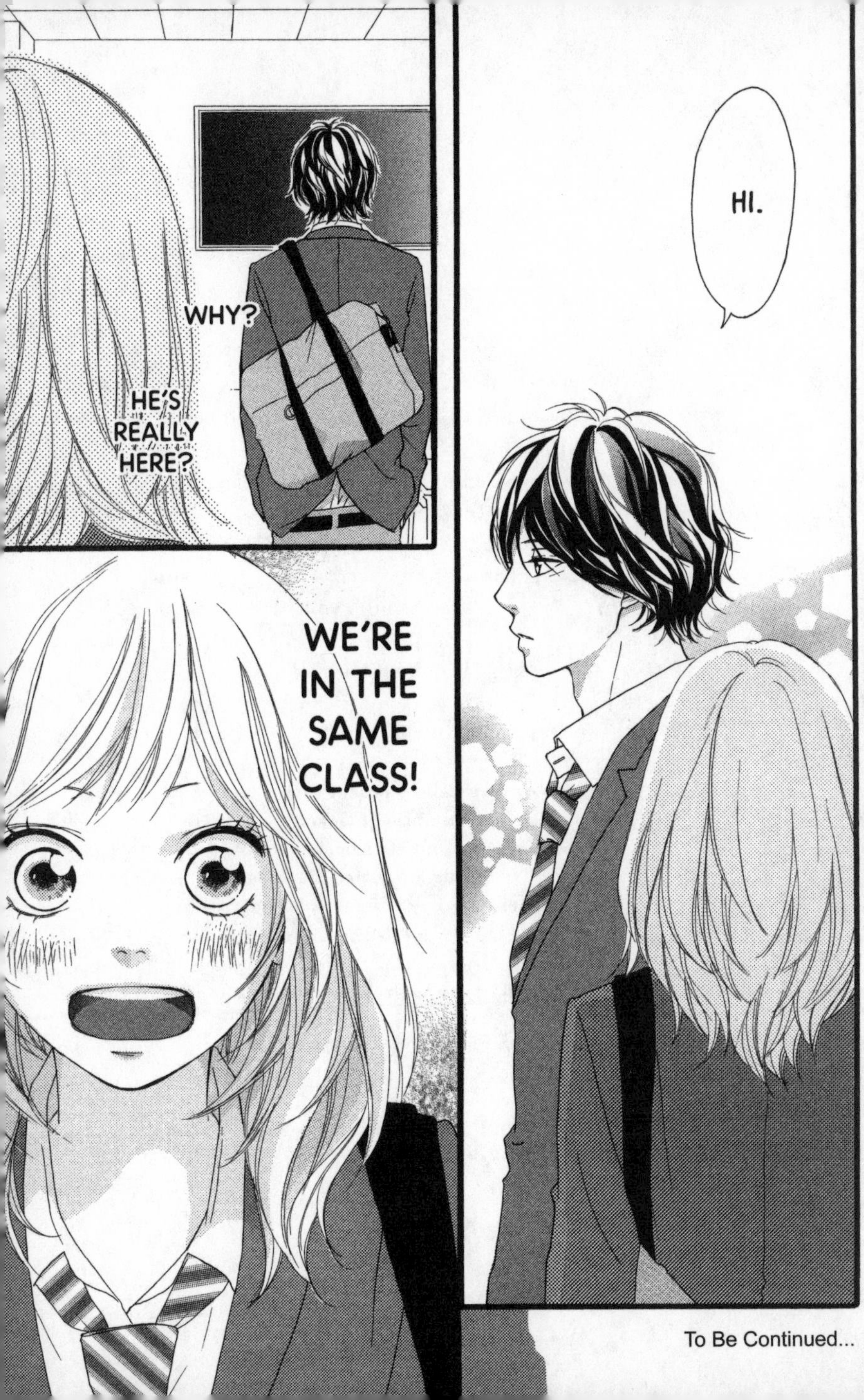
HI.
WHY?
HE'S REALLY HERE?
WE'RE IN THE SAME CLASS!

To Be Continued...

I love the springtime, and it makes me happy that volume 1 is coming out in the spring in Japan. I feel excited whenever I start something new, no matter what it is. All aboard! The *Ao Haru Ride* Express is leaving the station! Hurry—don't miss this ride through youth!

IO SAKISAKA

Born on June 8, Io Sakisaka made her debut as a manga creator with *Sakura, Chiru*. Her works include *Call My Name*, *Gate of Planet* and *Blue*. *Strobe Edge*, her previous work, is also published by VIZ Media's Shojo Beat imprint. *Ao Haru Ride* was adapted into an anime series in 2014. In her spare time, Sakisaka likes to paint things and sleep.

Ao Haru Ride

VOLUME 1
SHOJO BEAT EDITION

STORY AND ART BY **IO SAKISAKA**

TRANSLATION **Emi Louie-Nishikawa**
TOUCH-UP ART + LETTERING **Inori Fukuda Trant**
DESIGN **Shawn Carrico**
EDITOR **Nancy Thistlethwaite**

Printed in the U.S.A.

Published by VIZ Media, LLC
P.O. Box 77010
San Francisco, CA 94107

10 9 8 7 6 5 4
First printing, October 2018
Fourth printing, March 2021

ratings.viz.com RATED T TEEN

PARENTAL ADVISORY
AO HARU RIDE is rated T for Teen and is recommended for ages 13 and up. This volume contains the awkwardness of youth.

VIZ MEDIA
viz.com

Shojo Beat
shojobeat.com

STOP!

YOU MAY BE READING THE WRONG WAY.

In keeping with the original Japanese comic format, this book reads from right to left—so action, sound effects and word balloons are completely reversed to preserve the orientation of the original artwork.